ENTERTAINMENT MANAGEMENT
Towards Best Practice

CABI TOURISM TEXTS are an essential resource for students of academic tourism, leisure studies, hospitality, entertainment and events management. The series reflects the growth of tourism-related studies at an academic level and responds to the changes and developments in these rapidly evolving industries, providing up-to-date practical guidance, discussion of the latest theories and concepts, and analysis by world experts. The series is intended to guide students through their academic programmes and remain an essential reference throughout their careers in the tourism sector.

Readers will find the books within the CABI TOURISM TEXTS series to have a uniquely wide scope, covering important elements in leisure and tourism, including management-led topics, practical subject matter and development of conceptual themes and debates. Useful textbook features such as case studies, bullet point summaries and helpful diagrams are employed throughout the series to aid study and encourage understanding of the subject.

Students at all levels of study, workers within tourism and leisure industries, researchers, academics, policy makers and others interested in the field of academic and practical tourism will find these books an invaluable and authoritative resource, useful for academic reference and real-world tourism applications.

Titles available

Ecotourism: Principles and Practices
Ralf Buckley

Contemporary Tourist Behaviour: Yourself and Others as Tourists
David Bowen and Jackie Clarke

The Entertainment Industry: An Introduction
Edited by Stuart Moss

Practical Tourism Research
Stephen L.J. Smith

Leisure, Sport and Tourism, Politics, Policy and Planning, 3rd Edition
A.J. Veal

Events Management
Edited by Peter Robinson, Debra Wale and Geoff Dickson

Food and Wine Tourism: Integrating Food, Travel and Territory
Erica Croce and Giovanni Perri

Strategic Management in Tourism, 2nd Edition
Edited by L. Moutinho

Research Methods for Leisure, Recreation and Tourism
Edited by Ercan Sirakaya-Turk, Muzaffer Usyal, William E. Hammitt and Jerry J. Vaske

Facilities Management and Development for Tourism, Hospitality and Events
Edited by Ahmed Hassanien and Crispin Dale

Events as a Strategic Marketing Tool
Dorothé Gerritsen and Ronald van Olderen

Entertainment Management: Towards Best Practice
Edited by Stuart Moss and Ben Walmsley

ENTERTAINMENT MANAGEMENT

Towards Best Practice

Edited by

Stuart Moss

Carnegie Faculty, School of Sport,
Leeds Metropolitan University, Leeds, UK

Ben Walmsley

School of Performance and Cultural Industries,
University of Leeds, Leeds, UK

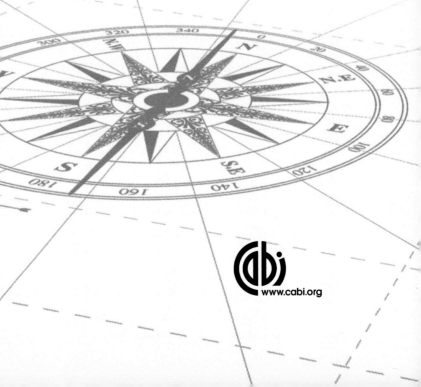

www.cabi.org

CABI is a trading name of CAB International

CABI
Nosworthy Way
Wallingford
Oxfordshire OX10 8DE
UK

Tel: +44 (0)1491 832111
Fax: +44 (0)1491 833508
E-mail: info@cabi.org
Website: www.cabi.org

CABI
745 Atlantic Avenue
8th Floor
Boston, MA 02111
USA

Tel: +1 671 682 9015

A catalogue record for this book is available from the British Library, London, UK.

Library of Congress Cataloging-in-Publication Data
Entertainment management: towards best practice / [Stuart Moss, Ben Walmsley, editors].
    pages cm. -- (CABI tourism texts)
  Includes bibliographical references and index.
  ISBN 978-1-78064-022-8 (hardback : alk. paper) -- ISBN 978-1-78064-023-5 (pbk. : alk. paper)
1. Performing arts--Management. I. Moss, Stuart, 1972- editor of compilation. II. Walmsley, Ben editor of compilation.
  PN1584.E58 2014
  790.2068--dc23

                        2014000447

ISBN-13: 978 1 78064 022 8 (hardback)
         978 1 78064 023 5 (paperback)

Commissioning editor: Claire Parfitt
Editorial assistant: Emma McCann
Production editor: Lauren Povey

Typeset by SPi, Pondicherry, India.
Printed and bound in Great Britain by Severn, Gloucester.

First printed in 2014.
Reprinted 2018.

Contents

Contents

Contributors

Maria Barrett

Maria is a senior lecturer at Liverpool Institute for the Performing Arts where she teaches on the BA (Hons) Music, Theatre and Entertainment Management degree. She has been consultant to a range of companies including Cartwheel Community Arts, Arts Culture Media Enterprise, Merseyside and the Independent Theatre Council. Maria directed, managed and performed with a range of theatre companies including a performance at the Institute for Contemporary Arts, London. She was founder and Chief Executive of Theatre Resource Centre, a management resource for small-scale theatre companies across the North West. Maria is a Director of Liverpool Lantern Company and has served on the boards of the Unity Theatre and Urban Strawberry Lunch, and is a former member of LIPA's Council. She is a sometime contributor to The Guardian's Live Chats on employment in entertainment. Maria is currently studying for a PhD at the Centre for Cultural Policy Studies at Warwick University looking specifically at audiences' experiences of theatre-going.

Shirley Beresford

Shirley is an experienced educator and consultant who specializes in Arts Marketing and Strategic Communications. She is currently a senior lecturer in Public Relations and Marketing at Leeds Metropolitan University, where she enjoys a portfolio of responsibilities in undergraduate, post-graduate and professional course leadership and teaching, including the MA Strategic Communications for the NHS and the MSc Corporate Communication. With management experience in consultancy and board-level roles in the arts, regeneration and cultural industries, Shirley is currently a Board member of imovearts, an Olympics legacy organization for the Cultural Olympiad for Yorkshire. Shirley has held positions as Deputy Chairman of AXIS, the national database of the contemporary visual arts, Head of Marketing for Yorkshire Tourist Board and Director of Wakefield City Regeneration Partnership, and she has led Communications teams for Bradford City Council and Leeds City Council's Leisure Services. Shirley is an active member of the Chartered Institute of Marketing, the Academy of Marketing and Chartered Institute of Public Relations, for whom she holds diverse roles as an examiner, conference organizer, academic and board external adviser, researcher, writer and awards judge.

Lisa Devine

Lisa Devine is a senior lecturer in Entertainment Management at Leeds Metropolitan University. She has been involved in entertainment and artist management for more than 10 years. Her research interests focus upon the customer service experience within a live entertainment setting. Other research interests include the student experience, specifically relating to learning environments. Prior to becoming a lecturer, Lisa ran her own entertainment agency as well as managing and performing within one of the most successful and in demand corporate live bands within the UK.

Dr Peter Dewhurst

Peter has worked in higher education since 1987, taking on senior management roles first at the University of Wolverhampton and then in 2007 at the University of Derby's Buxton Campus, first as Assistant Dean, then Dean and most recently as Strategic Director with responsibility for higher education and commercial operations. Peter's vision is for the University of Derby, Buxton, 'to deliver the highest quality of student centred experiential learning, providing all students with an opportunity to develop their knowledge and skills within real working environments'. Peter sits on numerous advisory committees and is a board member of Business Peak District, Visit Peak District and the Local Nature Partnership. Most recently Peter accepted a role as Director of Vision Buxton and Chair of the Peak District Partnership.

Lisa Gorton

Lisa's 17-year industrial background has seen her manage at all levels from team leader to company director in a range of travel industry roles. Her background is in sales management and directorship with an emphasis on the provision of excellent customer service. Lisa is currently the Course Leader for the BA Honours in International Tourism Management at Leeds Metropolitan University. She teaches at all levels of the undergraduate curriculum, focusing mainly on the theoretical, operational and strategic elements of management and employability. She is currently working on an innovative online learning project which will allow the School of Events, Tourism & Hospitality at Leeds Met to take the lead in the area of online higher education provision for these subjects.

Professor John Horne

John is Professor of Sport and Sociology in the School of Sport, Tourism and The Outdoors at the University of Central Lancashire. He is the author, co-author, editor and co-editor of numerous books, edited collections, journal articles and book chapters. His books include *Sport and Social Movements: From the Local to the Global* (Bloomsbury Academic, 2014), *Understanding Sport: A Socio-cultural Analysis* (Routledge, 2013), *Understanding the Olympics* (Routledge, 2012) and *Sport in Consumer Culture* (Palgrave Macmillan, 2006). He was selected as a member of the panel for Sport and Exercise Sciences, Leisure and Tourism in the 2014 Research Excellence Framework, elected as an Academician of the Academy of Social Sciences (AcSS) in 2012, is convenor of the British Sociological Association Sport Study Group and Founding Editor of the Globalizing Sport Studies book series with Bloomsbury Academic.

Peter McQuitty

Peter is Head of Policy, Culture and Communications at Oxford City Council. He began his professional career in academia, teaching and researching English literature in Australia and the UK. The charms of academia could not compete with his long-standing interest in practical politics, which led him inexorably into political organization and public relations in his native Australia. Since returning to the UK he has worked in a social housing consultancy and, for the last several years, at Oxford City Council. He is passionate about the Museum of Oxford because it is the only organization that tells the story of the city and its people and how industrial development shaped modern Oxford.

Dr Dinusha Mendis

Dinusha is a senior lecturer in Law and Co-Director of the Centre for Intellectual Property Policy and Management (CIPPM) at Bournemouth University. Dinusha is involved in teaching and research in the areas of Intellectual Property (IP) Law and Entertainment Law and specializes in digital aspects of IP law, in particular copyright law, and has published widely in this area. Dinusha is an Associate Editor (Copyright) for *Script-ed, A Journal of Law, Technology and Society* published by the AHRC/SCRIPT Centre, University of Edinburgh; an Executive Committee Member of the British and Irish Law Education and Technology Association (BILETA); a Council Member of the Society of Legal Scholars (SLS); and a Visiting Academic at University of Krakow, where she is involved in the teaching of Intellectual Property Law. Dinusha has been called to the Bar of England and Wales, and is a Member of the Honourable Society of the Middle Temple Inn, London.

Stuart Moss

Stuart is the Course Leader for the BA (Hons) Entertainment Management at Leeds Metropolitan University as well as being a senior lecturer in entertainment entrepreneurship and a Teacher Fellow specializing in employability skills development, the student experience, and social media usage in education. Stuart has previously edited *The Entertainment Industry: An Introduction* for CABI, as well as co-authoring two editions of 'Employability Skills' for Business Education Publishers. A member of the Society of Authors, Stuart is a keen writer and journalist and keeps an entertainment industry blog called 'Entertainment Planet', which can be found at http://www.entertainmentplanet.eu, as well as 'Issues in Contemporary Entertainment & Arts Management (ICrEAM)', a website linking to news and discussion features about developments in the global entertainment industries, which can be found at http://www.icream.eu. Stuart's current research interests involve nightclubs, music, entrepreneurship and entertainment consumer behaviours.

Amanda Peacock

Amanda is a Senior Consultant at PLB Ltd, one of the UK's leading consultancy firms serving the heritage and tourism sectors. She holds a BA (Hons) in English and Modern History and has an MA in Archaeological Heritage Management from the University of York. Amanda works on a range of planning projects for PLB's consultancy and design teams including feasibility studies, options appraisals and business plans, interpretive plans, conservation plans, audience development and community engagement strategies. She is particularly interested in the integrated management of cultural and natural heritage assets across a landscape. Amanda has considerable experience of facilitating community consultations, talking to different stakeholder groups about their perceptions of heritage and using interpretation to break down cultural and intellectual barriers to accessing heritage. Amanda is a member of the Association for Heritage Interpretation and the Local Access Forum for the North York Moors National Park.

Dr Martin Piber

Martin studied at the University of Graz and at the University of St Gallen in Switzerland. He is currently Associate Professor in the Department of Organization and Learning and Head of the research centre of Organization Studies at Leopold-Franzens-Universität in Innsbruck, Austria. He teaches on several Bachelors, Masters, PhD, MBA and further education programmes in Austria, Germany, Italy, South Africa, Spain and Sweden. His research and publications focus on the management of cultural organizations, the practices and theory of management control and performance measurement, the relevance of culture for society, aesthetics and business ethics. In 2009/10 he was Visiting Professor at the University of Cape Town in South Africa and the University of Stockholm in Sweden. Since 2012 Martin has been the Director of the Controlling (Management Accounting) programme at the Center of Science and Training in Bregenz, Austria. His background includes change management projects and consulting work for several private and public organizations, especially in the fields of culture and the arts.

Professor Dirk Reiser

Dirk is a Professor for Sustainable Tourism Management at Cologne Business School (CBS) in Köln, Germany. He is also an Honorary Senior Lecturer at the University of Tasmania in Australia and a lecturer at the European Overseas Campus of the University of Flensburg in Bali, Indonesia. His fields of interest include a variety of topic areas of sustainable tourism such as ecotourism, corporate social responsibility, animal ethics, green events and festivals, climate change and the future of mobility. Other areas of interest are World Heritage tourism and museums and tourism. He has published in a range of different books and journals.

In the past, he lived and taught in a variety of different countries including New Zealand, Australia, Indonesia and Nicaragua. His PhD studies on the impact of tourism, globalization and localization on the Otago Peninsula were conducted at the University of Otago in Dunedin, New Zealand. He also holds a Postgraduate Diploma in Tourism from the University of Otago, New Zealand, a Master of Social Sciences from the University of Wuppertal, Germany, and a certificate of Tertiary Teaching from the University of Canberra, Australia.

Dr James Roberts

James is a lecturer in strategy and innovation at Leeds University Business School. Before becoming an academic, James spent 15 years in strategy consulting, latterly with Oliver Wyman, working for entertainment, technology and media clients on strategy and innovation projects. His clients included the BBC, Sony Entertainment, Viacom, Walt Disney and Warner Bros. His research work focuses on the analysis of organizational capabilities in entertainment and media firms, specifically how such firms make sense of, and react to, often discontinuous and radical changes in their commercial environment.

Volker Rundshagen

Volker is a lecturer in Business and Tourism at Cologne Business School. In his early career stages he completed an apprenticeship at a travel agency in Germany, and then held sales support positions with tour operators and in the airline industry. In 2001 he completed his Master of Arts in Tourism Management at the University of Brighton, followed by tourism consultancy assignments for a German tourist destination and a Swiss travel intermediary start-up. In 2006 Volker joined his current employer, transferring his industry experience and his passion for the field into a new career in higher education. Upon the successful pursuit of part-time studies in Germany and in Kentucky he received his MBA from the University of Louisville in 2007. Currently, Volker is studying towards the DBA degree in Higher Education Management at the University of Bath. His research interests comprise the sociology of business education, responsible business, tourism education development and contemporary business school critique. He is a member of the Academy of Management, focusing on the divisions of Management Education and Development (MED) and Critical Management Studies (CMS).

Dr Andreas Schwarz

Andreas is a senior lecturer and Head of the Department of Media Studies at Ilmenau University of Technology in Germany. Since 2006 he has been Managing Director of the International Research Group on Crisis Communication. Andreas has served as founding chair of the Temporary Working Group on Crisis Communication at the European Communication Research and Education Association (ECREA) since 2011. His research has been published in a range of academic journals including *Public Relations Review*, the *International Journal of Strategic Communication* and the *Journal of Public Relations Research and Communications*. His research interests include crisis communication, public relations, journalism and cross-cultural communication. Andreas teaches in the areas of public relations, journalism, communication theory, public diplomacy and crisis management, and has several years of experience as a consultant to government authorities, NGOs and private companies, mainly in the field of crisis communication management.

Professor Guido Sommer

Guido is Professor of Tourism at Cologne Business School. He earned his first business degree at the University of Trier in Madrid. Between 2002 and 2007 he worked as research assistant at the Market Intelligence Institute at the University of Trier, cooperating with the Austrian National Tourist Office and completing his PhD in target group choice for tourism destination marketing. After working in business consulting for 3 years Guido joined his current employer where he built up the Tourism Management department accrediting new Tourism programmes at both bachelors and masters levels. His research interests comprise destination marketing, new technologies in tourism and transportation issues. He is a member of the competency network Tourism North Rhine-Westphalia.

Edwin Thwaites

Edwin has spent over 30 years in higher education emphasizing the people issues in management and organizations. In particular, the emphasis of his teaching and research has been in the area of crisis management and service operations management. He was one of the team that developed hospitality and tourism education at the University of Central Lancashire, and he retired in 2011 after 10 years as Division Leader for Tourism, Hospitality and Events.

An obsession with customer service and the role and importance of front-line workers in delivering exemplary service continues to be at the heart of Edwin's professional life. He currently works as a consultant for his own company specializing in executive coaching, organizational development and management learning. His aim, as ever, is personal and organizational improvement.

Dr Ben Walmsley

Ben lectures and researches in arts management and cultural engagement in the School of Performance and Cultural Industries at the University of Leeds. Prior to this, he worked as a Producer at the National Theatre of Scotland, before moving to Leeds Metropolitan University as a senior lecturer in Arts and Entertainment Management. Ben is a Fellow of the Higher Education Academy, an Artistic Assessor for Arts Council England, and an active member of the Arts Marketing Association and the Academy of Marketing. Ben has published widely on arts marketing, arts and entertainment management, cultural value and cultural policy, and recently edited an acclaimed book entitled *Key Issues in the Arts & Entertainment Industry*, which was published by Goodfellow in 2011. Ben is currently evaluating a £1.4m ACE/ National Lottery funded action research project at West Yorkshire Playhouse and a national £2m Transforming Arts Fundraising grant. He was recently awarded an AHRC grant as part of a University of Leeds consortium to explore cultural value as a complex system through a case study of the LoveArts Festival in Leeds.

Dr Beccy Watson

Beccy is a Principal Lecturer in the Carnegie Faculty at Leeds Metropolitan University. She has extensive experience teaching and researching across leisure and sport, including sociology, media, the creative industries, leisure and consumption. She has a particular research interest in gender and leisure, social (in-)equalities and difference, and the intersections between different social categories, and is currently engaged in researching dance and masculinities. She is one of the Managing Editors for the Routledge journal *Leisure Studies*.

Dr Simon Woodward

Simon is Principal Lecturer in Tourism at Leeds Metropolitan University and has worked as a consultant to the leisure, tourism and heritage sectors for some 25 years. His experience includes preparing feasibility studies for new leisure attractions, reviewing the operational and management performance of a wide range of businesses, preparing management plans for protected areas and historic buildings, and working with national and regional government agencies on the preparation of strategic tourism planning documents. Public sector clients include UNWTO, the World Bank and the EU as well as national agencies such as VisitEngland, Historic Scotland, CADW, the Corporation of London and the Saudi Commission for Tourism & Antiquities. Since 2001 Simon has been a member of the ICOMOS-UK Cultural Tourism Committee and in 2009 he was co-opted onto the ICOMOS International Tourism Committee. His current research interests include student engagement with World Heritage Sites and the commodification of 20th-century military heritage by tourism organizations.

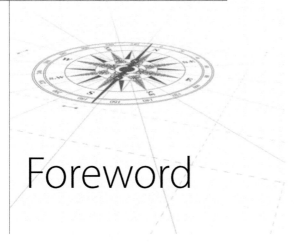

Foreword

Management has acquired a considerable literature, ranging from authored monographs to edited books and articles published in specialized management journals. Over the last 30 years most scholarly attention has been devoted to the non-profit domain of arts management, providing a rich landscape in a once barren field. These materials are supplemented by autobiographies, biographies and histories by and of leaders in the field, of how they changed their institution to one focused on strategies and structures through people management rather than being focused on the art work itself, or their lament that the former is fading into the background. However, entertainment management has a scant literature, making this book a much needed addition to the marketplace.

Entertainment Management: Towards Best Practice redresses the imbalance in the literature globally. Edited by Stuart Moss and Ben Walmsley, this book is divided into 15 chapters and its principal sources have been provided by primary and documentary research by scholars in the field, located in the major universities around the globe. The question needs to be asked: is this research justified in the case of entertainment management, which has a relatively short history and a comparatively modest impact on business? The answer is provided by the way in which Moss and Walmsley have constructed the task and divided it among their co-authors, and by the nature of the offerings in each part of the book.

Entertainment Management encompasses a significant set of industries from an economic, employment, social and even political perspective. The industry as we know it has flourished and evolved through 20th-century technologies and is now changing at a faster pace than ever before and becoming increasingly competitive. This is why effective management in the field is so necessary.

Moss and Walmsley have structured the book around the development of the entertainment industries within the broader context of cultural and economic growth. They focus in particular on key areas of enquiry, including the environment of entertainment, marketing entertainment, managing live events, human resource and artist management, creativity and business, entertainment law, performance management, consultancy and visitor attractions. In other words, this book provides a comprehensive coverage of a domain previously overlooked. The chapters are written to provide an overview of each of the main topics from a teaching and learning perspective, with case studies used to apply theory to practice and highlight areas of best practice. The book touches on subjects that are often missing from standard texts on the arts, such as equal opportunities and anti-social hours of working. Readers are left with an excellent understanding of the nature of the entertainment industries and the peccadilloes that abound for those employed in them. Each chapter also includes a helpful list of anticipated learning objectives and seminar activities.

The book breaks new ground by revealing insider perspectives on entertainment management in a dynamic, changing environment. It is co-authored by scholars in a number of universities in the UK and Europe, making it relevant and responsive to the needs of an enthusiastic body of potential students, managers and artists in a fast-paced and growing industry that has been waiting for a book to meet its needs.

Ruth Rentschler OAM, BA Hons, PhD
Chair and Professor in Arts Management
Deakin University
Australia

chapter 1

The Entertainment Industries: A Re-introduction

Stuart Moss

LEARNING OBJECTIVES

After reading this chapter you should be able to:

- appreciate that things which are novel or unique are more likely to capture the attention of an audience;
- have learned that entertainment affects people emotionally;
- realize the broad range of emotions that entertainment can have upon audiences;
- understand the key mediums by which entertainment is delivered; and
- know the composition of the entertainment industries.

INTRODUCTION

If the average person was playing a word-association game and were given the word 'entertainment' to associate other words with, it is highly likely that the associations they would make would include one or more of the following: fun; comedy; performance; television; movies; laughter; music; singer; stage; or show. In a short experiment that was carried out with my students doing just this, these were the top ten general responses I received from 50 that I asked. By general responses I mean responses that were not specific to a particular entertainer, band, brand, venue, location, television programme or product. What the experiment demonstrated is that in the mind-set of the people asked, entertainment is a word that has a largely positive resonance and is something that provides an overall enjoyable experience to those who are being subjected to something that has been created for them, which captivates and engages them.

In French the word 'divertissement' is used to describe the phenomenon of entertainment as a distraction, while in Italian 'divertimento' provides a similar translation, and these are perhaps more accurate indicators of the true meaning of entertainment. In the English language the word 'entertain' has 16th-century origins and was used to label the action of getting the attention of somebody and keeping them in a certain frame of mind. The suffix 'ment' forms nouns and has Latin origins to label the result or product of an action. Entertainment as a word first appeared in the 16th century, where originally it was used to label: retaining attention, public performance and amusement. The word 'attainment' has a number of meanings including acquisition and accomplishment (Etymonline.com, 2013). Anything seeking to be entertaining needs to acquire an audience before entertainment can be accomplished. The definition of entertainment offered by Moss (2009, p. 1) remains unchanged and will be used in this book: 'Entertainment is something that can engage or captivate an audience through sensory stimulation, which can invoke an emotional response amongst that audience'.

NOVELTY

Not everything that we consider entertaining is a part of the entertainment industry. Multiple occurrences daily can attract audiences; these may be created by man or occur in the natural environment. Consider graffiti and what the purpose of it is. Graffiti is intended to be seen (and often read) by passers-by; depending on what it is, some audiences may consider it repulsive, others may admire it. Most graffiti does not make money but has been created as a form of self-expression for others to see. Some graffiti does make money, sometimes considerable sums, e.g. Banksy. A rainbow or a very colourful sunset is naturally occurring and attracts spectators in the same way that a piece of art might. For those who witness and emotionally resonate to such a spectacle, the feeling within that it can generate can be a powerful one. Whilst graffiti, rainbows and sunsets are not rare, they are not witnessed continually and do stand out from their surroundings as being different, novel or unique. This is a key challenge faced by organizations within the entertainment industries, captivating audiences, in that they must provide something that does stand out from the surroundings.

In a perfect and somewhat academic scenario (and particularly from a business perspective), entertainment should provide a level of distraction that is beyond everything else in the background, in order to first capture and then captivate an audience above and beyond the competition and every other distraction that this potential audience may be exposed to. Providers of entertainment who collectively make up the entertainment industry are continually providing products that are intended to be highly visible and have customer appeal. This is often achieved through novelty or uniqueness. Something that is novel is something that in the eyes of the audience is interesting because it is 'different' and not the norm, and therefore draws attention. Figure 1.1 is a perfect demonstration of this; the image shows two examples of novelty attracting audiences. In the top image, the London 2012 Olympic Torch whilst on its journey around the UK is being taken through the town of Much Wenlock in Shropshire, England, which has historical associations with the modern Olympic games. The novelty

Fig. 1.1. Novelty attracts audiences. Top photograph courtesy of Alan Machin.

of being witness to the Olympic Torch drew large crowds to the town who wanted to see something that for many would be a once in a lifetime experience. In the bottom image, an audience comprised of one person gets up close to a white tiger at Bioparc Fuengirola on Spain's Costa Del Sol. The white tiger is an animal that is an extremely rare sight to anyone, but to be able to get so close and witness one in safety is quite unique.

The premise that novelty attracts audiences is not a new one and has been exploited by those wanting to attract audiences for hundreds of years; consider the travelling 'freak shows' and circuses of the past, where people who looked 'different' were paraded as 'freaks of nature' (often in cages) in front of fee-paying audiences. Notable examples of people paraded in such a way include John Merrick 'The Elephant Man' and Frederick Kempster 'The English Giant'. Today, ethics dictate that such exploitative travelling shows are rare in modern 'Western' societies. Although, those who look or behave 'different' to what are deemed societal norms are showcased by documentary makers in various forms of reality television, e.g. *Bodyshock* (Channel 4, UK), which, whilst questionable, is seemingly more morally acceptable to audiences who are drawn to it. Further discussion around morality and ethics in entertainment can be found within Chapter 10 of this book.

Whilst novelty attracts, audiences are varied and may not all share the same opinions.

Normality is extraordinary through other people's eyes, so what one person considers to be novel or unique may be an everyday sight to somebody else and considered less of an entertaining spectacle. Much 'cultural' entertainment is based upon this premise and is a key motivator amongst audiences, many of whom travel to witness particular spectacles in other cultures; specific examples include cultural events such as: La Tomatina held in Buñol, Spain; The Changing of the Guard held outside Buckingham Palace, London, UK; and Oktoberfest held in Munich, Germany. All of these draw in visitors from nearby who wish to celebrate and participate, as well as tourists from afar who wish to witness something that is culturally unique and different to what they are used to seeing.

EMOTION

An emotion is 'positive or negative experience that is associated with a particular pattern of physiological activity' (Schacter, 2011). Emotions are triggered through sensory input, be that sight, sound, smell, taste or touch, and entertainment experiences of any quality generate emotions amongst audience members. Vogel (2007, 2010) makes this point and presents an entertainment industry that is truly varied and encompassing numerous sectors and sub-sectors, all of which attract, captivate and emotionally impact upon audiences who experience entertainment as part of a wider recreational undertaking. For recreation think re-creation, as emotional impacts are created through conscious and subconscious mental activity, some of which may be cognitive but all of which stimulate or relax the mind, re-creating the mental state of audience members to something different to what it was prior to being entertained.

It is important to consider that the emotional response experienced by an audience need not be a positive one; it is a popular misconception that entertainment should be 'happy and clappy', but this is certainly not the case. A horror movie may terrify, a painting in a gallery may cause unease and a museum exhibit may provoke shock; these emotions are demonstrated in Fig. 1.2.

In terms of audiences, it is typical to consider an audience as being a group of people; however, it is important to clarify that an audience can be as small as one person and as large as the largest audiences on the planet, which could be international audiences of millions captivated by a solar eclipse, or, in terms of man-made entertainment industry provision, the global television audiences tuning into mega-events such as the Olympic Games and the football (soccer) World Cup.

THE INDUSTRIES

An industry is typically considered to be a sector of economic activity, based upon a specific branch of manufacture or trade. Industries involve inputs of raw materials, labour, finance and skills as well as processes such as engineering, remixing, manufacturing and packaging to create product outputs that are predominantly products (tangible or intangible) aimed towards a fee-paying consumer market. Numerous industries create entertainment products, which are products that are designed to attract, captivate and emotionally resonate a mostly fee-paying audience.

Whilst the majority of the entertainment industries economically exploit entertainment, it is important not to forget that a great deal of entertainment provision is not-for-profit and may have been created for a variety of

Common emotions associated with entertainment

Positive ← → Negative

Adoration	Affection	Acceptance	Anticipation	Agitation	Aggravation	Agony
Amazement	Attraction	Amusement	Astonishment	Anxiety	Annoyance	Anger
Bliss	Bonded	Assurance	Awe	Anxious	Bitterness	Disgust
Delight	Confident	Calm	Comprehension	Apprehension	Consternation	Dread
Desire	Courage	Caring	Surprise	Boredom	Contempt	Fright
Ecstasy	Dignity	Cheer	Thoughtful	Dejection	Depression	Fury
Elation	Eager	Compassion		Disappointment	Despair	Hatred
Euphoria	Empowered	Content		Displeasure	Despondent	Horror
Exhilaration	Enjoyment	Elegance		Distress	Disliking	Insulted
Glee	Enthralled	Empathy		Embarrassed	Dissatisfaction	Mortified
Infatuation	Excitement	Eustress		Envy	Disturbed	Outrage
Inspiration	Happiness	Friendship		Exasperation	Fear	Panic
Love	Jolliness	Gladness		Frustration	Greed	Shock
Lust	Joy	Gratified		Grumpiness	Grief	Suffering
Motivation	Liking	Harmonious		Guilt	Hostility	Terror
Victorious	Longing	Honourable		Insecurity	Humiliation	Torment
	Positivity	Hope		Irritation	Loathing	Vengefulness
	Pride	Interest		Jealousy	Misery	
	Relaxation	Nostalgia		Nervousness	Mourning	
	Respect	Optimism		Regret	Remorse	
	Satisfaction	Pleasure		Resentment	Revulsion	
	Security	Relief		Rivalry	Sadness	
	Thankful	Responsible		Troubled	Scorn	
	Thrill	Sentimental		Unease	Shame	
	Wonder	Sympathy		Worry	Woe	

Fig. 1.2. Emotions commonly associated with entertainment (Moss, 2009).

other purposes, including learning, celebration, commemoration, tradition, community engagement or just to bring people together. A great deal of art (traditional/performance/contemporary) is created as expression by the artist, and this may not be for profit. The motivation of artists and creative people is quite varied and is often intrinsic in the satisfaction gained from producing something that other people appreciate. The contemporary rise of the 'prosumer' (somebody who produces and consumes content) through various social media channels demonstrates this perfectly. Creators of content on platforms such as Facebook, Twitter, Instagram, Foursquare, Tumblr and WordPress do not gain financially for their endeavours but may get 'likes', 're-tweets' and 're-blogs' for the content that they have created and shared.

In this example the financial gain is made by the social media networks themselves, and largely at very little of their own effort.

In creating a sectoral model of the entertainment industry based upon the unique aspects of areas within it, Moss (2009) attempted to present a seemingly disparate range of industries under one umbrella term called 'the entertainment industry'. Sayre and King (2003), Donaton (2005), Vogel (2007) and Perebinossoff (2008) (amongst many others) have also (with varied opinion) presented their idea of what the entertainment industry actually is. In some academic texts, 'entertainment' is too narrowly focused as consisting only of products of 'the stage', music, film and television, without properly considering that so many more things captivate and emotionally resonate amongst audiences.

In the predecessor to this book, what was identified as entertainment industry sectors by Moss (2009) are in fact each an assortment of industries that collectively create products that are intended to attract, captivate and emotionally resonate amongst audiences. Collectively all of these bodies make up the entertainment industries (note the plural) and share an over-riding commonality, which is how audiences experience and interact with their products, namely:

- at a live event;
- via a form of media; or
- at a visitor attraction.

Events, media and visitor attractions all engage audiences who are seeking to be captivated and emotionally involved with what it is that they are experiencing, whether it be a tragic play, a song on the radio or a painting in a gallery. The rationale for the plural 'industries' (above) is simply down to the disparate nature of the plethora of industries that collectively make up the entertainment industries, and to give credence to the fact that each industry deserves to be recognized and identified as such. To try and claim that industries as varied as basketball, stand-up comedy, satellite television, social media and opera are merely sub-sectors of a larger body called the entertainment industry is perhaps doing those industries a dis-service.

The entertainment industries consist of a great deal more than entertainment at the point of delivery. Organizations that provide entertaining events, media and visitor attractions have physical locations and facilities to manage, such as premises where production, manufacturing and retail/delivery take place. In order to attract audiences, promotion is essential; if potential audiences are not made aware that the entertainment exists they will not buy into it. The industry is also highly competitive so promotion is essential for organizations to showcase their products over the products offered by their competitors. Ironically, the majority of promotional mediums are entertainment in their own right, in that they must also attract, captivate and engage audiences to get their messages across and generate 'buzz' about the entertainment that they are promoting. All of these processes are supported by specialist support organizations and agencies that offer expertise, services and outsourcing to the organizations that create entertainment. This is demonstrated in Fig. 1.3.

COMPETITION

With technological advancements, there has been unprecedented growth in the number of avenues by which people can spend both their increasing levels of disposable income and free time. The arts and entertainment industries have never shrunk, surviving wars and recessions alike. Competition amongst organizations to supply consumers with products to keep them occupied, interested and emotionally involved has never been fiercer, both within the home and outside it. The recognition of this and the industry's value to the economy has led to a global reverence of the industry by governments, making it an attractive proposition for imitators and followers and a 'hotbed' of creative entrepreneurship.

Competition within the entertainment industries involves like-for-like competition, where organizations creating similar products are competing for the time and money of audiences. This also involves substitution competition where audiences may choose one form of entertainment over another, for example going to the theatre or buying a video game.

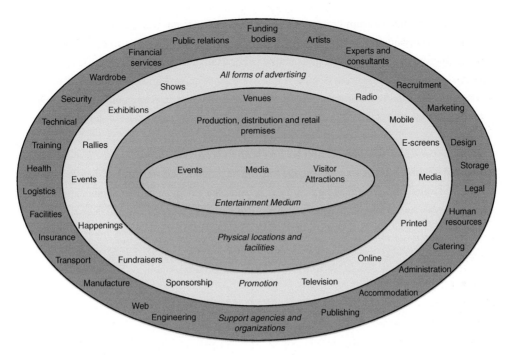

Fig. 1.3. The composition of the entertainment industries.

The reality is that audiences are extremely diverse, and a broad range of products is created for those audiences. Figure 1.4 is a competitor map, demonstrating the intensity of competition within the entertainment industries. Like-for-like competition is at its strongest when similar products are targeted at similar markets. Where products and markets differ there is little competition, and where there is some difference in either markets or products there is some competition, which is when substitution is most likely.

EVENTS

'Events are temporary occurrences…they have a finite length, and for planned events this is usually fixed and publicized' (Getz, 1997, p. 4). Events can bring economic benefits to areas by drawing in audiences whose ancillary expenditure can support shops, food outlets, bars, restaurants, hotels and public transport. Events can also help boost both tourism and the profile of the locations in which they take place. The coastal town of Whitby (UK), once a bustling fishing port, has seen recent fortunes shaped from the 1897 book *Dracula* by Bram Stoker. In the book, Dracula came ashore at Whitby after his boat is shipwrecked off the town's coast. Followers of the 'gothic' subculture (goths) now descend on the town twice each year to attend the 'The Whitby Gothic Weekender' (WGW) and are reportedly worth £30–40 (US$46–61) per visitor per day to the Whitby economy, where 25% of the town's population work in tourism-related roles (BBC, 2012). Events can also bring disruption through interference with 'normal' life; this may be through congestion of road and footpaths, vehicles not being allowed to use roads, temporary changes to public transport, closure of certain premises, restrictions placed upon businesses and environmental issues (see 'The Rural Environment', Chapter 2, and Chapter 10 for 'responsible' management initiatives). Figure 1.5 is a sign that demonstrates how a sporting event caused temporary road closures in Edinburgh, UK.

Recent growth in live music events and festivals in particular has been stemmed due to saturation and competition. This has led to some planned major events not running.

Examples of this are 'The Big Chill' and 'Sonsiphere', which were due to be held in the UK but were cancelled in 2012 and 2013 due to both competition and a weak economy, demonstrating how sensitive events can be to forces within the industry as well as the wider business environment. Chapter 6 of this book is dedicated to the planning and management of live events.

Table 1.1 shows an A–Z typology of common live events, which may draw audiences of

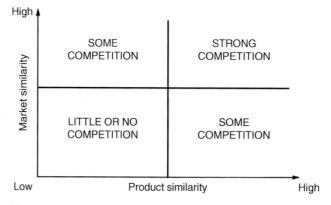

Fig. 1.4. Competitor map.

Fig. 1.5. A sign in Edinburgh indicating parking restrictions due to an event.

Table 1.1. An A–Z typology of common live events.

Type of event	Description and example
Astrological events	Anything that naturally occurs in or emanates from outer space that can be seen from earth, e.g. the Perseid meteor shower.
Auctions	A gathering of people who may wish to either competitively bid or witness competitive bidding for items that are on sale, e.g. an art auction at Sotheby's in London, UK.
Award ceremonies	A formal ceremony where a gathering of people including award nominees, friends of nominees, sponsors and interested others gather to see awards in a specific field given to winners of particular categories, e.g. The Academy Awards (more popularly known as the Oscars), held annually in Hollywood, USA.
Cinema screenings	Film shown at a cinema, e.g. any film being shown at the IMAX cinema at The National Media Museum in Bradford, UK.
Club nights	Any event held in a nightclub where the DJ is the main entertainer, e.g. 'Together', a weekly club night at Amnesia, Ibiza, Spain.
Competitions (non-sport)	An event that attracts an audience of competitors and onlookers who wish to compete to win a prize in a structured game or scenario that involves rules and fairness, e.g. a beauty pageant such as Miss World.
Conferences	A meeting of people who gather to listen to speakers give presentations around a particular theme, e.g. The International Medieval Congress, which is held annually in Leeds, UK.
Conventions (trade shows)	A meeting of people with a shared interest who gather to network with like-minded individuals, listen to speakers and make purchases of related products, e.g. a science-fiction convention such as Worldcon.
Culturtainment events	Societal/cultural celebrations, commemorations, spectacles and displays. These may involve religion, worship and/or tradition and are routinely performed at set times in accordance with cultural norms, e.g. the Feast of St Julian known as the 'Gostra', which is held annually in Malta and involves residents attempting to run up a greased pole.

(Continued)

Table 1.1. Continued.

Type of event	Description and example
Educational demonstrations	An event at which a performer demonstrates and explains something to an audience of interested onlookers; this commonly involves either a particular skill, a craft or animals, e.g. a falconry display.
Exhibitions	A temporary display of a curated collection of objects that have a particular theme and may draw interested onlookers, e.g. the travelling Bodyworlds exhibition.
Festivals (all types)	A communal celebration that involves a central theme, where practitioners and consumers gather to socialize and celebrate, e.g. The Glastonbury Festival of Performing Arts, UK.
Historic re-enactments	Themed events that depict a moment from history, where costumed performers re-enact a past occurrence, e.g. the annual Battle of Waterloo re-enactment, which is held in Belgium.
Live music concerts/gigs	A show where the predominant form of entertainment is live music, e.g. The BBC Proms.
Live screened events	Live events that are broadcast and screened to audiences, e.g. sporting events screened in bars.
Natural phenomena	Anything that occurs in the natural world that may attract an audience of onlookers, e.g. a waterspout over a lake.
Rallies	A rally is a meeting of people who are commonly gathering to show support for a particular cause. Rallies often involve speakers who address the audience. Many rallies have a political affiliation, e.g. Democrat and Republican rallies prior to an election in the USA.
Sales parties	Typically smaller events that take place in the home or a communal setting; sales parties also serve as social occasions where products are demonstrated to attendees, e.g. a 'Pampered Chef' party.
Showcase events	A hybrid of conventions and exhibitions, showcase events are designed to attract audiences of enthusiasts to witness a themed temporary collection and display; themes are extremely varied but commonly involve transport, animals or industry, e.g. The Paris Air Show (Salon International de l'Aéronautique et de l'Espace, Paris-Le Bourget) held bi-annually in France.

(Continued)

Table 1.1. Continued.

Type of event	Description and example
Spiritual shows	Shows that have a religious or spiritual theme where the audience believe that religious or supernatural forces may play a part in events that take place, e.g. séances, evangelism and fortune telling.
Sporting fixtures	Events where spectators watch athletes compete at sports that involve physical exertion and fair competition, e.g. the Olympic Games.
Staged story and variety performances (all theatre forms)	An extremely diverse set of events that are theatrical and involve the performance of a rehearsed routine; these are extremely varied in nature but may include: magic shows, plays, opera, ballet, ventriloquism, puppet shows, dance shows, readings and recitals, sportertainment, theatre, pantomime, musicals, new work, happenings, stand-up comedy, after-dinner speaking, flaring, clowning, circus performances, cocktail flaring, juggling, talent shows, parkour, acrobatics, daredevils and feats of endurance, e.g. The Royal Variety Performance, held annually in London, UK.
Tours	An event that takes place in a specific location or locations over a period of time and involves a guide taking an audience around and explaining to them facts about their surroundings, e.g. A Jack The Ripper tour around Whitechapel, London, UK.

spectators that may be captivated and entertained at them (this list is comprehensive but not exhaustive). The majority of these events are planned, man-made events that require specific venues at which the events take place. There are some exceptions to this, with astrological and natural events being out of man's direct control, but venues such as viewing galleries and interpretive visitor centres may still be provided as facilities or visitor attractions in order to enable audiences to experience and understand the event taking place.

MEDIA

The majority of audiences regularly experience entertainment through the media. Those media forms that are intended to communicate information or data to large audiences are known as mass media, which may be both tangible storage devices or intangible communication mediums. Tangible media consist of storage mediums that can hold visual, audio or audiovisual data or information. This may be static data such as text or graphics, audio data such as spoken word or music, moving images such as silent film, or a combination of all of the above such as video. Media does not have to be electronic, nor does it need to have an electronic device to access the information upon it. Printed media for example simply needs to be looked upon by the user. Media may be stored in analogue or digital formats on discs, cassettes, cartridges or other mediums, and then accessed via electronic player devices such as CD/DVD/Blu-ray players, record players or cassette players, which allow for the communication of the data/information stored on the tangible media formats.

Schumpeter (1934) is responsible for coining the term 'creative destruction'; this is a term used to demonstrate how innovation can lead to new and improved design, rendering older designs obsolete. This is a continual process and is something that is easily demonstrated by the rise and fall of numerous tangible media formats throughout the 20th century and into the 21st century.

Nowadays it is increasingly common for the data/information contained on all tangible media forms to be available in intangible media-less electronic formats that are accessed via the Internet and played back on computer devices, such as desktop computers, laptops, tablets, phablets, smartphones,

Internet-ready televisions and personal video recorder (PVR) units. The continued cycle of creative destruction has meant that now usage of all tangible formats is in decline and intangible e-formats are on the rise. This is demonstrated in Fig. 1.6.

Other intangible media include:

- broadcast media, which is radio and television broadcasts created at a distance and then transmitted to be played. Transmission is most commonly through analogue or digital air-wave frequencies, satellite or cable;
- cinema, which is predominantly (but not only) movie-based entertainment played to large audiences of attendees in movie-theatres;
- telephonic, which is predominantly communicative data and information transmitted from and to telephone devices; and
- the Internet, which is capable of communicating all of the above tangible and intangible media formats through the use of specific programs or applications (apps).

Media convergence is the term used to define the 21st-century phenomenon that has seen information technology companies, telecommunications networks and content providers from the publishing worlds of

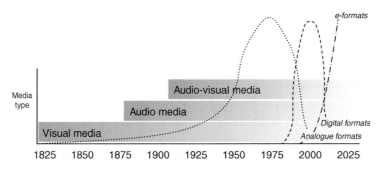

Fig. 1.6. The rise and fall of audio and visual media formats.

newspapers, magazines, music, radio, television, films and entertainment software bring together the 'three Cs' - computing, communications and content (Encyclopedia Britannica, 2013). A prime example of this is with Apple Inc., who currently are the world's leading online retailer of e-media content, direct from their iTunes program and App store, to consumers who can play this content on their computers and mobile devices. Apple also holds a dominant position in the gaming, e-literature, audio, video, web browsing and social media markets using Apple devices such as the iPhone, iPod Touch and iPad, which run 'apps' for these varied purposes. Apple Inc. are not the only company to work on converging media through e-formats; indeed both Google and Microsoft also offer devices for this purpose, although Apple's success with its devices and particularly its iTunes store has given it an extremely dominant foothold in this market. Apple, once only a computer manufacturer, is now one of the world's leading entertainment retailers.

VISITOR ATTRACTIONS

A visitor attraction is an 'excursion destination, a primary purpose of which is to allow access for entertainment, interest, or education' (VisitEngland, 2011). Visitor attractions attract both tourists and visitors from their own locale; hence the term 'tourist attraction' has not been used to label these entertainment facilities. The debate as to what constitutes a tourist attraction varies along with the definition as to what constitutes being a tourist, with some definitions focusing on distance travelled and others about duration spent at a destination, with tourists needing to have

an overnight stay. This is a largely philosophical and academic debate, which makes little difference to industry; however, the term visitor attraction is more relevant in terms of the physical attraction premises, which are a part of the entertainment industry and attract audiences from both near and far. Page and Swarbrooke (2001) state that the majority of visitor attractions attract the majority of their audiences from within a 50 mile radius or a 2 hour drive time, which gives them a 'regional' focus in their promotional activities and outlook.

Mintel (2012) identified that the economic climate, particularly high inflation and low earnings, can have a marked impact upon visitor attractions. During these periods, overall visitor numbers fall, particularly from international visitors. Proportionally, domestic visitor numbers may (but do not always) increase through the rise in the number of people holidaying domestically rather than abroad, or taking 'staycations'. Contemporary management issues associated specifically with visitor attractions are given detailed coverage in Chapter 15 (this volume) along with a typology of visitor attractions.

ENTERTAINMENT VENUES, PREMISES AND FACILITIES

Both event-based entertainment and visitor attractions require venues and facilities within which audiences may interact with the entertainment that has attracted them there. Such venues may be considered to be visitor attractions in their own right or simply premises where live entertainment events can take place. Making the distinction as to when a venue becomes a visitor attraction may be done on several parameters: the size of the venue, with larger venues being more likely to be considered visitor attractions; the distance that visitors will travel to visit the venue, with those venues who attract visitors from further afield more likely to be considered visitor attractions; and whether they attract visitors even when they are not in use as events venues, as is the case with the Santiago Bernabéu Stadium in Madrid, Spain, which contains a number of informative displays for visitors and also allows visitors to sit in the Manager's dugout (Fig. 1.7).

Some venues may not operate primarily as entertainment venues but still host live entertainment as a part of their operations. An example of this is a bar or pub, where the core business function is the sale of drinks and food. Bars and pubs use live entertainment as a means to attract more customers to enter the premises where they invariably spend money while in the premises; some examples of pub entertainment include live music, karaoke, DJs playing music, live quizzes, bingo, card-game tournaments, stand-up

Fig. 1.7. The Santiago Bernabéu Stadium, Madrid, Spain.

comedy and small theatrical performances. In the UK, bars and pubs are where the majority of people experience live entertainment (Mintel, 2007). Larger venues may offer the space and facilities for a number of entertainment events or attractions to occur simultaneously; for example, many large-scale casinos may also operate live music and nightclub venues within them, and theme parks may have multiple shows and events taking place at the same time alongside their usual operation of ride attractions. The larger the venue and the wider the array of events and attractions offered, the greater the diversity and number of people who will be attracted to it.

AN ACADEMIC DISCIPLINE

The word 'entertainment' is still not fully appreciated by those who may wish to express an opinion without giving the subject proper consideration. This is nothing new, and other more established academic disciplines such as tourism management and events management also once faced similar issues. Some may consider the subject of entertainment management a sub-set of a discipline that is more established such as business and management, events management, leisure management, tourism management, media studies, cultural studies or arts management. The reality is that aspects of all of those academic disciplines collectively contribute towards the subject of entertainment management. The purpose of this book is to draw upon the most pertinent areas of each of those disciplines and present, as best practice examples, relevant management information that an effective manager in the dynamic and ever-changing entertainment industry should know, in order to help effectively guide their organization through the challenges of the 21st century. If you are of the opinion that entertainment management is solely about managing entertainers, then think again. Entertainment management involves entrepreneurship, responsibility, marketing and promotion, event planning and review, strategy, venue management, human resource management, fundraising, finance, consultancy, research, legal awareness and a whole lot more.

Welcome to the entertainment industries.

SEMINAR ACTIVITIES

1. Over the next week, make a list of 'things' that attracted your attention or made you look twice. Consider why they attracted your attention and how they made you feel.
2. Consider what your favourite book is, and ask yourself *why* it is your favourite book. How does the book make you feel emotionally as you read it?
3. In a group, discuss the last event that you each attended; discuss the type of event, your motivations to attend the event and how reflecting on the event makes you feel.
4. Which visitor attractions have you been to in the past year? What type of attractions were they? And how were audiences kept entertained whilst there?
5. How do you consume media at home in a typical week? In a group, discuss your television, music, Internet, radio and reading consumption, including when you consume these media forms, for how long and which devices you most commonly use to consume media.

REFERENCES

British Broadcasting Corporation (BBC) (2012) Goths descend on UK seaside town of Whitby. Available at: http://www.bbc.co.uk/news/uk-17885655 (accessed 18 April 2013).

Donaton, S. (2005) *Madison & Vine: Why the Entertainment and Advertising Industries Must Converge to Survive*. McGraw Hill, New York.

Encyclopedia Britannica (2013) Media convergence. Available at: http://www.britannica.com/EBchecked/topic/1425043/media-convergence (accessed 15 April 2013).

Etymonline.com (2013) Online etymology dictionary. Available at: http://www.etymonline.com/index.php?allowed_in_frame=0&search=entertainment&searchmode=term (accessed 10 November 2013).

Getz, D. (1997) *Event Studies*. Taylor & Francis, London.

Mintel (2007) *Live Entertainment*. Mintel Group Limited, London.

Mintel (2012) *Visitor Attractions*. Mintel Group Limited, London.

Moss, S. (2009) An introduction to the entertainment industry. In: Moss, S. (2009) *The Entertainment Industry: An Introduction*. CAB International, Wallingford, UK, pp. 1–17.

Page, S. and Swarbrooke, J. (2001) *The Development and Management of Visitor Attractions*, 2nd edn. Butterworth-Heinemann, Oxford, UK.

Perebinossoff, P. (2008) *Real-world Media Ethics: Inside the Broadcast and Entertainment Industries*. Focal Press, Abingdon, UK.

Sayre, S. and King, C.M. (2003) *Entertainment and Society: Audiences Trends and Impact*. Sage, London.

Schacter, D.L. (2011) *Psychology*, 2nd edn. Worth, New York.

Schumpeter, J.A. (1934) *Fundamentals of Economic Development*. Harvard University Press, Cambridge, Massachusetts.

VisitEngland (2011) Visitor attraction trends in England. VisitEngland, London. Available at: http://www.visitengland.org/Images/11536%20VA%20Trends%20in%20England%20Full%20Reportv3_tcm30-33874.pdf (accessed 13 April 2013).

Vogel, H. (2007) *Entertainment Industry Economics: A Guide for Financial Analysis*, 7th edn. Cambridge University Press, New York.

Vogel, H. (2010) *Entertainment Industry Economics: A Guide for Financial Analysis*, 8th edn. Cambridge University Press, New York.

chapter 2

Entertainment Environments

Stuart Moss

LEARNING OBJECTIVES

After reading this chapter you should be able to:

- appreciate the range of geophysical location types and spaces within which the entertainment industries are present;
- realize the range of entertainment types that are commonly found in particular entertainment environments;
- be informed of a range of contemporary issues that exist in particular entertainment environments;
- understand the benefits that the entertainment industries can bring to each environment;
- become aware of some of the negatives that the entertainment industries can bring to particular entertainment environments; and
- appreciate some strategic decisions adopted within the entertainment environments to

minimize any harmful effects that entertainment provision may have there.

INTRODUCTION

Entertainment surrounds us; quite literally it is everywhere – in our homes, on transport, in urban centres, in the countryside, in the places we go on holiday and in our own personal spaces. We interact with products of the entertainment industry in a plethora of physical environments and for a variety of reasons. We may use entertainment in order to enhance the experience that we are having in a particular location such as listening to a city audio tour on a mobile device while exploring, or we could choose to use entertainment to mentally escape our surroundings and be taken elsewhere by the cognitive and emotional processes that can be triggered by entertainment interaction, such as reading a book whilst commuting to work.

Both scenarios highlight how entertainment is used for experiential enhancement by providing additional sensory inputs to accompany or to combat the environment we are within.

The entertainment environments are the range of geophysical location types and spaces within which entertainment may be encountered or utilized. The environments that are detailed within this chapter are the urban environment, the rural environment, the home environment, the transport environment and the cruise ship environment. Each of these environments is sensitive to the impacts that the entertainment industries can have upon them and each of these environments can influence the types of entertainment encountered within them, often through their physical nature. From a business strategy perspective, it should be noted that the environments within this chapter, the issues that are caused or created by entertainment and the (often resulting) influences that these environments can have upon entertainment would be considered to be in the macro-sphere (Johnson *et al.*, 2010).

It should also be noted that whilst environment from a 'green' or responsible perspective is a theme throughout this chapter, it is not the core focus of this chapter, and an in-depth discussion around green and responsible entertainment can be found in Chapter 10.

THE URBAN ENVIRONMENT

An urban area can be defined as one that has a high population density and a concentration of buildings and man-made infrastructure such as roads and footpaths within what is known as the 'built environment'. We commonly refer to urban areas as towns and cities, and when these areas grow and merge to become a larger 'urban-sprawl' the term conurbation is often used to describe them. Within the majority of urban areas there are focal points where the concentration of buildings often provide a service, cultural, commercial or business purpose; these areas attract people to them from surrounding areas and often further afield. There are several types or categories of these areas, which include: central business districts; cultural quarters; creative hubs; business hubs; leisure and entertainment parks; out-of-town shopping centres; and retail parks. All of these areas have characteristics that give them an identity and help them stand apart from each other, and all of these areas share the commonality that they are designed to draw visitors towards them.

The urban environment is the most concentrated entertainment environment, which attracts the most people to the widest number of entertainment providers per square unit of area than any other environment. The following attractions and events can often be found in urban areas:

- adult entertainment venues;
- art galleries;
- bars, pubs and clubs;
- big wheels;
- big screens for broadcasting major events;
- buildings that are iconic or unique;
- casinos;
- cathedrals and churches;
- cinemas;
- fairgrounds;
- festivals (numerous varieties);
- guided tours (on foot or by vehicle);
- live music venues;
- museums;
- spectator sport stadia and arenas;
- street entertainers;

- tall towers with observations decks;
- temporary and seasonal attractions and events such as Christmas markets; and
- theatres.

Please note that the above list is not definitive and that some of the above can also be found in non-urban areas.

Entertainment attractions and events draw visitors into urban areas. There are a number of benefits that increased visitation can bring, some of which are listed below:

- economic benefits through increased expenditure on goods and services;
- job creation;
- regeneration of 'run-down' and ex-industrial areas into new 'destinations';
- rejuvenation of existing facilities and infrastructure; and
- restoration of local pride.

There are also some negatives associated with visitors being drawn into urban areas for entertainment:

- increases in crime and anti-social behaviour;
- over-use of facilities and infrastructure;
- rises in prices of goods and services to match demand;

- pedestrian congestion of pavements and streets;
- pollution through vehicle emissions and littering; and
- traffic and road congestion.

The supporting transport infrastructures of roads, car parking and mass transit transportation systems (metro systems, subways and trams) offered within the urban environment enable the rapid movement of people into, out of and within urban areas, as do footpaths, pedestrianized areas and signage. Urban areas are often architecturally rich, providing 'architainment' through the grandeur or uniqueness of their buildings and infrastructure, as well as public displays of art including sculpture and statues, all of which is designed to enhance the environment from a visitor's perspective; for example, Fig. 2.1 (left) shows a sculpture of Polish Second World War resistance fighters in Warsaw and is designed to help educate visitors to a dark time in Poland's history, and (right), a shining golden-coloured statue of August the Strong in Dresden commemorates the life of the former ruler of Saxony in the early 18th century.

Fig. 2.1. Sculptures and statues in urban locations.

Town and city 'centres' where a high proportion of the buildings or 'units' have traditionally served a retail purpose, supported by services such as banks, employment agencies and insurance brokers, have become known as central business districts (CBDs). These often also feature a varied entertainment offering that can include venues such as theatres, cinemas, bars, pubs, nightclubs, themed restaurants, live music venues and gaming arcades, as well as visitor attractions including museums, art galleries, statues, monuments and fountains. The variety of offerings within CBDs ensures that visitor numbers, whilst highest during the daytime, can often also remain buoyant in the evening and throughout the night. The CBD, whilst dominant in being the busiest of urban areas, is itself undergoing transformation – established retail and service types such as media retailers, home-electronics shops, travel agents, gaming shops, DVD rental outlets and banks are in decline. This has been blamed on the rise of both Internet retail and supermarket chains in out-of-town areas.

What this means for the 'high street' is that more shop units are becoming vacant, which (often in particular areas of CBDs) can push prices for rents down and open up the possibility of 'newer', less corporate and more-independent units opening. What this also means is the possibility of more spaces being made available that can be utilized for leisure and entertainment purposes, and certainly the ratio of bars and restaurants to retail units particularly within what were once considered 'shopping' malls is on the increase (Ruddick, 2012), as are bookmakers and betting/gambling facilities (Sims, 2012; Barford and Judah, 2013). It certainly is not all doom and gloom for the high street as shopping arcades and malls are transforming 'worn and tired' CBDs into bright and often architecturally stunning and unique places to visit, which draw visitors to them as much to gaze upon their spectacle as to visit the retail and service units within them. These arcades and malls often feature various art forms in their design as well as open spaces that can be used for performance. This is highlighted in Fig. 2.2, which shows the Trinity Leeds shopping and leisure mall, which opened in Leeds, UK, in March 2013. In the figure, crowds are entertained by an aerial performer, and also a prominent sculptured artwork entitled Equus adorns a highly visible space within the mall. Trinity Leeds plans to have permanent art pieces on display as well as temporary installations, and states on its website 'Trinity Leeds is more than just a world-class retail destination. It's the heartbeat of a city built on a long legacy of creativity, culture and innovation. This is reflected in our art programme, which brings exceptional art and creativity into the city and the scheme, connecting people and place in ways that will inspire everyday' (Trinity Leeds, 2013).

Open pedestrianized spaces are also frequently a feature of urban areas and provide a focal point as an event space; these typically include 'squares', 'plazas' and 'piazzas', which can hold large crowds and provide local councils, private promoters and related organizations the opportunity to generate revenue through the staging of events. Spracklen *et al.* (2013) noted that where city centre spaces have become 'eventized' and commodified for branded and corporate leisure and entertainment purposes, spaces for alternative (predominantly 'left-wing' or subcultural) leisure and entertainment are marginalized and often displaced from city centres.

Fig. 2.2. Trinity Leeds on opening day, Leeds, UK.

A contemporary example of this is parkour being banned from a number of locations including Moreton in the Wirral (UK) and Battery Park in Manhattan (USA). An example of a major city centre event taking place in an urban open space is demonstrated in Fig. 2.3, where a rock concert is being held in Millennium Square, Leeds, UK.

Open pedestrianized spaces and areas with a high pedestrian flow are often targeted by impromptu entertainers who seek exposure or financial reward, such as 'buskers'. Where numbers of buskers have grown to a point where they have either become a nuisance or have attracted negative feedback from both locals and visitors, a system of local-level regulation may be put in place and enforced, requiring buskers to buy permits or licences and then follow strict rules and guidelines. Figure 2.4 demonstrates a teenage busker in Birmingham, UK (left), and police officers in Dresden, Germany, checking the permits of street musicians in the city (right).

Many visitors to urban areas, who are there to sample the entertainment offering of the location, are often engaged and captivated as visitors by their sometimes new and novel surroundings. Activities engaged in by such people often include photography, film-making and simply gazing as an audience member. Visitors to urban centres can spread the word very easily, particularly through social media, which helps to promote destinations and has been embraced by some localities who have provided free Wi-Fi networks for visitors to use; two examples include Warsaw's Old Town (Poland) and Briggate in the City of Leeds (UK); these networks are known as Municipal Wireless Networks (MWNs) and are set to increase in proliferation as more local authorities globally seek to 'add value' to the experience of their visitors.

Engagement in tourist activities can lead to momentary lapses in awareness with regards to self and surroundings, leaving visitors vulnerable to those willing to take criminal advantage

Fig. 2.3. Example of an urban open space being used to hold an entertainment event, Millennium Square, Leeds, UK.

Fig. 2.4. Buskers in urban centres.

of this. Many urban centres (particularly areas within large cities) around the world, which are considered 'tourist hot-spots', are also synonymous with pickpocketing; examples include Covent Garden (London), Las Ramblas (Barcelona) and Piazza del Plebiscito (Napoli). Persistent pickpocketing of both visitors and staff at the Louvre art museum in Paris led to a one day strike by staff in April 2013 (BBC, 2013). It is a true adage that increases in tourism can lead to increases in crime, particularly petty opportunistic crime against those who are distracted. Figure 2.5 is a warning sign to tourists who are visiting Auschwitz in Oświęcim, Poland.

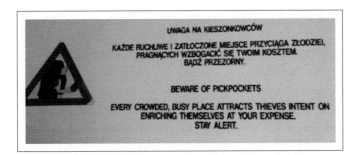

Fig. 2.5. Warning sign about pickpockets, Oświęcim, Poland.

More severe crimes against visitors to urban areas also occur, and when this becomes a regular occurrence it can lead to the reputation of such an area suffering, as is currently the case in a number of Mexican urban locations where crime exacerbated through drug trafficking has made some locations unsafe to visit, including the city of Ciudad Juárez, which the UK foreign office 'advise against all but essential travel to Ciudad Juarez. There is a high level of drug-related violence and criminal activity in the area' (Foreign and Commonwealth Office, 2013). People who visit urban areas for the purposes of recreation in their leisure time want to feel relaxed and at ease; in any new environment the 'unknown' is always going to lead to a degree of visitor stress, but having the enjoyment of visitors suffer, either through negative experiences or simply by being overly vigilant of potential threats, lessens their ability to immerse themselves in the experience that they want to have whilst in these areas.

It is a fundamental human need to feel safe in the environments that we are in, and urban centres that attract leisure seekers need to make their visitors feel safe by taking measures to minimize threats against them. In preparation for the football World Cup in 2014, and the Olympic Games in 2016, the Brazilian Government is currently restoring law and order within, and removing gangs and criminal elements from, 'favelas' (ex-shanty towns), which are urban neighbourhoods that form parts of cities, in preparation for the arrival of large tourist numbers.

This was the case in South Africa, which in the early 2000s had experienced a boom in visitor numbers in coastal and countryside areas but a decline in urban centres. The then South African Tourism Minister Marthinus van Schalkwyk said in a speech to tourism industry leaders that about one-third of potential tourists had mentioned fears about safety as one reason for not visiting South Africa. 'Crime is an issue we as industry have to deal with if we want to reach our target of 10 million arrivals by 2010,' van Schalkwyk said (Associated Press, 2007). South Africa's solution was to boost police and security personnel by almost 25% between 2007 and 2010, which was also in time for the country to host the football (soccer) World Cup competition.

One type of urban area in South Africa where tourists and visitors were once ill-advised to enter was the slums around major cities such as Cape Town and Johannesburg. But even these are now opening up to visitors who wish to gaze upon the unique cultural heritage that the slums and their occupants offer. Under various schemes aimed at helping the slum communities and spreading visitor spend to benefit areas that would not normally receive tourists, people in the slums have been trained as guides and now take paying visitors on educational guided tours. This example of so-called 'slum tourism' highlights two areas of best practice: it demonstrates pure entrepreneurship (turning nothing into something) to turn an urban area once bereft of tourists into a visitor attraction; and it also demonstrates the involvement of the local community in creating a visitor attraction that ultimately benefits themselves both financially and in terms of community safety and pride. Once the benefits of in-bound visitor spend became apparent, the community themselves took pride in their unique urban area and ensured that the area was safe, so that visitors would not be dissuaded from returning and telling others about their experience (Briedenhann and Ramchander, 2006).

Cultural tourism involves the visitation of locations specifically to sample the differences that exist between the ways of life and social norms of the visitor and the host community, and it has a greater financial impact than many other forms of tourism (Hughes, 2000), making it a favourable option for those responsible for the management of destinations, particularly in terms of regeneration to destinations boosted by tourist revenue; 30% of destinations in Europe are visited due to their cultural heritage sites (Bellini et al., 2007).

The entertainment industry is vast, and many urban destinations have a range of entertainment offerings, which may be culture or heritage based, or based upon more hedonistic pleasures including drinking alcohol and engaging in sexual activities. Whilst the tourism under discussion in this section so far has been mainly cultural and heritage focused, many urban destinations that are favoured by cultural tourists are also favoured by both alcohol and sex tourists due to the availability of bars, pubs, clubs and adult entertainment venues within these destinations. An alcohol tourist (or alco-tourist) is one who travels to a destination with the intention of consuming alcohol; this may be due to the type of alcohol or an associated novelty of it, or due to cheaper prices or relaxed 'rules' around its sale and consumption in relation to the region from where the tourist has travelled. Bell (2008, p. 291) refers to this as 'alcotourism', which is 'the practices of travelling to drink, drinking on holiday, drinking to travel and drinking while travelling'. A sex tourist is one who travels to a destination 'to have sex with a stranger at the destination' (Bauer and McKercher, 2003, p. 4) or to experience sexual desire from the adult entertainment on offer at the destination (Griffiths, 2009).

The motivations of tourists differ. Ryan (1991) placed tourist motivations under the following categories: escape; relaxation; play; strengthening family bonds; prestige; social interaction; sexual opportunity; educational opportunity; self-fulfilment; wish fulfilment; and shopping. Figure 2.6 demonstrates that there are many similarities in motivations between cultural tourists and alcohol and sex tourists, as well as a number of differences. It is the resultant behaviours of fulfilling these motivations, and the impacts of these upon the host community and the urban environment, that is the key issue, with the most negatively perceived impacts being associated with hedonistic behaviour. Whilst hedonistic behaviour may also be demonstrated by cultural tourists, it is largely alcohol and sex tourists who are perceived as doing the most harm to urban destinations.

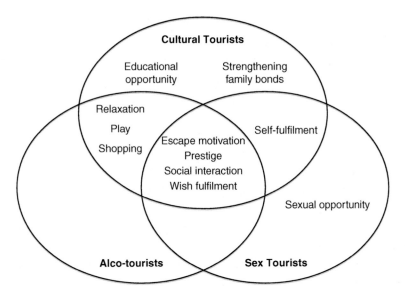

Fig. 2.6. The motivations of cultural, alcohol and sex tourists, based upon the original work of Ryan (1991).

Hughes (2000) states that a large proportion of cultural tourists with an interest in visiting destinations for their arts and heritage are of a post-retirement age. Tallinn, Estonia, is an example of a European city with a medieval old town, which is a UNESCO world heritage site, that has seen the nature of tourists to the city change from high-spending over-50 year olds, who were there for the architecture and culture (Hickman, 2008), to many more younger people and particularly same-sex parties of young adult males. This was as a result of budget airlines commencing operations to the city from the early 21st century. The downtown area of Tallinn, which encompasses the medieval old town, is less than a mile wide and is where the majority of the city's bars are concentrated. At its worst, Tallinn experienced 'hundreds of drunk, leery men each weekend, singing and stumbling their way from bar to strip club in search of alcohol and sex' (Hickman, 2008, p. 314), which caused

disquiet amongst many destination stakeholders such as the authorities, residents and business owners.

The image of Tallinn as a cultural tourism destination suffered as a result of this and led to a number of bars, hotels and restaurants in Tallinn no longer accepting large same-sex parties. It is highly likely that even if cultural tourists and groups of young people have travelled from the same destination, their age difference will mean that there is a significant 'culture gap' between them in terms of their behaviours, norms and values. Therefore, when both groups meet in a confined destination it is possible that conflict could arise. Richter (2010) noted that where entertainment and leisure pursuits were seen to be damaging to the corporate image of urban centres, policies are often introduced that displace or ban them from these locations.

The problems experienced by Tallinn have also been experienced by numerous coastal towns that promote themselves as being beach resorts, where the primary recreational offerings are beach activities, sea swimming and sunbathing. Resorts generate wealth for their host populations predominantly through tourism-related industries such as accommodation, transport, leisure services and entertainment provision. The population of a resort is typically swelled during 'seasons' when a relatively large number of people visit either for days, short breaks or longer holidays. One key geophysical factor is the weather; beach resorts are particularly sensitive to this and are at their busiest periods in the summer when the weather is at its hottest. Seasonality brings challenges to beach resorts where much employment and income generation is only for the short period of the season, which can sometimes be only for several weeks.

The majority of entertainment provided for visitors to beach resorts is geared towards those who stay overnight as tourists. Visitor spend can be greatly increased with the provision of a night-time entertainment offering, which can positively benefit the local economy and even 'stretch' the main tourist season. However, the amount and type of entertainment offered can result in concentrations of particular groups of visitors, which in relation to bars, pubs and nightclubs has proved problematic in some beach resort destinations, when large concentrations of these establishments has led to a change in visitor demographics, typically more younger people and same-sex groups. This can change the image of a destination and then lead to a further knock-on effect of more 'untraditional' and for local residents 'unwanted' entertainment establishments opening, such as gambling venues including casinos and adult entertainment venues such as strip clubs and lap dancing bars. For some beach resorts, the beach and sea have

become secondary to the nightlife in attracting visitors, which can have a detrimental effect in 'putting off' certain other groups of visitors and causing irritation to the host community through behaviour associated with drunkenness or other 'anti-social' problems.

'When travelling away from home, tourists come in contact with the places they visit and with their inhabitants, and social exchange takes place' (Burkart and Medlik, 1981, p. 59); it is important that this social exchange is not considered harmful or an 'irritant' (Doxey, 1975) to the host population of areas that are developed for tourism purposes, as the presence of tourists and their social background can affect the lives of those within destinations. These impacts should therefore be either minimal or beneficial to the host population. Initial visitation by income-generating visitors and tourists to an area is often welcomed by the host population, who Doxey (1975) described as being in a 'euphoric' state in the early days of inbound tourist visitation but who after time become 'apathetic' towards tourists as they become familiar with them, which becomes 'annoyance' when tourist behaviours begin to impinge upon local traditions and lifestyles, and from there to 'antagonism' when the reputation of the locality suffers as a result of tourist activity and behaviour. This positive to negative transgression of local feeling towards tourists is known as Doxey's Irridex.

The addition of bars, pubs and clubs in destinations provided for tourists can also alter the social fabric of destinations. Moore's (1995) study of the Greek town of Arachova demonstrated that over time, drinking practices brought to the town through tourism actually changed the habits of young people (particularly men) in the town by giving them a taste for world beers that they had largely never experienced before, and forever changing the social structure of the town with an increased visitation by the town's young people to bars and nightclubs that had been provided as part of the tourist infrastructure.

In summary, urban locations have a large and diverse concentration of entertainment offerings, ranging from their very own architecture and art works to an extremely diverse range of entertainment venues, including theatres, museums, themed restaurants, adult entertainment venues, bars and nightclubs. Urban destinations can add value to the visitor experience by providing entertainment spaces and facilities such as Municipal Wireless Networks. High concentrations of visitors are attracted into urban areas, and these visitors require careful management as well as protection from harm, particularly crime, in order to make urban locations safe and appealing to those who visit them. The balance of entertainment offered needs to attract a blend of visitor types, and this needs to be monitored in order to protect the image, reputation and social fabric of destinations. Ultimately, visitor spend in urban areas can benefit the host community and lead to improvements within urban destinations.

THE RURAL ENVIRONMENT

A rural area is one that has a low human population density and typically man-made infrastructure is minimal, although man's influence upon the environment may be seen in agricultural areas. Common types of rural land areas include: woodland/forests; beaches; mountainous and 'rocky' areas; desert; wetlands/marshes; and grasslands/savannah. 'Countryside' is commonly used within the English

language to generically refer to several of the above areas, particularly in relation to those areas where man's influence has managed rural lands for agricultural purposes.

In terms of physical area, the rural environment has the least density of entertainment industry provision of all of the entertainment environments, but attraction and event-based entertainment does exist in rural areas, some common examples of which are as follows:

- archaeological or historic sites;
- factory shops with craft demonstrations;
- gardens and garden centres;
- music and arts festivals;
- natural parklands and nature reserves;
- open-air museums;
- pubs and restaurants;
- stately homes, historic buildings and castles;
- theme parks;
- traditional cultural events;
- visitor centres including educational and interpretation facilities; and
- zoos and wildlife-based attractions.

Entertainment in the rural environment can bring a number of benefits, these include:

- cultural exchange between visitors and the local community;
- demand for products created in rural areas;
- job creation in rural areas;
- preservation of rural services including bus routes, pubs, restaurants and shops in rural areas;
- raised awareness of wildlife and habitat conservation; and
- revenue streams to rural communities.

The rural environment is sensitive to the influences of man, particularly in relation to numbers, so for its protection visitors to rural areas require careful management.

Some of the negative influences that man can have upon the rural environment are as follows:

- changes to local culture;
- damage of agricultural land;
- damage to the natural habitats of species;
- degradation of footpaths;
- harm to wildlife;
- increased crime levels, including vandalism;
- overuse of infrastructure that has not been created for large numbers of people, e.g. rural roads, leading to traffic congestion;
- pollution, including littering and the introduction of substances that are alien to the natural environment, which may cause harm to it; and
- population increases in rural areas, which can lead to inflated property prices.

Whilst small-scale operations such as farm shops and craft demonstrations may not attract significant numbers of visitors or do great harm to the rural environment, larger scale operations such as music and arts festivals can. Financially, entertainment, whether attraction- or event-based, is reliant on an audience, so the more expensive the entertainment is to provide, the larger the audience needs to be to pay for it. Large-scale entertainment attractions and events in rural areas need to provide amenities for substantial numbers of visitors. Basic considerations include sanitation, fresh water, signage, car parking, transportation, accommodation, electricity, security, waste disposal and recycling facilities. This is covered in more detail in Chapter 10.

Case Study: The Glastonbury Festival of Contemporary Performing Arts

The Glastonbury Festival of Contemporary Performing Arts has been running on farmland near the village of Pilton in the county of Somerset, UK, since 1970. The festival has steadily grown in popularity, size and scope, and is now the world's largest festival of contemporary performing arts. In 2005 the festival sold 153,000 full weekend tickets, although in more recent years they have reduced this number to 135,000. The festival is held on most years, although there are years when it has not, including 2006 and 2012, which are 'fallow years' intended to give the land on which the festival is held more time to recover and to give those who live near the festival site a break from the disruption caused by the festival. Where a festival attracts such a large number of people into a rural area, it needs to provide an infrastructure and facilities to cater for these visitor numbers, including toilets.

However, providing toilets does not necessarily mean that festival goers will actually use them, and urinating in public places has proved to be problematic at the festival site, particularly as urine has polluted not only the ground but also the local streams. The media reported that after the 2003 festival up to 4000 fish had died in local streams and rivers as a result of public urination at the festival. It was also reported that much urine contained traces of alcohol and illegal drugs, which affected the frog and toad population. This level of environmental damage could have led to the festival losing its licence, so a solution had to be found. This was a three-pronged strategy: first, more toilets were provided for festival goers; secondly, signs and posters were made to deter people from urinating on the land

(Continued)

Case Study. Continued.

and into streams; and thirdly, the 'Green Police' were formed. The Glastonbury Festival Green Police are performance artists who 'patrol' the site looking for those committing environmental 'crimes' such as littering and urinating in public. Upon spotting a 'criminal' the green police run towards them with sirens blaring pointing flowers rather than guns to publicly chastise them for their crimes. This works not only through enforcement but by education with a little humiliation thrown in for those who are caught in the act. The net result of the Green Police's endeavours has been a reduction in public urination, littering and other environmentally unfriendly acts. Figure 2.7 (below) demonstrates the sheer size of the festival by providing an aerial view of part of the site (left) and the Green Police ready for action (right).

Fig. 2.7. Glastonbury Festival of Contemporary Performing Arts, UK; aerial view of part of the site and Green Police. Photographs courtesy of Jason Bryant.

In summary, the rural environment has a low population density and its natural spaces are sensitive to the impacts of man. Entertainment attractions and events are present in the rural environment and can provide a number of benefits, including economic benefits, jobs and cultural exchange. Rural areas can provide wide spaces in which large-scale entertainment attractions may be based, or events may be held that can attract very large audiences. Such numbers can have a detrimental impact upon rural areas from both a 'green' and conservation perspective, so careful management and amenity provision is necessary in order to preserve the rural environment.

THE TRANSPORT ENVIRONMENT

Transport is a medium by which people (passengers) or items (freight) can be moved from one location to another. Passenger transport as both a spectacle to behold, and more significantly as an experience for those fare-paying passengers, has suffered the same fate as many spectacles and experiences that may have once been considered entertaining, in that familiarity with it has bred contempt. Once upon a time, watching the landscape 'fly by' at the heady speeds of 20+ miles per hour (mph) was entertainment enough, but a journey today (particularly a lengthy one) may be perceived as being more of a chore than a pleasure. This is especially the case with journeys such as daily commutes and the drudgery that such a repetitious experience may bring, which is why passengers often seek entertaining distractions to ease such negatively perceived experiences.

Entertainment that can be found in the transport environment includes (but is not limited to) the following:

- at-seat audio points;
- carriage-mounted display screens;
- children's play areas;
- impromptu variety performers;
- live music;
- newspapers and magazines;
- seat-back television screens; and
- table-top games.

In terms of advantages and disadvantages of entertainment in the transport environment: the main advantages are that it can add value to the passenger experience and alleviate passenger boredom; the main disadvantages are the cost of providing entertainment, and that due to the confines of limited space, entertainment may prove to be an annoyance for those passengers who do not want it.

Newspapers have provided a mental distraction and therefore entertainment for passengers for over a century; and since the 1930s, the rise of the paperback book, through publishers such as Penguin, and later imitators and competitors, has provided passengers with a conveniently pocket-sized mental break from the tedium of their journey and their sometimes overcrowded/unpleasant surrounding environment. Free newspaper titles, which

have become known as 'Freesheets', funded by advertising, are now often available on public transport. One such example of this is 'The Metro', which is owned by Associated Newspapers Ltd and distributed to transport hubs, trains, trams and buses around the UK. Over 1.3 million copies of the newspaper are distributed daily, with an estimated readership of 3.8 million people (Associated Newspapers, 2013). Many transport providers 'give away' their own printed publications, which are directly funded through advertising and indirectly through on-board retail, which occurs due to promotions contained within the magazines and also indirectly through passenger fares.

Games have also proved popular amongst passengers on journeys, from simple games needing no equipment such as 'eye-spy' to card games, and from the 1980s onwards, handheld electronic games, which have grown in capability and shrunk in size ever since. Games are especially important to keep children entertained on journeys; this keeps them occupied and often gives their parents and surrounding passengers a more 'harmonious' transport experience. To assist this, some transport-operating companies provide accessories to help make journeys more 'fun'. Two examples where this happens are Deutsche Bahn in Germany who have children's areas within certain carriages on Inter City Express (ICE) trains, and Grand Central Trains in the UK who provide imprints of game boards on table tops, with retail opportunities on board to buy the game pieces.

At-seat audio is available on some public transport, where passengers can listen to music by plugging their own headphones into at-seat sockets; however, since the 1980s, personal cassette players such as the Sony Walkman gave passengers on public transport another entertainment option. This was followed by a period of creative destruction in analogue and digital media formats to format-less media, which saw the rise of the Disc-Man in the 1990s where passengers could listen to compact discs (CDs), followed by the short-lived mini-disc and then hand-held battery-intensive personal DVD players, until the MP3 player rose to prominence in the late 1990s (a market which was championed by Apple Inc.'s iPod range). Early iPods only played audio, but video-capable machines also appeared in the early 2000s. In recent years, the rise of the laptop, smartphone and tablet computer has given passengers a personal multimedia audio-visual entertainment option, which with the increase in proliferation of Wi-Fi networks, 3G and 4G, means that passengers can now be entertained by words, audio, video, photographs and games from their one personal device. At-seat audio has been phased out by a number of transport providers as a cost-cutting measure and also so that the power and cabling infrastructure can instead be used for Wi-Fi transmission. The strategy of many transport providers has been to facilitate passengers to entertain themselves rather than to provide entertainment. A disadvantage of Wi-Fi on board some public transport is its slow speed and limited bandwidth. This is due to the fact that many trains and buses actually connect to the Internet through the 3G mobile telephone spectrum, so the speeds passed onto passengers are not greatly faster than what their own device could give. The main advantage of using on-board Wi-Fi over passengers using their own 3G signal is that most trains and buses scan all networks at once, thus providing greater coverage and less drop-out.

Television and video on board land-based public transport such as trains, trams and buses is available, and it is not uncommon to see television screens on luxury coach transport. However, in many cases the provision of such services has been downgraded, again due to passengers having their own devices that are capable of playing video. In the UK, Great Western Trains 'High Speed' services offer 'Volo', video on-demand, which operates from screens on seat backs in certain carriages. More widespread on land-based public transport are video displays where video can be played to a largely captive audience, but such resources are often for use in advertising and the provision of 'infotainment'; however, their level of quality is sometimes questionable. Figure 2.8 demonstrates (left) popular board games reproduced on table tops on Grand Central Trains (UK) as well as power outlets for customer use, and (right) video-based visitor attraction advertising on board a tram in the city centre of Amsterdam, the Netherlands.

Live performed entertainment is a rarity on land-based public transport due to the practicalities of providing such spectacle safely and to the genuine passenger benefit in the confines of a typically seated coach/carriage. It does happen but often more for novelty on special workings rather than a long-term sustainable entertainment source. In the UK, Northern Rail run an occasional music and real ale train between the town of Huddersfield and the city of Sheffield. Passengers on board may be treated to acoustic or jazz performances, and have the additional option to purchase real ale (traditionally brewed British beer) to drink and savour the performance. The whole train becomes a moving theatre and people ride the train just

Fig. 2.8. Some rail transport on-board entertainment.

for this experience, but this is only done occasionally otherwise the novelty value of this experience would lessen and audiences would dwindle. The music and ale trains run on normal scheduled services, upon which passenger numbers are increased by around 400% (Drew Haley, 15 March 2013, personal communication); one such train is featured in Fig. 2.9.

Other less-common examples of entertainment that can be found on trains include: cinema cars; children's play areas; DJs and dance floors; at-seat entertainers for children such as clowns; DVD and games console hire; on-board information including leaflets distributed about points of interest passed en-route; and art exhibitions.

With air travel, a different set of circumstances exists around passenger expectations, journey length, practicalities, legalities and safety concerns which means that there is more rationale for airlines to invest in entertainment for their passengers than for train, tram or coach companies. In terms of the provision of media-based 'at-seat' entertainment, airlines lead the way with on-demand television

Fig. 2.9. Jazz musicians on a Northern Rail music train. Photograph courtesy of Northern Rail.

and films, music and gaming (Fig. 2.10). The provision of entertainment on aircraft is more of a necessity where mobile phones cannot be used and where a minority of passengers have a window seat. Long journeys can become tedious and off-putting, so entertainment can help improve the passenger experience.

Whilst the use of mobile telephone networks is currently banned on the vast majority of global airlines due to safety concerns,

Fig. 2.10. Airlines lead the way in terms of audio-visual on-board entertainment provision. Photograph courtesy of Stuart Rhodes.

on-board Wi-Fi Internet is now being rolled-out by some airlines including Delta, United Airlines and Lufthansa. While this is not yet commonplace globally, it will eventually become so, and for airlines the onus to provide at-seat entertainment will be less as passengers choose to take advantage of this. An even newer technology called Earth Stations on Mobile Platforms (ESOMPs) is currently being developed, which will allow aircraft to communicate directly with satellites that will then offer Internet speeds up to ten times faster than current Wi-Fi networks (Miller, 2013). New innovations such as Google Glass (a wearable head-mounted computer and display) and smart paper, which offers micro- thin flexible screens, will only increase the penetration of entertaining gadgetry that passengers carry and will also contribute to a lesser need for airlines to provide entertainment.

Passengers using airlines need to use airports, and with security, check-in and often a lot of queuing, there is a need to arrive early – in some cases up to 3 hours before a flight is due to take-off. The majority of airports now offer passengers Wi-Fi (either free or as

a paid service), and many airports have luxury lounges where, for a price, passengers can relax with complimentary drinks, films, television, computer games and even 'Scalextric' racing car games, as in the case of the passenger lounge at Manchester Airport. Some airports offer viewing facilities so that passengers can relax and watch aircraft take-off and land; these prove popular as the sight of aircraft taking off and landing is still novel for many. All of the above helps to improve the passenger experience and alleviate boredom. Figure 2.11 demonstrates the mobile phone screen (left) of a passenger 'checking in' to Vilnius Airport (Lithuania) with the iPhone Foursquare game app (not to be confused with checking in for a flight); upon checking in, the app promotes the airport's free Wi-Fi network. Figure 2.11 (right) shows at Krakow Airport (Poland), access gates to the unstaffed runway viewing gallery, which is coin-operated by customers, providing the airport with a small income stream.

Water-borne transport such as boats and ferries also face a unique set of challenges. However, as these are broadly similar to the entertainment challenges faced by cruise ships (which are more than transport alone), these will be covered in that particular section of this chapter.

Whilst the focus of this section has focused on public transport, the humble car should not be overlooked in terms of entertainment provision. In-car entertainment has mostly focused upon audio entertainment, and this has quite rightly been for safety reasons. However, the car of the future will certainly focus on more visual entertainment options. Innovations are already happening; in January 2013 the new Volkswagen Golf was being promoted as having a '5.8" colour touch screen infotainment system', and it

Fig. 2.11. Entertainment provision at airports.

may not be long before tablet computers are integrated into car dashboards, seat backs, windows and ceilings. The car of the future will most likely drive itself; Google is already trialling this technology, so with less need for people to drive, the car will become more of a varied personalized entertainment space to move passengers from one point to another.

In summary, entertainment in the transport environment does allow transport providers to differentiate and strategically add value to their transport product, particularly in the face of much like-for-like competition. There is arguably a necessity for transport providers to invest in entertainment that is cost-effective and sustainable, but this needs to be contrasted with providing passengers with the facilities to use their own entertainment devices.

CRUISE SHIP ENVIRONMENT

It may seem an oddity to differentiate cruise ships from the transport environment but a cruise ship is much more than transportation. Cruise ships take passengers from one location to another, and usually on a cruise there are multiple destinations. Cruise ships also offer accommodation in terms of cabins, which on modern cruise ships are akin to hotel bedrooms, but a cruise ship is also an attraction and a destination in itself. People book cruises based upon both the itinerary of the cruise and also which ship will be making the cruise. The combination of what a cruise ship offers in terms of transport, hospitality, tourist attraction, leisure facilities and entertainment provision has generated a decades old academic debate as to where a cruise ship should be located within the tourism 'system'.

Leiper (1979) identified three distinct regions that make up the tourism system: a tourist generating region, which includes mainly tour operators and travel agents; a transit route region, which includes all forms of transportation and infrastructure for facilitating the movement of tourists to and from their destinations; and a tourist destination region, which includes accommodation, visitor attractions, leisure and entertainment amenities. From Leiper's model it is clear that the transport environment lies within the transit route region, and that the urban and rural environments lie within the tourist destination region, but as cruise ships are both destinations and transport, they could be considered to be in both the transit route region and the tourist destination region of Leiper's model. Cruise ships are large floating contained resorts, and their passengers provide a perfectly captive audience. Cruise ships actually demonstrate a flaw in Leiper's model, which can be seen in Fig. 2.12.

The issues within this section, which are based specifically on cruise ships, may also be applied either wholly or partially to some large ferries, which may also provide accommodation and entertainment for their passengers but which typically are used by their passengers to get from one location to another and not as the location for a holiday. These issues are largely not relevant to small ferries that undertake short journeys and are transport alone.

According to the European Cruise Council (ECC) (2012), the cruise industry has enjoyed dynamic growth over a period of 30 years. The ECC is an industry body, which was established in order to represent the leading cruise operators in Europe. Its 2012 report, entitled 'The Cruise Industry: Contribution of Cruise Tourism to the Economies of Europe 2012 Edition', reveals a number of statistics (European Cruise Council, 2012, p. 12) that demonstrate how the global cruise industry has grown, particularly in recent years:

- From 2001 to 2011 cruise passenger numbers have increased from 9.91 million passengers to 20.60 million (+108%) with 9.6% growth achieved in 2011.
- In 2011, North America represented 56% of global market share (a drop from 70% in 2000) in the cruise industry with 11.5 million passengers; Europe came in second place with 6.18 million passengers; and the rest of the world had 2.91 million passengers on cruise ships.

What the above information tells us is that demand for cruising is increasing globally, and where once cruising was considered a mainly North American market, the rest of the world is catching up. This has largely been achieved through popular North American brands such as Carnival, Celebrity and Royal Caribbean International entering European and other global markets, as well as many European brands emerging, which are emulating the success of the North American cruise industry and their extremely large and

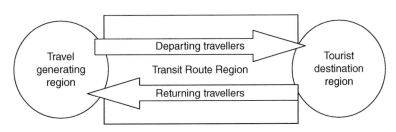

Fig. 2.12. Leiper's model of the tourism system (Leiper, 1979).

glamorous cruise ships. Notable European cruise brands include MSC, Aida and P&O Cruises.

Cruise ships are getting bigger, carrying more passengers and offering more in the way of leisure and entertainment options. It is not untypical now to find the following entertainment facilities provided for passengers on 21st-century cruise ships:

- art galleries;
- casinos;
- children's areas;
- cinemas;
- games rooms;
- health entertainment and wellness services such as massage;
- in-cabin television with movie channels;
- Internet cafés;
- libraries;
- live music;
- nightclubs;
- simulator rides;
- spectator sport arenas;
- theatres (of varying sizes) that showcase a range of performances; and
- themed bars and restaurants.

There are invariably more entertainment facilities than listed above on cruise ships, but the list does serve as an indicator to the breadth of what is actually available to audiences of potentially thousands of passengers, who when the ship is at sea are a captive audience.

Cruise companies generate headlines and publicity by offering 'new' forms of entertainment to their passengers. In 2012, two new high-profile cruise ships both offered on-board entertainment innovations in terms of 4D cinemas; these ships were the *The Carnival Breeze* and the *MSC Divina*. Such high

profile entertainment also helps to attract the increasing family market and can generate revenue by charging for their use.

The majority of entertainment provided on cruise ships is complimentary and comes as part of the cruise package, and may include nightly theatre shows, stand-up comedy, nightclubs and live music. Where this occurs, passengers are continually offered retail opportunities including drinks and the purchase of souvenirs and photographs. It is a fact that the longer passengers stay on board cruise ships, the more likely it is that they will spend money on board the ship, and this is how cruise operators increase their profit margins. Many cruise operators include additional taxes with transactions, and these are often what pay staff wages. Quite simply, it makes perfect sense to provide a wide range of entertainment on-board cruise ships; the passengers feel that entertainment adds value to their cruise experience, but the reality is that it adds profit for cruise ship operators.

Carnival Corporation PLC is the world's largest cruise ship operator, owning the following brands: AIDA Cruises, Carnival Cruise Lines, Costa Cruises, Cunard Line, Holland America Line, Ibero Cruises, P&O Cruises, P&O Cruises Australia, Princess Cruises and Seabourn Cruise Line, which between them have 100 cruise ships – half of those operating in the world today. According to Carnival Corporation PLC (2012) in their annual report, 23% of revenue that the company generated in 2012 was from on-board spend. This amounted to US$3.5bn, which divided by 100 cruise ships equals US$35m per ship; each ship had an average of 1 day in port per week, so with 314 sailing days, this amounted to US$111,465 in sales per day or US$4644 per hour. With an average ship holding 2500 passengers, this roughly equated to US$1.85 per passenger per hour.

Some cruise holidays are sold at little profit, particularly with new ships that need to establish a reputation, so on-board spend is extremely important to cruise operators in terms of them remaining profitable, particularly when new ships can cost upwards of US$700m, as was the case with the *MSC Divina* (Ship Building Tribune, 2012). Modern cruise ships, like modern shopping malls, place a large emphasis on themed and artistic leisure and entertainment spaces, often with artworks, sculptures and signature furnishings. Figure 2.13 highlights three distinct entertainment spaces on board the *MSC Divina*, including the Pantheon Theatre (top images), MSC Arena for spectator sport fixtures (bottom left) and the Galaxy Disco (bottom right).

A growing trend, particularly in North America, has been to book big-name musicians to play on cruises and even to combine the cruise experience with that of a music festival, attracting dedicated music fans who are willing to pay a premium price for such a unique experience. This also opens up cruising to people who may not have before considered this type of holiday. Bands and artists such as Kiss, Weezer and R. Kelly have all played their own themed cruises, which attracts their fans, who not only get to see them perform but also share social space with them in a way like no other. In 2012, the long established Californian Coachella Music Festival launched a cruise called the S.S. Coachella on board the *Celebrity Silhouette* cruise ship. This cruising music festival featured numerous bands, artists and DJs including Pulp, Yeasayer, Gaslamp Killer, James Murphy and Hot Chip, who played two festivals over 3 days, the first around the Bahamas and the second around Jamaica, both in December 2012 (Coachella Music Festival, 2012).

Whilst themed cruises featuring such high profile artists are still comparatively rare, they are innovative and demonstrate how

Fig. 2.13. Some entertainment facilities on board the *MSC Divina*.

entertainment can help differentiate an existing product to potential new markets.

In summary, the cruise environment is distinct from the transport environment in that cruise ships offer more than transportation and are attractions/destinations in themselves. Entertainment is used on cruise ships to add value to the cruise experience and to encourage passenger spend. New and innovative forms of entertainment such as 4D cinema and themed big-name music cruises are attracting more families and people who may not have considered cruising before, to ships that are increasing in size and, with this, increasing in the leisure and entertainment facilities that they offer.

HOME ENVIRONMENT

The home is where the majority of people spend increasing amounts of their time (particularly, according to Mintel (2009) in the current economic climate) and where most media-based entertainment is consumed. This largely incorporates:

- broadcast media (television and radio);
- games and gaming;
- literature;
- music;
- movies;
- social media;
- streaming media; and
- web browsing.

Homes are no longer merely functional areas for sleeping and eating, and increasingly incorporate entertainment facilities to help occupants enjoy and make the most of their home spaces. In wealthy industrialized nations, once upon a time, people sat around a fire; from the mid-20th century, people sat around radio

sets; and from the 1960s the television became the focal point of home social spaces. A period of renewed wealth in the 1980s, combined with a rise in affordable home entertainment products from Asia, meant that many homes contained multiple electronic entertainment devices, including televisions, stereos, video recorders and games consoles. Children began to have their own televisions and stereos in their bedrooms, allowing occupants of the same household to enjoy what they want to be entertained by in their own spaces.

In the 1990s, the rise of home computing and the Internet began to shift the focus away from purely broadcast media for entertainment, something which affordable laptops, tablets and home Wi-Fi have continued to do in the 21st century. In terms of media, a continual wave of creative destruction has witnessed media change from being analogue to digital to now media-less software files, which are stored at a distance on servers or locally on the device that plays them. Homes are becoming less cluttered with entertainment paraphernalia as all traditional media forms, from CDs to DVDs, Blu-Rays, books, games and newspapers, are shifting online and are becoming physically format-less. There is reduced need for 'television cabinets' upon which a television may have stood, and in which DVDs and various peripherals may have been stored, which suits the design of new homes, which are getting smaller (Mintel, 2009). Electrical items becoming obsolete is helping to feed a rise in consumer expenditure on new entertainment gadgets: between 2009 and 2012, 50% of UK adults purchased a computer or a mobile phone, and these two items were the most purchased electrical products by UK adults during this period, followed by televisions (Mintel, 2013).

In the 21st-century home, people are most likely to spend their leisure time watching television, browsing the Internet, reading and listening to music (Mintel, 2009). Televisions are likely to be wall-mounted large-screened high definition sets, and shrinking peripherals are either becoming obsolete or are integrated into new technologies such as tablet computers, which can easily be connected to TVs to play movies or watch video on-demand. People are watching live television less, on-demand services more, and using technology to create tailor-made, social and interactive entertainment environments in shared living spaces, either in living rooms or in purpose-built 'media rooms', as in Fig. 2.14.

When watching television, it is now common practice to share this experience with online associates through social media, and it is just as likely that in a 21st-century home, games will be played with somebody in another location as in the same room. Games are becoming more physical for inter-activity and often require larger spaces for proper engagement. The home environment is being shaped by the entertainment that is being consumed, entertainment that is chosen which allows consumers to interact with friends near and far. The only certainty with the home environment is that it will continue to become more entertainment focused, and as technology continues to develop it will generate entertainment that is seemingly more real, which attempts to compete with the experiences offered by out-of-home entertainment. Interactive multi-use 'screen walls' and virtual reality are no longer the stuff of science fiction, and the home of the future will be an even more entertaining environment.

In summary, the home environment offers occupants a more affordable and secure environment to relax and consume media in a social way, not just with other occupants but also with friends, family and associates in other locations. Its use as a media entertainment hub will continue to increase as technological advancements allow occupants to enjoy entertainment experiences, which compete with many of the experiences that people can experience outside of the home.

SEMINAR ACTIVITIES

1. Consider your nearest urban centre. What types of entertainment venues exist within it?

Fig. 2.14. A 'home cinema'-style media room. Photographs courtesy of Alan Machin.

How does the location of the entertainment venues within your nearest urban centre benefit them? How does the location of the entertainment venues within your nearest urban centre impact negatively upon them?

2. Which forms of entertainment do you prefer when using transport? Why?

3. What strategies could you suggest to cruise ship operators that may help them increase their average passenger expenditure per hour?

4. What other suggestions could you make to the operators of the Glastonbury Festival to get them to better educate their visitors about the harmful effects of environmental damage through littering and urination?

5. What initiatives could you suggest to the managers of European destinations, which are popular with 'stag' and 'hen' parties, which would separate alcohol tourists from cultural tourists?

REFERENCES

Associated Newspapers (2013) Metro UK. Available at: http://www.associatednewspapers.com/free-division (accessed 11 March 2013).

Associated Press (2007) South Africa's crime rate causes tourism to decline. Available at: http://www.heraldnet.com/article/20070819/LIVING05/708190305/-1/headlines2 (accessed 20 November 2011).

Baeur, G. and McKercher, B. (2003) *Sex and Tourism: Journeys of Romance, Love and Lust*. Howarth Press, Binghamton, New York.

Barford, V. and Judah, S. (2013) The street with 18 betting shops. Available at: http://www.bbc.co.uk/news/magazine-22934305 (accessed 18 June 2013).

Bell, D. (2008) Destination drinking: toward a research agenda on alcotourism. *Drugs: Education, Prevention and Policy* 15(3), 291–304.

Bellini, E., Gasparino, U., Del Corpo, B. and Malizia, W. (2007) Impact of cultural tourism on urban economies. Available at: http://ageconsearch.umn.edu/bitstream/8220/1/wp070085.pdf (accessed 30 November 2008).

Briedenhann, J. and Ramchander, P. (2006) Township tourism: blessing or blight? The case of Soweto in South Africa. In: Smith, M.K. and Robinson, M. (eds) *Cultural Tourism in a Changing World*. Channel View Publications, Clevedon, UK, pp. 124–142.

British Broadcasting Corporation (BBC) (2013) Paris Louvre shuts as staff strike over pickpockets. Available at: http://www.bbc.co.uk/news/world-europe-22098102 (accessed 10 April 2013).

Burkart, A.J. and Medlik, S. (1981) *Tourism: Past, Present and Future*, 2nd edn. Butterworth-Heinemann, Oxford, UK.

Carnival Corporation PLC (2012) 2012 annual report. Available at: https://materials.proxyvote.com/Approved/143658/20130219/AR_155681.pdf (accessed 27 March 2013).

Coachella Music Festival (2012) S.S. Coachella. Available at: http://ss.coachella.com/index.php (accessed 27 March 2013).

Doxey, G. (1975) A causation theory of visitor-resident irritants: methodology and research inferences. *Proceedings of the Travel Research Association, 6th Annual Conference*. San Diego, California, pp. 195–198.

European Cruise Council (2012) The Cruise Industry: Contribution of Cruise Tourism to the Economies of Europe, 2012 Edition. Available at: http://www.ashcroftandassociates.com/downloads/EIR_2012_Report.pdf (accessed 23 March 2013).

Foreign and Commonwealth Office (2013) Mexico. Available at: http://www.fco.gov.uk/en/travel-and-living-abroad/travel-advice-by-country/north-central-america/mexico1 (accessed 16 March 2013).

Griffiths, P. (2009) Adult Entertainment. In: Moss, S. (ed.) *The Entertainment Industry: An Introduction*. CAB International, Wallingford, UK, pp. 346–364.

Hickman, L. (2008) *The Final Call: Investigating Who Really Pays for Our Holidays*. Transworld Publishers, London.

Hughes, M. (2000) *Arts, Entertainment and Tourism*. Butterworth-Heinemann, Oxford, UK.

Johnson, G., Whittington, R. and Scholes, K. (2010) *Exploring Corporate Strategy: Text and Cases*, 9th edn. Pearson, Harlow, UK.

Leiper, N. (1979) The framework of tourism: Towards a definition of tourism, tourist, and the tourist industry. *Annals of Tourism Research* 6(4), 390–407.

Miller, J. (2013) High-speed in-flight internet possible by 2014. Available at: http://www.bbc.co.uk/news/technology-23768536 (accessed 21 August 2013).

Mintel (2009) *Home Lifestyles*. Mintel International Group, London.

Mintel (2013) *Electrical Goods Retailing*. Mintel International Group, London.

Moore, R. (1995) Gender and alcohol use in a Greek tourist town. *Annals of Tourism Research* 22, 300–313.

Richter, A. (2010) Exploiting 'an army of friendly faces' – contemporary policy debate. *Journal of Policy Research in Tourism, Leisure and Events* 2(2), 184–188.

Ruddick, G. (2012) Capital Shopping Centres boosted by restaurants. Available at: http://www.telegraph.co.uk/finance/newsbysector/retailandconsumer/9101200/Capital-Shopping-Centres-boosted-by-restaurants.html (accessed 10 February 2013).

Ryan, C. (1991) *Recreational Tourism: A Social Science Perspective*. Routledge, London.

Ship Building Tribune (2012) STX France shipyard delivers MSC Divina. Available at: http://shipbuildingtribune.com/2012/05/21/stx-france-shipyard-delivers-msc-divina (accessed 27 March 2012).

Sims, P. (2012) March of the bookies: Betting shops, pawnbrokers and loan firms join invasion of ailing high streets. Available at: http://www.dailymail.co.uk/news/article-2157406/Betting-shops-pawnbrokers-loan-firms-join-invasion-ailing-high-streets.html (accessed 10 February 2013).

Spracklen, K., Richter, A. and Spracklen, B. (2013) The eventization of leisure and the strange death of alternative Leeds. *City: Analysis of Urban Trends, Culture, Theory, Policy, Action* 17(2), 164–178.

Trinity Leeds (2013) Public art. Available at: http://www.trinityleeds.com/centre-information/public-art (accessed 21 March 2013).

chapter 3

Marketing Entertainment

Ben Walmsley

LEARNING OBJECTIVES

After reading this chapter you should be able to:

- define and describe the role and purpose of entertainment marketing;
- discuss what differentiates entertainment marketing from marketing in other sectors and industries;
- define and explain the marketing process and the marketing mix;
- discuss the benefits and challenges of market research and articulate the expectations and desires of 21st-century audiences;
- explain and apply the principles of market segmentation, pricing and product positioning;
- plan a strategic marketing and communications campaign;
- consider the pros and cons of digital and social media marketing; and
- evaluate the strategic importance of branding and re-branding.

INTRODUCTION

This chapter will explore the role of marketing in the entertainment industries and focus on what differentiates the marketing of entertainment-related products and experiences from other forms of marketing. After a review of various definitions of marketing and of the key underlying principles of the marketing concept and mix, it will apply some of the theories and frameworks of experiential marketing to the entertainment industries and explore how these relate to the needs, expectations and desires of the audiences, visitors and consumers of 21st-century entertainment.

In order to understand what audiences, visitors and consumers seek and expect from entertainment, we will need to consider the different types of market research that inform entertainment organizations about their customers. To make effective use of these insights into consumers' attitudes and behaviour patterns, we will also need to study the role that strategic planning plays in designing, implementing, monitoring and evaluating marketing campaigns. Part of this planning process involves segmenting our markets into distinct customer groups and pricing and positioning our products, services and experiences accordingly. To achieve this, we will also need to understand how marketing communications work – how our audiences and visitors receive and decode the messages that we send them. Increasingly, these messages are sent and decoded through digital channels, so we will also be focusing in this chapter on the benefits and challenges of digital marketing, which will take us into the realm of social media marketing. Finally, we will consider the roles that brands and brand management play in the entertainment industries and discuss the process of re-branding.

DEFINITIONS

Marketing has been defined as 'managing profitable customer relationships' in order 'to create value *for* customers and to capture value *from* customers in return' (Kotler and Armstrong, 2010, p. 26). However, this definition is problematic in the entertainment industries, where sectors such as arts and heritage are often less concerned with generating profit than with creating quality experiences. Kotler and Armstrong's definition also raises the question of what kind of value entertainment organizations should expect from their customers: in an era of increasing collaboration and co-creation, the nature of this value is evolving all the time. If we consider a definition from a predominantly non-profit sector of the entertainment industries, Hill *et al.* (2003, p. 1) define arts marketing as 'an integrated management process which sees mutually satisfying exchange relationships with customers as the route to achieving organizational and artistic objectives'. This definition succeeds in avoiding the supposition of profit and incorporates the realization of artistic objectives, but it lacks the helpful focus on value evident in Kotler and Armstrong's definition.

A specific definition for entertainment marketing is provided by Sayre (2008, p. 2), who defines it as 'techniques and strategies developed to sell tickets for activities that amuse and involve us'. At face value, this is a useful definition, as it incorporates the *nature* of the experiences that entertainment organizations aim to create and market. But it falls down in its supposition that entertainment marketing is only related to ticketed events. In the UK, for example, many museums and art galleries are subsidized to enable them to offer free entry to their visitors; and on a global level, digital music downloads never involve the sale of a ticket. So to provide an accurate and appropriate definition of entertainment marketing, we will have to conflate the existing definitions to produce an all-encompassing definition. For the purposes of this chapter, then, entertainment marketing will be defined as: *strategic activities designed to develop and manage mutually satisfying value-based relationships with audiences, visitors and customers in order to entertain them and achieve organizational goals.*

As a strategic activity, marketing is often confused with promotion and sales. So an important point to emphasize here is that marketing is a broader function than promotion; it encompasses communication, which includes promotional activities, and its aim is to generate engagement or sales. As a function, it has historically struggled to compete with the more established disciplines of finance and sales, and perhaps for this reason, it occasionally suffers from the misguided perception that it is all about common sense. This is perhaps due to the fact that marketing is a softer discipline than either finance or sales, lying somewhere between an art and a science. Marketing is about *people* rather than figures; it is a *dialogue* with audiences, visitors and customers; and it involves *pulling* intelligence from the market rather than pushing products into it. So the marketing process resembles that shown in Fig. 3.1.

THE MARKETING MIX

Marketing is based around what is generally called the *marketing mix*, and there are two main variations on this. Marketing scholars and practitioners often talk about the 4Ps of marketing, and these refer to the elements of product, place, price and promotion. *Product* refers to an organization's market offering, which it tailors to meet the needs and desires of its customers. Products are affected by their features, quality, variety, design, branding, and related services. In the entertainment industries, this focus on products is again problematic as much of the sector is more focused on producing memorable experiences rather than tangible products. The second element of the marketing mix is *place*, which defines where the product or experience is available to buy and/or be presented to the audience. As many sub-sectors of the entertainment industries are based on live performances, this element is hugely important as it covers the significant experiential role played by venues: stadia, theatres, museums, art galleries, cinemas, concert halls, etc. The third element of the marketing mix is *price*, which we will consider in detail later in the chapter. The fourth and final element of the mix is *promotion* – the mechanisms and activities that promote the product or experience to audiences and customers and persuade them to buy or engage with it. We will explore this further in our exploration of the communications mix.

The other version of the marketing mix is the 7Ps model, also referred to as the services marketing mix. This extended version of the mix includes the extra three elements of people, process and physical evidence. The *people* element covers customer service and

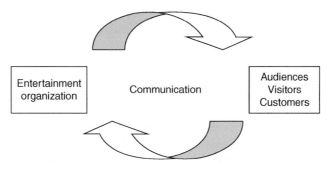

Fig. 3.1. The entertainment marketing process.

any personal interaction between the product or experience and the customer or audience member. Its inclusion in the marketing mix represents an acknowledgement of the significant role that people play in selling and promoting products and augmenting experiences. In the entertainment industries, this could refer to a whole host of workers, from front-of-house staff to actors, curators and musicians, although arguably these are an essential part of the product or experience itself. The inclusion of the *process* element highlights the importance of the marketing process we described above – the integrated range of marketing activities that comprise the ongoing dialogue between an organization and its customers. The final element is *physical evidence* (sometimes called the physical environment) – this refers to buildings, packaging, flyers, uniforms, tickets, programmes and logos. Although these elements are important in positioning, promoting and enhancing a product or event, it could be argued that they are covered in the product, place and promotion elements of the mix and therefore do not require their own separate element.

You might well still be asking yourself why these elements are referred to as the marketing *mix*. The idea behind this is that the individual elements are like ingredients in a cake that combine together in different proportions and configurations depending on the product or desired outcomes. For example, the most popular bands such as U2 or Coldplay are able to rely more on their product to sell their tickets and are less dependent on promotional activities than lesser known or emerging artists. However, they are quite dependent on a certain size of venue, so place is still important; and as they are market leaders and in such high demand, they can charge a premium for their tickets, so the price element is also relevant here. The marketing mix therefore needs to be tailored specifically to each individual product and organization.

THE NEED FOR STRATEGIC PLANNING

Because marketing is a strategic business activity that aims to promote and achieve organizational objectives, it needs to be carefully planned. Byrnes (2009) argues that planning should be an integral part of an organization's daily operations. He identifies the different types of planning as a series of oppositions including strategic/operational, single-use/standing-use, top-down/bottom-up and contingency/crisis. What we are concerned with here is strategic planning. Strategic planning enables organizations to ensure that their value and capabilities fit as closely as possible with changing market opportunities. Effective planning involves organizations asking themselves a series of simple questions:

1. Where are we now?
2. Where are we going?
3. How are we going to get there?
4. How will we know we have arrived?

To answer these questions, an organization will have to undertake both internal and external analysis. However, marketing planning should not need to start from scratch: it should be in line with the organization's mission statement and reflect its strategic goals and objectives. For example, if an entertainment organization's mission is to 'delight and challenge' its audiences, the role of the marketing department is to plan how to support this through a marketing campaign.

Considering the four planning questions we mentioned earlier, this might involve:

1. Analysing some previous survey data to determine to what extent existing audiences are reporting being 'delighted' and 'challenged'.
2. Determining the marketing objectives of a forthcoming show, production, exhibition, etc., taking on board the aim to delight and challenge audiences.
3. Planning and agreeing marketing tactics and activities that will enable these objectives to be achieved, e.g. incorporating an image of a 'delighted' audience member and using the word 'challenging' in an e-flyer.
4. Agreeing a monitoring and evaluation strategy, for example by agreeing a percentage of survey respondents you would like to report being 'delighted' by the show.

When determining a monitoring and evaluation strategy, it is worth bearing in mind that unless your goals and objectives are measurable it will be hard to assess the extent to which you have achieved them. Chapter 13 (this volume) covers performance measurement in much more detail, but for now it is important to consider the utility of SMART objectives. However, SMART objectives do not have to be numerical, and one danger of marketing planning and evaluation is to rely too heavily on quantitative box office data such as sales or visitor numbers rather than spending time undertaking deeper qualitative evaluation based around more holistic objectives. Using our earlier example, if our objective was to delight and challenge our audiences, we will not be able to evaluate our success in achieving this by looking at sales figures and capacity rates; we will need to watch and interact with our audiences

and listen to what they say about their experiences.

The usual way to formalize the planning process is to create a marketing plan. A marketing plan generally has the following sections:

1. Introduction and executive summary.
2. Vision, objectives, targets and projections.
3. Internal analysis (objective assessment of organizational strengths and weaknesses).
4. External analysis (including a customer analysis, competitor/industry analysis and a macro-analysis).
5. Strategy and approach (based around the marketing mix).
6. Monitoring and evaluation.
7. Conclusion and action plan.

In the entertainment industries, a strategic marketing plan normally covers a 3–5 year period, but it should be revised and updated on at least an annual basis. A small and simplified version of the marketing plan should be used to create a marketing campaign plan for a one-off production or event.

MARKET RESEARCH AND CONSUMER BEHAVIOUR

If marketing is all about developing and managing mutually satisfying value-based relationships with audiences, visitors and customers, it follows that we need to ascertain what it is about entertainment that satisfies audiences and how they derive value from it. To achieve this, we need to ask them questions about their motivations and behaviour and listen carefully to what they say.

In other words, we need to carry out *market research*.

There are three main types of market research:

1. Internal or desk research.
2. Secondary research.
3. Primary research.

Desk research involves analysing existing information from within the office and tracking data such as audience surveys and previous sales reports over time. This can be time consuming but the data are inevitably relevant to your organization and it costs nothing to access it. However, the effectiveness of internal research depends on the quality and quantity of existing data. Secondary research involves collecting, collating and/or analysing existing data from external sources and applying your findings to your own organization and research questions. It is usually free, quick and easy to collect, but the drawbacks are that it is not always up-to-date or wholly relevant to your own situation or campaign. Primary research involves generating new data by either interacting directly with your audiences, visitors or customers through surveys, focus groups and interviews etc. or by outsourcing your research questions to an external market research company. The main benefit of conducting primary research is that it produces up-to-date information that is highly tailored to your organization and to any specific research questions you might have. The drawbacks are that it can be costly and time consuming, and there is sometimes a risk that audiences can grow weary of questionnaires and such like.

Primary research can be divided into two main approaches: quantitative and qualitative. Quantitative research is based on the systematic measurement and analysis of statistics,

numbers and figures. It aims to identify patterns and trends in data over periods of time and/or between different groups of people. It is useful for answering specific questions and evaluating SMART objectives, and its main advantage is that it often produces objective, robust and statistically valid answers to specific research questions. Qualitative data, on the other hand, seeks depth rather than breadth and aims to elicit rich, authentic and nuanced attitudinal data. Qualitative research is all about garnering personal views through extended interaction with willing participants who can provide insights (rather than answers) to complex questions. Although based on small samples and therefore not statistically valid, these insights can often be generalized to generate hypotheses that can be tested in future research. Typical examples of qualitative methods include focus groups, depth interviews, participant observation and virtual ethnography. Figure 3.2 provides an insight into the kind of participant observation that a researcher might experience through an ethnographic approach.

When conducting primary research, there are a number of ethical considerations to bear in mind. If you are undertaking research

Fig. 3.2. Audience members captivated by a Divine Performing Arts show in Boston, USA. Image by Bing Yuan, courtesy of *The Epoch Times*.

from a college or university, you will generally require ethical approval for any primary research. But even in industry, there are a number of ethical standards and guidelines that should be followed. This is especially important if you are working with young people or other potentially vulnerable individuals. At the very least, written parental consent must be obtained before interviewing these groups or carrying out a focus group, and ideally you will need to be accompanied by a carer, teacher, parent or authorized chaperone.

The main principles of research ethics are transparency and informed consent. Transparency involves ensuring that all participants in your research have a clear and unambiguous understanding of the purpose(s) for collecting the data and are fully aware how it will be used. Informed consent means that at the time the data are collected, participants must acknowledge that the aims are transparent and give their consent to their data being collected and used in specific ways and under specific conditions. In the UK, the most important of these conditions is the Data Protection Act, which was established in 1998 to protect the public's right to privacy regarding the processing of their personal data, including all electronic data such as e-mail addresses.

A final point to make about market research is its connection with studies into consumer behaviour. In the past few decades, consumer behaviour has emerged as an important field of study in its own right and there is now a rich body of academic literature, complemented by industry intelligence such as Mintel reports, that provides organizations with invaluable insights into how people spend their leisure time and why they make the leisure choices they do.

Motivation theory such as Maslow's hierarchy of needs can be useful here, as it illustrates the kinds of needs that all human beings have and which needs they might be trying to fulfil when they engage in entertainment. Other theories, such as hedonic consumption (Hirschman and Holbrook, 1982) and flow (Csikszentmihalyi, 1988), have also produced rich insights into how and why people engage with entertainment, highlighting audiences' general search for emotional, sensual, imaginative, intellectual and captivating experiences (as illustrated in Fig. 3.2). More recent studies have also shown that audiences often seek challenging and impactful experiences that provide a meaningful means of escapism (e.g. Walmsley, 2011).

You might have realized by now that marketing is all about knowing your customers. This involves keeping up-to-date with the latest trends and developments in their behaviour and attitudes. As we saw in Chapter 1, the entertainment industries are diverse and fast-changing and it is not always easy to keep abreast of the latest trends, especially where technology is concerned. But we do know that global audiences have an increasing amount of leisure time, and although many countries have been hit hard by the downturn of 2008, globally, GDP and disposable income is on the rise. Entertainment consumers and audiences are increasingly interactive and tech-savvy and many younger audiences are interested in playing and gaming and in co-creating and co-curating their entertainment products and experiences. This market intelligence can help marketers to tailor their products and experiences to suit the changing needs of their audiences as effectively as possible.

SEGMENTATION, TARGETING AND POSITIONING

One of the most important functions of a marketing department is to identify the best ways to divide up the organization's potential audiences. This process is known as *segmentation*, where a segment refers to 'buyers with similar needs and wants' (Hill *et al.*, 2003, p. 54). Segmentation is the first and most important part of a three-step process, which involves segmenting, targeting and positioning. The idea is that once you have successfully segmented your potential market, you can then start to develop tailored marketing strategies specifically for different segments and position your products and experiences accordingly. The logic behind this stems back to the above definition of a segment: if people have different needs and wants, it makes sense to target them in a different way and market different products to them. For example, a theatre might post out a flyer to a retired couple promoting a Shakespeare play or a modern classic, whereas they might send a recent graduate an e-flyer for a more experimental show.

There are many benefits to this segmentation-based approach to marketing. First, it promotes a better, deeper, richer understanding of customers and audiences; it encourages marketers to find out what makes audiences tick and ask them the right questions through targeted primary research. Second, it facilitates a more effective allocation of resources: staff and marketing spend can be allocated according to likely returns on investment from different target groups. Third, segmentation supports the strategic planning process, as it requires smarter

objectives and more targeted strategies than a generic or mass-marketing approach. Finally, it can improve internal communication as it embeds a better understanding of marketing across the organization.

There are four main types of segmentation:

1. Geographic segmentation (based on people's home addresses, usually postcodes).
2. Demographic segmentation (based on age, gender, income, education and ethnicity).
3. Behavioural segmentation (based on previous buying or attendance patterns).
4. Psychographic segmentation (based on consumers' attitudes and predispositions).

Each of these methods has its relative strengths and weaknesses, so we will now explore them in turn. Geographic segmentation is relatively easy for entertainment organizations that sell tickets or products or gather data systematically from visitors, as all it requires is some basic database analysis based on postcodes. It is also useful for attracting potential customers who live within a certain area. For example, if a theatre were putting on a new play based on a certain area of its city, it might consider doing a leaflet drop to all the postcodes in that location. The problem with geographic segmentation is that it is relatively crude and indiscriminate – based on the assumption that many people in a given area will share an interest in a certain product, service or event.

To circumvent this problem, demographic variables can be introduced to narrow down the segments. This is known as geo-demographic segmentation and a good example would be a music venue targeting local men between 35 and 60 for a folk music gig. This approach can provide a powerful and effective means of targeting groups most likely to attend a certain event, and there are two main commercial marketing tools in the UK that can help marketers to segment using geo-demographic variables: ACORN and MOSAIC. Both of these use the latest census data, together with information from store-card applications etc., to provide a detailed picture of consumers' behaviour relative to their geo-demographic profiles. ACORN breaks down the population into five main categories: wealthy achievers, urban prosperity, comfortably off, moderate means and hard pressed. These general categories are then subdivided into 17 key groups (e.g. 'aspiring singles' and 'prudent pensioners') and then again into 56 different types (e.g. 'student terraces' and 'older people flats'). MOSAIC works in a similar way, distinguishing 15 key groups, which are then divided into 67 'household types' and then 155 'person types'. These geo-demographic classification tools can be particularly helpful for venues in helping them better understand the demographic make-up of their surrounding neighbourhoods and region. But they are less useful where only certain specific demographics are being targeted. In these cases a purely demographic segmentation might be more effective – for example to just target the Afro-Caribbean community of Leeds.

The third segmentation method is based specifically on consumers' behaviour. It considers information such as: booking and attendance patterns; motivations for attendance (e.g. a family occasion or Christmas show); show preference; and average spend. It is based on the basic assumption that past behaviour is a relatively good predictor of future behaviour, and again, it can be combined with other types of segmentation to be even more effective (e.g. combining age with frequency of attendance). A good example of

behavioural segmentation would be targeting frequent attenders of dance for a forthcoming new production from an international ballet company.

The final and most sophisticated type of segmentation is psychographic segmentation. As its name suggests, this method is based on psychological concepts such as values and beliefs and therefore demands a deep level of customer engagement. There are some generic models that marketers can use to help them to profile their audiences psychologically, such as the VALS™ framework, which classifies individuals into the following ladder comprising eight groups differentiated by their resources and primary motivation:

- innovators (highly resourced and innovative);
- thinkers;
- achievers;
- experiencers;
- believers;
- strivers;
- makers; and
- survivors (poorly resourced and lacking in innovation).

VALS can provide a useful framework for segmenting a population or audience into meaningful psychological segments. But there are three main problems with the framework: (i) it takes considerable time for users to learn about the groups sufficiently to apply the framework effectively; (ii) as it cannot be appended to existing datasets, it can be time-consuming and costly to encourage a sufficient number of audience members to complete the survey from scratch to make the results useful or valid; and (iii) like other motivational frameworks, VALS is based on subjective value judgements and implies a hierarchy of consumer, where audiences with high educational and social capital who like to innovate are placed higher than those with lower resources who are said to be more passive and cautious. This of course goes against the principles of audience development, which aims to attract new and diverse audiences to arts and entertainment events.

At first sight, segmentation might sound like a uniquely positive activity (and even like pure common sense). But there are problems with the segmentation approach to marketing, which have been flagged up by its critics. Some of these have been mentioned above; but more generally, it is argued that segmentation can be crude and judgemental and can perpetrate stereotypes and generalizations. For example, ask yourself if you would like to be labelled under 'high rise hardship' or 'crowded Asian terraces'.

PRICING

Kotler and Armstrong (2010) define price as 'the amount of money charged for a product or service' or 'the sum of the value that consumers exchange for the benefits of having or using the product or service' (p. 314). The first of these definitions encapsulates perhaps how most people would conceive of a price and is therefore useful for its simplicity. But the second definition is particularly useful within the context of marketing entertainment because it defines price in a broader sense and equates it with the notion of *value*. This is important for several reasons, not least because the concept of value does not necessarily refer to financial value. Some products or events in the entertainment sector are free (although they may of course incur an opportunity cost), so the value

exchanged is not always monetary. It is also a useful definition because it regards consumption as a *value exchange* between consumers and producers. This is appropriate if we consider our earlier definition of marketing as the process of *developing and managing mutually satisfying value-based relationships with audiences, visitors and customers*. So pricing is not just about money; it is about all the elements of value exchanged between producers and consumers.

Price is made up of various different *elements* that dictate how a product is sold (e.g. discounts and supplements) and it is subject to a range of *controls* (such as costs, supply and demand, competition and legislation) that determine its final value. Some good examples of controls in the UK's entertainment industries are free museum entry and cultural exemption on VAT. These various elements and controls help arts and entertainment organizations to set their pricing structures for their products, services and events.

There are a number of popular pricing policies and strategies at play in the entertainment industries. Perhaps the simplest strategy is the cost-plus approach, which is based on the following calculation: Price = fixed costs + variable costs + profit margin. This is often used for tangible products such as CDs, where unit costs can be calculated very simply. Other popular pricing strategies include:

- competitive pricing, where prices are based on what direct competitors are charging;
- value-based pricing, where consumers decide how much they want to pay for a product or experience;
- discriminatory pricing, where prices vary according to variables such as times (e.g. matinée shows), consumer segments

(e.g. student discounts) and locations (e.g. stalls or balcony seats); and

- dynamic pricing, where ticket prices fluctuate with demand to encourage early booking (often adopted by airlines and train companies but increasingly popular in the entertainment sector).

It should be noted that these different pricing strategies are often complementary. For example, a music venue may rely on a combination of competitive, discriminatory and dynamic pricing to sell tickets for a gig. Sayre (2008) encapsulates this combined approach nicely in her 7-step plan for setting price in the entertainment industries:

1. Set price objectives (e.g. to cover costs or develop audiences).
2. Estimate demand.
3. Calculate costs.
4. Analyse competitors' prices.
5. Select a pricing policy.
6. Determine price-setting methods.
7. Decide on a final price.

Like marketing in general, pricing is both an art and a science and it can take years of experience, intuition and careful market research to get it right.

COMMUNICATIONS

When we talk about communications in marketing, we are referring to all of the elements of the marketing mix that involve communication between an organization and its target audiences (Pickton and Broderick, 2005). Many people confuse marketing communications with the activities of promotion or advertising, or use the terms interchangeably, so it is important to be aware of the essential differences between these three terms. We noted earlier that promotion was a key part of the marketing mix and it is generally the most visible aspect of marketing activity, used to communicate the key benefits of a product, service or experience to a target market. An obvious example of promotional activity is a poster, flyer or e-mail. Advertising refers specifically to media-based promotion and it generally takes the form of adverts on television or radio, in newspapers and magazines and, increasingly, online. Communications is a wider concept – an umbrella term covering all forms of interaction between an artist or organization and audiences or consumers. Communications therefore comprises not only promotional activity, such as advertising or a flyer campaign, but any form of exposure or contact including social media, PR and branding. Promotion and advertising are thus only part of the wider marketing communications process; and unlike promotion, communications is not limited to promoting the benefits of a product or experience.

There is a widespread misconception in the entertainment industries that as communications steadily migrate online, print is dying as a communications tool. While the rise of digital communication should certainly not be underestimated, in many instances it is actually complementing rather than replacing print, and print is gradually becoming a more nuanced and valuable tool, used to enhance audiences' experience both before and after an event (e.g. via image-rich season brochures and souvenir programmes). If we bear in mind the age demographics of some sub-sectors of the entertainment industries (e.g. opera), we can appreciate how print still has a major role to play in reaching older demographics who have not yet migrated online, and many theatres and opera houses still report significant sales spikes after a direct mail drop of season brochures.

But as ever in marketing, and particularly in the communications area of marketing, the important thing is to tailor the message to the target audience, regardless of the medium. The challenge for marketing communications is to communicate the right message in the right way to the right people in the right place at the right time, and this requires some insight into the science of communication. It is generally acknowledged that the communication process comprises four stages or components, which can be illustrated as follows:

sender → message → media → receiver

Pickton and Broderick (2005) explain how this process should ideally form a communication loop, where the receiver responds in a way that is discernible to the sender, who may then tailor their messages accordingly in future communications. In any case, the message will ideally trigger a response from the receiver, as long as it is well timed and tailored and channelled through an appropriate medium. The aim of a well-targeted message is to effect a change in behaviour in the receiver, and it has been argued that this process occurs through a hierarchy of effects, which was most famously theorized by E.K. Strong in 1925 in his AIDA model, illustrated in Fig. 3.3. The AIDA model illustrates a possible hierarchy of effects resulting from an effectively tailored message and demonstrates how over time, communications can function as a powerful call to action. Although Strong's model has been criticized for being over-simplistic by predicting everyone's behaviour, it does provide

a useful checklist for structuring a message (Hill *et al.*, 2003). But of course, this ladder of effects can go wrong at any time and for any number of reasons (not least competing messages and other 'noise'), which may result in no action being taken on behalf of the respondent. On the other hand, desire and interest may spark positive word of mouth, which will spread the sender's message to other (often unanticipated) receivers. This peer selling is the ultimate goal of an effective marketing communication.

Pickton and Broderick (2005) provide a useful summary of the different forms of marketing communications in their Integrated Marketing Communications (IMC) Mix Model (Fig. 3.4). This model categorizes the multifarious forms of marketing communications under four main headings (advertising, public relations, personal selling and sales promotion) and illustrates the overlap between them. It also highlights the importance of integrating marketing communications so that a consistent message is given and received.

This integrated model of communications takes us back to the need for strategic planning, which must be at the heart of any marketing communications campaign.

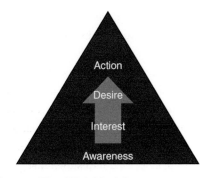

Fig. 3.3. The AIDA Model.

Fig. 3.4. The IMC Mix Model. (From Pickton and Broderick, 2005, p. 17, courtesy of Pearson Education Limited.)

DIGITAL MARKETING

As discussed above, digital marketing is becoming an increasingly significant element of the marketing communications mix and it therefore warrants specific attention in this chapter. Digital marketing refers to online and other electronic marketing tools such as e-mail, SMS, MMS and websites. It also covers viral and social media marketing through online forums such as YouTube, Facebook and Twitter. The Digital Marketing Institute defines digital marketing as 'the use of digital technologies to create integrated, targeted and measurable communications which help to acquire and retain customers while building deeper relationships with them'. This definition is useful in highlighting the intrinsic benefits of digital marketing such as its ability to reach mass audiences and retain them through interactive communication. If we think back to the importance of the communication loop, we can easily see how digital marketing might facilitate this.

Apart from its mass, global reach and ability to retain audiences, the other key benefit of digital marketing is that it encourages active participation and co-creation. This fits with the modern concept of marketing as a people-based process based on building relationships through interactive dialogue. Ancillary benefits are that: it is green; it is easy to track, monitor and evaluate through increasingly sophisticated tools such as Google analytics; and it facilitates digital word of mouth – or what Sayre (2008, p. 219) calls 'word-of-mouse'.

However, digital marketing is certainly not the Holy Grail and it has a number of significant drawbacks. Activities like social media marketing can be very time-consuming (if not indeed invasive and intrusive) for marketing staff, and their indirect benefits can be very difficult to measure or quantify. Because it is perceived to be 'free', e-mail marketing is often used badly, with distribution lists often not properly segmented or de-duplicated and customers often stalked with too much inappropriate information. Platforms such as Twitter have also increased the risk of mixed messages coming from different staff, which threatens the integrated messaging paramount to effective communication. It can be also be quite scary to relinquish control to audiences, and, if not handled properly, digital marketing can lead to major PR disasters, including abuse!

But in order to appreciate the growing significance of digital marketing, it is important to consider some key facts and figures regarding the online behaviour of consumers. It has been estimated that in the USA, people now spend more time online than watching television (AmbITion Scotland, 2011). The same source reports that 200 million people now access Facebook on a mobile phone and that sales of smartphones have now overtaken notebooks and PCs combined. So, despite our earlier caveat about the persisting benefits of print, we can see that the future is online and mobile, and this is therefore where entertainment organizations will need to focus their future communications training and resources, as illustrated in the case study below.

Case Study: Digital engagement at Brooklyn Museum

Brooklyn Museum is one of the oldest and largest cultural organizations in the USA. Located in the New York borough of Brooklyn, its mission is 'to act as a bridge between the rich artistic heritage of world cultures, as embodied in its collections, and the unique experience of each visitor'. The museum describes itself as 'dedicated to the primacy of the visitor experience' and draws on 'both new and traditional tools of communication, interpretation, and presentation […] to serve its diverse public as a dynamic, innovative, and welcoming center for learning through the visual arts' (Brooklyn Museum, 2013).

The digital engagement strategy at Brooklyn Museum is overseen by its Chief of Technology, Shelley Bernstein. Shelley's role is to enhance the museum's visitor experience and community engagement through the innovative use of digital communications technologies. Over the past few years, this has resulted in a series of digital initiatives including free public Wi-Fi, video competitions, user-generated content, projects designed specifically for mobile devices and digitizing the museum's vast collection of artwork.

According to Bernstein (2013), one of the museum's most successful technology projects has been its 'comment kiosk' (Fig. 3.5). These iPad-based kiosks sit in every exhibition, gather visitor comments and e-mail them automatically to the museum's curatorial and visitor services staff. Visitors' comments are moderated, but a selection (containing both positive and negative feedback) are posted on the kiosks in the gallery, on the website and on the exhibition pages for other visitors to respond to. Bernstein argues that the kiosks offer the museum a novel way to learn from its visitors, as well as facilitating visitor to visitor communication.

The kiosks have recently become more interactive and the technology has enabled artists, curators, conservers and educators to both pose and answer questions, which are then threaded into themes, ranked by popularity and posted on exhibition websites. This has facilitated a deeper, two-way engagement between visitors and the museum staff and led to what staff estimate as a 40% rise in inspiring and insightful comments.

This case study highlights how modern arts and entertainment organizations are starting to harness digital technology to realize the fundamental goal of marketing: to develop and manage mutually satisfying value-based relationships with audiences, visitors and customers. By entering into a dialogue with its visitors, Brooklyn Museum is engaging in an effective communication loop and consequently receiving high quality feedback, which it can use to continually improve its visitor experience to help it to achieve its mission.

(Continued)

Case Study. Continued.

Fig. 3.5. An interactive comment kiosk at Brooklyn Museum. Image courtesy of Brooklyn Museum.

BRANDING

A brand is 'a name, term, sign, symbol or a combination of these, that identifies the maker or seller of the product' (Kotler and Armstrong, 2010, p. 255). In the entertainment sector, it involves 'creating mental structures for a product and helping audiences organise their knowledge about entertainment experiences in a way that clarifies their decision making and provides value to the producer' (Sayre, 2008, p. 182). The ultimate aim of branding is to differentiate an organization and its products, services or experiences in order to place them uniquely above the competition, at the forefront of the audience's minds.

Creating a powerful brand is important because it has been estimated that the core product itself only accounts for about 20% of a product's impact on the market (Macdonald and Wilson, 2011). As the above definitions indicate, branding is a complicated business and brands themselves are complex hybrids, which combine both tangible and intangible assets. For example, a brand could incorporate an organization's mission, vision and values, its organizational culture and ethos, and the stories that people recount about it, as well as its products, buildings, services or events. Many people wrongly attribute a brand solely to a logo, but as we can see, a brand is far more than an organization's visual identity. A successful brand needs successfully to bring together the following elements:

- a brand identity (e.g. its name, crest, logo, colours and symbols);
- a strong personality (which combines rational, sensual, and emotional appeal and delivers *meaning*); and
- tangible and intangible customer benefits (e.g. quality, reliability or wellbeing).

A strong brand can deliver significant *brand equity* to the organization that owns and develops it. Brand equity is another complex construct that is often challenging to define and quantify, but it basically refers to the value that a brand brings to a product, service, event or organization *over and above its specific attributes* (e.g. price, quality, performance, etc.). Brand equity is notoriously difficult to measure (just think how you might decide as a manager how much to pay for the Cirque de Soleil brand, for example) but tools such as Young & Rubicam's Brand Asset Valuator exist to help organizations calculate their own or other companies' brand equity.

There are many benefits to be gained from building up a successful brand (and the related brand equity). A strong brand can increase brand loyalty and lead to competitive advantage; it can enable companies to charge premium prices and increase their profit margins; it can enable organizations to invest in brand extensions; and it can ultimately generate substantial marketing efficiencies, because well-branded organizations are less reliant on external communications such as advertising. Benefits such as these often motivate organizations to re-brand, but Aaker (2010) highlights five other reasons for organizations to consider re-branding:

1. The brand was poorly conceived in the first place.
2. It became obsolete.
3. The brand appeals to a limited or shrinking market.
4. Its identity needs modernizing.
5. Its identity is tired and boring to consumers.

In the arts and entertainment industries, branding is often treated with suspicion, especially by artists and other creative practitioners. This is because although it can reap significant marketing benefits (as we have seen

in this chapter), it can also be guilty of commodifying what are actually complex cultural entities. As O'Reilly (2011) points out, 'brandspeak' can be reductive and comes with limitations: it is perhaps more challenging to brand experiences than it is to brand products. O'Reilly argues that a brand is really just another word for a *sign*, and that the discipline of semiotics (the science and language of signs) fits much more closely with cultural products than does commercial branding. This semantic challenge is indicative of fundamental tensions in the wider field of arts management, which aims to marry the passion and creativity of the arts with the commercial discipline of management.

CONCLUSION

We have seen in this chapter how marketing entertainment engenders its own specific issues and challenges that can sometimes separate it from other, more commercial forms of marketing. This is largely due to the intangible, experiential nature of many of the products produced by the entertainment industries, which confer specific types of value on those who consume and experience them. At the beginning of the chapter, we explored a range of definitions of marketing and combined them to generate a new definition that is tailored specifically to the entertainment industries. This led us to define entertainment marketing as *strategic activities designed to develop and manage mutually satisfying value-based relationships with audiences, visitors and customers in order to entertain them and achieve organizational goals.*

We have seen how entertainment organizations need to tailor their marketing mix to their products, services and experiences, and we have discussed how important strategic planning, market research, segmentation, positioning, communications and branding are in developing value-based relationships with audiences. We have also seen the increasing role that digital communication technologies are playing in facilitating interactive dialogue between producers and consumers. For example, the short case study on Brooklyn Museum illustrated how digital marketing can be used effectively to deepen and broaden engagement with visitors.

We have discussed how entertainment marketing is both an art and a science and entertainment marketers thus need to draw from a broad skill set to excel in their chosen careers. To market entertainment, we need above all to understand consumers and what makes them tick. This requires deep insights into human psychology and in particular a sound knowledge of consumer behaviour theory and practice. Marketing entertainment is a challenging pursuit; but an awareness of the key concepts behind it, a passion for its products and a desire to understand its audiences can go a very long way!

SEMINAR ACTIVITIES

1. What would you say differentiates entertainment marketing from marketing in other sectors?
2. Discuss the concept of 'mutually satisfying value-based relationships'. What do you think value looks like in the entertainment industries and how might you market it?
3. Why are consumer behaviour studies so important to market researchers in the entertainment industries?
4. What are the main benefits of a segmentation-based approach to marketing and which segmentation method do you find the most effective and pragmatic?
5. Do you think that print will survive as a marketing communications tool? If so, in what format and for how long?
6. Which elements of the marketing mix do you think Brooklyn Museum`is harnessing most effectively and why?
7. Which brands do you think are the strongest in the entertainment sector and which elements of them make them so effective?
8. How might you critique the marketing theories surrounding segmentation and branding, and what problems can these approaches cause in the entertainment industries?

REFERENCES

Aaker, D.A. (2010) *Building Strong Brands*. Simon and Schuster, London.
AmbITion Scotland (2011) Home. Available at: http://www.getambition.com (accessed 10 March 2011).
Bernstein, S. (2013) Moving toward a conversation. Available at: http://www.brooklynmuseum.org/community/blogosphere/2013/06/11/moving-toward-a-conversation (accessed 5 August 2013).
Brooklyn Museum (2013) Mission statement. Available at: http://www.brooklynmuseum.org/about/mission.php (accessed 5 August 2013).
Byrnes, W.J. (2009) *Management and the Arts*, 4th edn. Elsevier, Oxford, UK.
Csikszentmihalyi, M. (1988) The flow experience and its significance for human psychology. In: Csikszentmihalyi, M. and Csikszentmihalyi, I.S. (eds) *Optimal Experience: Psychological Studies of Flow in Consciousness*. Cambridge University Press, Cambridge, UK, pp. 15–35.

Hill, L., O'Sullivan, C. and O'Sullivan, T. (2003) *Creative Arts Marketing*, 2nd edn. Butterworth Heinemann, Oxford, UK.

Hirschman, E.C. and Holbrook, M.B. (1982) Hedonic consumption: emerging concepts, methods and propositions. *Journal of Marketing* 46(3), 92–101.

Kotler, P. and Armstrong, G. (2010) *Principles of Marketing*, 13th edn. Prentice Hall, Upper Saddle River, New Jersey.

Macdonald, M. and Wilson, H. (2011) *Marketing Plans: How to Prepare Them, How to Use Them*, 7th edn. John Wiley & Sons, Chichester, UK.

O'Reilly, D. (2011) Branding the arts and entertainment. In: Walmsley, B. (ed.) *Key Issues in the Arts and Entertainment Industry*. Goodfellow, Oxford, UK, pp. 47–65.

Pickton, D. and Broderick, A. (2005) *Integrated Marketing Communications*, 2nd edn. Pearson, Harlow, UK.

Sayre, S. (2008) *Entertainment Marketing & Communication: Selling Branded Performance, People, and Places*. Upper Saddle River, New Jersey and Pearson Prentice Hall, Harlow, UK.

Walmsley, B. (2011) Why people go to the theatre: A qualitative study of audience motivation. *Journal of Customer Behaviour* 10(4), 335–351.

chapter 4

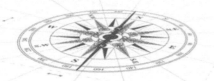

Managing Public Relations

Shirley Beresford and Andreas Schwarz

LEARNING OBJECTIVES

After reading this chapter you should be able to:

- appreciate debates surrounding definitions of Public Relations (PR) in contemporary theory and professional practice;
- describe how PR differs from marketing in its contribution to strategic management at boardroom level;
- define and articulate PR's strategic and tactical contribution to the arts and entertainment sector;
- describe and provide examples of distinct aspects of PR activity, including media relations in publicity and promotion, stakeholder engagement, co-creation and issues/crisis communications; and
- critically evaluate the use of PR in professional practice.

INTRODUCTION

In this chapter we will consider Public Relations (PR) and its contribution to the arts and entertainment sector, focusing particularly on three distinct areas of activity: media relations in publicity and promotion; stakeholder engagement and co-creation; and issues and crisis communications. Related case studies will be incorporated and discussed to illustrate these specialist areas.

According to Sir Martin Sorrell, CEO of WPP, the world's largest communications services group, 'Editorial publicity has resumed its rightful place as one of the most powerful, if not the most powerful, marketing medium today' (Sorrell, 2010). 'Even if we focused only on "media relations", the evolution of the media we are seeing today ensures a greater influence – and even greater responsibilities – for the public relations professional and has expanded the scope of the public relations function' (University of Southern California, 2011).

PR has evolved from a simple promotional tool to an invaluable contributor to the strategic management of the reputation of institutions and individuals in every walk of life, and the arts and entertainment industries are no exception to this evolution. For a relatively young profession, PR receives a considerable amount of attention in the media and elsewhere, attracting very public criticism and plaudits. What is undoubted is that the promotion of art and entertainment has taken place in every setting in which the two are found throughout history. From Greek comedy to Grimaldi, PR has played a significant role. As culture has become professionalized, so has the PR that supports it, and today, the professional practice of PR has become an essential element of any successful film, show, exhibition, tour or event.

In this chapter, we will consider some of the key territories of PR practice and reflect on how both practitioners and academics define the activity. Specifically, we will consider how PR differs from marketing in its contribution to strategic management and explore examples of successful and less successful practice in an attempt to shed some light on why PR as a contemporary practice continues to divide opinion.

DEFINING PUBLIC RELATIONS

Much has been written about what PR actually is, but many academics take their lead from successful practitioners, who believe that PR is essentially about creating narratives and telling a story that attracts people to support an organization or an individual. Stories can be told in many ways and through many media. The variety of PR channels (and consequently how a story is relayed, translated and interpreted) has exploded in the past few years. What is more, the media through which a story passes has an unquenchable appetite. These stories (or messages) create the bedrock on which PR builds and protects reputations.

As the UK's Chartered Institute of Public Relations (CIPR, 2012; Fig. 4.1) explains:

> Public relations takes many forms in different organizations and comes under many titles, including public information, investor relations, public affairs, corporate communication, marketing or customer relations. To add to all the confusion, not all of these titles always relate accurately to public relations, but all of them cover at least part of what public relations is.

No matter what the activity, however, storytelling and narrative are implicit components of PR from the perspective of practitioners.

Entertainment PR agencies pride themselves on the expertise they offer clients in the industry. At a purely tactical level, PR agents promote albums, tours, exhibitions, events, products, artists and celebrities. Their activities include the organization of

Fig. 4.1. CIPR's logo.

digital conversations, managing the media profiles of clients, brand building and protection, image development and publicity. The practice of PR is rarely exclusively separated from other forms of communication such as web/app design, advertising and videos; it is generally integrated into the whole marketing communications process and mix.

STRATEGIC PUBLIC RELATIONS – WHEN MARKETING IS NOT ENOUGH

The image of PR both as a profession and as a scholarly area of study continues to be complex, contradictory and evolving. Despite growing professional and academic focus in the last 20 years, some practitioners, researchers, teachers and trainers remain of the view that PR is mainly a tool in the marketing communications mix or a replacement label for media relations. So, what is PR? The following represent a selection of PR specialist activities that can be claimed to be incorporated in the practice:

- media relations for publicity and promotion;
- reputation management;
- corporate image and identity;

- corporate social responsibility (CSR);
- stakeholder relations;
- social media, digital and viral PR;
- issues and crisis management;
- public affairs;
- internal communications and employee engagement;
- financial affairs and lobbying (campaigning);
- strategic planning; and
- social marketing.

With the exponential growth of the Internet and social media, organizations and individuals in the arts and entertainment sector are increasingly focusing on reputation as the key to sustainable success. In recent years, the concept of reputation has been increasingly adopted by marketing professionals and academics and framed as an extension of the marketing discipline. While until relatively recently marketing was mainly concerned with satisfying customer needs profitably (Chartered Institute of Marketing, 2009), PR practitioners maintain that PR engages and interacts with a broader range of stakeholders and publics, occupying a professional space that marketers cannot fill (McKie and Willis, 2012). This space is claimed and defined as Strategic Public Relations or Corporate Communications by the PR profession and academic community (Hutton, 2001).

Case Study: Leeds Teaching Hospitals and *One Born Every Minute*

The fundamental difference between PR and marketing is that PR focuses on *the enhancement and protection of reputation* whereas marketing's focus is on enhancing and protecting the financial return on products and services offered. These are both of benefit, but the profit motive is not a primary driver for some institutions. The UK's National Health Service (NHS) hospitals do not 'market' product in a traditional marketplace; they are mainly financed by the state. The enhancement of a hospital's reputation is, however, very important to stakeholders,

(Continued)

Case Study. Continued.

including the general public. This case study illustrates how a public sector institution and a television production company can mutually benefit through a well-designed entertainment product: *One Born Every Minute* (Series 3). For the television production company, Dragonfly, the collaboration produced a critically acclaimed, internationally popular and financially successful series. For the Leeds Teaching Hospitals NHS Trust, the series improved the profile of its maternity unit and significantly improved staff morale.

The hospital group had a long and well established track record of working with entertainment companies in both drama and fly-on-the-wall documentaries. Leeds Teaching Hospitals had played host to the first highly successful UK fly-on-the-wall hospital programme, ITV's *Jimmy's*, which was filmed between 1987 and 1994. Dragonfly's *One Born Every Minute* was already a successful TV format. However, the production team wanted to refresh the format. They were looking for a busy host maternity unit at a hospital with engaging characters and found both at Leeds General Infirmary. A series of promotional activities assisted in making the show a success. For example, as part of the deal, a small amount of money was given to the maternity unit to compensate for disruption during the 8-week filming period. This was used to redecorate the birthing pool facility, which was opened with the celebrity endorsement of Myleene Klass (see Fig. 4.2).

For Dragonfly, Series 3 proved to be the most successful ever, with viewing figures regularly topping 5 million on Channel 4, making this the UK's most successful week-night post-watershed show. The programme was also sold internationally and won several TV awards and nominations, including being shortlisted for a prestigious BAFTA. The programme was immediately re-commissioned by UK's Channel 4 and Dragonfly achieved its objective of producing a refreshed, commercially successful series.

Fig. 4.2. Myleene Klass's birthing pool visit. Image courtesy of Leeds Teaching Hospitals NHS Trust.

(Continued)

Case Study. Continued.

The benefit to the hospital was mostly reputational. During the 2 months of screening, the positive press coverage (measured in terms of column inches) increased ten points to 92% in February and March 2012 and staff morale amongst midwives increased by 19 points according to the NHS staff survey 2011. Leeds General Infirmary received thousands of positive recommendations, both online and in letters and thank you cards. The hospital was approached by three other documentary producers wishing to scope new projects. Leeds Teaching Hospitals therefore achieved its objective of increasing its reputational standing with its internal and external stakeholders.

THE ROLES AND REACH OF PUBLIC RELATIONS

Definitions of PR, both as an area of communications practice and as an academic discipline, continue to be hotly debated by its professional bodies and academic communities (Gregory, 2009). In practitioner circles, this has resulted in recent attempts at 'up-dating'. In March 2012, following an intense blog debate and public vote, the Public Relations Society of America's (PRSA) campaign to agree an updated definition of PR announced the winning statement as follows: 'Public relations is a strategic communication process that builds mutually beneficial relationships between organizations and their publics'. Other contenders stated that: 'Public relations is the management function of researching, communicating and collaborating with publics to build mutually beneficial relationships' and 'Public relations is the strategic process of engagement between organizations and publics to achieve mutual understanding and realize goals'.

The organization's chair and CEO Gerard Corbett (2012) commented that the winning definition was simple and straightforward, focusing on 'the basic concept of public relations as a communication process, one that is strategic in nature and emphasizes mutually beneficial relationships':

'Process' is preferable to 'management function', which can evoke ideas of control and top-down, one-way communications. 'Relationships' relates to public relations' role in helping to bring together organizations and individuals with their key stakeholders. 'Publics' is preferable to 'stakeholders' as the former relates to the very 'public' nature of public relations, whereas 'stakeholders' has connotations of publicly-traded companies.

(PRSA, 2012)

Although this is a US-dominated perspective of stakeholders, all the PRSA definitions build on a view that PR as a discipline goes beyond a tactical tool for the marketer or solely a media relations activity (although no-one denies the importance of PR to media relations). In the UK, the Chartered Institute of Public Relations (CIPR) joined the debate and has increasingly defined the activities of its membership around reputation:

Public relations is about reputation – the result of what you do, what you say and what others say about you. Public relations is the discipline which looks after reputation, with the aim of earning understanding and support and influencing opinion and behaviour. It is the planned and sustained effort to establish and maintain goodwill and mutual understanding between an organization and its publics.

(CIPR, 2012)

So, although very few workers in the arts and entertainment sector are members of any professional body, or indeed involved in the professional bodies' debates about what PR is or is not, what they do under the title of PR can range from the tactical to the strategic, from a short-term social media campaign for an emerging new band to a strategic brand repositioning for a major entertainment corporation. And at the centre of any strategic or tactical plan will be the enhancement of the image and reputation of the organization or individual.

Undoubtedly, PR and social media are now inexorably intertwined in practice and the boundaries between journalism and PR are becoming more and more blurred. As journalists and the media become increasingly pressurized by 24/7 rolling deadlines, the role and importance of PR in providing copy for arts and entertainment pages just increases. The relationship between the arts and entertainment media and PR has always been symbiotic, and this has just increased with the expansion of social media.

Systems theory perspectives of PR suggest that a boundary-spanning role for PR can create a bridge between the internal and external environments of an organization, a link between the organization's stakeholders or publics and its dominant coalition, those who determine its goals (Moss and Warnaby, 2003). For some, the boundary-spanning role of PR is also potentially enhanced by the emergence of the importance of social media to practitioners. This special role and expertise gives PR practitioners a degree of power and influence in arts and entertainment organizations and is a distinctly different role from that of the marketer. It is a role that is essential to identifying and understanding the issues and problems facing an organization or individual. So PR can act as a strategic device to inform and frame the internal direction of communications strategy and policy. It has the potential to inform and support the decision-making process for the organization at Board level. This interpretation and vision of PR as a strategic function places PR specialists within the boardroom rather than merely acting as an additional tactical tool for marketing.

However, it is difficult to assess how common or consistent this strategic view of PR is in arts and entertainment organizations. As we have seen, there are many interpretations and definitions of titles and names given to these activities. For example, are entertainment celebrity agents perhaps functioning in the realm of strategic PR when they are operating to protect their clients from harmful press attention in a crisis situation? By managing their clients' issues, are they operating as a boundary-spanner between the entertainer and his or her publics?

As global economic uncertainty and turbulence continue, many publically funded arts and entertainment organizations in the UK and Europe are facing new austerity measures. As a result, there are emerging signs of a refocusing of PR activity. Research into the broader PR profession in Europe suggests that agency clients across various industry sectors are adapting to the new fiscal environment with the strongest growth being in online reputation management and crisis management (EUPRERA, 2012).

Company performance and reputation management clearly remain a priority to both organizations and individuals; and given the continued growth in social media and communications technology, and the continuing pressures in journalism, there is little doubt that PR remains a healthy growing profession in the arts and entertainment, as its activities increasingly transcend the narrow scope of 'media relations'.

PUBLIC RELATIONS' CONTRIBUTION TO AUDIENCE DEVELOPMENT AND CO-CREATION

So as PR continues to be seen as highly necessary for reputation protection and enhancement for many entertainment corporations, it is also contributing increasingly to the creative process itself. PR has become part of the process of developing an entertainment product and is essential to the concept of audience development and content co-creation. Recent examples show a trend in the use of PR to engage stakeholders, publics, audiences and customers in the development of new creative ventures and to create an extended and integrated experience between producers and audiences (Fig. 4.3). Opportunities to use online PR and new social

media platforms for distribution enable a new kind of dialogue and conversation between creative forces and audiences over periods of time, thus building and developing relationships. PR and co-creation can be seen as operationalized in this way. If PR is enacted in its most authentic and strategic form it seems to enable organizations and audiences to converse, discuss, disagree and agree in a new space that facilitates creative feedback and increases the potential to develop long-term relationships.

Producer Ridley Scott's crowd-sourced documentary film *Life in a Day* (2010) illustrates the growing importance of online PR to co-produced arts and entertainment. Comprising an edited series of video clips selected from 80,000 individual submissions to YouTube, the film recounts personal stories from 140 nations on a single day. Thousands of people around the world uploaded videos of their day to YouTube to take part in *Life in a Day*, which was promoted as 'a time capsule' and 'a historic cinematic experiment' to

Fig. 4.3. Co-creation at the HUB Network Milan. Image by Filippo Podestà, courtesy of the HUB Network.

create a documentary film about a single day on earth (Fig. 4.4). Oscar-winning director Kevin Macdonald edited over 4500 hours of footage into a 90-minute film that won admiration and plaudits at numerous international film festivals. After a year of editing and largely online PR, the film premiered in theatres and was streamed live on YouTube in 2011. It is now free to view online. PR was used to first generate interest, gain engagement and encourage involvement by participants, then to maintain support, and finally to enhance and promote the finished film. The majority of the film's content came from people contacted through YouTube, some traditional advertising, media relations on TV shows, and newspaper editorials. This integrated mix of techniques produced a continuous online dialogue with participants and audiences for over a year.

The powerfully effective use of PR and technology made the production possible. The film's director believed it would not have been possible to produce 10 years before, as it allowed film-makers to tap into pre-existing communities of people around the world and bring about real-time distribution of information and discussion about the film as it developed. As Macdonald stated: 'It just wouldn't have been organizationally or financially feasible to undertake this kind of project pre-YouTube'. Online digital PR underpinned the entire process.

Fig. 4.4. *Life in a Day* promotion campaign.

Case Study: PR and audience development

PR also increasingly plays an essential role in audience development. In a range of recent community-based UK arts and entertainment projects, PR has been used to uniquely engage and stimulate new audiences and generate new experiences. *Frankenstein's Wedding*, *Live in Leeds*, and *The Passion* in Port Talbot, are industry examples where PR has played a pivotal role in initiating, establishing, generating and sustaining communications and dialogue between new and existing communities of audiences and arts and entertainment organizations through the creative process and beyond.

Frankenstein's Wedding was a BBC live drama, music and dance event that took place in 2011 at Kirkstall Abbey, Leeds, and was broadcast on BBC Three. The event, which re-imagined the well-known gothic horror story, was a collaboration between local organizations in Leeds, including Leeds City Council, Welcome to Yorkshire, Marketing Leeds and Phoenix Dance Theatre. Online communications with participants resulted in the audience playing real roles as wedding guests wearing their best wedding outfits and taking part in the wedding dance and other moments of audience participation. The event

(Continued)

> **Case Study.** Continued.
>
> included thousands of people recruited from local dance workshops and culminated in a flash mob-style dance by more than 2000 dancers as part of the night's performance.
>
> Communications about local free dance workshops and online tutorials took place in advance for audience members to learn the routine for the mass audience dance scene. Phoenix Dance Theatre was responsible for the choreography of the main event and worked with key regional partners to run the dance workshops. Twitter and Facebook were used effectively to generate instant feedback on development of the project over pre-production months and during the event as it happened and was broadcast live on the BBC network.
>
> Similar PR activity underpinned the audience development and profile of *The Passion*, which starred and was directed by Hollywood actor Michael Sheen. The play, produced by National Theatre Wales, was performed at Easter 2011 on the streets, beaches and hills of Port Talbot. Hundreds of local people became involved in the play, which used the whole of Port Talbot as a performance site. Most of the cast were local volunteers and included choirs, youth theatres and voluntary groups. More than 1000 people took part in scenes that were held at locations including the seafront, a shopping centre, a social club and the civic square. Social media and local media relations activity provided up-to-date information and again created a dialogue to engage the community in the project, which in turn generated commitment to the project's legacy.

THE ROLE OF PUBLIC RELATIONS IN CRISIS MANAGEMENT

In the past two decades, the management of crisis communication has become one of the most important sub-disciplines of PR. The growth of academic publications as well as surveys among European PR professionals (Zerfass *et al.*, 2012) are indicative of this trend. As in all sectors of society, crises are a frequently observed phenomenon in the entertainment industries and they are often related to reputational damage or a downturn in profits and employment. They can even trigger life-threatening situations. Examples of this are: celebrity scandals (drug abuse, sexual harassment, etc.); theme park accidents; the economic crisis faced by the music industry after 2001; the allegations against the video games industry in the aftermath of school shootings like the Columbine High School case in 1999; and the accident of the Italian cruise ship *Costa Concordia* in January 2012. Most of these crises can be described as an 'organizational crisis', a term which can be defined as 'a low-probability, high-impact situation that is perceived by critical stakeholders to threaten the viability of the organization and that is subjectively experienced by these individuals as personally and socially threatening' (Pearson and Clair, 1998, p. 66). History teaches us that organizational crises can lead to disillusionment or the loss of psychic and shared meaning, as well as to the shattering of commonly held beliefs and values; and during a crisis, decision making is often pressed by perceived time constraints and coloured by cognitive limitations (Pearson and Clair, 1998).

Scholars and practitioners have recognized the significance of communication in crisis situations as they can be conceived as socially constructed or even as terminological creations by the people and organizations involved. Hearit and Courtright (2004) conclude that communication actually constitutes the quintessence of crisis management. This underpins the importance of PR in the context of crises, which will subsequently be termed 'crisis communication'.

Like PR in general, crisis communication can be conceptualized and practised as a strategic management process as opposed to a reactive and unplanned use of communication once a crisis has hit. Coombs (2007) suggests an ongoing approach to crisis management and identifies the three stages of pre-crisis, crisis and post-crisis. In the pre-crisis stage, crisis managers should take actions to:

1. Detect early warning signals of crises.
2. Prevent crises from occurring.
3. Prepare for crises that may happen in the future.

In the post-crisis stage, PR managers should evaluate their crisis communication activities and learn for the future in order to prevent further crises or at least be better prepared for them. In the acute crisis stage, the main functions of crisis communication include the collection and dissemination of information to protect people affected by the crisis from harm (instructing information) and help them to cope psychologically with threatening situations (adjusting information) (Sturges, 1994).

In addition, organizations can use crisis communication strategies to protect and defend their reputations. Crisis communication strategies refer to the verbal and nonverbal response of organizations to address a crisis situation, usually with the goal of protecting or strategically shaping their reputations in the eyes of stakeholders (Coombs, 2007). Several scholars have analysed such strategies and proposed different typologies. Coombs (2007) suggests grouping these strategies into the four postures of denial, diminishment, rebuilding and bolstering. In the denial posture, organizations do not accept any responsibility for the crisis and try to remove any connection between them and the crisis situation. This posture includes the strategies of attacking the accuser, denial and scapegoating. The scapegoating strategy is often used by organizations trying to blame someone else for the crisis. Diminishment refers to organizations' attempts to reduce perceptions of organizational control over the crisis. Common strategies include excusing (minimizing the perceived responsibility of the organization) and justification (minimizing the perceived damage as a result of the crisis). In the rebuilding posture, organizations tend to accept responsibility for the crisis by trying to benefit stakeholders or attenuate the negative outcomes of the crisis. This posture includes the strategies of compensation (providing money or gifts to victims) and apology (where organizations take full responsibility and ask for forgiveness). The bolstering posture refers to strategies designed to supplement the previous three postures. Bolstering includes the strategies of reminding stakeholders of past good works, ingratiation (praising stakeholders) as well as 'victimage' (trying to present the organization as a victim of the crisis).

Although these strategies are the most common ones employed by individuals and organizations, there is an ongoing discussion about how to match the right crisis response to crisis situations to protect reputation most effectively. Coombs and Holladay (2004) have conducted several experimental studies that produced evidence-based guidelines for crisis managers. Their findings showed that in contexts of organizational crises, stakeholders make judgements about whether a certain organization is responsible for the crisis and its negative outcomes. The more they consider an organization to be responsible for such negative outcomes, the more negatively they evaluate organizational reputation. Depending on these perceptions, crisis managers and PR professionals should employ crisis communication strategies that match these perceptions. If stakeholders perceive an organization to be responsible for the negative effects of a crisis (e.g. human-error accidents and organizational misdeeds), organizations should accept responsibility and/or compensate stakeholders. If, on the other hand, organizations were not in control of a crisis (e.g. natural disasters, false rumours) then denial strategies should be employed. Experimental studies have indicated that matching crisis response strategies to crisis situations depending on perceptions of responsibility minimizes reputational damage for organizations as long as they follow ethical principles.

Case Study: How to respond to a crisis

Besides crisis response strategies, which usually refer to questions of responsibility, the crisis communication literature provides several recommendations for the right form of crisis response (Coombs, 2007). Organizations should respond quickly to crisis situations in order to control interpretation patterns and show stakeholders that they are willing to engage actively and responsibly in resolving the crisis. In addition, organizations should coordinate their public crisis response to disseminate consistent messages, as contradictive information or opinions reduce the perceived credibility of the sender. Crisis situations are shaped by substantial informational needs among affected stakeholders as well as the media. Organizations should respond to these needs by demonstrating their willingness to disclose important information; they should be open for media inquiries and interview requests; and they should tell the truth in any message that they address to stakeholders.

In the entertainment industries, crisis communication often lacks a strategic approach as organizations do not sufficiently prepare for crises, lack the necessary skills or are psychologically overwhelmed by crisis situations when they hit. In the context of more severe crises that threaten human life and thus endanger the very existence of an organization itself, the pivotal role of crisis communication becomes particularly apparent. The following case study of the Love Parade accidents in Germany 2010 is a telling example of such a crisis in action.

Case Study: The Love Parade festival in Duisburg, Germany 2010

At its peak, the Love Parade in Germany was one of the largest techno music festivals in Europe. It was initiated by the techno DJ Matthias Roeingh in 1989 and started out as a small party in the streets of Berlin with 150 participants that was officially declared a political demonstration. It rapidly transformed into an annual festival with steadily rising numbers of visitors from Germany and other countries, and at its peak in 1999, 1.5 million people participated in the festival. However, the festival organizers increasingly had to face financial problems, as after 2001 the Love Parade was no longer classified as a political demonstration. In 2006, Germany's largest gym chain, McFit Ltd, became the Love Parade's main sponsor. Its CEO, Rainer Schaller, bought the Love Parade trademark and organized the festival as CEO of Lopavent Ltd. In 2006, the parade took place in Berlin for the last time and attracted 1.2 million participants (see Fig. 4.5). As the senate of Berlin refused to authorize the festival in 2007, the event moved to cities in the German Ruhr Valley in 2007 and 2008. In 2009, the Love Parade was cancelled because the city of Bochum refused to authorize the festival. The official reason given for this was the lack of capacity of the city's train station.

Fig. 4.5. Love Parade 2006 seen from above. Image by Ioan Sameli.

(Continued)

Case Study. Continued.

On July 24 2010, Rainer Schaller and Lopavent Ltd organized and promoted the Love Parade in the German city of Duisburg with sponsorship from McFit Ltd. Instead of a procession through the city centre as in previous years, the whole event was planned to happen on the grounds of a former railroad depot, an enclosed area that could only be accessed from the east and west sides through tunnels. Both tunnels met at a ramp that was supposed to be the only entrance to the festival venue. This ramp was also the only exit point from the site. In the late afternoon of 24 July, a stampede injured 500 participants and killed 21 young people after mass panic broke out in one of the tunnels. Autopsies subsequently revealed that all of the 21 deaths were due to crushed rib cages: other participants, panicked by the pressure of the crowd, had trampled them to death.

The organizations who were responsible for the planning and security at the festival venue were the organizer Lopavent Ltd and its CEO Rainer Schaller, the authorities of Duisburg and its mayor Adolf Sauerland, as well as the police of Duisburg who were responsible for the security across the city. This group received most of the public attention and had to face accusations of wrongdoing.

Although the spokespersons of these organizations and the mayor of Duisburg expressed their compassion with the victims, they started to deny any responsibility for the accident from the beginning. The police insisted that they did an excellent job in coping with the situation. The mayor of Duisburg even started to speculate about the causes of the accidents and tried to downplay his own responsibility: 'We did everything possible in advance to have a safe Love Parade.' On the question of causality, he said: 'It was not due to the failed security plan, but probably to individual shortcomings.' This last statement caused particular outrage among the victims and the public, as it was perceived as an accusation levelled at the festival participants for having caused the mass panic.

The CEO of Lopavent Ltd did not appear in public until the next day when the second press conference was held. In his subsequent interviews and statements, he insisted that the police were responsible for security measures at the festival venue. The police on the other hand blamed Lopavent Ltd for shortcomings in the preparation of the event and in their own security measures. The mayor of Duisburg tried to assume the role of an active investigator of the case. He contracted an external law firm to review the available documentation, which according to the lawyers indicated that 'external actors' were responsible for the accidents. As a consequence of the extreme anger he caused with these statements, the mayor was actually attacked on the streets and received several death threats. Only 5 days later did the organizer, Lopavent Ltd, announce that it would pay 1 million Euros in compensation for the victims. This was later supplemented by a further half a million Euros, which was paid by the city of Duisburg in August 2010.

(Continued)

Case Study. Continued.

One hundred days after the Love Parade, a weblog journalist described the crisis as a 'catastrophe without consequences'. He referred primarily to the fact that none of the politicians involved in planning and authorizing the festival had stepped down. McFit, Lopavent and Rainer Schaller all escaped paying any further damages. No high ranking police officers had lost their job and no-one had been taken to trial. Only in February 2012 did the Mayor of Duisburg finally step down following the long-term consequences of the Love Parade tragedy.

Media reports, Internet user comments and reactions to public appearances of the actors in question indicated that they suffered substantial damage to their reputation and trust. Two major reasons led to this outcome. First of all, the Mayor of Duisburg, the police, Lopavent and its CEO were all perceived as being responsible for the crisis to a certain extent. A content analysis of social media postings on message boards related to the Love Parade crisis produced evidence for this assumption (Schwarz, 2012). The causes mentioned most frequently were failures in planning the festival, actions taken at the festival venue, and the characteristics of the festival venue itself. Hence, the perception of the crisis as an accident due to human error prevailed among the message board users.

According to Coombs (2007), this type of crisis is related to high levels of responsibility attributed to the organizations involved by the crisis stakeholders. This case study demonstrates that blame games in crisis communication do not pay off: usually, these strategies are zero-sum games that nobody is able to win. Rather, shifting blame to others in the context of a severe crisis usually provokes stakeholders and fuels negative media coverage, and as a consequence, reputational damage will be amplified. According to evidence-based recommendations in the crisis communication literature, the gap between responsibility as perceived by stakeholders and responsibility as publicly accepted by an organization should be as small as possible (Coombs and Holladay, 2004). Hence, in the case of the Love Parade crisis, denial strategies were clearly the wrong choice. The situation would have needed the actors involved to apologize, accept their share of the responsibility and offer compensation. Only this last strategy was applied in this case. The intent of the crisis communicators to shift or minimize responsibility resulted in a strong focus on technical details, and this discourse neither helped to clarify the actual causes for the victims and other stakeholders nor did it serve to manage reputation effectively. In addition, these tactics did not leave sufficient space to concentrate on stakeholders' concerns and the victims' needs to cope with the consequences.

Besides issues of crisis response, the Love Parade case study points to the fact that a strategic approach to crisis communication begins long before a crisis. Especially in the case of large music festivals and arts and entertainment events such as the Love Parade, organizations have to anticipate possible crisis scenarios and prepare for them adequately, which includes preparing for crisis communication. Such a strategic approach can even

(Continued)

Case Study. Continued.

serve as an early warning system to recognize crisis signals and, in some cases, may even prevent crises. In the case of the Love Parade, there were in fact many such signals: in the meetings between the Duisburg authorities, the organizers and the security staff before 24 July, several police and fire staff expressed their concerns about the tunnels and the festival venue; and even on the Internet, at least one social media user warned people not to participate in the festival because of the precarious security situation.

We can conclude from this case study that festival organizers should professionalize their PR in terms of crisis preparation and crisis communications. As a means of sensitizing people for possible dangers prior to crises, risk communication is woefully underused and underestimated by festival organizers in the entertainment industries. Usually, communication activities in the context of such events focus on marketing measures to increase sales and attendance. Several accidents and crises in the history of such events demonstrate that this approach is neither ethical nor strategically effective.

CONCLUSION

In this chapter, we have outlined current developments in strategic and tactical PR, both in the theory and in practice, and we have unpicked some of the definitions of the term. We have considered PR's strategic role as a boundary-spanner as part of the co-creation process and as a creative driving force behind the entertainment industries.

In organizations such as corporations and governments, PR has had serious image problems. This has arguably been a result of a lack of understanding or awareness of how to use it, and its potential communications power, properly and ethically. Sometimes it is depicted in the popular media as a dark art or spin, and in the entertainment industries it is often reduced to ephemeral media padding. As an activity, it is sometimes practised as an art rather than a science. But in recent decades PR has emerged as an acknowledged boardroom-level strategic management discipline, which can exert as much punch and

influence on the bottom line as the traditional marketing effort.

In the new world of social media and digital communications, PR has massive growth potential in the entertainment industries. Indeed PR should lie at the heart of the entertainment industries as a driver for publicity and promotion and as a potential tool for co-creation and audience development. It is also increasingly understood as an essential strategic management tool, which can develop the reputation of brands, artists, celebrities and entertainers and support them in areas of issues and crisis management.

SEMINAR ACTIVITIES

1. Describe the key differences between PR and marketing and discuss why these are important for an organization's approach to the management of its communications.
2. How can PR contribute to the strategic management of arts and entertainment organizations?

3. How would you describe the role of PR in contributing towards the co-creation of arts and entertainment products?

4. How would you describe the role of narrative for professionals working in PR? Why do you think storytelling plays an important role in communications between organizations and audiences?

5. Why is it important for PR professionals to engage and develop relationships with an organization's stakeholders? What value and benefit is there in this dialogue?

6. What are the key characteristics and issues related to crisis management that are faced by arts and entertainment organizations?

REFERENCES

Chartered Institute of Marketing (2009) *Marketing and the 7P's. A Brief Summary of Marketing and How it Works*. Chartered Institute of Marketing Publications, Berkshire, UK.

CIPR (Chartered Institute of Public Relations) (2012) The Chartered Institute of Public Relations Definition of PR. Available at: http://www.cipr.co.uk/content/about-us/about-pr (accessed 2 January 2013).

Coombs, W.T. (2007) *Ongoing Crisis Communication. Planning, Managing, and Responding*, 2nd edn. Sage, Los Angeles, California.

Coombs, W.T. and Holladay, S.J. (2004) Reasoned action in crisis communication: An attribution theory-based approach to crisis management. In: Millar, D.P. and Heath, R. (eds) *Responding to Crisis. A Rhetorical Approach to Crisis Communication*. Lawrence Erlbaum, Mahwah, New Jersey, pp. 95–115.

Corbett, G. (2012) A Modern Definition of Public Relations. Available at: http://prdefinition.prsa.org/index.php/2012/03/01/new-definition-of-public-relations (accessed 5 November 2012).

Euprera.org (2012) European Public Relations Education and Research Association, European Communications Monitor. Available at: http://www.communicationmonitor.eu (accessed 5 November 2012).

Gregory, A. (2009) Managing and organising of public relations. In: Tench, R. and Yeomans, L. (eds) *Exploring Public Relations*, 2nd edn. Pearson, London, pp. 147–273.

Hearit, K.M. and Courtright, J.L. (2004) A symbolic approach to crisis management: Sears defense of its auto repair policies. In: Heath, R.L. and Millar, D.P. (eds) *Responding to Crisis. A Rhetorical Approach to Crisis Communication*. Lawrence Erlbaum, Mahwah, New Jersey, pp. 201–212.

Hutton, J. (2001) Defining the relationship between public relations and marketing. In: Heath, R.L. (ed.) *Handbook of Public Relations*. Sage, Thousand Oaks, California, pp. 205–214.

McKie, D. and Willis, P. (2012) Renegotiating the terms of engagement: Public Relations, marketing, and contemporary challenges. *Public Relations Review* 38(5), 846–852.

Moss, D. and Warnaby, G. (2003) Strategy and public relations. In: Moss, D., Vercic, D.D. and Warnaby, G.G. (eds) *Perspectives on Public Relations Research*. Routledge, London.

Pearson, C.M. and Clair, J.A. (1998) Reframing crisis management. *Academy of Management Review* 23(1), 59–76.

PRSA (Public Relations Society of America) (2012) A Modern Definition of Public Relations. Available at: http://www.prsa.org/AboutPRSA/PublicRelationsDefined (accessed 25 November 2012).

Schwarz, A. (2012) How publics use social media to respond to blame games in crisis communication: The Love Parade tragedy in Duisburg 2010. *Public Relations Review* 38(3), 430–437.

Sorrell, M. (2010) Chartered Institute of Public Relations Keynote Speech. Available at: http://www.corporate-financial.com/events/agm2010.aspx (accessed 3 November 2012).

Sturges, D.L. (1994) Communicating through crisis: A strategy for organizational survival. *Management Communication Quarterly* 7(3), 297–316.

University of Southern California (2011) Strategic Public Relations Center's Generally Accepted Practices Study. Available at: http://annenberg.usc.edu/ResearchCenters/Strategic Communication and Public Relations Center.aspx (accessed 25 November 2012).

Zerfass, A., Verčič, D., Verhoeven, P., Moreno, A. and Tench, R. (2012) European Communication Monitor 2012. Challenges and Competencies for Strategic Communication. Results of an Empirical Survey in 42 Countries. Available at: http://www.zerfass.de/ecm/ECM2012-Results-ChartVersion.pdf (accessed 2 December 2012).

WEBSITES OF FEATURED ORGANIZATIONS AND ONLINE RESOURCES

http://media.prsa.org/pr-by-the-number
http://media.prsa.org/prsa+overview/industry+facts+figures
http://www.bbc.co.uk/news/uk-wales-south-west-wales-12326895
http://www.cim.co.uk/Resources/ResourcesHome.aspx
http://www.cim.co.uk/marketingresource
http://www.cipr.co.uk/CIPRMembershipSurveyReport
http://www.phoenixdancetheatre.co.uk/frankenstein
http://www.prca.org.uk
http://www.wpp.com
http://www.youtube.com/user/lifeinaday

chapter 5

Mass Media and Entertainment Management

Beccy Watson and John Horne

LEARNING OBJECTIVES

After reading this chapter you should be able to:

- outline key social and cultural contexts that inform how entertainment and media are directly interlinked;
- define core aspects of mass and new media and identify changes and continuities across the two;
- identify different aspects of production, messages and audiences as three core elements of media, whilst recognizing the links between and across them;
- outline different theoretical approaches to media; and
- assess how mega-events such as the Olympics and Paralympics offer opportunities and challenges to entertainment managers across local and global contexts.

INTRODUCTION

'Entertainment' is a term that always seems to be used with a hint of disdain: entertainment is always only entertainment. There are two implicit contrasts involved here. One rests on an aesthetic judgement: entertainment (fun, of the moment, trivial) is being contrasted to art (serious, transcendent, profound). The other on a political judgement: entertainment (insignificant, escapist) is being contrasted with news, with reality, with truth.

(Frith, 1996, p. 160)

This chapter focuses on mass media and offers a critical account of media–entertainment interrelationships that can usefully inform the broad contexts within which entertainment managers operate. The chapter outlines definitions of mass media and new media, and assesses changes and continuities between and across these to highlight some of the key ways in which mass media are theorized and explained. Of course there are caveats, as the topic itself is huge and there is variance across theoretical and conceptual approaches. So what we aim to do here is provide an outline of some of the key aspects that social scientists, in particular those from sociology and cultural studies backgrounds, offer in order to highlight areas that can usefully inform a deeper understanding of mass media for entertainment managers. We hope to offer insights to the social and cultural significance and complexity of media rather than a chapter based around facts and figures purporting to the size or scope of mass media.

In rapidly changing and technologically driven contemporary societies (in the West and/or northern hemisphere at least) it may seem rather burdensome to engage with critical accounts that question the plurality of media, of its endless possibilities for attracting and maintaining consumers of entertainment. However, for those involved in management and the generation of new ideas, new markets and outlets, an understanding of the social and cultural contexts within which mass media operates is vital. Entertainment after all is a constituent feature in, and a significant representative of, the social worlds we inhabit; how people choose to be entertained and/or how they seek to entertain themselves is inextricably linked to the proliferation of media that has occurred over the last hundred years. This chapter offers definitions of mass and new media; outlines a framework for how mass media has been conceptualized and researched, drawing on related theoretical approaches; and includes a range of examples to illustrate key arguments. The extended

case study of the Olympics provides a fruitful illustration of change and continuity and of competing views on the role and purpose of mass media.

MASS MEDIA TO NEW MEDIA: DEFINITIONS AND THEORETICAL PREMISE

Mass media and modernism

Commonly, the term 'mass media' is associated with the ways in which a single source or message can be communicated to the many, the mass. Social scientists continue to eke-out what the consequences and significance of media are. Initial accounts of mass media reflect what are referred to as modernist and structuralist accounts, that is, explanations of the world that seek to compartmentalize and attempt overall (macro) accounts of specific social phenomena. This has resulted in an emphasis on asking what/who mass media is for and what role and impact they have in society.

Mass media was increasingly considered by functionalist sociologists to be one of the key social institutions (along with family, education and the workplace) that underpinned the fabric of everyday modern life. Functionalists regard media as a potential mechanism for promoting and maintaining a plural and liberal society, as a means for maintaining the status quo. Sociologists in the USA in the 1940s and 1950s were particularly interested in aspects of human behaviour and interaction and the role media plays in socialization processes. European functionalists were focused on aspects of social order and how key social institutions operated in maintaining social consensus more broadly. This included the ways in which nation states developed and used mass media to communicate to their populace, which underpins the legacy of Public Sector Broadcasting (PSB) epitomized by the mantra of John Reith, the first Director General of the BBC in the UK, to inform, to educate and to entertain. Mass media could also result in dysfunctional appropriation of mass communication such as the propaganda associated with fascist ideology and Nazism in Germany prior to the Second World War.

From the 1960s onwards, Media Studies courses proliferated in universities and colleges. They tended initially to adopt *either* a more engineering, scientific approach to the technology and production aspects of media *or* a more social science based focus on, for example, psychosocial impacts of media (such as the effects of violent content on children), or the symbolic significance of cultural texts (genres, subcultural meanings); that is, some combination of assessing representations and their effects (Briggs and Cobley, 2002). Media Studies courses were and still are not the same as Journalism courses, which tend to be aligned with more literary-based training and have separate codes of professional accreditation.

Researching mass media has frequently been understood across three key platforms: (i) that focuses on media businesses and related industries, often including the 'hardware' and technological context of media; (ii) that analyses the representations (images and meanings) contained within mediated content; and (iii) that assesses impacts and effects on audiences. It is useful to bear this triad in mind in the analysis of the media, and we can think about it broadly as:

- *production* of mediated forms;
- *messages* broadcast through media; and
- *audiences* who receive and consume media.

These three areas are not mutually exclusive and by the end of the chapter readers should be able to identify and assess some of the interconnections across and between them. Links between mass and new media also inform our understanding of the interconnections.

New media and postmodernism

We have grown accustomed to the fact that media and communication technologies are a fundamental part of the fabric of our everyday lives. In contemporary contexts we experience levels of information generation and exchange, (potential) interactivity and localized self-production that simply was not envisaged 20, let alone 50, years ago. Developments in new media technologies and the ways in which communication has changed, both in terms of how that is enabled through technology and people's expectations of instant communication, is at the heart of much that is referred to as 'new media'.

> Increased and improved communication across the globe – through satellite technology, digital television, improved telephone links and the Internet – certainly means that we are now in touch with people and events internationally with a frequency, speed, quality and affordability never imaginable in the analogue age.
>
> (Creeber and Martin, 2009, p. 5)

What we tend to see in the literature on media currently is a discussion about *shifts* from mass to new media, particularly when related to new developments and a move from old (analogue) to new (digital) formats. One way in particular that the shift is explained is in charting the development of Web 1.0 technology to Web 2.0. (see Fig. 5.1) This, implicitly at least, suggests progress,

Fig. 5.1. Web 2.0 storytelling. Image by Bryan Alexander.

advance and potential that resonates with 'positive' aspects of media, aligned to functionalist analysis and a focus on how media 'works' in the maintenance of society.

Whereas the term 'mass media' is often associated with modernism and structuralist accounts, 'new media' sits fairly readily in accounts of postmodernism and fluidity, fragmentation and discourse. New media has continuities and links with mass and/ or traditional media yet there are also some contrasting features. Postmodernism reflects multiplicities in terms of the range and scope of media technologies, the context and content of representations, and recognition of a plurality of consumers and audiences. This point can be taken in consideration with developments in marketing entertainment (see Chapter 3). Modernist approaches to

understanding and analysing mass media were focused on finding meaning and overarching accounts (or grand narratives) and drew on conceptualizations of ideology to 'make sense' of and account for media practices. Poststructuralist theory contests underlying explanatory 'truths' and thus challenges attempts to describe and define media as a single entity. The modernist/postmodernist theoretical divide is particularly significant for understanding media because media practice from the 1980s began to be increasingly about multiple modes, to be deregulated and to seemingly require more detailed attention to the diversity of its audiences. Thus we have a change in theorizing, that is, developments in poststructuralist analyses that coincided with media itself arguably becoming more 'postmodern'. A key example of this is the dramatic shifts in the temporal and spatial contexts in which mediated content could be communicated and consumed. This is given some further consideration in the Olympics case study we discuss later.

CRITICAL THEORY AND CULTURAL STUDIES

Cultural Studies scholars offer accounts of the impacts of mass media as a feature of mass culture and the commodification of the 'cultural'

and the semiotic analysis of cultural texts and artefacts that mass media generates, such as music tracks, films, television programmes and so on. As we will see later in the chapter, cultural analysis of media is a fascinating, if somewhat complex, terrain – it engages highly critical and damning accounts of media and also incorporates alternative perspectives and sites of creative resistance. Much of this work is informed to some extent by the critical, Marxist-based, accounts of the Culture Industry proposed by the Frankfurt School in the mid-20th century (see Perspective 1).

Perspective 1: The Culture Industry

The term 'culture industry' is associated with the German scholars Theodor Adorno (1903–1969) and Max Horkheimer (1895–1973). These writers were active in what is known as the Frankfurt School, a body of theorists that drew on Marxist-based criticism of capitalist production and attended to the ways in which culture and creativity were key contexts for the maintenance of ideological control of the masses. A view of media and entertainment such as this reflects accounts associated with mass society theory. From this perspective, the commodification and massification of cultural products, including and in particular those associated with mass media, results in a range of negative outcomes including de-politicization, de-humanization and a 'brainwashing' effect. Adorno and Horkheimer, along with other theorists linked to the Frankfurt School, argued that the culture industry encapsulated how the creation and expansion of 'entertainment' forms of media dumbed down the masses and resulted in passive, malleable audiences. The concept of the 'culture industry' has had a profound influence on scholars seeking to account for the scope and impact of mass media and notably how entertainment is perceived and packaged. One of the lasting legacies of the 'culture industry' thesis is the contested notion of passive recipients of mediated cultural forms.

MASS SOCIETY THEORY

So why do those interested in entertainment and the entertainment industries need to know about the pessimistic outlook of some theorists writing over half a century ago? A 'critical' perspective on media, and on social

and economic relations more broadly, seeks to challenge the status quo rather than maintain it. Critical theory proposes change that ranges from outright rejections and a radical 'anti' based position (such as the Frankfurt thesis) to calls for change that work within existing systems. In part this engages modernist and postmodernist debates and questions the extent to which change can ever be overarching and lie 'outside' present systems and discourses. Mass society theory is more aligned to modernist challenges to dominant ideologies and has informed the development of a political economy model for understanding media.

POLITICAL ECONOMY MODEL

> One important approach to the critical study of communications focuses on the political economy of the media: their relation to the state and to the domination of the economy by giant corporations.
>
> (Downing *et al.*, 1995, p. 75)

Some key questions emerge from this perspective (Downing *et al.*, 1995, p. 76), including:

1. Are the media free and independent to present views, news and entertainment just as they want?
2. Are they free to be diverse from each other, not just in format but in the expression of opinion?
3. Does it matter if increasing numbers of both national and global media channels are owned and operated by large transnational corporations?

The bleak forecast of the Frankfurt School and other cultural theorists resonates with the political economy model but the focus here lies more centrally on overarching systems of political and economic power. Graham Murdock has been a key protagonist in the political economy model of mass media, as has Denis McQuail's 'mass communication theory' model. These theorists argue that the power of the state (nation states in modernist

contexts) and the demands and requirements of capitalist economies have the biggest and most profound impact on how media and communication have developed. In this respect 'entertainment' can be considered as a mechanism for generating major sources of profitability and act as a means of social control and 'dumbing down' of the masses.

This legacy informs how media, be it mass and/or new, operates in contemporary society and is evidenced in our discussion of the Olympics. We can see that questions of power, control and influence are central to analysing mass and new media and these can be traced across the three key aspects of production, messages and audiences. It is worth noting that analysis is not always distinctly modernist or postmodernist and that explanations of media vary dramatically, not least according to the focus under scrutiny. It is fair to say that there is usually some evidence of whether a functionalist tendency (we will add 'positive' for simplicity) or critical theory (negative) overall approach to media is being employed in explaining its social and cultural significance.

REPRESENTATIONS AND STEREOTYPES

If we turn our attention to the second aspect of the mass media triad of messages broadcast and conveyed through media, both mass and new, then a key concept used here is representation. Assessing representation, both as a concept and as a cultural text, is at the centre of much media analysis. It has been conceptualized across modernist and postmodernist contexts and continues to be referred to regularly in current media research.

From a basic definitional perspective, representation means a depiction or image of something or someone. Representations are ways in which meanings are conveyed, commonly through visual imagery, though they are also communicated through text and audio. If we think literally about 'text' as on a mobile phone, then the act of 'dropping a text' and the language and letters used is itself a representation of, for example, youth subculture. Representations in media may be regarded as: simply reflections of the world as-is (functionalist theory); reproductions (critical theory) of unequal power relations such as gender and race; or as processes under constant construction and negotiation (poststructuralist theory). Stuart Hall (1997) argues that representations are a dynamic interplay of production, consumption and reception. They do not have a fixed meaning rather a range of signifiers and signifying practices.

Analysing representations in media often relies on reference to stereotypes, identifying their persistence and/or highlighting and challenging the way in which meanings can be attributable to certain markers of identity. Challenges to stereotypical representations in media have commonly developed from critical theory-based perspectives, including, for example, feminist theorizing and critical theories of race and ethnicity. The box below illustrates how a feminist perspective problematizes dominant representations of femininity. It also illustrates how we need to look across the triad of practices, messages and people to more fully appreciate the interconnections between what is represented via media, by whom and to which audiences.

Perspective 2: Representations and audiences: the feminist perspective

A significant amount of audience research, as well as critical analysis of representations, has drawn on feminist and pro-feminist perspectives. These can be associated with critical theory in that they seek to challenge and change media practices, in this instance to overcome unequal power relations on the basis of gender. For some commentators this has meant identifying and challenging dominant ideologies of 'acceptable femininity' such as 'housewife'. Modernist feminist theory and poststructuralist feminist perspectives that deconstruct heterogeneous complexities contend that not all women (or men) seek or receive mediated texts and practices in the same way. They therefore argue that neither women nor men should be represented as a homogeneous (uniform) category in terms of representations. That said, there *are* commonalities in gender, most usually expressed and understood through stereotyping that often refers to and reproduces shared and dominant codes of behaviour. One of the key tenets of Hall's work on representations as dynamic constructions is that we *identify* with sameness and difference in contextually specific ways, largely through our exposure to the visual imagery by which we are surrounded.

We can think about women in the music industry as an example to highlight some key issues of representation. This arguably remains an under-researched topic, despite the highly visual representations of women in music. We can also link these to another aspect of
(Continued)

Perspective 2. Continued.

media, that of practices of production. If we think about rap as a genre, then some recurring representations come to the fore: women are commonly represented as overtly sexualized and at times in misogynistic ways; that is, they are over-represented as sexually available and they are under-represented as having roles outside of this limited scope. These types of representations can be linked to power and influence in social, economic and cultural relations more generally and much feminist analysis would seek to engage with these issues. Some feminists, particularly those interested in gender and other social factors, in this case race, would also trace other representations that reproduce such stereotypes, for example, how blackness intersects with gender that impacts negatively for women *and* men. Other commentators may link representations of women in rap to practices of production in the media industries and business more broadly – beyond a very small number of successful female producers there is very little presence of women in rap at executive levels, and there is little evidence of women in top positions in the music industry in general. Some analysts will focus on who these few 'successful' women are and assess how this has been achieved on an individual basis. This, it could be argued, offers new and alternative (potentially positive) representations of women in the industry. But its analysis may be limited to a very small part of media or it might inadvertently reinforce further stereotypes such as women performing as vocalists and 'looking good' or certainly looking a particular way. The point to note is that different perspectives will ask different questions regarding media and offer different explanations in their analysis; feminist theory does not offer a sweeping explanation about all women in music as an overriding feature of the entertainment industries.

AUDIENCES: DISCOURSE AND PLURALITY

Another aspect where it is important to recognize difference in relation to media is in thinking about audiences. Modernist material on media audiences focused on negative consequences, albeit in different and contrasting ways. Accounts of media impacts on audiences tended to draw either on behavioural psychological based assumptions on the impacts on identified groups of viewers (such as children) or on mass society theory, claiming wholesale negative social and cultural outcomes such as impacts of propaganda and/or fear of 'brainwashing'. Poststructuralist approaches that are more focused on the potential for meanings to be disrupted have prompted interest in sites of resistance to mass media and associated ideological meanings. Various writers engaging with critical theory, for example, have grappled with the extent to which audiences are active rather than passive in their reception of mediated texts.

> Media audiences are not 'masses' – anonymous and passive aggregates of people without identity. Nor are they merely 'markets' – the target groups of the media industries. [...] media audiences are active in the ways in which they use, interpret, and take pleasure in media products. [...] We cannot say in advance which meanings and

effects media content will have on audiences. It will depend on who those people are (e.g., in terms of class, gender, race, religious conviction, regional or national background) and the specific social and cultural contexts in which these media are embedded when they 'reach' their audiences.

(Ang, 1995, p. 219)

This assertion echoes early work by Stuart Hall who argued that people are not passive recipients of mediated messages and that they are active in receiving and 'de-coding' (Hall, 1973). It was also argued, in the context of television, that people use TV in different ways (Williams, 1974) and that audiences are diverse in make-up and in interests. These critiques laid an important foundation for audience research that draws on poststructuralist theorizing on difference and diversity and indicates how 'audience' shifts to plural rather than singular receivers of media. This continues to raise lively topics for debate particularly amongst theorists seeking to employ a critical lens whilst recognizing that messages and representations require deconstruction and do not carry or convey singular meanings. There are some interesting collections of key audience research in mass media and these are often, though not always, linked to analyses of representations. Examining representations and assessing their meanings draws on content and discourse analysis and these are popular and established ways of examining media texts. Content analysis can be very micro-specific, focusing on, for example, a single music track or piece of film through to broader analysis of genres and styles. Along with a research focus on what media do to audiences there has also been a research tradition that asked what audiences *do* with media. This has been particularly evident in work on youth subcultures and

associations with subcultural style and 'value'. The case study includes use of media as sites of resistance to challenge and subvert dominant discourses of Olympism. It is arguably the case that there continue to be key sites of power and influence within mass and new media and across the triad of producers, messages and people.

POWER AND INFLUENCE: TRACING CONTINUITIES

One of the ways in which we can trace further commonalities across notions of mass and new media is to consider how control and regulation has altered and, importantly, to acknowledge consistencies in power and influence. Some of the key influences include:

- changes in statutory regulations;
- deregulated economies;
- the rise of new technologies; and
- globalization.

NEWS AND INFOTAINMENT

One of the recurring themes in critiques of media is in relation to 'news' and the production of what shape and form this takes. We can certainly trace arguments of mass society theorists and those working with a political economy model in research into the news. It would appear that the ownership of major newspapers, television channels and entertainment and film companies irrefutably (still) revolves around power and control. 'Infotainment' is associated with ways in which some media practice (e.g. the treatment of newsreaders and other journalists as celebrities) and behaviour (particularly that of journalists) is centred round controversy and scandal. The creation and maintenance of celebrities is clearly a significant feature of mass and new media.

A contradictory concern that persists (and that was evidenced in the recent Leveson Inquiry in the UK) is the continuing reference to the notion of 'freedom of speech' associated with western, liberal democracies whilst at the same time attempting to reaffirm codes and parameters about what is considered acceptable in the production and exchange of information. To some extent, the development of new media technologies is regarded as an enabler, of the dissemination of 'news', of gossip, of what the public wants. Those working in entertainment are not directly responsible for such matters, though they often provide 'content' (in a multiplicity of ways) that needs to be 'in favour' with the public. Reality TV and the rise and rise of programmes that have emerged since *Big Brother* have established a 'bare all' type of programming that is now a taken-for-granted part of the global TV entertainment landscape.

GLOBALIZATION AND REGULATION

Regulatory forces that impact on media do still exist, but these are not always easy to trace in terms of lines of control and agenda setting. Any regulatory framework is irrevocably shaped by global contexts in which the role of the nation state appears to be blurred and where, in most cases, the state has stepped back from governing directly. There are some obvious contemporary divergences from this, such as China, where state control is being preserved (even though some commentators

argue this is untenable). In terms of technological developments, time and space have certainly 'shrunk' and been compressed via instant communications. For one country to set or impose specific regulatory frameworks is difficult to uphold, not least because of popular cultural signifiers, which are in constant production and exchange and which have their own value and cultural agenda.

In the context of globalization, entertainment is therefore particularly interesting when we look across the three aspects of media outlined in the opening sections of the chapter: media as institution/business; as representations (cultural texts); and as audiences (receivers and producers). It is of course pertinent to also consider the impacts of technological developments. The scope for the production and dissemination of media is vast and our very notion of producers and users has changed dramatically; conceptualizations of media, across mass and new, of convergence, ICTs and networks develop accordingly and require further scrutiny.

Despite technological change at unforeseen speeds and the global context of contemporary communication offered by digital interfacing, we need to bear in mind that there are lasting legacies and 'codes' that continue to underpin how media operates. In the European Union, a legislative framework for media is set out through a series of directives that are interpreted at national level and activated by member states. In the UK, Ofcom acts as the independent regulator and competition authority for communications industries and it describes its role as follows:

We are charged by the Communications Act with assessing the effectiveness of the designated public service broadcasters

(BBC, Channel 3, Channel 4, Five, S4C and Teletext), taken together, in delivering the public service purposes set out in the Act. *We are also charged with reporting on how the quality of public service broadcasting can be maintained and strengthened in future.*

(Ofcom, 2012, emphasis added)

We now turn our attention to some of the interrelationships between the Olympics and media as a means of further illustrating the key themes identified thus far. The following case study draws on Horne *et al.* (2013) and Horne and Whannel (2012).

Case Study: The Olympics and sport

The combination of the growth of jet travel, television coverage and commercial sponsorship triggered a transformation of sport in the 1960s (Whannel, 1986). Television, sponsorship, advertising and merchandizing became the dynamic forces underpinning the commercialization of sport. The transformation of sport by television and sponsorship between 1965 and 1985 was dramatic. At the start of the 1960s, television provided a grainy black and white image. By 1980, high quality live colour pictures were relayed around the world by satellite, augmented by slow motion action replay. Sponsorship was a major source of revenue for the elite level of sport. Sports agents became rich and powerful by intervening to manage relations between stars, managers, governing bodies, promoters, television executives and sponsoring companies. The impetus for the transformation of sport came from opportunist and maverick entrepreneurs who established themselves as sports agents, and who constituted the mediation point between sport organizations, sport stars, television, sponsors and advertisers. Horst Dassler of Adidas and Rupert Murdoch of News Corporation are two key figures in this process. Dassler taught the leading world governing bodies, like FIFA and the IOC, how to exploit television advertising and sponsorship, through his company ISL. Murdoch's Sky Television has been the driving force behind the transformation of football in England since the 1990s.

In the 1980s, sport became an international television spectacle, producing vast earnings for elite performers and strengthening the power of sports agents. In the process, traditional authority was undermined. The growing global visibility of major sport was of considerable appeal to advertisers and the 1984 Olympic Games made over US$100m from sponsorship, ten times that made in previous games. In the USA, only the McDonald's logo was more recognizable than the five rings of the Olympics.

In 1990, although the Internet had become established, the digital revolution had hardly begun. Television subscription channels for sport in the UK grew slowly at first, hampered by slow dish sales and competition between two providers, BSB and Sky. However, once Sky Television, into which BSB was 'merged', had the field to itself, the

(Continued)

Case Study. Continued.

rapidly growing revenue from the pay-per-channel services began to give satellite television enhanced scope to obtain the rights to major events. Since then there has been a shift toward satellite television and from broadcasting as a public service towards broadcasting as a commodity to be chosen and purchased. The launch of digital television and growth of pay-per-view transmission of major football matches and other big events provided a significant new impetus to the commodification of sport.

Since the mid-1990s, as media content of all kinds became digitalized, the Internet became central to the distribution of media content. Multiple channel television and deregulation have paved the way for the replacement of analogue television by digital television; and sport channels, with new access to extra channels, widescreen, high definition and 3D transmission have benefited. Although the convergence of the technologies of television and computing has been slower than predicted, it seems likely that more sport will be available on the Internet. Given ownership of its own rights, a sports club with a global recognition can now sell live games globally through its own website (see Rowe, 2011 for a discussion of media developments). Globalizing processes have ensured that the promotional culture, with its brands and iconic celebrities, has become one of the dynamic driving forces in the commercialization and commodification of sport.

As illustrated in Table 5.1, the Olympic Games could not have developed its global impact without television: the Olympics, as they currently exist, are a product of television's power to produce and distribute a live global spectacle. Indeed they are perhaps better understood as a television event rather than a sporting one.

As Whannel (1984, p. 30) stated nearly 30 years ago, the Olympics is the 'ultimate media festival'. Of the Olympic sports only athletics, tennis, football, basketball and boxing have any significantly large spectator following outside the Olympic Games, and in the case of tennis, football, basketball and boxing, the Olympics is only a minor part of their sporting calendar and competitive formats. Nor can the Olympic sports, for the most part, claim a broad base of participants. Although a fair proportion of Olympic sports can claim a solid degree of participation, in the UK at least, only football, running, swimming and cycling would count as mass participation activities, and even then only if one includes swimming and running and cycling for leisure rather than competition.

So the Olympics does not appear to be popular because of the regular following of its major component sports. Rather, it is because it is a *spectacular television show,* with the badge of being the *world's best show.* As *spectacular television entertainment,* the Olympic Games can be productively understood to have been shaped by the forces of commodification, globalization and digitalization; and, increasingly, it is shaped by

(Continued)

Case Study. Continued.

Table 5.1. Countries broadcasting the Summer and Winter Olympic Games 1936–2008. (From Horne and Whannel, 2012, p. 52.)

Summer Games			Winter Games		
Year	**Site**	**Countries**	**Year**	**Site**	**Countries**
1936	Berlin	1			
1948	London	1			
1952	Helsinki	2			
1956	Melbourne	1	1956	Cortina	22
1960	Rome	21	1960	Squaw Valley	27
1964	Tokyo	40	1964	Innsbruck	30
1968	Mexico City	n/a	1968	Grenoble	32
1972	Munich	98	1972	Sapporo	41
1976	Montreal	124	1976	Innsbruck	38
1980	Moscow	111	1980	Lake Placid	40
1984	Los Angeles	156	1984	Sarajevo	100
1988	Seoul	160	1988	Calgary	64
1992	Barcelona	193	1992	Albertville	86
			1994	Lillehammer	120
1996	Atlanta	214	1998	Nagano	160
2000	Sydney	220	2002	Salt Lake City	60
2004	Athens	220	2006	Torino	200
2008	Beijing	220	2010	Vancouver	220[a]

[a]Broadcasting Rights for consecutive editions of the Summer and Winter Olympic Games are now packaged so that increasingly the number of countries broadcasting the Winter Games has more or less equaled those showing the Summer edition.

(Continued)

Case Study. Continued.

the convergence of the once distinct technologies of television, computers and the Internet.

The Olympic Games has become an enormous event, not least in terms of its global reach via television, its massive revenues from commercial sources and its huge costs. The Olympic Games produces four main sources of revenue: ticket sales, sale of television rights, sponsorship and licensing, and merchandise. The IOC collects television rights payments and international sponsorships and redistributes these funds to the Organising Committee, the National Olympic Committees and the International Federations. The IOC retains a little less than 10% of commercial revenue to cover its own running costs, which include the lavish travel and accommodation available to IOC members. Local sponsorship and merchandizing revenue goes to the Organising Committee. In the 4-year quadrennium 2005–2008, the total Olympic revenue was over US$5 billion, of which 47% came from television rights, 45% from sponsorship and only 5% from ticketing (see Fig. 5.2).

N.B. The Olympic Partners (TOP) programme is the worldwide sponsorship programme managed by the IOC. The IOC created it in 1985 and it operates on a 4-year term – the Olympic quadrennium. The TOP programme provides each Worldwide Olympic Partner with exclusive global marketing rights and opportunities within a designated product or service category. Eleven corporations, including Coca-Cola, McDonald's, Visa, Samsung, Omega and Acer, were amongst the partners during the seventh quadrennium from 2009 to 2012, or 'TOP VII'.

Until recently, when the revenue from sponsorship grew exponentially, television rights payments provided the dominant share of Olympic revenue (see Fig. 5.3), and the bulk of the money came from the major American networks. Television revenue for 2010–2012 was expected to be over US$3 billion, of which two-thirds was estimated to come from NBC for the USA rights. Of the total television revenue, 88% comes from the Americas and Europe. Despite the massive growth in the reach and usage of the Internet, new media rights payments account for less than half of one per cent of this revenue (IOC, 2010). Ever since the first proper rights payments from USA sources, in 1960, the competition between the major American television

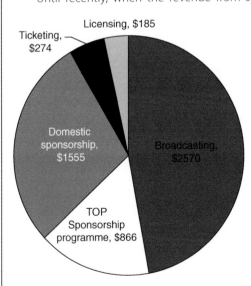

Fig. 5.2. Olympic Revenue 2005–2008 (US$m). (From Horne and Whannel, 2012, p. 48.)

(Continued)

Case Study. Continued.

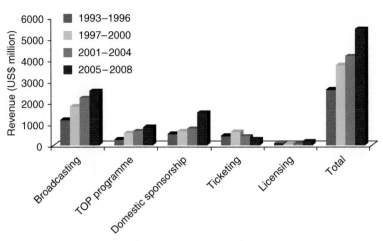

Fig. 5.3. Olympic Marketing Revenue 1993–2008 (US$m). (From Horne and Whannel, 2012, p. 49.)

networks has driven revenues upwards at a rapid rate. Only in the last decade can signs be detected that the rises are no longer enormous. However, in an era when broadcast television may be losing a little of its absolute primacy, the Olympic Games is still able to offer the live and unpredictable drama at which sport excels, and hitherto only broadcast television can adequately quench this thirst for global live entertainment.

Ever since 1988, the digitalized, computerized and globalized Internet dissemination of the Games has begun to emerge. The growth of the Internet and the emergence of the World Wide Web provided the IOC with both an opportunity and a threat. The Internet offered a radical new means to promote the Games, the sponsors and Olympism; but it also threatened to become a new means of dissemination that could potentially steal television's audience whilst not replacing its revenues. Just as the IOC had, in the 1980s, assumed greater central control of the negotiation of rights and sponsorship deals, during the 1990s it determined to take greater control of the international feed, the television pictures provided by the host broadcaster to the rest of the world. By 2001 it had established OBS (Olympic Broadcasting Services) to organize the televising of the Games. OBS is basically a committee that commissions established broadcasters and production companies from around the world to provide aspects of the coverage. After ISL collapsed in 2001, the IOC assumed a more central control of both television and marketing. In 2005 it established a separate company, IOC Television and Marketing Services SA.

In 2008, which Andy Miah has referred to as the first Web 2.0 Games (Miah *et al.*, 2008), Internet use and video streaming rose dramatically. The NBC website recorded an estimated 1.3 billion page views, 53 million unique users, 75.5 million video streams and

(Continued)

Case Study. Continued.

10 million hours of video consumption during the Games. The European Broadcasting Union delivered 180 million broadband video streams. In Latin America, Terra's Olympic site reported 29 million video streams and 10 million video-on-demand downloads (Hutchins and Mikosza, 2010). This substantial and rapid rise in digital video streaming is a strong indicator that the dominance of the Olympic Games by broadcast television could come under increasing threat.

The dilemma for the IOC is that it wishes to utilize all the new media resources of the Internet and social networking sites to promote the Olympics brand, while still remaining in control. But as Hutchins and Mikosza argue, there is a shift in the *media sport content economy* from the comparative scarcity of television channels to the 'digital plenitude' of the new media environment in which online media challenge both market driven logic and central control. As they graphically put it, 'the carefully designed and fertile "media garden" tended by the Olympic Movement over the past 25 years was sporadically beset by weeds – uninvited, unpredictable, socially-driven, participatory digital media' (Hutchins and Mikosza, 2010).

In the build-up to any Olympic Games 'the media coverage is often focused on two central questions: "Will it go over budget?" and "Will the facilities be ready in time?" The answer to both questions is usually "Yes"' (Horne and Whannel, 2010, p. 766). After the games commence, however, 'there is a massive turning inward of the media to events in the arena and the stadia' (ibid.).

Fig. 5.4. Building London's Olympic stadium. Image by John Horne.

(*Continued*)

Case Study. Continued.

The British print media and the London Olympics (July–August 2012)

Issues raised in the British media in the 12 months prior to the London Games included concerns over: 'legacy promises'; a potential 'crisis of legitimacy' because chemical company Dow was a sponsor of the IOC and the London Games; 'surveillance by drones' and 'rocket launchers on the roofs'; transport congestion; and ticket scandals. During the Games, initial concern at the lack of a Team GB gold medal after 4 days of competition led to the publication of a 'Keep calm and carry on… We've still got Wiggo' poster in *The Guardian* (referring to cyclist Bradley Wiggins, who had become the first British rider to win the Tour de France the weekend before London 2012 began). As sports journalist Rob Steen (Steen, 2012, p. 225) presciently commented before London 2012:

> The tone within the UK press […] will depend on the medal count and the impact of the Coalition Government's spending cuts […]. The expense of an Olympic Games must be justified by glory and, at the very least, organizational competence. Broadcasters […] are inclined to exaggerate the good.

Indeed, during July, August and September 2012, the British media became more like flag-waving fomenters of the feel-good factor than dispassionate critics. As the British medals accumulated, it was estimated that the British print media devoted an average of 46 pages daily to Olympic coverage, publishing more than 7200 pages of Olympic news (Edgar, 2012).

Despite the fact that the BBC's sport budget had been cut by 20% as the licence fee was frozen, the BBC produced 2500 hours of live Olympic TV and used 765 reporters

Fig. 5.5. London's Olympic stadium. Image by Alexander Kachkaev.

(*Continued*)

Case Study. Continued.

during the Olympics alone (compared with 550 Team GB athletes). There was blanket coverage from 6am to 1am daily across multiple digital channels. It was estimated that 90% of the population watched at least 15 minutes of coverage (Thomas, 2012). Television channel C4 were exclusive rights holders for the 2012 Paralympic Games and ran a series of advertisements featuring the strapline 'Thanks for the warm up' towards the end of the Olympics. Using the song 'Harder than you think' by American rap group Public Enemy as the theme tune, C4 produced almost an equal amount of saturation coverage of the Paralympics and was awarded with a BAFTA award for best televized sport and live event coverage.

Public and symbolic contestation

As the Olympic and Paralympic Games have grown as a media spectacle over the past few decades, so too has the level of public contestation. Localized resistance utilizes the media to resist the 'Olympic machine', and this raises questions such as:

- Who benefits from mega-events such as the Olympics?
- What sections of the community are potentially excluded and marginalized?
- What scope is there for contestation?
- How is symbolic contestation played out?

Mediated, symbolic contestation between mega-event supporters and activists, or 'boosters' and 'sceptics' (Boykoff, 2011), takes place and various forms of the media become a site of struggle between competing groups. In line with the creation of the Olympics as a spectacular form of family entertainment, London 2012 organizers commissioned cartoon animations named Wenlock and Mandeville as the mascots for the Olympic and Paralympic Games. The characters were named after Much Wenlock in Shropshire (which hosted a precursor to the modern Olympic Games in the 19th century) and the birthplace of the Paralympic Games, Stoke Mandeville hospital in Buckinghamshire. During the London 2012 Olympics there were 84 different Wenlock and Mandeville figures scattered across London, including this 'Pearly Mandeville' in Spitalfields (see Fig. 5.6), a costume design related to the charitable London working class cultural tradition of Pearly Kings and Queens.

Changes in contestation reflect different phases of the Olympics and Olympic-related politics but also different media forms and technologies: pre-TV (largely before the 1960s); TV (since the late 1960s); and the Internet (since the 1990s). In terms of politics, the Olympics have moved from being installed as part of the international political system (through, for example, the 1936 'Nazi' Olympics held in Berlin and the 1968 Games staged in Mexico City) to a more global, corporate, commercial and media-oriented 'prolympism' (Donnelly, 1996) best exemplified by Sydney in 2000 and Beijing in 2008 (Horne and Whannel, 2012).

(Continued)

Case Study. Continued.

Fig. 5.6. Pearly Mandeville. Image by John Horne.

News, including news about mega-events, needs to be understood as a social production (Hall *et al.*, 1978). One element of this has been the increasing use in sport of public relations (PR) expertise (Boyle, 2006), especially by 'boosters' for and promoters of large sports events. Increasing use of PR or 'spin' in Olympic sport took off during the 1990s as an attempt to manage the crisis of Olympism when a number of investigative journalists had uncovered corruption, for example in terms of the selection procedures for host cities (Jennings, 1996) as well as a way of harnessing sport to the promotional age of consumer culture (Horne, 2006).

Any attempts at 'seizing the Olympic platform' (Price, 2008) by sceptics or critics face uneven power relations. The sceptics typically lack resources, the initiative of timing, and the legitimacy that comes with being the 'official' body responsible for delivering large sports events. However, media 'agenda setting' is a dynamic situation in which some possibilities arise for criticizing official stories. For example, during the run up to London 2012, issues of security became prioritized ahead of the removal and evictions of people who lived in or on the land used for the Olympic Park. In addition, with the rise of corporate social responsibility (CSR) and legacy as a predominant discourse in sports mega-events, gaps opened up between rhetoric and reality that sceptics could sometimes exploit. Hence critics resorted to weapons such as satire, critical websites and creative (re-)designs of logos, mascots or Games-related slogans. During the London 2012 Olympic and Paralympic Games (in July–September 2012) many examples of these were available online that focused on ethics and sustainability. One such was the work of the anarchist group Space Hijackers (see for example http://www.protestlondon2012.com). The Internet also enables the promotion of causes transnationally, as can be seen with respect to campaigns about human rights and housing connected to the next Summer Olympics to be held in Rio de Janeiro in Brazil in 2016.

Assessing media coverage of the Olympics and Paralympics in 2012 and beyond in relation to the broad range of issues it generates will be an important focal point for

(Continued)

Case Study. Continued.

those interested in studying the media. Whether it is in tracing the creation or continuing coverage of sporting celebrities, of assessing sport in the context of 'infotainment' and sport as entertainment or examining social media usage and abuse there will no doubt be plenty of scope for discussion. For example if you were tweeting enthusiastically during the televized Opening Ceremony of the London 2012 Olympics, how do you know you were not caught up in an attempt to make us all feel good about ourselves and our country? As Glaser (2011, pp. 46–51) argues, national governments and politicians, as well as commercial enterprises, are increasingly using the informality of social media to deliver a carefully planned message via 'astroturfing', that is the creation of *fake* grassroots opinion, to project the appearance of a broad base of support for a product or message.

CONCLUSIONS: WHAT OF MEDIA AND THE FUTURE?

What happens in the future with regards to media depends on a number of key factors upon which this chapter has touched. Two central features that will continue to have substantial social and cultural consequences are:

- sources of power and regulation, both politically and economically, with a recognition that these are complex and fragmented; and
- changes in technology and the pace of such change in the context of global networks.

There are clearly enabling aspects of media, such as the potential for global promotion, on which entertainment managers need to capitalize. However, we have seen in this chapter that the media can also provide a global platform for protest and resistance, so entertainment managers need to treat it with great care. It may be that we have seen the most dramatic changes over the most recent decades in terms of technological developments. But what is intriguing for entertain-

ment managers is how central social aspects of mediated communication shape our uses and expectations of what media does and may do for us in the future. Humans appear to remain rooted to interaction, keeping in touch with one another and sharing information. That is one of mass media's most obvious continuities and it makes it hard not to draw in some respects from functionalist approaches. These uses operate in a complex context of potential that includes political and economic motivations and thus some reference to the political economy model of media retains some significance. The Facebook phenomenon illustrates the currency of both functionalist and critical approaches to media and reminds us how there are continuities across mass and new media, not just changes. The format of social networking for instance is at once individual, diverse, plural (postmodern) and yet it is arguably also uniform, bland and business-led (modern). It is difficult to make claims that this is wholly positive news for entertainment managers but it would be naive to paint only a negative picture of its uses and viability – and it is perhaps less significant than the user-generated content that YouTube and other online 'production' allows for.

We hope that as potential managers you will seek to persist in asking questions about the mass media's place in socio-cultural contexts and that you will ask questions about entertainment's symbiotic relationship with media. Entertainment might regularly be positioned as 'less serious', as the quote at the start of the chapter suggests, but nonetheless it requires serious attention in relation to what media is and how central it is to the study and management of entertainment.

SEMINAR ACTIVITIES

1. Trace some of the continuities and changes across mass and new media.

2. Select a cultural text/set of practices (from e.g. music, TV, film, social networking) and assess it across the triad of media business, representations and audiences.

3. Discuss the statement that being in control of the news can/has direct links to being in control of entertainment formats.

4. Drawing on examples across mass and new media, outline the relationship between major sports coverage and sponsorship.

5. How does a political economy model of media contrast with functionalist approaches and what are the strengths and weaknesses of each?

6. Select a media text or set of practices and outline and apply a feminist perspective.

7. Drawing on examples from mass and new media, examine the complex interrelationship between the Olympics/Paralympics and the media.

8. Outline your vision of media in the future incorporating at least one theoretical perspective to support your claims.

REFERENCES

Ang, I. (1995) The nature of the audience. In: Downing, J., Mohammadi, A. and Sreberny-Mohammadi, A. (eds.) *Questioning the Media: A Critical Introduction*, 2nd edn. Sage, London, pp. 207–220.

Boykoff, J. (2011) The Anti-Olympics. *New Left Review* 67, 41–59.

Boyle, R. (2006) *Sports Journalism*. Sage, London.

Briggs, A. and Cobley, P. (eds.) (2002) *The Media: An Introduction*, 2nd edn. Pearson Education, Harlow, UK.

Creeber, G. and Martin, R. (2009) *Digital Cultures: Understanding New Media*. McGraw Hill, Maidenhead, UK.

Donnelly, P. (1996) Prolympism: sport monoculture as crisis and opportunity. *Quest* 48(1), 25–42.

Downing, J., Mohammadi, A. and Sreberny-Mohammadi, A. (1995) (eds.) *Questioning the Media: A Critical Introduction*, 2nd edn. Sage, London.

Edgar, A. (2012) The future of reporting at the Olympic Games. Conference presentation at 'The Olympic Games: Meeting New Challenges' Conference, Oxford University Club, Oxford, UK 13–14 August.

Frith, S. (1996) Entertainment. In: Curran, J. and Gurevitch, M. (eds.) *Mass Media and Society*, 2nd edn. Arnold, London, pp. 160–176.

Glaser, E. (2011) *Get Real: How to Tell It Like It Is in a World of Illusions*. Fourth Estate, London.

Hall, S. (1973) *Encoding and Decoding in the Television Discourse*. Centre for Contemporary Cultural Studies, Birmingham, UK.

Hall, S. (ed.) (1997) *Representation: Cultural Representations and Signifying Practices*. Sage, Newbury Park, California.

Hall, S., Critcher, C., Jefferson, T., Clarke, J. and Roberts, B. (1978) *Policing the Crisis*. Macmillan, London.

Horne, J. (2006) *Sport in Consumer Culture*. Palgrave, Basingstoke, UK.

Horne, J., Tomlinson, A., Whannel, G. and Woodward, K. (2013) *Understanding Sport: A Socio-cultural Analysis*, 2nd edn. Routledge, London.

Horne, J. and Whannel, G. (2010) The 'caged torch procession': Celebrities, protesters and the 2008 Olympic torch relay in London, Paris and San Francisco. *Sport in Society* 13(5), 760–770.

Horne, J. and Whannel, G. (2012) *Understanding the Olympics*. Routledge, London.

Hutchins, B. and Mikosza, J. (2010) The Web 2.0 Olympics: Athlete blogging, social networking and policy contradictions at the 2008 Beijing Games. *Convergence* 16(3), 163–183.

IOC (2010) *Olympic Marketing Fact File*. International Olympic Committee, Lausanne, Switzerland.

Jennings, A. (1996) *The New Lords of the Rings. Olympic Corruption and How to Buy Gold Medals*. Pocket Books, London.

Miah, A., Garcia, B. and Zhihui, T. (2008) 'We are the media': Non-accredited media and citizen journalists at the Olympic Games. In: Price, M.E. and Dayan, D. (eds.) *Owning the Olympics*. Digital Culture Books/University of Michigan, Ann Arbor, Michigan.

Ofcom (2012) What is Ofcom? Available at: http://www.ofcom.org.uk/about/what-is-ofcom (accessed 5 May 2012).

Price, M. (2008) On seizing the Olympic platform. In: Price, M.E. and Dayan, D. (eds.) *Owning the Olympics*. Digital Culture Books/University of Michigan, Ann Arbor, Michigan.

Rowe, D. (2011) *Global Media Sport: Flows, Forms and Futures*. Bloomsbury, London.

Steen, R. (2012) The view from the press box. Rose-tinted spectacles? In: Sugden, J. and Tomlinson, A. (eds.) *Watching the Olympics: Politics, Power and Representation*. Routledge, London.

Thomas, L. (2012) Bigger than the Royal Wedding: 90% of Britons saw Games on TV, *The Daily Mail*, 13 August.

Whannel, G. (1984) The television spectacular. In: Tomlinson, A. and Whannel, G. (eds.) *Five Ring Circus: Money, Power and Politics at the Olympic Games*. Pluto, London.

Whannel, G. (1986) The unholy alliance: Notes on television and the remaking of British sport. *Leisure Studies* 5(2), 22–37.

Williams, R. (1974) *Television: Technology and Cultural Form*. Collins, London.

chapter 6

Event Planning and Management

Lisa Devine and Stuart Moss

LEARNING OBJECTIVES

After reading this chapter you should be able to:

- develop an understanding of the planning and processes involved in organising an event involving live entertainment;
- recognize the stages involved in choosing a suitable venue for a live event;
- learn project management techniques and identify events as the culmination of a series of tasks;
- discover how to identify, evaluate and hire live performers; and
- develop an appreciation of the fundamentals that contribute to producing a memorable event.

INTRODUCTION

An event is a gathering of individuals with a common interest who have been brought together for a shared unique experience. Events are often planned as one-off occurrences, although they can also be a regular occasion and may be organized for (amongst other reasons) celebratory, educational and/or fundraising purposes. Events are typically made up of mostly intangible offerings, which may include (but are not limited to): atmosphere, audience interaction, decoration, theming, entertainment, venue aesthetics and various additional novelties. As a result, each individual attendee will experience the event in a different manner depending on their personal perceptions and expectations.

Organizing a live event involving entertainment is much more than merely logistics and careful planning. It is equally important to design and create a concept that attracts and excites the potential audience as this will encourage them to attend. Entertainment can be used to enhance an event, e.g. a book launch for a romantic novel may be suited to a jazz band playing who can help create a stylish and classy ambiance. Entertainment can also be used as the primary focus of the event, e.g. a staged music performance. Where the entertainment forms the basis of the event, the venue, suppliers and theme need to be selected to reflect the genre and style of the showcased artists.

Events when properly planned and managed are more likely to be a success, and this chapter is designed to focus on best practice to create successful events. The foundation of any event relies on good planning in order to ensure that every eventuality has been considered and a contingency is in place, whilst the execution of a live event lies in effective management during the event itself. Organizing an event that involves live entertainment is challenging and not for the faint hearted. An event manager should be prepared to work extremely hard and communicate effectively with a wide range of event stakeholders including agents, artists, printing companies, marketing organizations, venue managers and potential audiences.

Chapter 1 of this book provides a narrative around the benefits of events and why live events are a part of the entertainment industry. This chapter is concerned with the practicalities and project management functions that need considering and implementing when running an event, from the initial conception of an event, to planning, running and managing the event, and then reviewing the event afterwards. This chapter should be read in conjunction with the chapters in this book on entertainment marketing, human resource management and performance management.

The success of an event can be measured in a number of ways, for example:

- the fulfilment of the expectations and needs of the audience, for example light relief through comedy or increased knowledge through an educational talk;
- financial profitability of the event, so that the event generates a greater revenue for those who invested into it than the sums that were initially invested;
- an intended behavioural change of the audience, for example an event intended to raise awareness of environmental issues may lead to audience members modifying their own behaviour;
- benefits that an event may bring to a third party, for example a charity event may raise money for a good cause; and
- the long term legacy of an event, for example regeneration of ex-industrial land and infrastructure for an event can then bring longer term benefits for the host community, for example the London 2012 Olympic Games were used to regenerate parts of East London that were considered to be deprived.

Events take place live, usually in front of an audience, and within the entertainment industry an event is likely to include as the key attraction an individual artist or team of artists/performers supported by other artists and performers. The majority of entertainment events aim to captivate and emotionally resonate with the audience often with the goal of providing a satisfying customer experience that generates a financial profit for the organizers (Carter, 2012). Whilst the on-stage entertainment is the main attraction of an event, an important consideration is the venue itself, particularly its size and ensuring that it is appropriate for the needs of the artists/performers and the audience. Figure 6.1 features a live band performing in a nightclub venue, which provides an appropriate stage area, a dance floor for the

Fig. 6.1. A band performing live in a nightclub. Photograph courtesy of Martyn Strange.

audience, sound and lighting equipment, and extra visuals including large screens.

ROLES AND SKILLS

An event team is the collection of individuals who must work together cohesively for the common purpose of planning, organizing, running and reviewing an event. It is difficult to define fully all of the officially designated roles that an event team will include, but typically in a well-organized team individual members will be aware of one another's roles and all will have duties delegated to them by a coordinating figure who is the event manager (although the actual job title 'event manager' may vary, with 'producer' and 'organizer' also often used). The job roles and size of an event team are dependent on the type of event and the event's size and scale. The team's duties will usually include liaising with suppliers, along with managing all elements of the event.

The event manager is often heavily involved in the initial planning and ideas stage of an event, drawing on the individual expertise of team members such as marketing, staffing, technical and health and safety specialists. Within a small live event, the boundaries between the roles and responsibilities of team members and managers may be blurred, with individuals taking on multiple roles. Event managers may also be employed as 'on the night' coordinators, whereby they are only required for the duration of the event taking place.

During an event, responsibilities can include: liaising with artists, performers and technical staff within venues, such as sound and light engineers; checking performance riders (a set of requests or demands made by an artist/performer) have been correctly fulfilled; ensuring power and staging requirements have been met; and liaising with other external suppliers and venue management.

The skills and personal traits required by an effective event manager share similarities with many general managerial roles. These include communication skills, problem-solving ability, working to deadlines and being a highly organized, energetic, adaptable, creative, flexible, passionate, motivational, imaginative, committed leader with a vibrant personality and an eye for detail. It is a reality of the industry that formal training is often not taken, and many staff working in an events management capacity often learn 'on the job' through experience. Since the 1990s the recognition of the value of the events industry and the need for effective events managers has led to a growth in formal education courses either specifically in events management, or that include an aspect of events management within them.

PLANNING AND PROJECT MANAGEMENT

Organizing a live event involves a much longer planning period than the duration of the event itself, although this does not mean that the shorter the event, the lesser the planning period; an event is a project in that it requires initial planning and preparation which can help to ensure the success of a live event. If the planning process is thorough, with the right questions being raised and potential problems and risks identified, contingencies can be planned for and often rectified in advance. Project management tools such as Gantt charts can help to visualize the planning stages of an event. Gantt charts show the scheduled and actual progress of projects, as they are horizontal bar charts denoting project tasks mapped against a timescale.

Gantt charts are used to try to work out the duration of a project; this is done by listing

how long each task that goes into a project should take. It is also necessary to establish which tasks are reliant on other tasks having already taken place (predecessors). Tasks are plotted along a horizontal time scale with a project starting date, which allows for the project planner to be able to work out the project end date from plotting the duration of the various tasks within the project. Tasks are plotted in sequence to the tasks on which they rely (predecessors) and in parallel to other tasks on which they do not rely.

When producing a Gantt chart, the first task is always to 'start' and the last task is always to 'finish'. As well as this, each individual task is given a unique identifier – commonly a number or a letter. A sample project of organizing a charity pub quiz would contain the tasks highlighted in Table 6.1. For this project there will be no venue hire charges, and the project manager is organizing this event alone. The venue will supply the public address (PA) system and also pay for publicity materials, as on the night of the quiz the venue will see increased sales, so it is in their interest to help promote it. In this project, the minimum task duration will be 0.5 days.

Table 6.1 demonstrates the number of tasks that need to take place in order to complete this project so that the event can run. The Task ID column contains merely an identifying number for each named task, the duration of each task is displayed in units of days, and the predecessor's column highlights which tasks need to have taken place in order for the particular task to happen.

To explain this further, tasks 1 to 3 are establishing the fundamentals of the event, including a venue and date. After this has happened, promotion can take place, which is

Table 6.1. Charity pub quiz task breakdown.

Task ID	Task name	Duration (days)	Predecessors (by Task ID)
1	Start	0	
2	Find a venue and fix a date	5	1
3	Contact potential sponsors for prizes	7	1
4	Create a Facebook event for the quiz, and invite attendees	0.5	2,3
5	Promote the Facebook event	14	4
6	Invite sponsors and representatives from the charitable cause that the quiz is being run for	0.5	4
7	Produce posters and flyers	0.5	4
8	Distribute posters and flyers	14	7
9	Promote the event on Twitter	14	4
10	Create the quiz questions and produce the answer paper	2	1
11	Repro sufficient blank answer papers	0.5	10
12	Test the venue equipment	0.5	2
13	Organize a selection of tracks for background music during the quiz	0.5	1,12
14	Decorate and theme the quiz venue	0.5	2,5,8
15	Run the pub quiz	0.5	14,13,11,9
16	Review the event's strengths and weaknesses	0.5	15
17	Publicise successes, make the charity donation and give thanks to sponsors, venue and attendees online	1	16
18	End	0	17

tasks 4 to 9. Producing the quiz is the next stage but realistically relies on nothing having taken place as the organizer could produce the quiz anyway even if the event did not happen. The venue equipment cannot be tested until the venue has been chosen, and music cannot be sourced until the equipment has been tested to see what is feasible (typically an MP3 player plugged into an amplifier or CDs supplied for an amplified CD player system).

The venue would not be decorated until the end of the promotional period in preparation for the quiz, and the quiz itself would not take place until all of the above had already happened. After the event had taken place there is time for reflection of what worked well during this project and what could have worked better, and publication of the event's successes, including the charity donation.

Once Table 6.1 has been transferred into a Gantt chart, it allows for a visual representation of the project tasks and duration mapped against a timescale. This is demonstrated in Fig. 6.2, which has been created using Microsoft Project 2010. Note that this software by default does not include Saturdays and Sundays as working days (this can

be changed). In reality this would be down to the project manager to decide.

In Fig. 6.2, the dark grey bar of the Gantt chart denotes the critical path of the project; these are the activities that must take place exactly on time otherwise the project will overrun and the event may not take place successfully, and on time. Tasks that are not critical have more flexibility in their timing. For Gantt charts to be of any use to an event planner, the event project planning stages must be mapped against a Gantt chart before the event planning takes place. The reality is that some event managers set a date for an event and then retrospectively try and make a Gantt chart fit into their timescale. This is a backwards approach and one that is not advisable, particularly to the inexperienced event planner.

EVENT PROMOTION

Event promotional mediums allow for communication of your planned event to the potential audience. Promotion should be consistent, and the promotional period varies

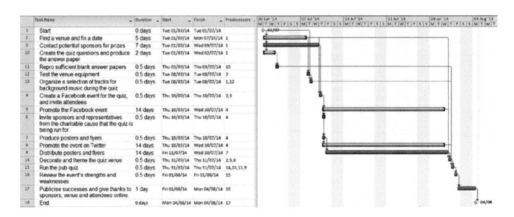

Fig. 6.2. Gantt chart for pub quiz event.

depending on the type and size of the event. The large rock music festival 'Download' begins promotion for the next year's event immediately following the current festival, so almost has a full year of promotion. Most club night events will begin promoting between 4 and 6 weeks in advance of the event taking place, with promotional intensity increasing as the event draws closer.

The most effective mediums for small-scale event promotion according to Moss (2011) are word of mouth, social media and flyers. Therefore, a sound social media strategy should underpin any other promotional techniques used; this is also cost effective but suffers from recipient apathy, where social media users are often bombarded by event promoters to the point that all event invitations may be viewed as spam. Therefore, personal contact through friends and friends of friends will mean that those invited to an event may take the invitation more seriously. A Facebook event, and Twitter use, promoting this are highly advisable, as are posters and flyers within and around the venue in which the event is taking place, and in locations likely to be frequented by the event's target audience.

Essential promotional information that should be contained on Facebook events, websites, posters and flyers includes the following:

- a logo;
- the event name and description;
- the location;
- contact details;
- time and date;
- a graphic illustration or photo;
- a brief benefit statement – why somebody should attend this event;
- a call to action – a slogan or something to motivate the reader;
- a positioning statement – what sets this event apart from other events;
- a web address where interested parties may then search for further information about what the event is about; and
- a small amount of event organizer information.

The theme of promotional materials including logos, design and wording should match other promotional mediums to enforce brand awareness by promoting a consistent identity, thus creating a cohesive promotional campaign (Carter, 2007).

THE 5 Ws

With regards to event planning, the application of Goldblatt's (2005) 5 Ws: 'What? Why? Who? When? and Where?' can help to organize and determine the feasibility of the event plans as follows:

1. WHY are you holding this event? What is the event's purpose and what do you aim to achieve? Is it to make money, raise awareness of a particular cause or charity, to cover costs, develop a sense of community or a celebration?

2. WHAT will be the entertainment that will be on offer? What will you need in order to provide this, including props, venue, licensing, advertising materials, staff, suppliers, online presence, insurance, permits, permission, and theming?

3. WHO do you want your audience to be? How will you contact them, and what would the audience seek from attending your event? Get to know your audience including their wants, needs, interests, lifestyle and leisure habits.

It is critical to identify who the audience will be very early on in the planning process in order to tailor the event specifically to the target market. Not doing this could have an impact on how many people actually attend and also their satisfaction of attending. A dissatisfied audience will publicly express their feelings through word of mouth and social media, which in turn can have an impact upon any future events you may plan through reputational damage.

Once you have identified your audience, you must also consider how they are likely to behave at the event. Will the audience be passive spectators, by simply being sat watching a live performance, or will they be participants who are likely to be dancing, crowd surfing (see Fig. 6.3) or interacting in other ways with the live entertainment? Depending on this, health and safety measures may need to be considered. If the audience are expected to do anything out of the ordinary, such as voting or spontaneous 'flash mob' type activity, it may be necessary to develop a communications strategy so that they are fully aware of this and what they need to do prior to attending the event.

4. WHEN would you like to hold your event? Before you make this decision, check what other events are taking place around the time of your event; the timing of your event is crucial, if it clashes with other events of a similar ilk in which your target audience may be interested, it may be a good idea to move your event.

Other unrelated events can also have an impact upon your audience, particularly televized events including major sporting events or royal events. If this happens and could impact upon attendance, it may be necessary to provide extra television facilities to allow audiences to view these, or public address system announcements to keep audiences informed. The weather and time of year may

Fig. 6.3. An active audience including a crowd surfer in a 'mosh pit' at a rock concert. Photograph courtesy of Gabrielle Riches.

also impact upon the event, particularly if an event is outdoors; if this is the case the risk of adverse weather impacting upon the event increases and risk contingencies for worse case scenarios should be planned for.

5. WHERE will the event take place? The event venue is absolutely crucial in terms of an event's success. Is it a suitable venue for the entertainment that you are providing and for the audience expectations and needs? Will the venue be suitable in terms of location, price and facilities?

Choosing the right venue is one of the most important decisions when organizing an event. Carefully considering the needs and wants of both audience members and performers should help to ensure that the correct venue is chosen.

It is advisable to construct a venue checklist and carry out a site inspection prior to booking in order to ensure both suitability and feasibility. Below are seven key considerations that should be made when choosing a venue.

1. *Location* – is there parking available? What is the area like? Is it easy to get to using public transport, including getting home from the venue? Is the venue easy to find? Ensure the address appears if using a GPS system.

2. *Reputation* – will the venue appeal to the intended audience? Will the venue dictate the type of audience that is likely to be attracted? Is it clean? Is it considered a 'safe' venue – does the venue have a security team in place?

3. *Price* – does it provide good value for money? Are there any special offers available for the audience at the venue, which can be promoted on publicity materials?

4. *Atmosphere* – does the style of the venue influence the atmosphere? Is the venue rustic,

modern, traditional, industrial, rural or something else? Will this match audience expectations? See the following case study for an example of how choosing the correct venue can benefit an event.

5. *Layout* – where are the key areas located within the venue, including the stage, audience area, bar and toilets? What is the route that the audience will take upon entering the venue? Is the entrance easily identified from the outside? What queuing systems are in place?

6. *Capacity* – is the venue a suitable size? Is it too big or small for the type of event you are planning? How many people does the venue comfortably hold? This is often a smaller figure to the official capacity of the venue in terms of safety requirements.

7. *Hire fee* – what are the cost implications for hiring the venue? Does this include security, technical staff, equipment, any of the entertainment and any theming décor? This will vary greatly from venue to venue, often depending on your own reputation as an event manager or promoter. The venue may simply agree a flat hire fee, although sometimes the venue may prefer to hire the venue through either a bar take agreement (where the deposit is returned on the condition that the bar takings are above a certain amount), or through a percentage split on door takings (if it is a ticketed event). Whatever the arrangement, ensure you are aware of this *before* booking, as you are unlikely to be able to negotiate further once you have confirmed.

It may be necessary to compromise on the suitability of some of the above as performers are likely to be less flexible in terms of their performance space and power/logistical requirements. There are additional technical and practical considerations that should be made when choosing an event venue. These can include the following:

- *Staging* – does the venue have a suitable performance area? Are the performers likely to require additional stage facilities? Is the stage large enough? Are there appropriate power sockets close to the performance area for plugging in equipment where necessary? (See Fig. 6.4.)
- *Light and sound* – does the venue have a good quality PA system and lighting rig installed? Is this suitable for the type of entertainment event that is planned? Are there any additional costs involved in using the venue's equipment, such as sound engineer and mixing boards? (See Fig. 6.5.)
- *Facilities and venue access* – will the performers require a changing area? How practical is the load-in/load-out for the performers? For example, carrying heavy equipment up a flight of stairs will be difficult – is there a lift available? Does the venue provide parking? As with the audience, the entertainment is also likely to require parking for the duration of the event.
- *Layout* – does the layout of the venue work for the type of entertainment that will be performing? For example, if the bar is in a separate area will this have an impact on whether people engage with the entertainment provided?
- *Licensing* – does the venue possess the required licence to allow entertainment to take place on the premises? In the UK this is less of an issue for smaller events since the introduction of the Live Music Act 2012, as licensed premises no longer require a separate entertainment licence, providing the audience is no bigger than 200 people and the live entertainment takes place between 8am and 11pm (Department for Culture, Media and Sport, 2013).

Fig. 6.4. Musical equipment will almost completely fill this stage and leaves limited room for performers to move around.

Fig. 6.5. A sound engineer prepares the mixing board prior to a concert in a theatre.

Case Study: Event Theming at the Leeds Steampunk Market, Leeds, UK

Leeds Steampunk Market (LSM) was held annually at Left Bank Leeds, which is an arts and events venue that was formerly a church. Steampunks are a subculture who have adopted fashions and accessories that involve a combination of Victoriana combined with gothic and science fiction. It is a relatively new subculture based upon 'a genre of science fiction that typically features steam-powered machinery rather than advanced technology' (Oxford Dictionaries, 2013). Steampunk markets are relatively uncommon and can attract like-minded attendees from a considerable distance, so have the potential to be well attended. Those with a good reputation are particularly likely to benefit from healthy visitor numbers.

For a steampunk market to be successful theming is vital, otherwise the market may just resemble any other market. Holding the LSM in an ex-church building contributes to the theme in terms of the gothic architecture and décor of the building, including tall columns and stained glass windows. Stallholders at the market are required to sell items related to the steampunk subculture, and many sell clothing and accessories, as well as Victorian themed food and drinks. Many stallholders additionally wear costumes related to the steampunk subculture, and the majority of attendees also wear steampunk costumes, as in Fig. 6.6.

At LSM steampunks and enthusiasts visit to sample the atmosphere and to look at the often original and elaborate costumes that other people are wearing. The audience themselves become a part of the entertainment spectacle, and it is common to see

(Continued)

Case Study. Continued.

Fig. 6.6. Leeds Steampunk Market.

costumed attendees posing for photographs for other attendees. LSM has been so successful that it has had to move to a larger venue and has now re-located to Leeds Industrial Museum at Armley Mills in Leeds, which in terms of event theming is in-keeping with the Victoriana aspect of the Steampunk subculture.

ADDING VALUE

It is important that the audience attending an event consider it a positive experience that they share with others after the event has taken place, through either word of mouth or social media, both of which are key in influencing the decisions made by other potential event attendees. Moss (2011) noted that word of mouth and social media were greater influences on the decision-making processes of those attending events at nightclubs than any traditional print promotional mediums such as flyers or posters. Adding value to the event experience by providing additional benefits to attendees is one way to generate positive word-of-mouth reviews and praise after the event has taken place. This is also more likely to attract repeat visitation to future events by attendees.

Value can easily be added by considering the smaller, often overlooked details, such as: efficient queuing systems; friendly door policy; visible security element; efficient cloakrooms with a fast turnaround; sufficient bar staff; a good selection of available food and drinks at reasonable prices; provision of special offers including loyalty and bulk purchase discounts; plenty of signage and information points throughout the venue (such as in Fig. 6.7) to help guide audiences; plenty of clean toilets; and additional post-event offers, discounts and promotional communications to attendees.

BOOKING ENTERTAINMENT FOR EVENTS

There are a number of considerations to make when booking artists and performers for an event; amongst other things cost, talent, venue space, power supply requirements, equipment requirements, day of the week and times that they are needed will all influence which artists and performers are booked. Using new and amateur artists and performers can be

Fig. 6.7. A sign informing customers that set times are available on their mobile devices via Bluetooth at a club night.

advantageous budget wise as they often cost less, but they are also likely to be unknown to audiences and therefore may not prove to be enough of an attraction. Professional artists and performers who generate the majority of their income from hiring out their services are likely to cost more, particularly at peak times, which includes weekends and around key holiday and celebratory periods such as Christmas, New Year and Valentine's Day. It is worth considering off-peak times if you are looking to use professional performers as they are more likely to negotiate on price when there is less demand for their services.

An artist's performance fee will vary depending on their level of expertise, travelling distance, length of performance and the arrival and finish times. If hiring the services of a professional band or solo artist in the UK, the fee of £144 (US$219) per musician for a 4-hour engagement is typical (Musicians Union, 2013). This would usually include around 2 hours of live performance time. Travel and accommodation costs are typically in addition to this fee. Some artists may ask for a percentage of the door take. Obviously artists who become well known and even famous command vastly higher fees, where quite literally there is no limit.

Artists are typically booked either directly or through an entertainment agency. If using an agency with a good reputation there is likely to be less chance of problems occurring such as artists not turning up or being double booked, and if this does happen there is more chance of an agency having a catalogue of replacement artists. When using the services of a booking agent, there is a commission fee to be paid and this is generally in addition to the artists' basic fee; this typically varies between 10% and 20% of the artists' fee. The benefit of booking direct with an artist rather than a booking agent is that there can sometimes be scope for negotiation on costs, which may be reduced by narrowing performance times, as well as arrival and finish times.

All agreements between event organizer and artist/agent should be in writing. It is generally good practice to have a contract agreed by all parties. A contract does not need to be a long, confusing document that is full of jargon. Quite often a simple written agreement that clearly states the name of both the artist and the hirer, the time and date of the engagement, the performance requirements, venue details and the artist fee will suffice. This will ensure that confusion and misunderstandings can be avoided. Figure 6.8 is a basic sample contract, which demonstrates the key details that a contract should contain.

Some artists will additionally have a 'rider', which is a separate document containing specific needs and special requests of the performers. The scope of a rider is fairly limitless, but typically a rider would include including performance space requirements, food requests, adequate changing space, parking and breaks required. It is important to try and meet these requests where possible and ensure that adjustments are made and the performers are informed if certain elements cannot be fulfilled to ensure that they are aware in advance of the event taking place. The importance of both a changing space and parking close to the venue should not be underestimated.

Before booking any artist the following is advisable:

- Go and see them for yourself to see what you think of their performance.

- Read reviews of the artist online from people who may have seen them perform.
- Talk to other promoters, venue managers and event organizers who may have used the artist in the past, particularly for artists that you are unaware of; testimonials from previous customers are important.
- Look at the artists' online profile through their websites and social media to ensure that they portray the correct image for the event.
- For singers and vocalists, do not be fooled by downloadable audio tracks of them performing; with today's technology, it is very easy to make anyone sound like they can sing and hearing them live is much different to a studio track. Check sites such as YouTube where actual attendees may have put up clips of them performing; this will help to assess their actual ability to sing live. There is a great deal of difference between a great singer that will perform well live, and someone whose voice has been doctored within a recording. Artists are becoming very aware of the need to invest in their online profiles as often this is the only point of contact with their clients before the actual performance, so gathering more independent and less biased views of their ability is strongly advised.

Most professional bands and artists will be fully self-contained, whereby they will provide their own public address (PA) system, amplifiers, lights and, in some cases, their own sound and light engineer, whereas amateur performers may not. If the venue does not have a sound system available then it is important to provide one. This will obviously have an impact upon the event budget. A dance troupe, magic act and compère will also expect a PA to be

---

Sample Contract

An agreement made on___/___/_____

Between_____(full name of hirer)

of_____(hirer's address)

and_____(full name of artiste)

of_____(artiste's address)

The hirer engages the artiste to perform at the following engagement_____

_____

at_____ (event address)

on___/___/_____   for an agreed fee of _____(include deposit if applicable)

The performance times are as follows:

Arrival time	Set up by (time)	Start time	Finish time	Performance Length
e.g. 18:00	e.g. 19:30	e.g. 20:00	e.g. 00:00	e.g. one hour long

Booking conditions: This may include details of final payment methods, cancellation clauses, any equipment provided by the hirer, food requests, and any technical requirements.

Signed (hirer)_____

Print name_____

Telephone_____E-mail_____

Signed (artist)_____

Print name_____

Telephone_____E-mail_____

Fig. 6.8. A basic sample contract.

provided if they do not have their own. The required specifications of this will be dependent on the size of the venue. If booking several artists to perform at the same event, it is beneficial to provide one single PA system and sound technician for all performers to use as this will create sound continuity; there will also be more performance space on stage with just one system, and the artist load-in and set-up times will also be slightly reduced. An event manager needs to be aware of the staging requirements at the event-planning stage. Simply assuming that all of the performers will just 'fit' is a recipe for the event experiencing trouble as it happens.

BEFORE THE EVENT TAKES PLACE

At least 1 week before the event, final checks will need to be undertaken, essentially to make sure everything is running to plan and that nothing is being left unaddressed or to chance. Confirmation of contract details should be made with all performers (particularly arrival times, technical requirement, performance times and payment) and any information not included within the original contract should be finalized. This is likely to include where they need to go on arrival at the venue and who will be their on-site contact. Thoroughness at this stage is key as once the event is underway it may be difficult to make any changes to what has been agreed.

Lighting can have a huge impact on the atmosphere at the event. It can add excitement, sophistication and create focus where required. Lighting can be used in many ways to enhance an event, including making a stage area appear less bare where much of the performance area is not covered by the on-stage entertainment (see Fig. 6.9). If the

Fig. 6.9. Lighting effects being used to add atmosphere and bring content to a largely empty stage.

venue is too bright people may feel awkward and unwilling to socialize, and the venue may feel rather stark to early arrivals. Equally, venues that are too dark can cause problems for audience members so it is essential to test the lighting in advance so that it is fit for the purpose and will contribute towards the right kind of atmosphere for the event.

Ensuring that the sound level is appropriate is normally dependent on the type of event that is being organized. If background music is being played it must be loud enough to hear, but at the same time it must not be too loud to drown out other sounds; for example, at a fashion show music is essential, but so is the ability of the audience to hear the compère. It is critical that the balance is just right; it should be tested in advance and will often require adjustment during the event.

Most stage performers will require a soundcheck prior to the event. A soundcheck is where the sound equipment is checked (guitars, drums, prerecorded music) and the levels mixed to maximize quality of sound

for both the performers and the audience. A soundcheck should ideally (but often does not) take place *before* the audience enter, and in terms of timing is typically 1–2 hours after the equipment load-in and set-up. As event organizer it will be necessary to schedule the soundchecks within the running order and inform the performers of the time constraints in place – especially when there is more than one artist performing. The last artist that is scheduled to perform (the headliner) should soundcheck first, with the last to soundcheck being the first to perform. Their equipment will then remain in place for when they begin (as demonstrated in Fig. 6.10).

Although it is not essential, and in some cases impossible, it is good practice for the performers to load-in and set up in advance of the guests' arrival. This makes for a far more professional event. It is also preferred for the load-out to take place once the event comes to a close, so the performers are not carrying equipment through the venue whilst the event is still taking place.

Fig. 6.10. A soundcheck taking place at an event. Photograph courtesy of Martyn Strange.

On the night of an event, it may appear that there is very little to do in terms of direction and coordination. This highlights good planning and organization. If something does go wrong, remain level headed and professional in order to deal with the situation calmly so that guests do not notice.

STAGING THE LIVE EVENT

Regardless of event size, close attention must be paid to every detail to ensure the event runs to plan. An event production schedule should be compiled, which will assist the event organizer during the final stages of planning and should cover all stages of an event from the moment the doors open to the public until all attendees have left.

It is advisable to begin compiling an event production schedule early within the planning process, so that all important documentation is set aside in one place. Each event will differ slightly with regards to what will be included; however, as a general rule an event production schedule will always include the following.

- *Running order for the event* – this should also include arrivals, set-up and load-out times for all performers and set times for each artist to perform; try not to make this too rigid, and build some slack time into it, so that if there are any problems, the slack time will hopefully absorb them.
- *Team roles and responsibilities* – this will include a full overview of who needs to be where at times throughout the event, and what individual members of staff should be doing.
- *Contact list* – an easy-to-absorb and quick-to-scan list of all artists and any

suppliers/contractors that are being used for the event, along with their mobile telephone numbers.
- *Emergency procedures* – this should include the venue's health and safety procedures in case of an emergency, and the venue layout with all fire doors clearly marked.
- *Contracts and riders* – signed copies of all contracts and riders should be included, along with payment details for all performers, including the payment schedule and whether it is an on-the-night payment, an invoice following the event or a split of door profits.
- *Technical lists* – these should detail technical requirements for each artist or performer including their required stage size and PA requests. This is more of a requirement when sound and light technicians and equipment are provided for the performers rather than them providing their own.

Some elements of a production schedule will need to be available for artists and team (if appropriate) to view. In particular, copies of the running order should be available in several places around the venue including the entrance, the backstage areas, sound and lighting booth and behind the bar.

POST-EVENT EVALUATION AND PROMOTION

The final stage in any live event is evaluation. This is often overlooked, especially when an event is a success. It is important to reflect on the successful elements and be fully aware of what they were in order to build upon this with any future events. It is also important to publicize either via websites, social media or press releases the successful elements of the event, in order to counteract any possible negative publicity that may be published about the event.

Some tips for evaluating the event are as follows.

- Gather feedback from the artists, performers and venue management as to how they perceived the event.
- For at least 2 weeks after the event perform web searches and check social media, particularly Facebook and Twitter, to gather the opinions of those who attended the event. These should be divided into three sections, positives, negatives and other comments. Where negatives have been raised consider methods by which these could be addressed for future events.
- Search out materials that may have been uploaded of the event to determine how they portray it, particularly photographs and videos which may have been uploaded to sites such as YouTube, Vine, Instagram and Flickr. Can you learn anything from studying these and any comments made upon them?
- Read reviews of the event in the local press and online.

Referring back to the original plans should provide a foundation against which to measure the event's success. Consider what went well, what did not, and whether any part of the event did not happen as planned or expected. Ask why this was the case. Try to learn from the experiences both good and bad in order to make improvements in the future. Learning on the job, particularly from what worked well at an event and what could have worked better, is an integral part of events management, which helps to create better future events. A truly effective event manager never stops learning from their own successes and failures – and the successes and failures of others.

SEMINAR ACTIVITIES

In small groups, work through the following tasks:

1. Focus on a live event that you have attended recently – write a list of ideas about how your experience could have been improved.

2. Construct a Gantt chart that includes all of the key tasks involved in planning a small-scale nightclub event such as a student party.

3. Apply Goldblatt's 5 Ws to your chosen event.

4. Consider five ideas that could add value to your live event, albeit on a limited budget.

REFERENCES

Carter, L. (2007) *Event Planning*. AuthorHouse, Bloomington, Indiana.
Carter, L. (2012) *Event Planning*, 2nd edn. AuthorHouse, Bloomington, Indiana.
Department for Culture, Media and Sport (2013) Entertainment licensing: changes under the Live Music Act. Available at: https://www.gov.uk/entertainment-licensing-changes-under-the-live-music-act (accessed 13 April 2013).
Goldblatt, J. (2005) *Special Events: Event Leadership for a New World*. John Wiley & Sons, Hoboken, New Jersey.

Moss, S. (2011) Results of the Leeds Clubber Survey 2010. Available at: http://entplanet.blogspot.
    co.uk/2011/02/results-of-leeds-clubber-survey-2010.html (accessed 30 June 2013).
Musicians Union (2013) National gig rates 2013. Available at: http://www.musiciansunion.org.uk/wp-
    content/uploads/2012/02/National-Gig-2013.pdf (accessed 3 May 2013).
Oxford Dictionaries (2013) Steampunk. Available at: http://oxforddictionaries.com/definition/eng-
    lish/steampunk (accessed 1 July 2013).

chapter 7

Management in Entertainment Organizations

Lisa Gorton

LEARNING OBJECTIVES

After reading this chapter you should:

- develop an increased understanding of what management is and what managers do;
- begin to appreciate the range of factors that have an impact on how we need to manage and work in order to be successful in the contemporary workplace;
- gain a fuller understanding of what makes the entertainment industries unique and how this, in turn, shapes how we manage our organizations; and
- be able to reflect upon the range of skills, qualities and attributes successful managers require in today's industry.

INTRODUCTION

This chapter will introduce and discuss the nature of management in today's entertainment industries. It is not my remit, nor would it be remotely possible, to discuss every aspect of management here, and there are of course thousands of textbooks dedicated to this topic. The business of this chapter therefore is not to explore every last sub-theme of this contested phenomenon but rather to offer a distilled perspective on some key themes within management that are relevant to today's entertainment industries.

This snapshot will be developed by considering four key questions about management and the wider context of the entertainment industries themselves.

© CAB International 2014. *Entertainment Management: Towards Best Practice* (eds S. Moss and B. Walmsley)

1. What is management and what do managers actually do?
2. What changes in business and wider society have led to changes in the way we manage?
3. What characterizes management in the entertainment industries?
4. To what extent do the above considerations impact upon the skills required to be an accomplished manager within the entertainment industries?

Perspectives, definitions, opinions and theories about many aspects of management change with great frequency and this academic field of study is exposed more than many to the vagaries of what is considered fashionable one day or outdated the next. It is therefore appropriate that some of the considerations that follow will trace the journey of these changing opinions.

It is also noteworthy that management is a subject that generates huge debate. This chapter does not seek therefore to be dictatorial in its approach but rather to present several perspectives surrounding the topic so that the reader's own ideas of what successful management might look like are stimulated. This individual approach to management is what makes it so fascinating – no two managers will be exactly the same just as no two individuals are exactly the same. I outline here some basic prerequisites of the discipline, a foundation upon which you as an individual can add your own 'layer' of interpretation and approach, taking into account many of the factors (e.g. the internal environment of the organization, the external context of the organization, the general operating climate of the time, etc.) that you will learn to appreciate along the way.

TOWARDS A DEFINITION OF MANAGEMENT

Despite the commonplace use of the term 'management', trying to achieve full consensus on a definition has, over the years, proved an elusive goal for many scholars and commentators. Mullins (2011, p. 296) states simply that management is about 'making things happen'. Kotter (1990) elaborates on this simplistic notion by describing good business management as bringing about order and designing organizational structures. He argues that management demands consistency and requires formal plans and monitoring of the organization's performance against these plans. In a reflective interview with Robert Allio (2011), Mintzberg points to management as being the way to influence actions by 'working through people and information'. Managers then are people who formulate plans, organize resources (including human resources) and control the performance of others in an effort to achieve organizational goals.

To supplement our understanding of the term 'management', we need to grasp what it is that managers actually do. Many frameworks and models have been formulated since the early days of management to try to help scholars understand the varied roles and functions of a manager. It is perhaps of little surprise to hear that this area has also long been contentious and total agreement about the full scope of which functions managers perform still seems a somewhat unattainable goal.

THE VARIED ROLES OF THE MANAGER

Most people have their own view about what a manager is and what a manager does.

Indeed the ubiquitous nature of the word in our everyday language use attests to this (just consider the wide variety of usage in our day-to-day lives: people management, anger management, time management, etc). Our own understanding of this word is subjective and based upon the extent to which we 'manage' in our own lives and it is fair to say in this context that we are all, to some extent or another, a manager of our personal lives. This chapter, however, seeks to move away from this form of self-management and concentrates on the management of others in an organizational setting where efforts are directed towards the achievement of organizational goals.

Since it was first distinguished from other organizational activity by Henri Fayol in the mid-20th century, the term 'management' has been open to many interpretations. Perhaps a logical place to start then is with this French industrialist turned author. Fayol's (1949) work identified five functions of management as outlined below.

1. Planning: preparing actions to enable the organization to meet future organizational goals.
2. Organizing: making sure that all resources and activities occur in such a fashion as to achieve stated goals.
3. Coordinating: ensuring a harmony between distinctive efforts within the organization to ensure success.
4. Commanding: putting plans into action by giving direction to subordinates.
5. Controlling: ensuring that all activities contribute to the achievement of the stated plan and agreed procedures.

Later theorists such as Brech (1975) analysed the functions of a manager as fourfold, encompassing planning, control, coordination and motivation. Drucker (1977) identified the five key areas of work for any manager as: setting objectives; organizing; motivating; communicating and measuring; and developing people. These theorists both agreed that employee motivation is a requisite of the successful manager (and indeed the sustainable and successful organization) and it is noteworthy that these two writers were undoubtedly influenced by the widespread and increasing awareness and acceptance of the importance of the work of the Human Relations School of Management (this is in direct comparison to the earlier Scientific School of Management, which focused managers on the task and the efficiency through which it could be completed by using standardized procedures). The Human Relations school of thought argues that the vital importance of the human and social activity of any organization is one of the key contributing factors to its success.

DOES THE REALITY OF MANAGEMENT REFLECT THE THEORY?

Mintzberg (1973) and Kotter (1982) were amongst the first commentators to test how managers actually spent their time. They investigated whether managers really did spend their time planning, organizing, coordinating, commanding and controlling, as was originally argued by Fayol (1949) or whether this was an outdated framework. The results of these respective empirical studies (which both followed different groups of managers and recorded and categorized their day-to-day activities) provided the starting points for revised thinking about what a manager actually does.

Mintzberg (1973) categorized managerial activities under the following three main headings: interpersonal, informational and decisional. Under these headings, he argued that the manager performed ten distinct roles:

Interpersonal roles

Figurehead – performs ceremonial duties

Leader – motivates and encourages subordinates

Liaison – networks externally

Informational roles

Monitor – ensures awareness of trends impacting business

Disseminator – communicates in many ways with employees

Spokesperson – shares information with superiors and external partners

Decisional roles

Entrepreneur – seeks to identify and exploit new opportunities

Disturbance Handler – solves problems and manages crises

Resource Allocator – places right resources with right people

Negotiator – makes deals and resolves arguments and disputes

Kotter's work (1982) was largely supportive of Mintzberg's. He summarized his findings by highlighting the fragmented nature of a manager's day and his study stressed the importance of effective communication in all areas of management activity, for example as a way to receive important information from colleagues and subordinates to underpin decision making.

So we can see that a manager's tasks are extremely varied, often require simultaneous consideration and must invariably be segmented to fit into small, available time slots.

It is perhaps necessary to pause for a moment or two here and reflect upon the use of the word 'management' thus far in this chapter. The use of this word rather than 'leadership' has been deliberate. It is now therefore opportune to consider whether or not these two entities are interchangeable terms or whether, as some commentators would argue, they should be considered quite separately.

MANAGEMENT AND LEADERSHIP: INEXTRICABLY LINKED OR QUITE DISTINCT?

Just as debate reigns over what is the exact, all-encompassing definition of management, there have been equally high-profile discussions about the nature of the relationship between management and leadership. Zaleznik (1977) was a key advocate of the idea that management and leadership should be considered as separate functions, demanding quite different attributes and skills. He argued that managers seek stability and feel safe when surrounded by processes and systems. When problems arise, their immediate urge is to resolve them as soon as possible so as to restore their sought-after status quo. In contrast to this, he maintained, leaders embrace chaos in an effort to understand underlying issues more completely and to develop requisite strategies to exploit in the achievement of the organizational vision. In essence, he claimed that management and leadership are different and therefore require different skills and abilities.

Kotter (1990) contrasted the functions of leadership and management in four areas of organizational success: creating an agenda;

developing people; execution; and outcomes. Leadership establishes direction, influences others, motivates and produces change, whilst management requires planning and budgeting, organizing, problem-solving and the production of order. For any successful organization, both parts of this process are as vital as the other to ensure success but they both require different skills, experience and expertise. The roles, Kotter maintained, are complementary.

The term 'business leader' is undoubtedly newer in our parlance and there are connotations of success and achievement in the very etymology of the word: 'to lead' means 'to go before' or 'to show the way', in contrast to the verb 'to manage', which means 'to handle, administer and govern'. Sveningsson and Alvesson (2003) established the 'anti-identity' of management or the 'not-me position', arguing that a lesser value had begun to be placed upon the management role (cited in Carroll and Levy, 2007, p. 77). A few years later, the respondents of a study by Carroll and Levy (2007) were in broad agreement. They discussed the default position of management as being 'mundane', 'boring', and not as 'challenging' as leadership, which, in turn, was described as being a vague and intangible position but one that was nonetheless perceived as more covetable than its lesser counterpart.

However, in reality, it is perhaps too simplistic to maintain that any individual is *either* a manager *or* a leader and can be labelled or pigeon-holed as such. It is becoming clear that the roles in practice cannot be distinguished quite as sharply, as the words can be defined differently. It is more likely, assert experts such as Handy (1993) and Mintzberg (1973), that there is great overlap and interdependence

between leadership and management. Readers will recall that Mintzberg argued that one (leadership) is merely one of the functions of the other (management). It could therefore be argued that the ability to lead is just one of the plethora of skills required by the contemporary manager.

This interdependence is highlighted in later work by Gosling and Mintzberg (2003), who argue that management without leadership is uninspiring and that leadership without management is a guarantee of nothing less than a disjointed, arrogant approach. Nearly 40 years after his earlier work, Mintzberg (2011, p. 4) supplemented his own theory and stated that 'an executive cannot lead without managing. If they're not coupled, the organization becomes dysfunctional'.

There is a high level of interdependence between leadership and management. I prefer this perspective because when I reflect upon the best leaders I have encountered, they have been able to appreciate how to create, implement and bring life to their vision (often viewed as the remit of so-called 'managers'); and likewise when I recall the qualities of the most successful managers, they have been able to influence others, to engage and inspire their people (often seen as the remit of the leader).

THE CHANGING NATURE OF THE WORLD OF BUSINESS

Seismic changes in the world of business and society as a whole have occurred in the last 150 years and these have impacted on the way in which organizations have been designed (which in turn impacts on the role of a manager). Three distinct eras of organizational structure design have been identified according to Anand and Daft (2007, cited in Buchanan and Huczynski, 2010):

Era 1: mid-1800s–1970s – The self-contained organizational structure

- people work in functions or departments;
- clear reporting mechanisms exist between people and departments;
- organizational activities are organized and integrated both vertically and horizontally by means of systems.

Era 2: 1970s–1990s – Horizontal organizational structure

- workflow processes rather than tasks should determine organization of work;
- flatter hierarchy;
- use teams for tasks and use team leaders to manage;
- team members have the authority to interact with external stakeholders;
- provision of required expertise from outside team.

Era 3: 1990s–present – The boundary-less organization

- organizational boundaries are penetrable;
- increased collaboration with external partners;
- flexibility to exploit market opportunities;
- outsourcing is normal.

It is important to note these changes at this point, as it is exactly these shifts that have had an impact on the skills and attributes required by managers and that will continue to shape the environment in which they will be required to perform. Today's business world is no longer dominated by production and manufacturing; the past 150 years have changed the landscape forever. The Chartered Management Institute believes these drivers will continue to mould industries as we proceed into the second decade of this century. In its 2008 report *Management Futures: The world in 2018*, it predicts a business world that will be characterized by six main drivers.

1. The new economies of Brazil, Russia, India and China will wield increasing power and influence in global markets.
2. A polarization of business structures will occur with global corporate enterprises at one end and community-led virtual enterprises at the other.
3. Improved technology will need to support an increasing amount of information-sharing both internally between employees and externally with customers and partners.
4. A more diverse workforce will require expert managers who are emotionally intelligent and who can facilitate creativity amongst disparate teams.
5. Boundaries will become increasingly blurred between work and home life with the best managers/organizations finding a way to facilitate work–life integration (which will replace work–life balance).
6. Personalized work contracts will become the norm as employee power rises. The workforce will be more culturally and age diverse.

Contemporary managers inhabit a world unrecognizable from that of their predecessors. New markets have merged and are growing exponentially; workforces and their working patterns and demands are more divergent; and yesterday's competitors have become today's collaborators as organizational boundaries become more fluid. All of these changes are underpinned by fast-paced technological advancements that show no sign of slowing down.

MANAGEMENT IN THE ENTERTAINMENT INDUSTRIES

As discussed in Chapter 1, the entertainment industries are extremely diverse. With offerings ranging from stage shows to sporting events and from adult entertainment to edutainment, their complex range of experiences make it difficult to generalize about how any one entertainment organization should best be managed. Although many organizations in the sector are run on a for-profit basis, a significant number are not and can be categorized as not-for-profit or as having charitable status. The diversity of underlying aims and strategies (e.g. to make a profit versus to produce art for the cultural benefit of all) also makes it more complicated to generalize about which management skills are most sought after. That said, the sub-sectors of the industry do share some common attributes, which can be delineated as (amongst others): the intangibility of the experience/service; the inseparability of the consumer from the experience purchased; and the often perishable nature of the offering.

Some writers argue, for example, that the creative industries are different – they do not deal in widgets like a manufacturer might but in 'symbolic, experiential goods of non-utilitarian value' (Townley *et al.*, 2009, p. 940). The experiences or services are produced in response to 'expressive and aesthetic taste' and their significance is 'determined by the consumer's coding and decoding of value' (ibid.). This inability to gauge reaction (and therefore demand) to a product builds, some writers argue, the case for the 'different' nature of the industry and it adds to the

managerial challenges facing this sector. It should be noted, however, that other commentators disagree with this perspective, arguing that uncertainty of demand is a characteristic of most forms of economic production.

These industry-wide attributes add to the existing and well-documented challenges of those employed to manage. This challenge is further compounded by the nature of the labour force within the entertainment industries, which are renowned for their high percentage of freelance workers, part-time and seasonal workers and volunteers.

CHANGING CONSUMER EXPECTATIONS

It is not possible to consider management of any organization in isolation as if it existed in a vacuum. It is not a discrete function, impervious to external organizational drivers and forces. Indeed, it is one of management's most important functions to anticipate, predict and exploit these external forces, despite being largely unable to exert any or little control over them.

One of the most critical drivers of change is the evolving practices and behaviours of consumers themselves. In its submission to the UK Government in 2010, The Work Foundation presented an overview of the contemporary consumer of the creative and cultural industries. Its authors described today's consumer as wanting 'to enjoy a greater degree of intangible and emotional value from the goods and services they buy and consume' (Brinkley and Holloway, 2010). They argued that 'art, entertainment, craft, brand and style values matter more (today) to those who consume them'. Clearly, ignorance of today's consumer is not to be recommended.

We can conclude that today's managers and leaders are confronted daily with an increasingly complex business environment and the challenges faced within organizations are more than matched by external forces of change. So what kinds of skills will be needed by managers to help them succeed in the entertainment industries?

SKILLS FOR THE 21ST-CENTURY MANAGER

Up to now, management and leadership have been portrayed as complicated, multifaceted and disjointed roles; and in real life, this is exactly what it is like. Anyone who aspires to take up a management position must acquire a wide range of skills and attributes if they are to enjoy any success at a senior organizational level. The world of management (including the element of leadership) is complicated, complex and confusing. It is full of paradoxes (think global versus local, for example) and full of imperatives (be strategic, be creative, show empathy, engage your co-workers). So you could be forgiven for thinking that no single person could ever live up to the exacting job specification of the manager.

Desirable attributes such as integrity, vision, judgement and persistence to be displayed by top executives were identified in the past by numerous leading experts (e.g. Stodgill, 1974 and Cannell, 2008, cited in Buchanan and Huczynski, 2010) and we are all familiar with top executive job advertisements requesting such demanding criteria. Ancona *et al.* (2007) argue that failure against such an exacting set of criteria is a given and

it is much more desirable that executives stop trying to achieve the unachievable and recognize their weaknesses (and in so doing, employ others who can complement their skills). That is not to say that Ancona *et al.* have not developed their own list of skills required by today's top executives; they have. But, as indicated in Table 7.1, this has evolved from the skills identified by earlier commentators. According to The Chartered Management Institute (2008), managers and leaders should be skilled in sense-making, relating, visioning and inventing, and key management skills for this decade and beyond will include interpersonal skills, building alliances, strategic planning and political skills. A comparison of these two skill-sets is outlined in Table 7.1.

As you can see from Table 7.1, there is some consensus amongst academics and practitioners regarding the skills required by today's managers. One cannot fail to notice the commonalities shared by key elements within these frameworks – for example, look how similar Ancona *et al.*'s skill of 'relating' is to the CMI's required skill of 'building alliances'.

To further our understanding, I have developed new categories drawn from these skill-sets. The highest skilled managers will be able to search out other ways, collaborate with many others, create new and other futures and get the most from others. The notion of 'otherness' here is important and should be interpreted to include not just the sense of an alternative but the new, innovative, challenging and improved. Prahalad (2010, p. 36) discusses the importance of 'non-conformity' for leading managers. This is a key concept to grasp and, as we can see here, its reach, which includes all areas of management, is extensive.

Table 7.1. Comparative skill-sets required by contemporary managers. Adapted from Ancona *et al.* (2007) and The Chartered Management Institute (2008).

	Searching out other ways	Collaborating with others	Creating new and other futures	Getting the most from others
Ancona *et al.* (2007)	Sense-making • Gather data from many sources – both internal and external to the organization • Check your perspectives with those of others • Look for new possibilities to explain the existing world	Relating • Build relationships that allow you to listen to others with pre-judgement • Allow others to voice their thoughts • Provide rationale for your views to aid others' comprehension	Visioning • Be creative and enthusiastic in your articulation of what the future should be like • Do not get bogged down in the day-to-day achievement of the vision – your enthusiasm for the project will inspire others to find ways to make it happen • Collaborate with others to create a shared vision	Inventing • Discourage the approach in yourself and others of 'this is the way we do things here' • Look for imaginative ways of people working/linking together • Encourage everyone to play a part in finding new productive ways to work
The Chartered Management Institute (2008)	Political skills • The skill to bring different teams and organizations together for the greater benefit of all • Be comfortable in many different arenas; be a catalyst for others to perform	Building alliances • Collaborate and facilitate collaboration between all organizational stakeholders	Strategic planning • Identify opportunities within the marketplace, utilize wisdom and judgement to make important business decisions	Interpersonal skills • The ability to motivate and lead many different 'types' of employee within the workforce, many of whom will follow a non-traditional work pattern

MANAGEMENT SKILLS REQUIRED TO SUCCEED IN THE ENTERTAINMENT INDUSTRIES

Given the unique nature of the entertainment industries, we must now determine whether the management and leadership skills outlined previously should be considered as an ideal, complete skill-set for the entertainment sector or rather as a starting point to which other key skills must be added. The skills outlined in Table 7.1 certainly have their place in the entertainment industries, and the following section outlines the opinions of key stakeholders and governing bodies that are directly related to the entertainment industries.

GETTING THE MOST FROM OTHERS

People1st (The Sector Skills Council for the Hospitality, Leisure, Travel and Tourism sectors, which therefore covers many sub-sectors of the entertainment industries) highlights the challenging nature of the labour force in this sector. In its 2011 *State of the Nation* report, it outlined that staff in this sector are far more likely to be part-time, young and transient. Managers must be highly skilled in motivating and engaging a diverse set of workers who are often required to work in non-traditional work patterns. Embracing more flexible work practices may suit the industry well to some extent, but managers must always be open to new ideas to ensure their front-line staff in particular remain engaged (it is they, after all, who are the interface between the organization and the consumer). Being open

to new approaches to labour market issues will, according to the Skills Council, be key to achieving employer engagement, and an ability to engage many others with your vision and plan is a key skill for any manager.

CREATING NEW AND OTHER FUTURES

The Department for Culture, Media and Sport (DCMS, 2011) stresses the need for management, leadership, business and entrepreneurial skills; it also encourages managers to exploit technological innovation and combine it with effective leadership and creativity to translate it into business intelligence. The Sector Skills Council for the Creative Industries, which includes sub-sectors such as film, television, radio, interactive media, music and the performing and visual arts, published its own list of requisite skills for industry managers and included 'business and entrepreneurial skills, especially project management for multi-platform development; the hybrid skills combining effective leadership with innovation, creativity and understanding of technology, and the analytical skills to understand audience interests and translate it into business intelligence' (Skillset, 2011, p. 6). Consider here, for example, the recent history of music distribution, where successful entrepreneurs and artists recognized the opportunities afforded by new technologies that have forever changed the landscape of music.

COLLABORATING WITH OTHERS

Arts Council England (2012) informs would-be arts managers that organizations providing artistic and cultural experiences for the public's entertainment and experience should better understand their communities; they should strive to build new public and private partnerships and work creatively with a wide range of commissioning partners. It would seem therefore that this skill is in demand in at least one sub-sector of our industry.

Indeed the ability to collaborate with others is cited by many experts as a key skill for any successful manager. As discussed earlier in the chapter, new working practices, supported by more flexible organizational structures, facilitate cross-boundary collaboration. Writing a guest article for the National Endowment for Science, Technology and the Arts (NESTA – a now independent charity formed to promote and bring innovative ideas to life), Gunatillake (2008) advocates such joint partnerships as daily fare in the arts and cultural industries. He points also to the collaboration potential with the sector's audiences and notes that some theatre producers are already using interactive production models. He wonders why, in the future, such collaboration models cannot extend to areas such as commissioning and programming (processes previously zealously guarded by the organizations themselves).

Such joint approaches arguably reinforce widely held beliefs of increasing participation and access to all, although Gunatillake wisely notes that it is unrealistic (and to a certain extent, undesirable) to seek to move all audience members as far along the engagement curve as possible. It is, he argues, through technology-facilitated collaboration that arts and cultural organizations can ensure the very best core and supplementary experiences for those members of the audience who are engaged.

We can conclude then that an understanding of and empathy with the audience, coupled with an ability to communicate in a meaningful way with the consumer, is already a skill of vital importance to today's entertainment manager. Given the dynamic pace of technological change evident in social media alone, the ever-evolving power of the consumer looks unlikely to diminish in the coming years.

THE SKILL OF THE PROJECT MANAGER

It has already been highlighted in this chapter that the nature of production in several sub-sectors of the entertainment industries can be characterized as event- or project-led. This being the case, we must add to the list of skills required by entertainment managers the ability to successfully manage projects and live events. To document fully every stage of project management and to produce a 'template' for success is beyond the remit of this chapter, but readers should at least appreciate the all-encompassing nature of such time-bound project management, and a good account of it is provided in Chapters 6 and 9. Many skills are drawn upon here, such as the ability to organize other people, to delegate and to negotiate, to name but a few. Underpinning all of these skills lies the imperative to communicate clearly and precisely. It is the manager who is responsible for bringing to life the creative vision for an event, administering all the processes that support it and facilitating the creative processes that give birth to it. To underestimate this all-encompassing skill is foolhardy and we should remind ourselves here of the work of Carpenter and Blandy

(2008, p. 64) who comment that 'leisure takes time, effort and energy. It takes a lot to look easy'.

CULTURAL LEADERSHIP

Cultural leadership is another addition to the list of skills required by any manager in the entertainment industries. Culture in its broadest sense is defined by Holden (2011, p. 182) as now encompassing a trio of closely related elements: 'publicly funded culture, commercial culture and home-made culture'; and Holden argues that these three areas are mutually dependent. This recent broadening of the term culture is important to us when we consider the skills of a manager. The cultural leader can no longer seek to impose their own notion of culture on a group of consumers. The new paradigm requires managers to listen and engage more actively with their formerly more passive audiences (Walmsley and Franks, 2011). This links closely with the notion of collaboration outlined earlier. Holden (2011) contends that cultural leaders should place themselves at the centre of a newer, flatter and non-hierarchical organization, where proactive collaboration can occur at all levels of the organization. The skill of working with varied and new stakeholder groups, all of whom are contributors in some way to the new broader concept of culture, will be a requirement of the new entertainment manager. Being amongst an elite, tasked with setting the cultural agenda (as may have happened in the past) will no longer be our reality. The new manager's modus operandi must be to seek new partners, solicit the views of many and enable others to deliver, whilst in turn offering innovative, desirable and sustainable products within the marketplace.

Case Study: Royal Shakespeare Company (adapted from Holden, 2011)

Consider the following two organizational charts from the Royal Shakespeare Company (RSC). Figure 7.1 dates back to 2003 and represents a typical organogram – a traditional hierarchical chart depicting chains of command as well as linear and sometime one-directional relationships.

Figure 7.2, however, illustrates the RSC's new structure from 2010. It depicts an organization where leaders are encouraging collaboration and boundaries for team-working and communication are broken down. Leaders within the organization sit at the centre, not at the top of the more traditional pyramid shape.

The new organization requires a different approach to working. Amongst the most vital prerequisites to the success of such a change in leadership and management style are the following organizational qualities:

- shared leadership;
- the inspirational use of language;
- values that are embedded and real at all levels of the organization (rather than just enshrined in a mission statement and pinned on to a notice board);
- practical solutions to the challenges faced every day by all organizational members;

(Continued)

Case Study. Continued.

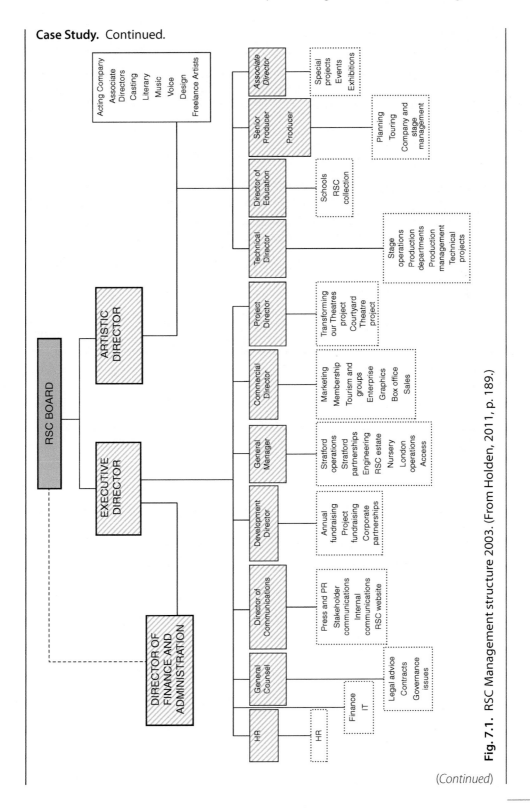

Fig. 7.1. RSC Management structure 2003. (From Holden, 2011, p. 189.)

(*Continued*)

Case Study. Continued.

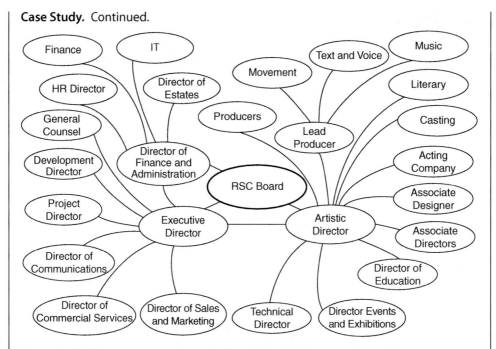

Fig. 7.2. RSC Management structure 2010. (From Holden, 2011, p. 190.)

- an appreciation that humans are emotional beings (even in our working lives); and
- the understanding that it is the leader's job to bring clarity where there is confusion and simplicity where there is complexity.

Distributed leadership has become the norm in the Royal Shakespeare Company. Leadership is flexible, shared and woven throughout a larger group rather than being concentrated in one role. If leadership is about influencing behaviour, then persuasive and meaningful language should be employed to facilitate that. The French term 'ensemble' (meaning 'together') embodies the approach adopted at the RSC. Given the nature of the wide body of contributing people, this is more complex than it sounds: how does such a large organization strike a balance between the undoubted contribution of a theatrical star and the perhaps less immediately visible efforts of a technical assistant working backstage?

Values have to be lived and evident in everyday practices rather than just used for rhetorical and promotional purposes. The RSC's former Artistic Director, Michael Boyd, talked about the need for honesty, altruism and tolerance. Leaders at the RSC have to ensure that they do not just make pronouncements from on high but rather that they *make things happen*. They manage the organization so that people can be effective and they achieve this by creating the space, opportunities and time for the aforementioned values to be discussed and embedded amongst all the team members. The style of leadership and

(Continued)

Case Study. Continued.

management adopted by the RSC is not afraid of recognizing the importance of emotions within organizational life. In contrast to most organizations, words such as 'fear', 'daring' and 'empathy' are used regularly.

Finally, leaders at the RSC must communicate effectively and with great clarity to allow issues to be understood by all. This allows individuals at all levels of the organization to buy into often complex tasks with full understanding of how they can contribute to the overall aims of the organization.

This case study illustrates that leadership should be shared and offer opportunities for new relationships and new ways of working between inspired colleagues. It should constantly adapt and, wherever possible, pre-empt change. It should facilitate rather than hamper and it should set an example rather than pontificate from on high. Leadership should bring clarity, focus and a readiness to embrace and overcome the challenges faced by an organization.

Fig. 7.3. The new Royal Shakespeare Theatre.

(*Continued*)

Case Study. Continued.

Fig. 7.4. The Royal Shakespeare Theatre's auditorium. Photographs by Peter Cook © Royal Shakespeare Company.

CONCLUSION

This chapter has portrayed management as a complex subject characterized by multitudinous and often conflicting opinions. It can be agreed, however, that management is generally accepted to be the discipline of achieving organizational goals through the direction of the efforts of others. Varied efforts have also been made to categorize the different functions of the management role and there is general accord on this point: managers must be able to perform a wide variety of roles, from representing the organization and spotting trends in the external environment to being an internal communications conduit. Whether leadership is merely another function of management or a separate, discrete role, requiring special skills and attributes, remains largely unresolved. There is, in my opinion, much to support the inter-dependence of the two functions.

There is a greater correlation of ideas when considering which skill-set is required of a progressive manager working in the 21st century. This chapter has proposed an overarching framework within which to consider the attributes, skills and experience of the entertainment manager. This frame of reference utilizes a common theme across all of the skills, namely that of entrusting in 'otherness'.

That is to say that diversity and non-uniformity should be celebrated, and the ability to seek new approaches to both old and new managerial challenges has become an imperative.

The chapter advocates that managers within the entertainment industries should seek out new ways to gather information, make decisions and seek agreement. Equally, it promotes building new internal and external partnerships and facilitating collaboration with others. It challenges managers to create a new and other future, where new opportunities are exploited and where the future can be populated by innovative and creative practices.

Finally, the ability to work with diverse types of people in imaginative and non-traditional ways is a clear precondition for success. It should also be acknowledged here that the unique nature and wide-ranging scope of the entertainment industries require an extension of the general list of managerial capabilities. For example, the function of project and event planning is an important addition, as is the sensitivity and understanding demanded to propose new cultural agendas to increasingly aware and active audiences.

Our opinions, thoughts and practices surrounding the subject of management, we can conclude, are constantly changing and being shaped by many wide-ranging forces and drivers. Although this can be in equal parts frustrating and invigorating, this change is a constant in itself. Management, managers, the organizations and resources they manage, and the skills required to manage them will continue to evolve, just as the RSC has done, and it is our task as scholars, practitioners and interested observers to ensure that we not only keep apace but set the pace in this exciting new world.

SEMINAR ACTIVITIES

1. We have seen that managers perform many activities and that management itself is a practical, integrating activity. As such, some observers argue that it cannot be learnt in a classroom and can only be learnt 'on the job'. Consider whether academic theories about management have any relevance at all in effective managerial practice today.

2. Identify as many ways as you can in which management and leadership are the same. Now consider in which ways they are different. Do you think we should use the terms interchangeably or not?

3. Consider which driving forces in society have led to the greatest changes in the ways in which successful managers must operate today.

4. Choose a managerial role in any sub-sector of your choice from within the entertainment industries. Rank, in order of importance, which skills you would consider to be the most important for that manager. What is the rationale behind each of your chosen skills?

REFERENCES

Allio, R.J. (2011) Henry Mintzberg: Still the zealous skeptic and scold. *Strategy & Leadership* 39(2), 4–8.
Ancona, D., Malone, T.W., Orlikowski, W.J. and Senge, P.M. (2007) In praise of the incomplete leader. *Harvard Business Review* 85(2), 92–100.
Arts Council England (2012) Strategic commissioning: what arts organisations and artists need to know. Available at: http://www.artscouncil.org.uk/funding (accessed 6 May 2012).

Brech, E.F.L. (1975) *Principles and Practice of Management*. Longman, London.

Brinkley, I. and Holloway, C. (2010) *Employment in the Creative Industries*. The Work Foundation, London.

Buchanan, D.A. and Huczynski, A.A. (2010) *Organizational Behaviour*. Pearson Education, Harlow, UK.

Carpenter, G. and Blandy, D. (2008) *Arts and Cultural Programming: A Leisure Perspective*. Human Kinetics, Illinois.

Carroll, B. and Levy, L. (2007) Defaulting to Management: Leadership defined by what it is not. *Organization* 15(1), 75–96.

Department of Culture, Media and Sport (2012) Arts and culture. Available at: https://www.gov.uk/government/topics/arts-and-culture (accessed 6 May 2012).

Drucker, P. (1977) *People and Performance*. Heinemann, London.

Fayol, H. (1949) *General and Industrial Management*. Pitman, London.

Gosling, J. and Mintzberg, H. (2003) The five minds of a manager. *Harvard Business Review* 11, 54–63.

Gunatillake, R. (2008) Advice for Arts and Cultural Organizations. London, NESTA. Available at: http://www.nesta.org.uk/publications/guest_articles/assets/features/advice_for_arts__cultural_organizations (accessed 5 May 2012).

Handy, C. (1993) *Understanding Organizations*. Penguin Books, Harmondsworth, UK.

Holden, J. (2011) Current issues in cultural and strategic leadership. In: Walmsley, B. (ed.) *Key Issues in the Arts and Entertainment Industry*. Goodfellow, Oxford, UK, pp. 179–193.

Kotter, J.P. (1982) What effective managers really do. *Harvard Business Review* 60(6), 156–167.

Kotter, J.P. (1990) *A Force for Change: How Leadership Differs from Management*. The Free Press, New York.

Mintzberg, H. (1973) *The Nature of Managerial Work*. Harper and Row, New York.

Mintzberg, H. (2011) The reinvention of management. *Strategy & Leadership* 39(2), 9–17.

Mullins, L.J. (2011) *Essentials of Organizational Behaviour*. Pearson Education, Harlow, UK.

Prahalad, C.K. (2010) The responsible manager. *Harvard Business Review* 88(1–2), 36.

Skillset (2011) Sector Skills assessment for the creative media industries in the UK. Available at: http://www.skillset.org/uploads/pdf/asset_16297.pdf (accessed 21 August 2013).

The Chartered Management Institute (2008) *Management Futures: The World in 2018*. Chartered Management Institute, London.

Townley, B., Beech, N. and McKinlay, A. (2009) Managing in the creative industries: Managing the Motley Crew. *Human Relations* 62(7), 939–962.

Walmsley, B. and Franks, A. (2011) The audience experience: changing roles and relationships. In: Walmsley, B. (ed.) *Key Issues in the Arts and Entertainment Industry*. Goodfellow, Oxford, UK, pp. 1–16.

Zaleznik, A. (1977) Managers and leaders: Are they different? *Harvard Business Review* 55(3), 67–78.

chapter 8

Human Resources and Artist Management

Maria Barrett

LEARNING OBJECTIVES

After reading this chapter you should be able to:

- understand and explain the basic principles of human resource management;
- apply these principles to recruitment and employment in the entertainment industries;
- understand the issues around equality of opportunity, specifically within the entertainment industries; and
- appreciate the roles and functions of the main entertainment unions and industry bodies.

INTRODUCTION

This chapter is about employing and being employed in the entertainment industries. It considers the context of that industry and then provides an introduction to the generic principles of human resource management, before applying these to the specific context of recruitment and employment in entertainment, while also exploring alternatives to employment. The chapter goes on to consider the issue of equal opportunities, before concluding with an introduction to the main entertainment unions and industry bodies. While it is impossible in one chapter to consider examples from every sector of the entertainment industries, the chapter does offer examples from music, theatre, film and television.

OVERVIEW OF JOBS IN THE INDUSTRY

The most prominent jobs in the entertainment industries are performance roles: actors, dancers, musicians, broadcasters and presenters; the people in front of the camera, holding the microphone and on the stage. It is evident, of course, that there is a whole range of jobs essential to running the sector. These include: those who initiate and commission the work (producers, writers, directors, managers, broadcasters, venue managers); those who present it (promoters, venue managers, broadcasters and increasingly Internet sites); those who sell it (marketing, press officers, box office); those who enhance it (sound, light, make-up, costume); and those who manage it (administrators, tour managers, stage managers and floor managers). Beyond this lie the ancillary parts of the industry, which could be characterized as the Business to Business (B2B) segment. These are the jobs that support and exploit the industry – the recording studios, prop and costume stores, post-production facilities, graphic designers, PR agencies, industry lawyers, accountants, financiers, critics, lighting hire, publishing, casting directors, agents, venue designers, seat upholsterers, wig makers, shower fixers, licensing enforcement bodies and many more.

JOB TITLES

Within individual industries, job titles and roles are not always 'fixed'. For instance, in theatre, the Administrator can be the Chief Executive Officer and the person who is responsible for its strategy and management or it can denote the person who does the general office work, similar to an office assistant or clerk. Similarly, a Producer in theatre, film and television can be the person at the top who initiates a project, takes the risk and sees the whole project through from beginning to end or the person or business who has had very little to do with the project other than contributing to its finances and getting its name 'above the title'. In the music industry, the word 'producer' can denote a great creative person who, through their input into the sound, selection and ordering of repertoire and influence on instrumentation and recording, can be seen as just as responsible for any subsequent success as the band members. On the other hand, they could be a jobbing staffer at a recording studio who engineers the work of a range of artists.

SCALE

Organizations in the sector range widely in scale. The recorded music industry, for instance, is dominated worldwide by three major labels (Universal, Sony and Warner), and the live music industry by Live Nation, which is a large promoter/producer owning many venues, US radio stations and festivals in the UK. Digitally, Apple's iTunes is a big player, and Google and Facebook are enormous and are very much changing how the sector works. At the other end of the scale, there are many small to medium-sized enterprises and many sole traders, such as session musicians, workshop leaders and so on. Theatre is defined by scale based on audience numbers: small-scale theatre plays to audiences of around 200 people, middle-scale around 500 and large-scale around 1000, although these numbers are not fixed. According to Creative Blueprint (2012), 85% of businesses in the creative and cultural sectors in the UK (and 86% in England alone) employ fewer than five people (see Fig. 8.1).

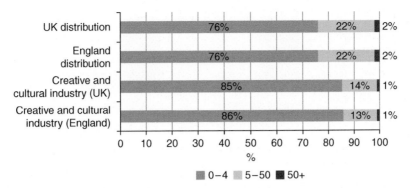

Fig. 8.1. The UK's creative and cultural businesses by size-band. (From Creative Blueprint, 2012.)

EMPLOYING AND BEING EMPLOYED IN THE ENTERTAINMENT INDUSTRIES

Competition

Work in entertainment is appealing and can even appear glamorous. This may be because it appeals to people's innate creativity, because of an assumed proximity to celebrity, or because of an overestimation of what those in the entertainment industries earn. Whatever the reason, it means that there is a lot of competition for many of the positions in the industry. In turn, this competition helps keep wages down.

A word about pay

There is a huge disparity in pay in the entertainment industries. Those at the top can command huge fees and salaries that would overshadow the top pay in many other industries. At the same time, according to the National Careers Service (2010), 73% of those working in the performing arts earn less than £20,000 per year. It would take an actor in small-scale theatre more than 311 years to earn Jennifer Aniston's fee for one film, and the same actor more than a thousand years to earn what Johnny Depp has been paid for the next instalment of *Pirates of the Caribbean* (based on ITC/Equity minimum of £400/ week 2011–12; film fees according to Vanity Fair, 2011).

A word about conditions

Self-employment, part-time and occasional employment and multiple job-holding are characteristic patterns of employment in the creative industries (see Fig. 8.2). While this has long been the case, according to the European Monitoring Centre on Change (EMCC, 2006), it is becoming increasingly pronounced. The EMCC goes on to say that work is 'fragmented and intermittent', reflecting the production patterns of the industry. Many jobs are short term, with some, such as a performer in an advert or a session musician, potentially lasting for even less than a day. There are few long term jobs; EMCC lists these as those 'in orchestras, acting groups, film production companies, as actors in television or radio soap operas'. There are also some in dance companies

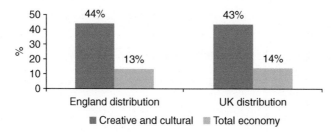

Fig. 8.2. Self-employment rates in the UK's creative and cultural industries. (From Creative Blueprint, 2012.)

such as the Royal Ballet, and in broadcast media there is also a 'relatively high proportion of workers on permanent contracts' at 79% (Randle *et al.*, 2007, p. 17).

Technicians, backstage and front of house staff in venues often fare rather better, with the potential for season-long or even year-round work. The same is true of those with management skills (e.g. fundraisers, marketers, chief executives) who can work in a variety of roles. Two-month contracts are common for performers in subsidized regional theatre, where the pattern is often 4 weeks' rehearsal and 4 weeks' performance. Commercial theatre usually has a shorter rehearsal period than subsidized theatre and, for instance in the West End, it is impossible to gauge how long a show might run as it is dependent on its ability to recoup at box office. A show that is apparently very good may still close early (e.g. *Spring Awakening* at the Novello Theatre, which received great acclamation, closed after 10 weeks), while shows that are panned by the critics can still sell (*We Will Rock You* is in its tenth year at the Dominion). This is a big challenge for all of the sectors in the entertainment industries – no-one can really know in advance which products will be successful.

However, even 8- or 10-weeks' work is long-term compared to some film or TV acting jobs, which could be less than a day,

although if this is for an advert it may still be lucrative. Similarly, a musician may go on tour for weeks or longer, while a session musician may just work for half a day. This is also true for non-performers: stage manager contracts in theatre often mirror performers' contracts, and a designer may work for one employer for the equivalent of a couple of weeks at a time, perhaps while working on other contracts.

Multiple job holding

This may mean embracing a main (or desired) job in the entertainment industries alongside a secondary job within or outside the industry; or it may mean having several short- or medium-term contracts either in succession or simultaneously. Stereotypically, that may be an aspiring performer who works in a restaurant or a bar, but it could equally mean a musician in a band who also works as a session musician and delivers workshops in schools; or a stage manager, director or designer who works for a succession of theatre companies. Television is similar: 61% of those in independent production companies are freelance or sole traders and 51% work in more than one sector (Skillset, 2005, quoted in Randle *et al.*, 2007, p. 17).

These working patterns, which may involve multiple contracts either simultaneously or in turn, lend themselves to self-employment. But they can make it difficult for staff to stay in the industry once they have families, and this is perhaps a reason why retention of women, for instance in film and television, is poor. This in turn has a negative impact on pensions (Sargent-Disc, 2012).

Tax and National Insurance

Self-employment or freelancing in essence means being a one-person business, where the worker is responsible for their own tax and National Insurance (NI). Those in employment have their tax and NI contribution taken from their pay by their employer through the PAYE scheme. In addition, the employer is obliged to add a contribution as proscribed by the Inland Revenue. Self-employed people have to manage their own tax and NI, filling in a self-assessment form and paying their tax annually rather than as they are paid. This is not as onerous as it may sound, and HMRC can be helpful if its advice is sought. It is not in the worker's or the employer's gift to describe an employee as self-employed though: the IR will confer this status based on their own definition.

Anti-social working

Work in the live parts of the sector is often antisocial in that by definition it has to take place when audience members have free time, i.e. at evenings and weekends, and for pantomime over Christmas. Work in television and film tends to have long hours and may be on location. Some workers, such as stagehands, have to start work before everyone else can, and finish after them. All producing sectors tend to have increasingly busy periods towards

deadlines, as in the gaming sector for example (Creativepool, n.d.; Prospects, 2011).

Entry routes and progression

Unlike many professions, there is no formal entry requirement or minimum standard that needs to be achieved to enter much of the industry and no formal progression structure once someone is in. It is, in fact, possible for people to enter the acting and singing professions at the top and with no training at all; and while that is rare, reality television perhaps encourages people to think it happens more often than it does. It is also possible to train for years and not find an entry point; and how good a practitioner is or the amount of time they have dedicated to their craft will not necessarily have a positive impact on pay, conditions, or even on whether they gain employment. Performers, particularly, are often valued for their ability to put 'bums on seats' over their technical ability.

Training

Multiple job holding and short-term contracts mean that training can be sporadic or non-existent, and even when in permanent employment, training can be very limited. According to the Creative and Cultural Skills' Workforce Survey (Creativity, Culture and Education, 2013), 30% of firms in the creative and cultural sectors spend less than £1000 pa on training, and another staggering 57% spend nothing at all. This may mean that there is much on-the-job training, and mentoring may be particularly important. Consequently, individuals need to be clear about their own training needs and take training where they can. Workers within the entertainment industries tend to be highly qualified, with 46% of creative and cultural workers in England having a qualification above Level 4 (Creativity, Culture and Education, 2013) and the majority of computer games designers being graduates (Creativepool, n.d.). There are many good courses now that train or educate people in a range of aspects including arts and entertainment management, stage management, performing, technical and media, and computer arts, games technology and animation, at degree level and beyond.

Subjectivity

For many performance positions, ability can only be judged very subjectively. How good a singer or actor one is, or how well a performer will fit into a band or theatre company, is arguably a matter of opinion, taste, whether or not they are liked by the 'gatekeeper' and even how they look. All of this means that as well as an industry that is overcrowded with people determined to break through and succeed, it can be easy for people who are not devoting their life to a performing career to enter the market on a temporary or part-time basis, adding to the competition. Anyone who has the knowledge and a couple of spare hours can contribute to a film crowd scene for instance, or even become an extra on a soap – something which may be interesting to them but a vital part of the annual salary to the jobbing actor. And of course the increasing sophistication of technology such as CGI means that filmed crowd scenes no longer need to use performers at all.

Family business

Sometimes people follow their parents into the industry and have relationships with others in the industry, creating dynasties, such as the great theatrical dynasties (Redgraves, Richardsons), musical families (Marleys, Carter/Cash, Arden/Osbournes, Gordys and Jacksons), those in film and television (Clooneys, Coppolas, Dimblebeys and Grades) and even in wrestling (Harts and McMahons). There is also a tendency for people to wish to work with people they know and like, or know from experience they can rely on. This is not significantly different from other industries where business is often kept in the family and professions from army to doctor are often followed by generations, but its visibility and lack of entry qualifications can lead to charges of nepotism.

Geography

Much of the industry's UK workforce is based in London and the South East: 45% of the performing arts workforce (Department for Business Innovation and Skills, 2012); half of the UK audio-visual industry (Randle *et al.*, p. 68); around half of the people working in the games sector (Creativepool, n.d.); and 57% of Britain's creative industry employees as a whole (Freeman, 2010, p. 55). Even within London, sectors cluster together, creating areas like the branded 'Theatreland' around Shaftesbury Avenue (see Fig. 8.3), or the music shops in Denmark Street. Businesses that make their money from entertainment may also cluster in these areas, such as Soho's internationally renowned film and media cluster (Freeman, 2010). Urban centres are also important (e.g. Sheffield for music; Liverpool and Dundee for games), and many regions have several theatres and

Fig. 8.3. London's Theatreland.

of course many clubs and small-scale venues. Many regional theatres still host their auditions in London however, and there are few respected theatrical or television agents outside the capital. Clearly, living in London can be a great advantage, particularly for multiple job holders.

To summarize: the entertainment industries are characterized by high competition, a disparity in wages, short-term and fragmented working, lack of clear routes of progression, multiple job holding, great subjectivity and possible nepotism, with many available opportunities concentrated in London and the South East. While some of these characteristics are clearly negative, many create an exciting and dynamic working environment. There are a number of strategies to ameliorate the worst effects including: joining unions and membership organizations to protect rights and negotiate for higher wages and better conditions; using agents to find work and to negotiate pay; and supporting organizations that help lobby for appropriate legislation, advocate for members or just provide information or a platform (e.g. Birds Eye View, Women in Film and TV, British Black Music, Women in Technology).

HUMAN RESOURCE MANAGEMENT

Put at its simplest, Human Resource Management (HRM) is the management of the most precious asset of the company, its people. People are often the biggest part of the running costs of an entertainment organization (see Chapter 13). More importantly, people are the essential means by which things are produced, whether goods or services. People drive a company forward, providing initial impetus and ongoing labour, as well as initiating innovation and change. Even in a technological age, people are needed to imagine all of the ways technology can be developed and exploited and to implement, evaluate, sell and distribute these applications. And of course there are many jobs where, for now at least, human beings are still better than technology.

So, if people are necessary to achieve an end result, such as putting on a show or building a set or producing music or designing a computer game, it is necessary to attract people to work on a project, to retain them and monitor how well they work, to reward them appropriately and perhaps incentivize them to work in different ways, to train them and to develop them. In a nutshell, this is HRM. This discipline used to be called industrial relations and then personnel management, and the change of phraseology reflects a change in emphasis, from the idea that employees were to be controlled from above to what Goss considers a more inclusive and open management style that recognizes the potential of the employee as a resource who adds value when s/he is involved at all levels (Goss, 1994, pp. 3–4).

THE PRINCIPLES OF HUMAN RESOURCE MANAGEMENT: ATTRACTING PEOPLE TO WORK FOR A COMPANY

At the outset of careers in entertainment management, many people will work with those they know and may be happy to work without payment. This is not always sustainable in the long term, as people need to pay bills and may want to further develop their work with people from beyond their immediate circle. The most usual way of doing this is for people to apply for jobs or to create companies and recruit people to work with them and to pay them to do so. Having said this, many people in the entertainment industries continue to work with people they know throughout their career, people they find stimulating, or fun to work with creatively, and sometimes this becomes permanent. Examples abound in the entertainment industries, partly because of the nature of bands and theatre/dance companies in providing, even necessitating, long-term relationships (some, like Keith Richards and Mick Jagger, go as far back as school). Many more will work with each other sporadically or when they can, or recall people they have worked with in the past for specific projects or roles. In their 2003 study of entry into film careers in London and Los Angeles, Blair *et al.* (2003, p. 265) maintain that 'the importance of building and maintaining a network of contacts was critical to progressing a career'. Networks are incredibly important throughout the entertainment industries, particularly at the point of entry.

RECRUITMENT

It is often necessary or advisable for companies to advertise employment opportunities so that the widest field of candidates is available for selection. Some funding bodies will insist on this as a condition of funding, and it will be the policy of many organizations to try to widen the pool of people applying to work with them. This is about more than equal opportunities: creativity can be inspired by new stimulus as well as existing relationships.

Nonetheless, and possibly because so many jobs are short-term, there is much word of mouth in the sector's job market. Consequently networking (through being a casual staff member, a volunteer or getting involved in workshops and training; through social media; or through going to parties and speaking to people) can often be most effective. Direct approaches can also work: performers, in particular, send CVs and a headshot to theatres, theatre companies, directors and casting directors, in the knowledge that plays are continually being cast. Performers, designers and directors also get work from decision-makers seeing their work. Performers therefore often contact decision-makers to invite them to performances. In theatre, it is often the case that people will not come to see a performer unless they are represented by an agent. In music, bands play not only for pay, enjoyment, to improve and to build an audience but also to be noticed by A&R people in the hope of getting a record deal. In addition they send their work to radio stations, as in the UK these are still huge influencers of record labels.

Many entertainment companies are not monolithic but are microcosms. While some industries largely need to recruit for the same sort of positions, individual organizations within the entertainment industries often recruit for a variety of people with a wide range of skills. For instance, a theatre may recruit performers, directors, writers, as well as stage managers, lighting and sound designers, alongside publicists, customer service staff, managers, cleaners and so on. How these are recruited falls into two main methods: a more typical recruitment system, whereby people apply for posts and explain how they would be able to fulfil them, usually at interview; and a recruitment system for performers, where the ability to fit into a role is demonstrated at audition. There is also some middle ground where for instance designers may show a portfolio of past work or even create work in response to a brief in order to demonstrate suitability at interview.

THE RECRUITMENT PROCESS

Jobs for performers, stage managers and technicians are advertised in specialist press such as *The Stage* (Fig. 8.4) and 'tip sheets'. Agents, Equity members and those who are in Spotlight can also access SBS (Script Breakdown Service), a specialist casting sheet, which is the only place some jobs are advertised. Online there is Equity, Castcall and Castweb. Backstage staff will also find jobs advertised on StageJobs Pro.

Musicians' jobs are advertised in *The Stage*, *Music Week* and *Bandit A&R Newsletter*. Local notice boards (for instance in music shops, rehearsal studios and band hangouts, and of course online) can still be effective for singers, instrumentalists, managers and so

Fig. 8.4. *The Stage* logo.

on looking for bands. There are also online notice boards such as Joinmyband and Musolist. Managers may find jobs in some of these places and also in *The Guardian* and specialist press such as *Arts Professional*.

CASTING

The recruitment process for performers in theatre, film, radio and television is called casting. Performers will usually be asked to audition for their jobs in front of the director, the producer and/or a casting director. This will be through open or closed auditions, or casting calls. Open auditions are advertised and anyone can attend. They tend to be for minor, non-speaking roles, or sometimes for people who are not (or not yet) professional performers (as has happened for some roles in the *Harry Potter* films). There is suspicion that some open auditions may be more about press and PR than they are about recruitment. Nonetheless, they are potential entry points to a competitive industry. They can therefore be very busy, and do not always give performers a lot of time to show their skills: as Natalie Gallacher (*See Me Now*, personal e-mail, 11 April 2012) of Pippa Ailion casting says: 'It's a quick in and out, 16 bars or a few lines of script'.

Closed auditions are much more usual. Here, performers will be invited to audition in response to one of the following:

- an approach by the performer's agent to the director, producer or casting director of a production;
- an approach, usually via the performer's agent, by a director, producer or casting director who has seen the performer's work, or their information/headshot in

Spotlight, or has had their work recommended to them and has done an availability check;

- by a director, producer or casting director having sifted through performers' CVs submitted in response to a casting breakdown;
- by a director, producer or casting director having looked at the performer's unsolicited CV; or
- a direct application by the performer, through their CV and headshot, for an advertised role.

According to Gallacher (*See Me Now*, personal e-mail, 11 April 2012), the first three routes are the most common. At auditions, performers will be asked to demonstrate their skills, often through set pieces. For a theatre actor, this is often two pieces of the actor's choice (traditionally a Shakespeare and a modern), but actors could be asked to sight-read a piece of the script that is being produced, or to improvise with other auditionees or with performers who have already been cast. This last is becoming much more common, as is directors sending text in advance so it can be properly prepared.

Dancers may be asked to take part in an observed class, or to learn a routine taught to them in a large group, which they will then demonstrate in smaller groups or alone. Singers auditioning for theatre roles will often be asked for two contrasting songs. Of course, those auditioning for musical theatre may be asked to do all of the above. Since the 1980s, this idea of the performer having the 'triple threat' has dominated, particularly in West End musical theatre. However, there are still many parts in British musicals where one skill, e.g. acting, is seen as being most important.

Those auditioning for minor and chorus roles may be seen for 5 minutes at their first audition. Performers auditioning for film will often be asked to sight-read and to do a screen test. Successful auditionees may be recalled to as many as five auditions, which will often increase in time and intensity and with successively more important people judging them, up to the producers. Similarly, musicians who want to join a band, pit band or orchestra will usually be asked to play or sing in an audition. For shows, musicians are usually asked to prepare two contrasting pieces. Musicians auditioning for bands may be asked to perform a song in a similar style to that of the band or play alongside the band. Figure 8.5 shows where casting comes in the process and gives an overview of the production process for live shows.

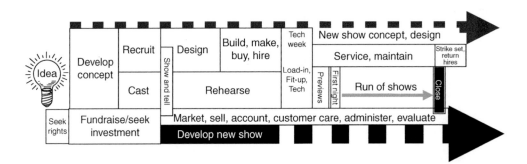

Fig. 8.5. The show development process.

SOLO ARTISTS, BANDS AND A&R

Bands and solo artists do not usually audition but traditionally strive to be signed by record labels or music publishers, either majors (EMI, Sony, Universal, Warner or BMG) or smaller independent labels ('indies'). A&R stands for Artist and Repertoire, but these days this actually means scouting for talent, and is the process by which bands and solo artists are selected to be 'signed'. The labels employ a (now somewhat reduced) number of A&R people whose job it is to recruit bands or solo singers for the labels to invest in, develop and exploit. A&R people (often known as 'A&R men', a perhaps historical reflection of the domination of men doing the job) go to gigs – on spec, on word of mouth, or by invitation – and go back to the label to make recommendations. They then have to convince a whole range of people back at the label to even come and listen to bands they recommend. If the band/artist is liked by the label, they may be offered a record deal. This usually involves the band being paid an amount of money up front to produce a number of tracks, an album or albums. This is then recouped by the record label when the artist releases the tracks.

For understandable reasons, getting signed is seen as a major goal for many unsigned bands. To get there means playing gigs that are not always profitable so bands can get on the radar to be heard. On top of the members' initial investment in the band (instruments, transport, marketing, time etc.), an investment in promotion to raise awareness amongst agents, managers and A&R is usually also necessary (see Fig. 8.6). While the 'signing fees' offered by record companies can look big, £60,000 is not a lot when split between band members. It also has to be remembered that this 'signing fee' is actually an advance against future sales, and while it is not repayable if the artist does not sell enough records, as it is recouped from sales, the artist sees no more royalty income until the debts have been paid back. In addition, the band needs to pay back some of the things the label are paying for on the band's behalf, such as producers, studios, legal advice, equipment, touring expenses, promotion costs, etc. And as music lawyer Ann Harrison (personal communication, 2012) reminds us, the manager has to be paid out of the gross income or advances too. This means a lot of sales in a market that is declining, at least for physical product, before a profit is reached. Harrison (2011) argues that bands are too often in a hurry to sign and can then spend a couple of years trying to back out of a bad deal. 'Signing isn't everything', she says: 'Go with your instinct and only sign if the

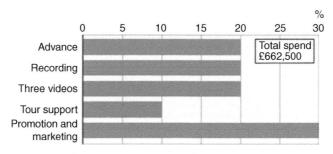

Fig. 8.6. Typical investment in a newly signed act. (From IFPI, cited in BBC News, 2010.)

deal feels right for you. And get some advice first, not after it has gone wrong!'

ENTREPRENEURSHIP

Not everyone working in the industry wants to go through processes such as this. Many arts and entertainment workers are highly entrepreneurial and want more freedom and control over their income, their work and the rights to their work. Some may even create their own company so that they can employ themselves rather than risking unemployment. So many actors, writers, directors, dancers, choreographers, musicians and so on therefore set up their own companies, and find ways to create, distribute and sell their own work.

MUSIC: DIY

Record labels no longer own the means of production, but they are the means of marketing and cash flow, and they have access to world markets. Advances in technology and related changes in the ways people discover and listen to music mean that musicians are now more able to record and distribute work themselves. This ownership of the means of production has benefits, including the possibility of bands retaining the rights to their own music, keeping any income and retaining artistic control. However, the mythology about artists such as the Arctic Monkeys and Sandi Thom who have 'made it' totally independently is just that. As Andrew Dubber (2007) says: 'PR, traditional media, record labels and money were all involved'. There are several reasons that 'do-it-yourself' is difficult. First there is a cash-flow issue in that the band has to invest in itself before the money comes in, something that a major label is in a better position to do. In addition, labels of all sizes have contacts and expertise, as well as established systems and routes to market including access to international markets. And many bands would rather spend their time creating music than managing, marketing and distributing.

The DIY model: A few case studies

There are many benefits of the do-it-yourself model. Ingrid Michaelson gained success in this way, although she then created her own label and made a global distribution deal with a major (RED, part of Sony). She says: 'It's virtually impossible to get an album into stores these days unless you have a distribution company – and you can't get that unless you have an actual label' (Widran, n.d.). Conversely, successful artists who have had major label backing such as Roger McGuinn of the Byrds have chosen to work independently making individual deals with distributors like iTunes and Amazon, or, like Prince, setting up their own label (although he still uses majors' distribution) (Reevers, 2011). And some musicians are doing it themselves. Bassist Steve Lawson feels that the record label model is 'broken', and sells his recorded music directly through Bandcamp, iTunes, Amazon and at gigs, and plays live, often duetting with singer/songwriter Lobelia, at 'house concerts' in the UK and the USA (Lawson, 2011). It will be interesting to see if more musicians manage without labels in the future and whether there are any high profile musicians who manage their whole career without the backing of a label.

REPRESENTATION: AGENTS

Agents are the go-betweens who find work and negotiate pay rates for many people working in the entertainment industries. Agents can specialize: there are, for instance, agents for walk-on parts for actors, for child performers, for session musicians, for dancers, for designers, directors and writers and so on. Whoever they represent, agents are regulated by the Department of Trade and Industry, and have to comply with the minimum standards set by The Conduct of Employment Agencies and Employment Businesses Regulations (2004). Unlike agents in other industries, who charge employers for finding suitable workers to fill vacancies, entertainment agents take their commission from the artists themselves. According to Equity (2011), this is usually 10–25% of what the worker is paid for the job. This is the only way an agent can be paid – they cannot take money up front or as a joining fee. Some agents may ask for a payment for a performer's entry in 'the Book'; this is a book showing photographs and details of everyone the agent represents, and is more usual for models and walk-ons. Any such payment should be commensurate with the cost of the Book, and artists should ask to see the last copy of the Book so they know what they are paying for.

Those seeking an agent usually need to be proactive and invite agents to see their work. Most large, reputable agents are based in London, and it is therefore easier to attract them to the London dates of a tour. Agents also go to showcases of performers in their final year in drama school. Agents will rarely see amateur work. When agents go to see work, they are not necessarily judging how good a performer is but whether they will be able to attract work and sustain a career in the short or longer term and whether they can assist with that.

MANAGING PEOPLE IN THE INDUSTRIES

Anecdotally, people in the entertainment industries, such as performing artists, 'creatives' and celebrities, can be difficult to manage, and there is a common stereotype surrounding the wild, unmanageable artist. While this is possible, it is difficult to find evidence that artists are more difficult to manage than anyone else. One big difference with other industries, however, is that the manager is often hired by those s/he has to manage. Bands and theatre companies will often appoint a manager and have the power to dismiss them or not to appoint them for future contracts, and yet the manager has to be responsible for the company and have some authority. In addition, the artist can grow bigger than the manager, having more power and earning more. This can make a traditional hierarchical management relationship a difficult balancing act. Another difference may be the different priorities of performers and managers, where managers may want to increase sales or grow markets and performers want to focus on performing or developing their product, sometimes in less marketable directions.

EQUAL OPPORTUNITIES

Traditionally, there have been two main arguments for equal opportunities: a business argument and a moral argument. I would like to posit a third argument. The entertainment industries not only provide role models like other industries in the public eye (sport, teaching and politics, for example), but they also reflect and even shape our society. I will call this the Cultural Argument.

Equal opportunities: the business argument

The business argument holds that employers would be remiss not to want to attract people from a diverse range of backgrounds in order to employ and retain the very best talent. Diverse talent brings with it not only the skills necessary to do the job but a cultural understanding that may also contribute to the business in different ways. In addition, according to the Chartered Institute for Personnel and Development (2011), employees want to work for good employers and feel valued at work. Further, there is legislation to ensure equality of opportunity, and it costs businesses in both cash terms and in loss of reputation to fall foul of the law.

Equal opportunities: the law

Legislation regarding equality has been developed gradually over time, but all previous legislation was superseded or absorbed by the Equality Act 2010 (Home Office, 2010), which now protects people from discrimination on nine counts (age; disability; gender reassignment; marriage and civil partnership; pregnancy and maternity; race; religion or belief; sex; sexual orientation). Employers in all sectors including entertainment need to comply with the law, not only in terms of employment practices but also in provision of goods and services. Equal opportunities law is not the same as positive discrimination. It does not allow for quotas and does not suggest that excluded groups are favoured in recruitment, training or promotion. Instead it aims to offer equality of opportunity by for instance encouraging employers to advertise in a wider range of publications so that information about job opportunities is available to a wider spectrum of potential employees.

Equal opportunities: the moral argument

The moral argument accepts that certain sections of our society have been and continue to be discriminated against and that this has led to some sections of society being under-represented in many sectors. This argument holds that all people should enjoy equality of opportunity and that it is the duty of all of us, whether individuals or companies, to address this.

Equal opportunities: the cultural argument

If entertainment holds a mirror up to nature, to paraphrase Shakespeare, it is important that what it reflects does not have missing pieces. Since the Equality Act 2010 (Home Office, 2010), all public bodies have a duty that goes beyond employment to 'promote equality and foster good relations' between people with protected characteristics and the rest of society. However, the entertainment industries hold a unique place in creating works that show us back to ourselves and that help us to conceptualize ourselves as individuals and as a society. As Miriam O'Reilly (2012) tweeted about television: 'Television has an enormous influence on shaping society. We can't leave fair representation of women to the whims of so-called creatives'. It is important, then, that the whole of society is represented, not only on stage and screen but in conceptualizing, making and managing our entertainment. If it is not, there is a danger that our view of ourselves is only partial and that a 'hegemony' is reinforced, where only the views, understanding and lifestyles of a dominant group are shared.

Equal opportunities policy

For all of these reasons, and in some cases because there is a level of encouragement (or what may be seen as coercion) by funders, many companies in the entertainment industries have an equal opportunities policy and many of these not only comply with but try to better the law. This is evident through extensions of policy to cover those who are not currently protected by law, including for instance those who are discriminated against on other grounds, such as socio-economic or HIV status.

Despite its adoption of such policies, the entertainment industries do not have a good record of employing the widest spectrum of people, nor of representing a variety of people of different genders and backgrounds. Women, for instance, 'make up only 6% of employees in the games industry' and ethnic minorities only 3% (Skillset, quoted in Prospects, 2011). Some sectors of society feel themselves to be invisible or depictions of them to be restricted, limited or stereotyped:

> Films are perpetuating harmful and out-of-date sexual, racial and gender stereotypes, according to the biggest-ever study of its kind into cinema audiences' opinions. Of 4,315 adults across the UK who were surveyed, a clear majority believe cinema too often falls back on discredited stereotypes,

including sexless older women, drug dealing, over-sexualized black people and gay people whose lives are dominated by their sexuality.

> (Hill, 2011)

Equal opportunities and portrayal: the case of film

The most recent survey of how people are portrayed in film was undertaken by the UK Film Council (2011). It found that people in some groups felt that film portrayal of them was partial, stereotypical and outdated. This is important if we believe that film has the power to shape our world – and most of us do: '69% of the general public say that films have the power to educate about real life issues... 1 in 2 of the general public also go further to say that film has the power to challenge stereotypes' (ibid, p. 9). If film educates and challenges us then we may feel it is important to get portrayal closer to real life. Some may even feel that we should use this power that is particular to the entertainment industries to shape a better society. Unions and industry bodies often play a key role in achieving this.

WORKING WITH ENTERTAINMENT UNIONS AND INDUSTRY BODIES

The main unions that represent the different sectors within the entertainment industries are Equity, the Musicians' Union, BECTU and The Writers' Guild. In addition there are many smaller unions representing the plethora of other workers, such as designers, directors, theatre technicians, etc. Good management should mean that managers work in cooperation with unions rather than in opposition, so it is useful to understand what unions do and what they are trying to achieve, in order to appreciate how they might impact on a company's work.

What entertainment unions do

The key aims of unions in the entertainment industries are the same as in other industries. They are there to represent their members, protect jobs, negotiate contracts with employers, improve pay and conditions of service, monitor safety in the workplace and campaign for increased equality. They often lobby governments on behalf of the entertainment industries. In addition, they publish house magazines and offer a range of benefits, from insurance discounts to personal advice. Unions have national offices, branches, divisions and representatives (or 'deputies') in companies.

What entertainment unions don't do

Unions are not agents. Membership of a union will not in itself guarantee work for a member nor does it vouch for the standard of the member's work. Membership of a trade union is voluntary. It is illegal to demand that a potential employee join a union before they can be employed or to demand they do or do not join one once they are employed.

Equity

Equity is the UK trade union representing professional performers and other creative workers from across the spectrum of the entertainment, creative and cultural industries. Equity negotiates minimum terms and conditions across the entertainment industries, allows performers to register their 'Professional Name', and collects and distributes royalties and other payments. Other benefits

of Equity membership include insurance and, for dancers and choreographers, the Dance Passport, which provides access to support and services from unions throughout Europe.

Musicians' Union

The Musicians' Union (MU) represents 30,000 musicians working in all sectors of the music business, from gigging to orchestras, jazz and musicals. While the MU provides the usual services of a union, many musicians join it initially for its generous insurance scheme, which entitles members not only to £10m of Public Liability Insurance but also up to £2000 instrument and equipment cover. In addition, it has championed many bands' rights protection and offers legal assistance for disputes over unpaid fees, cancellations, injury compensation, intellectual property rights, or help with contracts for recording, song-writing, touring or merchandizing. It also offers teacher services, recognizing not only those dedicated to teaching music but also the necessity of a portfolio career for many members.

Broadcasting Entertainment Cinematograph and Theatre Union (BECTU)

BECTU is the independent trade union for staff, contract and freelance workers working in broadcasting, film, theatre, entertainment, leisure, interactive media and allied areas, and its 25,000 members come from all aspects of the entertainment industries, including technicians, scenic artists, cinema artistes and game developers.

BECTU is recognized by many employers in the media and entertainment industries, from large-scale employers like the BBC, the

RSC and Odeon, through to smaller companies like the Eden Court Theatre, Inverness. In some cases, BECTU agreements are with groups of employers, such as with the Society of London Theatre (SOLT), which represents the West End, or the Producers' Alliance for Cinema and Television (PACT), which represents independent producers.

What about a union for managers?

Entertainment managers are not represented by a specialist union, but there are amalgamated unions such as Unite, which have traditionally attracted entertainment managers, for instance through their 'Finance & legal' and 'Community, youth workers & not for profit' divisions. Managers may also feel they are sufficiently represented and advised through their management associations such as SOLT, ITC and TMA for theatre managers, BPI and MMF for music and TIGA for managers in games development.

What unions mean for managers

Perhaps the most important ongoing impact that unions will have on a company and its management will be the negotiation of pay and conditions, or 'collective bargaining'. The large unions such as Equity, the MU and BECTU negotiate minimum terms and conditions across the entertainment industries. Where there is a major employer such as the BBC, they will do this directly with that company, and BECTU sometimes negotiates new House Agreements directly with individual managers. However, the industry is too fragmented with very many small and medium employers for each union to be able to do this with each individual company. Consequently, unions negotiate with industry bodies representing managements of different sectors and scales to agree terms, resulting in deals such as the ITC/Equity contract, the Equity/TMA Subsidized Repertory Agreement and the BBC/BECTU Agreement. These agreements stipulate pay and conditions of employment, which individual employers (or 'houses') can agree to vary to create 'house agreements'. It is important for managers to be aware of these as they will greatly inform budgets and schedules.

Trade associations

As well as collective bargaining, trade associations offer a range of benefits to members such as legal and management advice, research and lobbying.

- *ITC*: the Independent Theatre Council represents small-scale, often touring, performing arts organizations and their managements.
- *TMA*: the Theatrical Management Association represents middle scale and building-based theatre.
- *SOLT*: the Society of London Theatres represents theatre managers and producers in London's West End.
- *BPI*: British Phonographic Industry, now the British Recorded Music Industry, represents record companies. Its membership accounts for around 90% of all recorded music sold in the UK.
- *TIGA*: The Independent Game Developers' Association represents video and computer game developers in Europe.

Other entertainment unions, allied organizations and trade associations include:

- Association of British Orchestras.
- Association of British Theatre Technicians: (stage managers, production managers, administrators).

- Directors' Guild of Great Britain.
- Federation of Entertainment Unions (lobbies on areas that are of interest to all member unions, e.g. BBC Charter, tax breaks for British film production, training, equalities).
- NUJ (National Union of Journalists, of interest here for presenters).
- Society of British Theatre Designers.
- Writers' Guild (writers for television, film, radio, theatre, books, poetry, video games).

For a full list of guilds, unions and trade associations see the Skillset website (Skillset, 2012).

SEMINAR ACTIVITIES

1. Do you think the arts and entertainment industries behave as meritocracies? Does the 'cream' always rise to the top? Is this true of *Eastenders*? The Royal Shakespeare Company? *X Factor*?

2. Actors in crowd scenes have been replaced by CGI in films from *Star Wars Episode 1: The Phantom Menace* to *Titanic*. Will there come a time when actors are no longer needed in film, not even in principal roles? What about in live theatre? What about other performers – dancers or musicians? And what does CGI mean for others – makeup and hair artists? And what about designers?

3. Do you think the music industry is still male dominated? Why is this? Are other sectors dominated by one gender? Why?

4. Do you think there will be more successful, independent unsigned artists in the future? How will they market themselves? How will they make money from their work?

5. Do you think it is the responsibility of the entertainment industries to provide a diversity of role models? Do individual artists have responsibility to be role models, or to represent or be a spokesperson for their race, class, sexuality or gender?

6. Do you think that equal opportunities work? What are the downsides? Does representation in employment and within entertainment matter? If it does, would other measures, e.g. quotas, be more effective?

7. Do you agree that film has the power to shape what we think and to educate us? Can you give any examples? Does television, theatre, music, in fact the whole entertainment sector, have the power to shape our lives in this way? Has a piece of entertainment ever shaped the way you think? If this power exists, is there any downside to it?

8. According to Randle *et al.* (2007), the predominance of internships as a route of entry is an issue for equality in the UK film and television sectors. Why would this be an issue? For whom? What, if anything, would you do about it?

REFERENCES

BBC News (2010) What is a £1m record deal? Available at: http://www.bbc.co.uk/news/entertainment-arts-10654380 (accessed April 2012).

Blair, H., Culkin, N. and Randle, K. (2003) From London to Los Angeles: a comparison of local labour market processes in the US and UK film industries. *The International Journal of Human Resource Management* 14(4), 619–633.

Chartered Institute for Personnel and Development (2011) Diversity in the workplace: An overview. Available at: http://www.cipd.co.uk/hr-resources/factsheets/diversity-workplace-overview.aspx#link_2 (accessed 15 February 2012).

Creative Blueprint (2012) The Creative and Cultural Industries: England 2012/13. Available at: http://creative-blueprint.co.uk/statistics/reports/national-statistics (accessed 10 April 2013).

Creative Choices (2008) Creative and Cultural Industries Economic and Demographic Footprint. Available at: http://www.ccskills.org.uk/LinkClick.aspx?fileticket=S92bilQG9ZI%3d&tabid=600 (accessed 10 April 2012).

Creativepool (n.d.) Games Designer - Job Description, Salaries, Benefits and Useful Links. Available at: http://creativepool.co.uk/articles/?slug=games-designer-job description&parent=jobdescriptions (accessed 11 April 2012).

Creativity, Culture and Education (2013) Creative and Cultural Industries Economic and Demographic Footprint. Available at: http://www.creativitycultureeducation.org/the-footprint (accessed 10 April 2013).

Department of Business, Industry and Skills (2012) Guidance on the Conduct of Employment Agencies and Employment Businesses Regulations. Available at: http://www.bis.gov.uk/files/file24248.pdf (accessed 9 April 2012).

Dubber, A. (2007) New Music Strategies: The 20 things you must know about music online. Available at: http://newmusicstrategies.com/2007/03/16/the-20-things-you-must-know-about-music-online (accessed 20 February 2012).

Equity (2011) You and your agent. Available at: http://www.equity.org.uk/documents/you-and-your-agent (accessed 22 December 2011).

European Monitoring Centre on Change (EMCC) (2006) The performing arts sector – visions of the future. Available at: http://www.eurofound.europa.eu/emcc/content/source/eu06008a.htm?p1=ef_publication&p2=null (accessed 15 February 2012).

Freeman, A. (2010) London's Creative Workforce: 2009 Update. Greater London Authority, London.

Goss, D. (1994) Principles of HRM. Routledge, London.

Harrison, A. (2011) Music: The Business – The Essential Guide to the Law and the Deals, 5th edn. Random House, London.

Hill, A. (2011) Women, gay and black people still shown as stereotypes in film, says study. The Guardian, 18 March 2011. Available at: http://www.guardian.co.uk/film/2011/mar/18/women-gay-ethnic-stereotypes-in-film (accessed 10 April 2012).

Home Office (2010) Equalities Act 2010. Available at: http://www.homeoffice.gov.uk/equalities/equality-act (accessed 20 April 2012).

Lawson, S. (2011) A Skype Chat with Brad McCarty of TheNextWeb – Musicians And Money. Available at: http://www.stevelawson.net/2011/09/skype-brad-mccarty-thenextweb-musicians-money (accessed 26 April 2012).

National Careers Service (2010) Job Market Information: Finding out about performing arts. Available at: https://nationalcareersservice.direct.gov.uk/advice/planning/LMI/Pages/performing-arts.aspx (accessed 12 April 2012).

O'Reilly, M. (2012) Television has an enormous influence on shaping society. We can't leave fair representation of women to the whims of so-called creative. 6:36p.m. 22 February 2012. Available at: http://twitter.com/#!/OReillyMiriam/statuses/172389223603769344 (accessed 22 February 2012).

Prospects (2011) Games developer: Salary and conditions. Available at: http://www.prospects.ac.uk/games_developer_salary.htm (accessed 7 April 2012).

Randle, K., Kurian, J. and Leung, W.F. (2007) Creating Difference: Overcoming Barriers to Diversity in UK Film and Television Employment Report to EU ESF/EQUAL Programme. Available at: http://www.fdmx.co.uk and http://www.embracingdifference.co.uk (accessed 8 April 2012).

Reevers, C. (2011) 14 artists who launched their own labels. Available at: http://www.pastemagazine.com/blogs/lists/2011/03/kid-cudi-recently-announced-that.html (accessed 7 April 2012).

Sargent-Disc (2012) Age and gender in UK film industry. Available at: http://www.sargent-disc.com/sargent-disc-uk/news-insights/insights/uk-film-industry-age-and-gender.aspx (accessed February 2012).

Skillset (2012) Guilds, Unions & Trade Associations. Available at: http://www.creativeskillset.org/careers/further_resources/article_1910_1.asp (accessed 13 February 2012).

UK Film Council (2011) Portrayal versus betrayal. Available at: http://wftv.org.uk/userfiles/file/Portrayal%20Vs_%20Betrayal%20Research%20Report_UK%20Film%20Council%20March%202011.pdf (accessed 18 February 2012).

Vanity Fair (2011) Hollywood's highest paid stars. Available at: http://www.therichest.org/entertainment/vanityfairtop-40-highest-paid-stars-in-hollywood (accessed 19 December 2011).

Widran, J. (n.d.) Top Indie singer/songwriter Ingrid Michaelson talks about her album, 'Be OK', and her road to success. Available at: http://www.songwriteruniverse.com/ingridmichaelson123.htm (accessed 7 April 2012).

chapter 9

Arts and Cultural Management

Ben Walmsley

LEARNING OBJECTIVES

After reading this chapter you should be able to:

- define and contextualize the arts and cultural industries;
- articulate the key management and leadership roles in these industries and the skills required to fulfil them;
- discuss how arts and cultural management differs from management in other sectors;
- explain the funding, planning, programming and touring stages of producing arts and cultural activity;
- critically analyse the management and organizational structures of arts and cultural organizations; and
- understand the major operational and strategic issues facing arts and cultural venues.

INTRODUCTION

This chapter will focus on the specific issues faced by managers in the arts and cultural sector. The first part of the chapter will define the arts and cultural industries and discuss the roles of managers and leaders working in the sector. The second part will focus on how producing companies fund, plan, programme and tour their work, exploring the role that cultural policy plays in supporting artistic projects. The final part of the chapter will consider how arts organizations are structured and how they function operationally and strategically to fulfil their missions. This part of the chapter will focus predominantly on arts venues and explore the challenges and opportunities they are facing in a world of reduced public funding. The chapter will conclude with a case study on West Yorkshire Playhouse, one of the UK's largest regional producing theatres, which will illustrate how management works in practice and critically explore the major macro-environmental factors currently affecting the sector.

DEFINITIONS AND ROLES

Before we can start to explore and appreciate the challenges and idiosyncrasies of the arts and cultural sector, we need to define and contextualize some key terms and concepts. The cultural industries have been defined as those that produce tangible or intangible artistic and creative outputs (UNESCO, 2007). These include advertising, antiques, architecture, cinema and audiovisual products, crafts, digital and multimedia arts, entertainment, fashion, festivals, carnivals and community arts, graphic design, literature and publishing, museums and heritage, music, the performing arts, photography, television, radio and Internet broadcasting, and visual arts. Their importance to the global economy is reflected in the fact that cultural trade now represents over 7% of global GDP (UNESCO, 2005).

So now we know which products and art forms the arts and cultural industries comprise, the key remaining question is: what distinguishes arts and cultural management from other forms of management? What sets the arts and cultural industries apart is: (i) the particular role they play in society; and (ii) the type of value they generally aim to create. Let us just take these two differentiators in turn. So first, what role do the arts and culture play in society? The reason that many art forms are publicly funded all over the world is that they are deemed to provide a number of social benefits ranging from improved cognitive skills to moral rectitude and social cohesion (Belfiore and Bennett, 2008). If we return to

our definition of the cultural industries, we can appreciate that cultural products such as television, museums and music provide a vital social role, diffusing information, preserving and debating our heritage and entertaining us on an increasingly global scale.

The precise value produced and provided by the arts and culture has been debated for centuries. This debate has been marked by a traditional dichotomization of value into intrinsic and instrumental benefits, where intrinsic refers to the inherent value of art (art for art's sake) and instrumental covers tangible personal and social benefits. Research with arts audiences indicates that what they seek and gain from engaging with arts and cultural products is essentially to escape from the real world, to have a memorable emotional experience and to learn something about the world around them (Walmsley, 2011). The arts have also been shown to improve people's relationships by offering them quality time to spend with friends and family, to increase civic pride and social capital, and strengthen audiences' sense of cultural heritage and their sense of belonging (Brown, 2006).

Arts and cultural managers are therefore generally more concerned with making meaning rather than money and their strategic performance therefore needs to be evaluated on these terms. This important distinction is elaborated further in Chapter 13, where the need for a more holistic and balanced approach to performance management is discussed. But for now, it suffices to acknowledge that the primary concerns of arts and cultural managers are related to quality and accessibility rather than profit. This is why many arts and cultural organizations all over the world are established as charities – non-profit organizations that exist to promote cultural education and the arts.

MANAGEMENT AND LEADERSHIP ROLES

Successful arts managers need to balance business objectives against artistic objectives and this delicate equilibrium can often lead to tensions within arts and cultural organizations. The role of arts and cultural managers is often to manage the 'business side' of the organization (administration, strategy, finance, marketing, HR, contracting, operations management, etc.) while sharing and promoting the organization's artistic vision and managing artists and creative teams. This requires a specific set of skills, including high level diplomacy, communication and negotiation skills, along with a practical understanding of quality and talent management.

Leadership has become an increasingly important topic in recent years and, for the reasons stated above, is of particular significance in the arts and cultural sector. In the UK and the USA, there is an acknowledged crisis in cultural leadership (Hewison, 2004). In the UK, programmes like the Clore Leadership programme have been set up to solve this problem (see http://www.cloreleadership.org). Because the balance between the artistic and business sides of arts and cultural organizations is so delicate, many people argue that they should embrace a *dual leadership* structure. This is where the chief executive role is shared between an artistic leader (usually an Artistic Director) and a strategic leader (often a General or Executive Director). The main advantages of this structure are that it promotes continuity and sustainability, encourages critical reflection,

provides an in-built support network, shares power and responsibility, and doubles the available skill set. But drawbacks can include cost, power struggles, slower decision making, role ambiguity and even staff playing directors off against each another (Antrobus, 2011). Ultimately, this structure is dependent on excellent inter-personal relationships and effective communication so its pros and cons depend largely on the particular personalities involved. It should be noted that even in a sole leadership model, the opposing arguments for an artistic leader or an administrative director both retain their fierce advocates, and again, both of these models have their strengths and weaknesses.

As business models and practices are changing to suit new technologies, new ways of working and new demands from consumers, visitors and audiences, new styles of leadership are increasingly being advocated by practitioners, consultants and academics. For example, Knell (2005) characterizes modern cultural organizations as mobile, fluid, collaborative and well-networked; Hewison (2004, p. 157) argues that 'relational' leaders who work 'with and through others' will be more important in the future than 'transactional' or 'transformational' leaders; and Holden (2011) claims that successful cultural leaders lead across networks rather than down hierarchies. This leads Holden to promote the role of *distributed leadership*, where leaders sit in the centre of an organization and delegate power internally.

ORGANIZATIONAL STRUCTURE AND GOVERNANCE

As we shall see, this ongoing shift in leadership roles and styles is starting to impact on the way that arts and cultural organizations are structured. Traditionally, these structures can be divided into three main types:

1. Simple.
2. Complex/functional.
3. Project/matrix.

According to Byrnes (2009), there are four main benefits of a good organizational structure:

1. It clarifies who does what.
2. It establishes a reporting structure and delegates responsibility.
3. It defines appropriate communication channels.
4. It allocates human resources to defined objectives.

Organization is especially significant for arts and cultural entities, as they often work on a project-by-project basis to very tight deadlines with minimal resources. But the main point to note about organizational structure is that it should serve and fit the organization, not the other way round. This means that it should reflect the organization's mission and facilitate the achievement of its strategic goals and objectives. To illustrate how this works in practice, we will now analyse three different organization charts or *organograms*.

Figure 9.1 illustrates a typical example of a simple structure. It is based on a small organization of up to four full-time staff clustered around a key artist or artistic leader. The vast majority of organizations in the cultural industries are small and the sector is fragmented and under-managed, with many organizations relying on pro-am, semi-professionals, part-time and voluntary labour (Leadbeater, 2005). So this type of basic skeleton structure is the one most commonly found in the sector. This example also illustrates

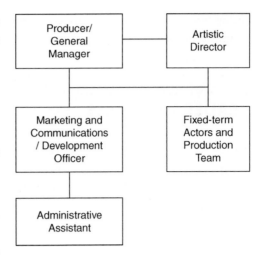

Fig. 9.1. Simple structure.

the dual leadership structure discussed earlier in the chapter; but often small organizations are led by an artist, choreographer, artistic director or entrepreneur, supported by a small team of administrators.

Referring back to Byrnes' theory, the advantages of this structure are that it facilitates excellent communication and encourages a clear allocation of roles and supervision. It is lean, flexible and highly efficient, based around a small core team who employ a larger fixed-term and/or freelance team on a project basis as and when appropriate – usually to rehearse, present and tour a new production. Employees working in this structure generally know everything that is happening in the company and have the opportunity to undertake a wide range of tasks. However, drawbacks can include poor resources and limited peer learning and promotion opportunities. It should also be noted that even a small structure of this nature is a luxury for many artists and cultural entrepreneurs, who often have to provide their own administrative support because of insufficient funding. This is one reason behind the rise of innovative producing organizations in the UK such as Artsadmin (http://www.artsadmin.co.uk) and Fuel (http://fueltheatre.com/home), who provide specialized support to creative artists, ideas and projects to bring them to fruition.

The second main type of structure is the complex or functional structure. As its name suggests, this structure is generally adopted by medium- to large-scale organizations and is based around their key functions or departments. In Chapter 7, we saw how the Royal Shakespeare Company had changed its management structure and Fig. 7.1 represented how the structure looked in 2003. Figure 7.1 depicts a typical functional structure with staff divided into clearly distinguished departments ranging from human resources and communications to producing and education. As before, the organogram illustrates a dual leadership structure and the organization is split quite neatly into an artistic side and a business side. The role of

the board should also be noted here: as registered charities, subsidized arts and cultural organizations in the UK are usually governed by a board of voluntary non-executive directors who appoint the chief executive(s), oversee top level strategy and policy, and ensure financial efficiency and probity.

Referring again to Byrnes' theory on the benefits of organizational structure, we can see here that although there are clear reporting and communication lines, and although staff are allocated according to the organization's primary objectives, this structure may well cause communication challenges and potentially lead to a silo mentality or even internal competition within departments. The structure also promotes a traditional culture of hierarchical, top-down management and communication, which could present a significant barrier to the new models of flexible networks and distributed leadership discussed earlier.

Case Study: A new business model at the RSC

As we saw in Chapter 7, it was for these reasons that the RSC revolutionized its structure in 2010 to produce the network structure illustrated in Fig. 7.2. Although not a direct example of a project or matrix structure, this structure clearly promotes and facilitates working across traditional departments, mitigating the risks of the functional structure and encouraging cross-organizational communication. It also illustrates what the concept of distributed leadership might look like in practice, with the board and chief executives sitting at the heart of the organization and leading across rather than down it. This radical new model reflects John Knell's point about the need for modern organizations to be fluid and collaborative and it is currently raising many eyebrows in the sector.

CULTURAL POLICY AND FUNDING

Since the times of the Ancient Greek festivals, nation states and local governments have taken an active role in funding artistic and cultural activity. This practice remains a strong European tradition, which has also been adopted by countries as far apart as Australia and Canada. Public funding is generally based on an acceptance of what is known as *market failure*, which refers to the inability of the open market system to create sufficient provision in sectors such as the arts and culture on its own. In the USA, there is much less support for public funding of arts and cultural activity so philanthropy and corporate sponsorship play a vital role here.

In the UK, public funding is distributed via the four national arts councils (Arts Council England, Creative Scotland, Arts Council of Wales and Arts Council of Northern Ireland), who work independently from Government following the so-called *arm's length principle*. Local authorities also fund arts activities and venues in most areas of the country. However, in light of the ongoing financial crisis, the UK Government is keen to introduce a *mixed economy* of funding in order to raise earned income and philanthropy to create a kind of hybrid model somewhere between the current UK and US models. The problem with this is that personal giving in the arts is not a cultural tradition in the UK and corporate sponsorship tends to be attracted by a small number of large organizations based in and around London (Mermiri, 2010). Organizations such as Arts & Business hope that future growth in private giving will come via friends' schemes, giving circles and crowd funding.

To understand the aims, processes and amounts of public funding distributed to arts and cultural organizations, we will now consider the role of the largest of the national funding bodies, Arts Council England (ACE). ACE's mission is to support 'great art for everyone' and it strives to achieve this by 'championing, developing and investing in arts and cultural experiences that enrich people's lives' (Arts Council England, 2012). Despite a funding cut of 29.6% announced in March 2011 and a further 5% cut announced in June 2013, between 2011 and 2015 ACE will invest around £2.25 billion of public money in the arts and culture. This will include (Arts Council England, 2011):

- £1.4 billion to the 696 new National Portfolio Organizations;
- £440 million in Strategic Funding mainly focused towards touring and capital development;
- £202 million in Grants for the Arts to support work by individual artists and arts organizations who are not regularly funded; and
- £35 million Renaissance in the Regions funding to transform England's regional museums.

The two guiding principles behind ACE's investments are artistic excellence and public access. So applications for funding must demonstrate not only the highest artistic standards but also a clear public benefit, financial viability, and sound management and evaluation. Ideally, funded projects should also make an original contribution to their art form.

ARTISTIC POLICY AND PROGRAMMING

Organizations funded by one of the national arts councils need to base their artistic policies around these core funding principles, but when it comes to detailed artistic mission statements and objectives, organizations are free to determine their own artistic values. Because arts and cultural organizations usually do not exist primarily to make money, their mission statements tend to focus on the type of product or experience they want to produce, how they want to produce it, and the value it will have for their consumers, audiences and visitors.

But deciding on an artistic policy is not always an easy task. This is partly because organizations often have to respond to multiple stakeholders (funders, staff, audiences, artists, etc.) who may have conflicting expectations and demands; and partly because there is no fixed rule about who should determine the policy. In many organizations, the Artistic Director or Producer will lead on artistic policy and programming, supported by the senior management team. But in other organizations, there may be a more democratic structure where even audience members are involved. Boards of directors should also play a fundamental role here, shaping, influencing and questioning policy, and ensuring that key artistic objectives are met.

Programming is also a complex process and varies considerably between producing and presenting organizations. For producing companies, programming is all about implementing their artistic plans and realizing their ambitions. For core-funded organizations, a 3-year programme of activity will have normally been funded by the arts council and this is what forms the basis of their funding applications. For project-funded organizations, decisions are made on a project by project basis.

There are ten key questions to consider when choosing which artistic projects to pursue.

1. Why are you doing it? Are you passionate about it?
2. Does it fit your mission, aims and strategic objectives?
3. Will it be high quality and accessible?
4. Where does it fit within your programme, season or portfolio?
5. Can you afford to do it? Can you afford *not* to?
6. What are the associated risks?
7. Who will want to see it: will it attract an audience?
8. Who will be in the creative team?
9. Will it develop your art form?
10. What will it look like on stage, in print, in a gallery, online, etc?

For presenting venues (also known as receiving houses), many of the same questions apply. Like their commercial counterparts, arts and cultural organizations should aim to develop a strong brand that responds to their customers' needs and offers something special and unique (see Chapter 3). This means that arts venues need to programme work that reflects and ideally strengthens their artistic vision and brand.

Beyond this artistic need is the more practical requirement to schedule work to create a balanced season, and for larger venues this may mean filling two or more spaces. This type of programming is a complex juggling act, which requires experience, patience and negotiation. Good venues are constantly on the lookout for the next best thing and they balance this support for new work against developing relationships with audiences and regular artistic collaborators. Venues that both produce their own work and present other companies' work have the further challenge of programming incoming work around their own in-house productions, events, concerts or exhibitions.

Touring companies face slightly different challenges. They are on the other side of the programming process and have to negotiate with venues to get the slot they want, while fitting this around the schedules of other venues on their tour. We will explore the process of tour booking in detail in the following section.

TOUR BOOKING

Tour booking is a vital activity in many sectors of the arts and cultural industries, notably in music and the performing arts. It is a complex but exciting activity, which demands excellent planning, sales, budgeting and negotiation skills. Although tour booking involves scheduling an intense period of artistic activity, the real skill behind it lies in cultivating long-term relationships with venues. The first stage in tour booking is to plan, and the best way to start this process is to set clear aims and objectives for the tour. For example, if an organization is trying to develop relationships with certain venues or with audiences in certain cities, it may want to target these first.

There are ten key considerations when booking a tour.

1. The reputation of venue: is it well respected in your art form and by your potential audiences?
2. Financial viability: what is the venue's capacity and average ticket yield? Can you make enough income?
3. What is its artistic policy? You should find this on its website or in industry publications.
4. Is it the right size and format? Will your show fit in, both literally and artistically?
5. What are your technical requirements (e.g. regarding the get-in and get-out)?
6. Location: what is the geography of the tour? Does it make sense?
7. Travel times and public transport: can you get there and back on time?
8. What is the venue's audience/visitor profile and what marketing support will it offer you?

9. Fulfilling funding conditions: are there certain venues or cities you *need* to tour to?
10. For international tours, are there any visa or entry requirements or restrictions?

Once you have thought through and discussed these issues with all the relevant people (especially with marketing and production staff) then you are ready to start booking the tour. As tour booking is essentially a B2B (business to business) sales activity, it is imperative that you know the product/experience/activity you are selling inside out and that you are personally enthusiastic (and ideally passionate) about it. Enthusiasm is infectious, and if you are not enthusiastic about your work then it is unlikely you will be able to convince promoters and presenters to take it. Tour booking is a logical, if time-consuming and sometimes frustrating, process, but it can be broken down into ten simple steps.

1. Create a draft or dream tour.
2. Obtain feedback on your ideas from colleagues in different departments.
3. Create a show information sheet and distribute it to the promoters on your wish list with a covering letter or e-mail.
4. Create a tour booking diary.
5. Contact the promoters (ideally in person or by phone) and gauge their interest.
6. If they are interested, check your dates and try and find a slot.
7. Negotiate the deal (see the following section) and pencil in a slot.
8. Once all your venues are pencilled, start to confirm them one by one and exchange contracts.
9. Draft, check and sign the venue contract (see the following section).
10. Pass on the contract to the relevant staff/departments and file it.

BUDGETING, NEGOTIATING DEALS AND CONTRACTING

One of the main responsibilities of an arts manager or producer is to create, manage and reconcile production or exhibition budgets. Indeed in the commercial sector this is a key role of producers who often have to raise the funds for a show themselves. The main point of budgeting is to set, monitor and control expenses and project accurate revenue, so when booking a tour, you should know in advance what you need to make from each tour venue. This will inform your negotiations with venues.

In order to budget accurately, there are certain things you may need to know:

- How big is the show/exhibition; how many people/exhibits etc. are in it?
- What wages, fees, royalties and insurance do you need to pay?
- How many production staff will you need?
- Where is the show rehearsing and for how long?
- Where is it touring to and for how many days/nights?
- What deals will you get from the venues? Are there any *contras* (charge-backs)?
- How much will you spend on marketing?
- What are the audience figures likely to be?

To answer these questions, you will again have to liaise closely with production and marketing staff. You can already appreciate how important excellent communication and interpersonal skills are in arts and cultural management!

Once you have budgeted your show, you will then need to negotiate your deals with venues. There are five main types of deal that are generally agreed in music and performing arts venues.

1. *The fee*: the venue gives the producer a fixed sum per performance.
2. *The split*: the producer and venue each receive a fixed percentage of the box office income.
3. *Calls*: the producer receives the first tranche of income; the venue the second; the producer the third and so on. The idea here is to share risk and return.
4. *The guarantee + split*: the producer receives an agreed percentage of the box office income but a minimum amount is guaranteed.
5. *The guarantee + calls*: as in deal 3 above but a minimum amount is guaranteed.

Beyond these typical deals, further considerations you will need to check or agree are issues such as:

- Tax: are both organizations VAT registered? Are they culturally exempt?
- Royalties: who will pay the artists' royalties? How will any live or recorded music royalties be paid? In the UK, this is governed and collected by the Performing Rights Society (PRS).
- Does the venue charge any contras for technical or marketing support?

When the deal has been agreed, the next step is the formal contracting stage, which makes the agreement legally binding. There are two types of contracts you may need to deal with. The first is the venue contract, which will include the financial deal and cover other essential legal, operational and financial matters. The following checklist includes the key points of agreement that make the venue contract useful and enforceable:

- names and addresses of both parties;
- name of production and production schedule;
- general responsibilities of both parties;
- financial deal/payment and when payable;
- ticket prices, concessions and comps;
- capacity of venue on sale;
- technical arrangements and special requirements;
- marketing arrangements and requirements (audience data, print, press, programmes, retail, etc.);
- insurance (public and employers' liability and third party);
- licensing and health and safety;
- copyright, PRS and withholding tax;
- exclusivity;
- cancellation;
- disputes; and
- partnership and assignment.

The second batch of contracts you might need to issue comprises artists', production and freelance contracts. The essential information you will need to cover here includes the precise nature of the assignment, the dates of the engagement, the remuneration (including any holiday pay, pension, subsistence and touring allowance), intellectual property arrangements and grievance procedure. Many of these engagements are covered by wider union agreements (such as Equity, BECTU and the Musicians' Union; Fig.9.2), so you need to ensure that you are respecting any minimum agreements on pay and conditions. You should also note that all contracts must be signed and dated by both parties in hard copy to be legally binding.

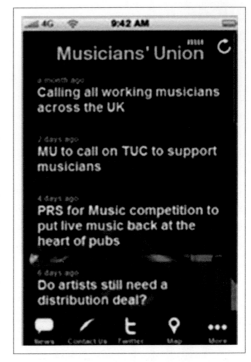

Fig. 9.2. Musicians' Union new app.

CASTING AND AGENTS

As discussed in Chapter 8, arts managers and producers may also be involved in a casting process. Casting can happen either directly, where directors and/or producers cast a show themselves, or indirectly, where the services of a casting director are engaged. Casting usually takes place through a process of auditions, where actors and other artists are called to read or perform for a part in a production. This may take the form of a casting workshop where a director might try out some ideas with a group of actors and see how they respond. This is particularly common in dance and in musical and physical theatre. There are several tools that can assist directors, producers and casting directors. In the UK, for example, Spotlight (http://www.

spotlight.com) is a very useful database of over 40,000 artists, which enables casting teams to search by categories including location, playing age, height, hair colour, accents and key skills such as the ability to play a musical instrument.

Once a production has been cast, the next stage is to make a formal offer to the actors or artists selected to take part in it. Most artists are employed through an agent (see Chapter 8), so this process usually involves approaching and negotiating with professional agencies. A good casting director can again be invaluable here as they can act as a broker between the company and the agent. When the agent has checked the availability of the artists and accepted the deal, the manager or producer then needs to issue a deal memo confirming in writing the details of the offer before passing to the contracting stage.

However, contracting is not always the happy end of the story! The nature of the entertainment industries is such that occasionally an artist will get a better deal or become injured and withdraw from the production. This can sometimes happen well into rehearsals or even during a tour, which is where careful contingency planning and understudies come into play. It should also be noted that in many countries, actors have a special tax status. In Ireland, for example, visual artists, composers and writers do not pay income tax on their earnings; and in the UK, they pay full (Class 1) National Insurance but for tax purposes are classed as self-employed. These exemptions do not apply to artists who are based outside the UK, in which cases income tax must be withheld and paid to the Foreign Entertainers Unit.

PRODUCTION, STAGE AND COMPANY MANAGEMENT

In producing companies, production, stage and company managers play a vital role in coordinating the technical, physical and human resources of a show. The main role of a production manager is to budget and coordinate the physical staging of a show. This involves hiring a production team (sound and lighting technicians etc.) and supervising the technical elements of the show (set construction, sound and lighting and any special effects). Production managers chair production meetings, manage technical rehearsals and lead on health and safety issues. Their overall goal is to liaise with the director and the set, lighting and sound designers to realize the artistic vision of the creative team and ensure that the production looks as slick and professional as possible.

The role of the stage managers is to coordinate the rehearsal process and ensure that any resulting performances and tours run as smoothly as possible. As Maccoy (2004) points out, stage management is a dynamic process that demands a unique range of skills including intuition, adaptability, intelligence and discipline. This is because stage managers work with a wide range of artists, technicians and craftspeople to find creative solutions to technical and human problems. Stage managers' duties include: managing rehearsals and the rehearsal space; maintaining discipline on stage and backstage; managing calls for fittings, rehearsals and performances; acquiring and managing props; booking transport and accommodation; and prompting. The stage and production management team is supervised by a company manager, who manages the team's calls, working hours, time sheets and pay, and ensures compliance with any contractual and health and safety requirements.

VENUE AND OPERATIONS MANAGEMENT

Many of the issues we have explored thus far affect both small, touring organizations and large, producing organizations. But some issues relate specifically to venues and merit further attention. Running a large theatre, gallery, concert hall, opera house or museum comes with its own particular set of challenges. Perhaps the most significant of these is the time and cost required to heat, light, maintain and upgrade the building itself. Many European arts and cultural venues are landmark 18th- or 19th-century listed buildings, which are often poorly suited to modern performance and audience needs and yet very difficult to modernize for practical or legal reasons. This is compounded by the increasing pressure to reduce carbon emissions, which has led to interesting initiatives such as London's Green Theatre Plan, which aims to reduce London theatres' CO_2 emissions by 60% from their 1990 levels by 2025 (Greater London Authority, 2008).

Considering the challenges of running, programming, presenting and producing in a building, there has been a move away from the traditional building-based model in recent years, with new national companies such as National Theatre of Scotland and National Theatre Wales opting for a touring model and smaller touring companies like Kneehigh and Paines Plough even commissioning their own light-weight, portable venues. But arts venues form a major part of many nations' cultural heritage and still house many of the world's most prestigious arts and cultural organizations. Running them to meet the needs of modern artists and audiences requires highly trained facilities and operations managers who understand the importance of customer service, hospitality, accessibility, ticketing, security, ambience and logistical issues such as heating, transport and parking.

In the UK, in an era of reduced public funding, where some local councils are even cutting arts funding altogether, there are particular challenges facing regional theatres, which as we saw earlier often find it hard to attract private donations and sponsorship. These challenges will be explored further in the following case study.

Case Study: West Yorkshire Playhouse

Introduction

West Yorkshire Playhouse (WYP; see Fig. 9.3) first opened its doors in March 1990, following a 20-year incarnation as Leeds Playhouse housed in a disused hall at the University of Leeds. In its first 24 years, WYP has established itself as a strong force in contemporary British theatre, with a national (and increasingly international) reputation as one of the UK's leading theatres. Based in a modern building in the Quarry Hill area of Leeds, it is one of the UK's largest regional producing theatres outside London and Stratford.

(Continued)

Case Study. Continued.

Fig. 9.3. West Yorkshire Playhouse by night. Image reproduced courtesy of West Yorkshire Playhouse.

The Playhouse comprises two auditoria: the 750-seater Quarry Theatre and the smaller, 350-seater Courtyard Theatre. As well as its administrative offices, it runs an award-winning bar, a café, a gallery, three rehearsal rooms, two function rooms, technical workshops, a recording studio and a costume hire department. In 2009, it expanded over the road to open its new dedicated space for young people, First Floor.

Funding and mission

West Yorkshire Playhouse is a National Portfolio Organization and currently around 34% of its income comes from Arts Council England and Leeds City Council (see Chapter 13, Fig. 13.3). The remaining income has to be earned directly from the box office, sponsorship and fundraising, room hires, trading and hospitality sales. West Yorkshire Playhouse is a company limited by guarantee and represents one of Leeds' largest registered charities. It is funded to produce and present theatre of the highest quality for audiences in West Yorkshire and beyond. Its vision is to be a world-class playhouse, which is rooted in its community; its mission is to make great theatre that illuminates, entertains and challenges and to be a creative spark for artists, audiences and local communities. To this end, WYP produces around 12 shows a year, about one-third of which are UK or world premieres. Each year it stages over 1000 performances, workshops, rehearsed readings and artistic events, attracting an annual show audience of around 200,000. The number of people who engage

(Continued)

Case Study. Continued.

with the Playhouse through engagement and community initiatives increases this annual audience to 300,000.

Policy, structure and leadership

The inaugural Artistic Director of WYP was Jude Kelly, who is currently Artistic Director of London's Southbank Centre. In 2002, Jude was replaced by Ian Brown, who held the role until summer 2012, when he was replaced by James Brining. With the support of their staff teams and boards, the Artistic Directors have developed the company's artistic policy from scratch to establish a brand associated with diverse, high quality theatre. The venue programmes and co-produces with some of the best theatres and touring companies in the UK and produces a wide range of work from classics and children's work to acclaimed musical theatre. Several of its biggest hits have transferred to London's West End, including *The 39 Steps* and a recent co-production of *Othello* with Northern Broadsides, starring Lenny Henry.

As one of the UK's largest regional theatres, WYP currently has a staff base of around 200, including over 100 permanent staff but not including actors, designers and other project-related freelance staff. The company employs a traditional functional structure for the day-to-day running of the organization, with staff separated into departments. However, the Playhouse has also embraced a matrix structure to implement a 2-year action research project funded by the National Lottery, which is intended to 'open up creative opportunities and open out the building's talent and resources' (West Yorkshire Playhouse, 2012). The aim of the matrix structure is to encourage staff to work together with colleagues from across the organization in temporary 'houses', each tasked with finding creative solutions to some of the key challenges currently facing the Playhouse.

From 2008 to 2012 the Playhouse followed a dual leadership model with Artistic Director Ian Brown and General Director Sheena Wrigley sharing the role of Chief Executive. This model changed with the appointment of James Brining in 2012, when Sheena Wrigley became sole Chief Executive in order to ensure continuity and facilitate long-term strategic planning and to free up the incoming Artistic Director to focus on developing the future artistic policy.

Education and outreach

Publically funded organizations are expected to develop new and non-traditional audiences and enhance their artistic programmes with education and outreach activities. Despite its size and growing international reputation, WYP remains at heart a community institution, and in this area of its work the organization has shown particular innovation. This is demonstrated by First Floor, a creative arts space dedicated to young people. First Floor offers a range of activities for local young people and introduces them to the many different careers available in theatre and in the other creative industries. It also delivers creative arts classes and accredited courses, targeting specifically young people with

(Continued)

Case Study. Continued.

learning disabilities and youngsters not in education, employment or training. First Floor aims to bridge the gap between education, training and the world of work, opening doors and unlocking opportunities for young people on the fringes of society. First Floor sits within WYP's Arts Development department, which includes a Creative Education Manager, a Creative Communities Manager, a Creative Education Consultant and a Creative Education Officer. This demonstrates the link between organizational structure and culture – in this case reflecting the Playhouse's creative approach to engagement and outreach.

For many arts organizations, education and outreach is generally restricted to programme-related activities such as workshops, competitions and schools tours, which encourage attendance at a theatre, museum or art gallery. But for WYP, education is viewed in its widest sense and the theatre aims to open its doors to its whole community. On Wednesdays, for example, the foyer and café are taken over by Heydays, a creative arts project run for people over 55. As opposed to many arts organizations, there is no pressure to convert a participant in an educational activity into a ticket-buyer; WYP's approach is to build new and open up existing spaces to entice its diverse local communities over its threshold in order to engage with them in a culturally creative way. An excellent example of this is the Dandy Lion Club, an afternoon of creative taster sessions of acting, dancing, singing and DJ-ing designed specifically for young people with learning disabilities.

The Future: challenges and opportunities

Many of the Playhouse's 200,000 annual visitors are first-time attenders and one of the main challenges for the company is to convert these curious theatre-goers into second-time, third-time and ultimately regular attenders. Another challenge is to attract younger audiences and broaden the appeal of WYP beyond the urban centres of Leeds, Wakefield and Bradford to engage with new audiences from the less wealthy areas of Calderdale and Kirklees.

To this end, the Playhouse is keen to get to know what its audience members think rather than just count them as faceless statistics. Former Communications Director Su Matthewman referred to her audiences as customers – a term sometimes regarded as commercial and even distasteful in the wider artistic community. But for Su, visitors to the Playhouse are paying customers who should enjoy the building's myriad facilities, from the bar and café to the theatres and workshops.

Su is interested in the 360-degree experience that her customers receive and she is passionate about the need to measure this not just by surveys and figures but also by talking and listening to her visitors both individually and through focus groups. This audience-focused approach typifies the culture at WYP, which aims to demystify the theatre-making process by opening up its walls and doors both literally and metaphorically. It achieves this principally through creative artistic development and co-creative projects such as *Transform* and *Furnace,* and through accessible services such as backstage tours, touch-tours and signed and audio-described performances.

(*Continued*)

Case Study. Continued.

Another increasingly important way of breaking down the so-called fourth wall is via the company website. Featuring a range of free services such as online booking, press reviews, audience reviews and subscription to a monthly e-bulletin and adding value to past, current and forthcoming productions via blogs, online interviews, rehearsal footage and free downloadable programmes, WYP's website provides a useful portal for all its stakeholders, from seasoned theatre-goers to potential sponsors.

However, in an era of swingeing funding cuts, the theatre faces a number of significant challenges. As discussed earlier in the chapter, regional arts organizations are struggling to attract the corporate sponsorship and/or philanthropy necessary to make the transition to the mixed funding economy so prized by the Government. On top of this, the financial crisis has led to a sharp reduction in household income, which has impacted on ticket sales. So the Playhouse is being financially squeezed from both ends. In response to this, it recently appointed a new Director of Fundraising and Development, who joined the senior management team in 2011.

Another challenge the Playhouse faces is to develop and improve its structure and external networks. We explored earlier the need for modern arts organizations to be mobile, collaborative and well networked and saw how this can be hindered by a rigid, functional structure that can impede communication. WYP is facing this challenge head on through its action research project, which is aimed at opening the venue up and out. Particular goals here are to develop relations with the press and wider media, such as regional television networks, and to work more collaboratively with a diverse range of artists.

Finally, the Playhouse needs to keep responding to the changing expectations, needs, demands and desires of modern audiences, who increasingly want to participate interactively in artistic creation rather than sit passively in an auditorium. Chief Executive Sheena Wrigley is aware of the trend towards event theatre, and a further challenge for the Playhouse is therefore how to cater for younger audiences while not alienating core older audiences, who are often opposed to recent developments such as 'tweet seats'. The creative projects and festivals discussed earlier represent a considered response to this challenge; but the real dilemma facing all large regional theatres is how to be all things to all people while simultaneously differentiating their work and developing a strong, identifiable theatre brand that will last well into the 21st century.

SEMINAR ACTIVITIES

1. How does arts and cultural management differ from management in other industries?

2. What are the key roles and skills required of an arts manager?

3. How would you define and describe *dual leadership*? What are its pros and cons?

4. What is *distributed leadership* and why do you think it is in vogue?

5. Which type of organizational structure would you prefer to work in and why?

6. How would you describe the *arm's length principle* and why do you think it was introduced?

7. Why do you think there are tensions between ACE's two guiding principles of artistic excellence and public access?

8. Carry out a detailed SWOT analysis for West Yorkshire Playhouse and then for an arts organization of your choice.

REFERENCES

Antrobus, C. (2011) Two heads are better than one: what art galleries and museums can learn from the joint leadership model in theatre. Available at: http://www.claireantrobus.com/publications (accessed 22 February 2012).

Arts Council England (2011) *The Arts Council Plan 2011-2015*. Arts Council England, London.

Arts Council England (2012) What we do. Available at: http://www.artscouncil.org.uk/what-we-do (accessed 16 February 2012).

Belfiore, E. and Bennett, O. (2008) *The Social Impact of the Arts: An Intellectual History*. Palgrave Macmillan, Basingstoke, UK.

Brown, A.S. (2006) An architecture of value. *Grantmakers in the Arts Reader* 17(1), 18–25.

Byrnes, W.J. (2009) *Management and the Arts*, 4th edn. Elsevier, Oxford, UK.

Greater London Authority (2008) *Green Theatre: Taking Action on Climate Change*. Greater London Authority, London.

Hewison, R. (2004) The crisis of cultural leadership in Britain. *International Journal of Cultural Policy* 10(2), 157–166.

Holden, J. (2011) Current issues in cultural and strategic leadership. In: Walmsley, B. (ed.) *Key Issues in the Arts and Entertainment Industry*. Goodfellow, Oxford, UK, pp. 179–193.

Knell, J. (2005) *The Art of Dying*. Intelligence Agency, London.

Leadbeater, C. (2005) *Britain's Creativity Challenge*. Creative & Cultural Skills Sector Council, London.

Maccoy, P. (2004) *Essentials of Stage Management*. A&C Black, London.

Mermiri, T. (2010) *Arts Philanthropy: The Facts, Trends and Potential*. Arts & Business, London.

UNESCO (2005) *International Flows of Selected Goods and Services, 1994–2003*. UNESCO Institute for Statistics, Montreal, Canada.

UNESCO (2007) *Statistics on Cultural Industries: Framework for the Elaboration of National Data Capacity Building Projects*. UNESCO, Bangkok.

Walmsley, B. (2011) Why people go to the theatre: A qualitative study of audience motivation. *Journal of Customer Behaviour* 10(4), 335–351.

West Yorkshire Playhouse (2012) Biography. Available at: http://www.wyp.org.uk/about-us/what-we-do/biography (accessed 27 February 2012).

chapter 10

Responsible Entertainment Management

Dirk Reiser and Stuart Moss

LEARNING OBJECTIVES

After reading this chapter you should:

- be able to appreciate the meaning of responsible entertainment management holistically as well as specifically in relation to corporate social responsibility, dark entertainment and from a sustainable/green perspective;

- be able to realize the benefits that responsible entertainment management can bring to organizations within the entertainment industries;

- be informed of a range of practices and examples that allow entertainment providers to manage their organizations and outputs more responsibly;

- become aware of some of the sensitivities surrounding dark entertainment; and

- learn how to create greener and more sustainable entertainment events.

INTRODUCTION

In a modern, arguably moralistic and increasingly litigious society, where worldwide headlines can be generated from a Tweet on a phone, it is no longer possible to hide from working responsibly when negative impacts may be caused by something that you as a manager within the entertainment industries are responsible for. Organizations and managers need to minimize the unwanted impacts of anything that they do, in order to prevent negative publicity that could potentially be harmful to an organization/business or its reputation, as well as minimizing the risk to their organization of litigation because something unforeseen has occurred as a result of what they are doing.

Whilst many organizations within the entertainment industries strive to work more responsibly, there is a continual stream of headlines generated due to the exposure of unethical or irresponsible management practices and entertainment product output. Table 10.1 highlights some varied examples from the last 15 years of potentially irresponsible management or behaviour within the entertainment industries.

The entertainment industries historically have been most irresponsible and highly unethical. Child stars of the screen and stage during the 1930s such as Judy Garland and Mickey Rooney were habitually given amphetamines and barbiturates in order for them to have the stamina to meet the gruelling demands of what was expected of them. Thankfully this practice has been outlawed in the majority of the world for a long time, but there are still many contemporary examples of where irresponsible practices have occurred within the entertainment industries.

Going further back in time throughout Europe from the 16th century, boys from the age of 8 onwards were castrated so that they could be used as castrato opera singers. Castration prevented many of the effects of puberty including the voice deepening. The consequence of this was a singing voice that was able to reach the highest notes (soprano, mezzo-soprano and contralto), powered by large male lungs. In Italy alone up to 4000 boys a year were castrated, many of whom were from poor families. Castration of boys for this purpose was banned in Europe in 1870. The most famous castrato singer of his day was Farinelli, who has been described as the world's first musical superstar. Born Carlo Broschi in 1705, Farinelli's singing ability of master composer's work (including Handel) drew audiences that included France's King Louis XV and Spain's Kings Philip V and Ferdinand VI. In later life Farinelli gained a reputation for being a bitter and wicked man, most likely due to his

castration; he died in 1782 (BBC, 2006; Centro Studi Farinelli, 2012).

Even longer ago in ancient Rome, gladiators fought to the death for the amusement of the crowd, slaves were thrown to lions, and hundreds of thousands if not millions of animals were slaughtered in the very name of entertainment. The modern-day legacy of such bloody sacrificial entertainment is bullfighting, which was originally practised by Roman soldiers and over centuries has been popularized in Spain and Portugal and then exported to South and Central America. In Spain, bullfighting has been banned in the region of Catalonia, which includes the city of Barcelona. This is due in the main to the growing awareness of animal rights and disinterest in bullfighting amongst younger generations of Spaniards, and a stance by Catalonia against a tradition that is viewed as being culturally Spanish rather than Catalan (Vajda, 2012).

Spracklen (2013) noted that morals differ amongst cultures and change over time. In the UK, 200 years ago, dogfighting was commonplace; however, after the passing of the Cruelty to Animals Act (1835), which made dogfighting an illegal activity, it now only exists on a minor scale amongst criminal elements. The majority of Britons are appalled when a news story breaks about an illegal dogfighting ring being exposed in the UK, and show disdain towards other countries that allow dogfighting when stories of it break in the media.

As populations become more globally aware, certain practices of the past become less acceptable. Comedy is a form of entertainment that is reliant on spoken and visual jokes and gags; many jokes and gags are made at the expense of societal sub-groups, obvious examples include racist jokes, sexist jokes, homophobic jokes and so-called 'sick'

Table 10.1. Some contemporary examples of potentially irresponsible management or behaviour within the entertainment industries.

Year(s) this occurred	Organization(s) involved	What happened
1999	20th Century Fox	During filming for the movie *The Beach* the beach where much of the film was set on the Thai island of Koh Phi Phi was remodelled, including the cutting down of trees and removal of sand dunes. This caused much controversy and a lawsuit, which 20th Century Fox lost.
2000	Sony Pictures Entertainment	Sony's films were performing poorly, with many severely criticized by influential film critics. Sony Corporation created a fictitious film critic, David Manning, who gave numerous positive reviews for releases from Sony subsidiary Columbia Pictures. These same films generally received poor reviews amongst real critics. Suspicions led to investigations and Sony was exposed for the fraud and removed adverts featuring the 'words' of the critic. Sony was fined in the USA for this action.
2000–2011	News International	Journalists working for News International newspapers were found guilty of hacking into the voicemail of mobile phones of a number of high profile figures and crime victims. The legacy of this was the closure of the newspaper *The News of the World*, numerous arrests and the Leveson Inquiry into press conduct in the UK.
2009	Ambassador Theatre Group	The group, which owns several theatres in London, has been criticized in the media and by performers' union Equity for the conditions 'backstage' for performers. This includes a lack of toilet facilities, rat infestations and cramped dressing rooms.
2012	2Day FM	Australian DJs Michael Christian and Mel Greig made a prank phone-call to a London hospital where Kate Middleton (wife of Prince William of the British Royal family) was being treated for severe morning sickness. The DJs pretended to be Queen Elizabeth II and Prince Philip. A nurse took the call and gave out personal details about Kate. After a story about the hoax broke in the media, the nurse committed suicide. Both DJs were suspended for a period but faced no legal action.

(Continued)

Table 10.1. Continued.

Year(s) this occurred	Organization(s) involved	What happened
2012–2013	Arnoldo Mondadori Editore	Italian magazine *Chi* controversially printed unauthorized bikini photos of a pregnant Kate Middleton on two occasions, invoking legal action from Prince William and Kate.
2013	Joss Stone, Craig David, Lisa Stansfield (artists)	The three British singers have faced criticism for promoting the aims of 'Big Tobacco' by agreeing to perform at Indonesia's Java Jazz Festival, which is sponsored by Djaram, the country's third largest tobacco producer.
2013	Google	Internet firm Google has been heavily criticized by British politicians and in the media for allegedly not paying sufficient tax on its UK earnings.

jokes. In many societies these types of jokes would once have been acceptable, and their subsequent use in mainstream published and broadcast entertainment would have been considered the norm. In the UK and beyond, 40 years ago, jokes and sketches based around race were regularly broadcast on television. A very popular British prime-time sit-com in the 1970s was *Mind Your Language*, which was set at a language school where the pupils were immigrants to the UK, and was littered with jokes based around racial stereotyping. In 2012 and beyond, a sit-com of this nature would most likely be considered wholly unacceptable, racist and something that mainstream programme makers and broadcasters would not touch, for fear of criticism and alienating audiences and advertisers.

As well as certain entertainment outputs becoming less acceptable over time, others may become more acceptable. British and American television programmes now include more scenes of a sexual nature than ever before, and the proliferation of swearing and bad language is now commonplace; programmes such as Channel 4's *Shameless* or HBO's *True Blood* demonstrate this point perfectly, as both of these programmes have now broken the final swear-word taboo of the English language in mainstream entertainment with use of the 'c' word, which even now in 2013 I as the author of this section (Moss) do not feel comfortable writing in this academic text. The 'c' word will become more commonplace in entertainment, just as the 'f' word has done since the late 1980s.

In 1979, the Monty Python film *The Life of Brian* was banned in many countries including Ireland and Norway, and given 'X' certification in the UK due to its perceived blasphemous content. The bans were eventually lifted and today it is considered a classic of the comedy genre. A more recent comedy offering to court controversy is the 2006 mockumentary film by Sacha Baron Cohen entitled *Borat*, which while regarded as a cult comedy classic in many parts of the world is outright banned in the entire Arab world (apart from Lebanon) for reasons of indecency, as well as in Kazakhstan for poking fun at Kazakh society and people. Globally, what constitutes acceptable and responsible entertainment output differs greatly.

Where there is demand for material that some members of society may consider unethical or unacceptable there will always be a supply, particularly where potential profitability may outweigh losses through reputational damage. Alongside this there is also a backlash against what some critics see as 'nanny state' political correctness that subjugates freedom of thought and expression. An example where this has occurred is Sickipedia – both a website and smartphone app, which publishes user-generated jokes that are categorized by joke type, e.g. racism and sexual humour. Sickipedia is a part of the B3ta community (online publishers of user-generated content that is often highly controversial in nature), and despite containing numerous jokes that may be considered highly offensive including racist jokes and jokes about sexual abuse, it is available as a downloadable app from both the Android Marketplace and Apple App Store. A book of Sickipedia jokes entitled *The Bumper B3ta Book of Sick Jokes* has also been made available by mainstream publisher HarperCollins.

Recently and particularly in the tourism field, the term 'responsible' has been given a largely environmental and sustainable remit. However, partly due to the complexity and breadth of the entertainment industries, the concept of responsibility requires a more expansive remit than this alone, and this chapter seeks to address responsible entertainment management from several perspectives.

It should be noted that whilst this chapter will mention issues associated with responsible and particularly ethical management, it will not include detailed aspects associated with the ethical human resource management of artists and employees, which is embedded within Chapter 8.

CORPORATE SOCIAL RESPONSIBILITY

The concept of responsible behaviour by entertainment organizations is not a new one, indeed entertainment, morality and ethics have been uncomfortable partners since the first stories were told that may have caused offence to particular audience members. Every corporation causes impacts that it is responsible for, which can affect their employees, customers or wider society, as well as the environment within which the entertainment industry operates.

Entertainment organizations 'are no longer governed by shareholder value alone; increasingly, their decisions are influenced by their responsibility towards employees, customers, the environment and the society they operate in' (Büchner, 2012, p. 41). This is driven by an increasing demand from consumers for the products that they purchase to come from ethically sourced suppliers and for the organizations with whom they buy from to behave in a way that is responsible socially and environmentally, which is particularly the case amongst North American and Western European markets (Waller and Conaway, 2011). It is not just consumers who are taking an interest in how responsible organizations are being, 'analysts and rating agencies no longer just look at revenue and profit, they are also starting to examine whether a company's profits were generated in a sustainable manner; that is, applying ecologically and socially sound principles' (Büchner, 2012, p. 42). This is the ethos of corporate social responsibility (CSR), which is 'the economic, legal, ethical and discretionary (philanthropic) expectations that society has of organizations at a given point in time' (Buchholtz and Carroll, 2008, p. 40). Within newly formed organizations, CSR may not always seem a priority to management, who will be more pre-occupied with organization survival. At this time, the responsibilities an organization has are to its employees, investors and creditors. CSR initiatives take time to become embedded into an organization's ethos, as demonstrated by Fig. 10.1.

Figure 10.1 also demonstrates that as an organization matures and begins to prosper, legal responsibilities with regards to all management practices are then more likely to be embraced and incorporated, as more resources are made available to assist compliance. As an organization continues to prosper, expansion could become a consideration. This may need the backing of a variety of stakeholders, including members of the public. So at this time it is crucial that a whole range of CSR activities are being undertaken and that the organization is seen to be working ethically in order to help secure the support of those who may otherwise object or place obstacles in the way of the organization's plans. Beyond expansion, organizations may diversify their product offerings through the creation of new ventures. Alongside this a greater support

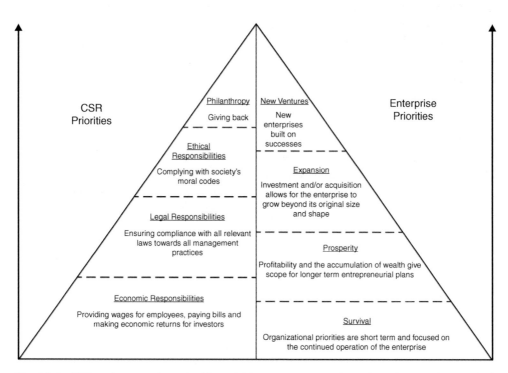

Fig. 10.1. CSR and enterprise priorities within new organizations. Based upon the original work of Carroll (1991).

for the environment and society in which the organization operates, with an emphasis upon shared value initiatives may also be integrated. This could include schemes such as programmes to help train or employ local people, or environmental programmes that are designed to make positive and sustainable changes in the areas in which the organization operates.

Organizations that embrace CSR are likely to benefit from a 'halo' response from consumers. 'A halo response can occur when perceptions of a brand's performance on one attribute are influenced by performance perceptions on another attribute' (Madden *et al.*, 2012, p. 42). The implications of this for the entertainment industries are that consumers may choose a particular entertainment product based upon an organization's image and reputation from a CSR perspective. This demonstrates not only the necessity of CSR to obtain competitive advantage but also the need for public relations and communications departments to make consumers aware of the positive CSR work that the organization is undertaking. Positive publicity about CSR helps to create stronger brands leading to increases in positive product evaluations by consumers, commitment to purchase a particular product and customer satisfaction (Hoeffler and Keller, 2002). Considering this, CSR should not only be a value of management but it should also be an integral component of an organization's marketing strategy. In terms of communicating positive CSR messages, language that is understandable and not academic in outward communications can be persuasive in influencing consumer choice (Font, 2013). Stanford (2013), using the context of a Wise Growth toolkit in responsible tourism, stated that an effective strategy for communicating initiatives that have a responsible remit should consider the following points:

- what is to be told;
- who it should be told to;
- why it should be told;
- how it should be told;
- where it should be told; and
- when it should be told.

It is essential that such communications are approached strategically so that they maximize benefits to the organization.

CSR as a concept is often criticized for being reactive rather than pro-active; however, this is entirely influenced by the way organizations approach it. A responsible organization will fully integrate CSR practices into the way that it operates, and will constantly be looking forward towards new avenues of responsibility. This does come at a cost to organizations in terms of finance, human resources, time and expertise. However, the benefits of working as a responsible organization should make these an investment that will ultimately benefit the organization.

From a responsible entertainment management perspective the following recommendations are made to organizations in order to be more responsible.

- Know the legal and moral rules of the society within which you are working. If you work within them you should be safe.
- Strive to align your management practices with recognized 'best practice' in your area of working, seek out independent certification for the positive work that you are doing.

- Know your customers and consider how they would react to your management practices if they were aware of them, and how they will react to your entertainment product output.

- If you do decide to push the boundaries of acceptability, be prepared for what may follow.

- Pre-empt anything from your management practices and entertainment output that may be deemed controversial, and be prepared to answer your critics.

- If you are judged to be in the wrong, be prepared to make the necessary changes and apologies.

- In rectifying any situation where you are considered to be in the wrong, ensure that your efforts to make amends are positively publicized.

- Do not repeat your mistakes.

Case Study: Best Bar None by Dr Alexandra J. Kenyon and Sallyann Halliday

There has been an expansion of the night-time economy in recent years. The media portrayal of the night-time economy is a 'chaotic' one, with tabloids often littered with stories of drunken behaviour in towns and cities at night, with particular reference to the UK having a 'binge-drinking' culture featuring heavily within such stories (Tierney and Hobbs, 2003).

The Best Bar None (BBN) Scheme was established in Manchester (UK) in 2003 and was set-up to facilitate and enable the licensed alcohol trade to engage quality controls, demonstrate commitment to socially responsible practices and connect with more communities and stakeholders in the 'night-time economy'. The scheme is administered nationally by the British Institute of Innkeeping (BII).

BBN encourages bars, pubs, nightclubs and other licensed alcohol retailers to sign up to a set of standards, which are designed to invoke best practice in the responsible operation of venues and particularly the retail of alcohol within venues. The scheme is completely voluntary, and after signing up, participants are assessed and given advice as to how to bring their premises up to the required BBN standard. If they do so, they are awarded Best Bar None certification. The schemes are supported at local levels by city councils and local police forces, and consequently BBN-certified premises are more likely to succeed with future licensing applications.

Best Bar None is seen as having huge potential in that it is perceived as an initiative and 'vehicle' to drive through changes within the night-time economy since it provides

Fig. 10.2. The Best Bar None logo

standards and benchmarking for all licensed venues in town and city centres. It is heralded by some local authorities as the 'bedrock' that helps many stakeholders reduce crime, alcohol-related harm, alcohol-related hospital admissions and improve the perception of town centres 'after dark'. Figure 10.2 demonstrates the Best Bar None logo, which holders of this award may display within their premises.

RESPONSIBLE SUPPLY CHAINS

Responsible entertainment does not only include entertainment at the point of audience interaction, the entire supply chain of products and services must also come under scrutiny. A supply chain incorporates all elements of input, process and output, which combined lead to product creation, processing and supply to the customer. In the entertainment industries, the sheer number of different entertainment products means that there is no one set type of supply chain; however, all will feature common elements including raw materials, finance, human resources and technology. Figure 10.3 demonstrates one possible model of a responsible supply chain that could be applicable to a range of organizations within the entertainment industries.

Figure 10.3 demonstrates that managers of entertainment organizations have a direct responsibility for responsible initiatives within their organization and that they should also have sufficient knowledge about the entities with which they do business to know that they also work in a responsible manner.

Because of the complexity of the entertainment industries and the variety in the type of products produced by the industry, it is difficult to impossible to produce one single supply chain model to represent this. Figure 10.3 is offered as one possible supply chain for tangible entertainment products such as a music CD or a book, where services and products are supplied, which are then processed and modified, and then output to the consumer market via retailers. The entertainment product producer could represent a music label or book publisher, who have immediate control over

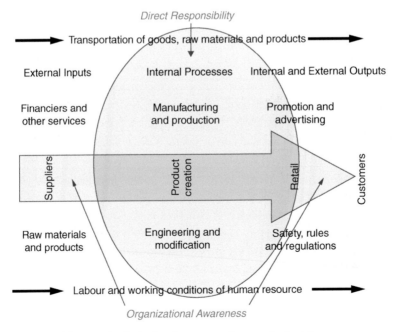

Fig. 10.3. Responsible supply chain for the entertainment industries.

the parts of the supply chain that they directly manage; however, there are also parts of the supply chain that they do not directly manage including their suppliers and some retailers. A responsible entertainment organization should also have an awareness of the organizational practices employed by the other entities along their supply chain, and whilst they may not directly manage these, should be in a position to influence them.

The more complex the product then the more complex the supply chain. As an example, a theme park purchases a wide range of both tangible and intangible products. Tangible products may include (but are not limited to) rides, props, costumes, cuddly toys, food, drink, souvenirs, fixtures, fittings, buildings, printed materials, clothing, utilities, decorating materials, tools, signage, wristbands, cleaning materials and vehicles. Intangible products may include (but are not limited to) designers, animators, technicians, legal services, financial services, insurance services, web services, security services, marketing services and employment agencies.

A truly responsibly managed theme park would ensure that all suppliers of products to them are themselves responsible in their behaviour and the way that their employees are managed, treated and paid. So, for example, if it transpired that suppliers of cuddly toys to a theme park were employing children and working them in 'sweat shop' conditions (long hours, brutal management and little pay) to create the cuddly toys, the theme park should threaten to switch supplier, thus punishing the irresponsible supplier through reduced business, unless the supplier changes the way that it operates. The same may be said of an employment agency, who may sell the services of people on their 'books' to theme parks at a vastly higher rate than what the agency pays the people. Agency staff may also be made to work under more unfavourable conditions than employees of the park itself, in aspects such as holiday entitlement and pay. A responsibly managed theme park would ensure that persons employed through agencies are treated the same as their own employees by pressuring the agency to adapt its practices.

It is perhaps a sad fact, but it is often not until exposure of irresponsible management along the supply chain is given via the media that companies take action to try and make changes along the supply chain. For organizations with a global reach this can prove to be embarrassing and taking action is often associated with counteracting negative publicity. In 2012, Apple were criticized in the media for the working conditions in Foxconn factories in China where some components of the iPhone and iPad were being made. Whilst Apple had no direct control over what is effectively a product supplier, the media still spread stories (of varying accuracy) forcing Apple to intervene. Apple commissioned an investigation by the US Fair Labor Authority (FLA), who found 'significant issues' in the factory, after which Apple requested Foxconn reduce hours, protect pay and improve staff representation. Following this, Apple Chief Executive Officer (CEO) Tim Cook visited the factory, which provided a positive publicity opportunity to counteract the previous negative press given to Apple, as allegedly working conditions were improved at Foxconn due to Apple's intervention, although subsequent news stories have put this in doubt (New York Daily News, 2013).

REGULATION OF ENTERTAINMENT INDUSTRIES

Globally, entertainment organizations are rarely entrusted to self-regulate their output and are bound by laws, rules, regulations and guidelines, which vary from country to country, around what is socially acceptable and what is not. The bodies that oversee and enforce these rules are known as regulators. It is the remit of regulators to ensure that certain standards are adhered to so as not to offend, harm or mislead audiences; ensure that management are operating in a legal and responsible manner; and to ensure that the supply chain of entertainment products is both legally and ethically sound. Where breaches of rules occur, regulators often have the power to levy punishments, including fining organizations and censoring or outright banning output, as well as forcing rule breakers to broadcast or publish apologies. Organizations, particularly in the media, may cause rule changes by pushing the boundaries of acceptability. Some examples of regulators from around the world are featured in Table 10.2.

Where breaches of rules are made, regulators will typically investigate and often take action. In the UK in 2011, Scottish comedian Frankie Boyle was censured by Ofcom, and broadcaster Channel 4 were highly criticized following an episode of Boyle's TV show *Tramadol Nights* during which he made a joke about the disabled child of a well-known British celebrity. Over 500 complaints were made to Ofcom by members of the public after the show was broadcast. Whilst Ofcom were highly critical of Channel 4 for sanctioning the joke, the regulator fell short of forcing

the television channel to broadcast an apology (BBC, 2011). In 2007, Channel 4 were forced by Ofcom to broadcast an apology on three occasions after an episode of *Celebrity Big Brother* was broadcast that featured perceived racial bullying of Indian actress Shilpa Shetty. This also resulted in the show's sponsors terminating their contract.

DARK ENTERTAINMENT

Death is a part of life, and in certain societies, particularly religious ones, it is a sacred subject that may be prohibited from discussion and certainly not under any circumstances associated with entertainment. As (globally) societies become more secular, subjects such as death that were previously taboo are becoming more open for discussion (Stone, 2013). Even in a secular society, one of the greatest responsible challenges faced by the entertainment industries is their sensitive representation of actual human tragedy, particularly death and suffering. This is principally the case where audience members may have a personal connection or resonance with something tragic that has occurred, and where commodification of these occurrences may be perceived as being ghoulish. The modern-day entertainment industry has to some extent de-sensitized audiences to death and suffering through their continual portrayal of these through the media, in particular dramatization and fiction in television, films and books. However, dark entertainment is not about fiction, and its responsible provision should consider that when tragic or dark occurrences have taken place, audience members may be genuinely

Table 10.2. A selection of entertainment regulatory bodies from around the world.

Name of regulator	Country of responsibility	Remit
Australian Communications and Media Authority (ACMA)	Australia	ACMA is an Australian governmental department that carries responsibility for broadcast media and the Internet in Australia, ensuring that codes of practice, standards and legislation are adhered to. See http://www.acma.gov.au/ for full details.
Canadian Radio-television and Telecommunications Commission (CRTC)	Canada	The CRTC regulates all Canadian broadcasting and telecommunications activities and enforces the Canadian content rules, which state that broadcasters must air a certain percentage of content that has been written, created or produced in Canada. The rules also stipulate a need for a percentage of content to be Canadian culturally in nature. See http://www.crtc.gc.ca/ for full details.
Conseil Supérieur de l'Audiovisuel (CSA)	France	The CSA regulates electronic media in France with a remit to ensure fairness of competition as well as standards and decency. It has been responsible for censorship and the closing down of broadcasting organizations accused of inciting hatred. See http://www.csa.fr/ for full details.
Federal Communications Commission (FCC)	United States of America (USA)	The FCC is a US government agency; from an entertainment perspective it has responsibility for all US electronic media and communications, and regulates fairness of competition and diversity, as well as facilitating the move to digital delivery of entertainment output. See http://www.fcc.gov/ for full details.
Kuwait Ministry of Information (KMI)	Kuwait	KMI oversee all entertainment and cultural/art output to ensure that it complies with the country's strict Sharia law. KMI regularly ban or heavily censor all audio-visual entertainment forms in Kuwait. See http://www.moi.gov.kw/ for full details.

(Continued)

Table 10.2. Continued.

Name of regulator	Country of responsibility	Remit
Office of Communications (Ofcom)	United Kingdom (UK)	Ofcom is the government-approved regulator for broadcasting, telecommunications and the postal industry in the UK. They apply rules governing decency and standards and are the body who deal with complaints from the public about output through all electronic media formats. See http://www.ofcom.org.uk/ for full details.
Press Council of India (PCI)	India	The PCI oversee all of India's print media for standards, accuracy and fairness. There are currently over 50,000 newspapers in circulation in India. India has no regulator for television, although one is planned. The government exert some control over private radio stations. See http://www.presscouncil.nic.in/ for full details.
State Administration of Radio, Film and Television (SARFT)	China	SARFT is a governmental department responsible for ensuring that all Chinese organizations involved in electronic entertainment media output comply with governmental rules and Chinese cultural standards. SARFT also research Chinese public opinion with regards to output and approves programming pre-broadcast. See http://www.chinasarft.gov.cn/ for full details.

affected by interaction with entertainment based upon that occurrence.

Dark entertainment has been happening for millennia, consider Roman gladiators fighting to the death or slaughtering animals in the name of entertainment for crowds of cheering spectators, or public executions that drew spectators from far and wide. The very notion that in this day and age dark entertainment could and should be responsible itself presents a paradox, when what is generating an audience activity is (typically) human suffering in the first place. However, dark entertainment is created to meet a demand in interest around tragic occurrences that have happened 'in the past', and not for the specific purpose of entertaining an audience by causing additional suffering or prolonging a tragic event.

As discussed in Chapter 1 of this book, there is a general misconception that entertainment is something that should be happy or have a positive resonance. The true meaning of entertainment is much deeper and involves audience captivation with something that emotionally resonates with that audience. Not all emotions are positive or happy ones, and many are the exact opposite. Dark entertainment through the provision of media products, the staging of events, or the development of facilities through the preservation and commodification of sites that have become visitor attractions due to their association with tragedy, death or suffering, is perhaps one of the most controversial and contested areas within the entertainment industries.

Dark entertainment is a part of dark leisure, which according to Rojek (2000) describes leisure choices made by individuals that go against what may be seen as traditional societal norms and that may disturb other members of society. Spracklen (2013) states that dark leisure rejects the mainstream and transgresses norms and values. Some may consider providers of, and audience participants in, dark entertainment as being deviant. Williams (2009) defined leisure activities that 'violates criminal and noncriminal moral norms' (p. 208) as deviant leisure; however, it should be noted in secular society that those society members who would consider participants in dark entertainment as deviants are in a minority (Stone, 2013).

Like all forms of industry-created entertainment, the vast majority of dark entertainment is media borne, be that through broadcast media, the Internet or print media. Dark media based upon a tragic occurrence reduces in volume and changes in focus over time. At the time of a dark occurrence, dark media is news focused, which subsides as time passes and is replaced by 'special' outputs that are dedicated to the occurrence explaining it in greater detail. Following this, documentaries are often made and memorial outputs produced. The volume of these depends on the scale of the dark occurrence and the number of people who have been affected by it. Over time, dark occurrences may be dramatized leading to outputs that may incorporate fictitious elements. An example of this in practice would be the 26 December 2004 Indian Ocean earthquake, which triggered a tsunami that had tragic effects in Indonesia, Sri Lanka, Thailand, India, the Maldives and the east coast of Africa, leading to deaths in the region of 280,000 (BBC, 2005b). In the immediate aftermath, news bulletins were filled with footage taken by tourists as well as interviews with survivors and experts. Eventually extended bulletins began to be produced and documentaries made such as *Seconds from Disaster* Season 3, Episode 13 *Asian Tsunami* and PBS NOVA's *Wave That Shook The World*. Alongside this, countless amounts of literature were produced in global newspaper and magazine pages as well as online, from a human interest, environmental and socio-political perspective. Numerous factual books about the tsunami have been published, including: *The Asian Tsunami 2004: When Disaster Struck* (2007) and *The Asian Tsunami: Aid and Reconstruction After a Disaster* (2010). In 2012, *The Impossible*, the first big-screen movie featuring a dramatized account of actual events that occurred during and after the tsunami was released, almost 8 years after the original tragedy.

Dark media needs to be accurate and factual; after the 2005 floods in New Orleans caused by Hurricane Katrina, various media outlets promoted stories about rapes, paedophilia, sniper attacks and murders, all of which proved to be false (Devine, 2005). There are also boundaries that should be considered in relation to taste and legality, particularly in relation to showing images of the dead; television channel Al-Jazeera faced heavy criticism for showing the dead bodies of British and US serviceman in Iraq in its news bulletins, something that was possibly in breach of the Geneva Convention (Kafala, 2003).

Dark entertainment is closely interlinked with dark tourism through the creation of visitor attractions or staging of events to mark or commemorate dark occurrences. Tarlow (2005) defines dark tourism as 'visitations to places where tragedies or historically noteworthy death has occurred and that continue to impact our lives'; similarly, Stone (2006, p. 146) defines dark tourism as 'the act of travel to sites associated with death, suffering and the seemingly macabre'. The relationship between dark leisure, dark entertainment and dark tourism is highlighted in Fig. 10.4.

Dark tourism involves people travelling to destinations or events specifically because of their connection with a historic

dark occurrence, for example the small town of Lockerbie in Scotland is synonymous with the bombing of PanAm Flight 103, which was flying from London Heathrow to New York John F. Kennedy Airport on 21 December 1988. The aircraft was a Boeing 747, which crashed after being bombed by terrorists, with much of the wreckage from the crash falling on Lockerbie. In total, the tragedy took the lives of 270 people, making it the worst terrorist atrocity on British soil to date. Today, dark tourists visit Lockerbie for a variety of reasons, particularly to see the town and to visit memorials, which were created as a focal point for grievers, respect payers, pilgrims and those interested by the event. The Lockerbie Air Disaster Memorial and Garden of Remembrance was created at Dryfesdale Cemetery near the town (see Fig. 10.5) and is the main memorial to the disaster; the site also now has a visitor centre. In addition to this, there is a memorial in Lockerbie Roman Catholic Church, where a plaque lists the names of all 270 victims. There is also a book of remembrance at the town's library and a second book at nearby Tundergarth Church. Lockerbie Town Hall has a stained-glass window, which depicts flags of the 21 countries whose citizens lost their lives in the disaster.

Van Maanen (2013) stated that heritage belongs to those who claim it and identify with it. This is certainly true in Lockerbie where the air disaster is a major historic event and has become a firm part of the cultural heritage of the town of Lockerbie in that it continues to shape and influence the town's present character. Considering this, Fig. 10.6 denotes dark tourism as a subset of heritage tourism, which Ryan (1991) classified as a part of cultural tourism. Figure 10.6

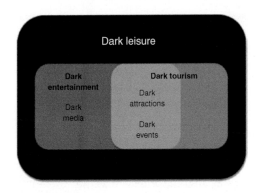

Fig. 10.4. Dark leisure, dark entertainment and dark tourism.

Fig. 10.5. The Lockerbie Air Disaster Memorial and Garden of Remembrance.

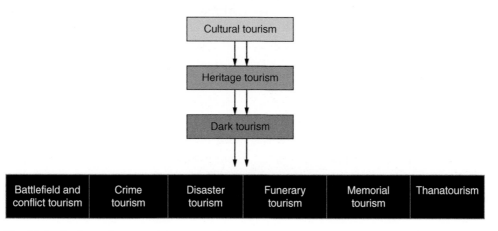

Fig. 10.6. Dark tourism typology.

also demonstrates a range of types of dark tourism, based upon the work of Lennon and Foley (2000) and Sharpley and Stone (2009), all of which may have an association with a dark historic occurrence or occurrences.

Figure 10.6 highlights the key subdivisions of dark tourism. These are explained as follows.

- Battlefield and conflict tourism: the visitation of sites associated with war, where battles or significant events may have occurred, e.g. the battlefields of Lexington and Concord, USA, where the first military engagements of the American Revolutionary War took place.
- Crime tourism: the visitation of sites that are synonymous with crime and criminality, e.g. mafia tourism in Sicily, Italy.
- Disaster tourism: the visitation of sites that have been the locations of a disaster, either natural or man-made, e.g. people visiting New Orleans after the flooding caused by Hurricane Katrina in 2005.
- Funerary tourism: this is the visitation of events and attractions relating to funerals, e.g. the funeral of Diana, Princess of Wales in London, UK, which took place on 6 September 1997, attracted over a million people along the route of the funeral cortege (BBC, 2005a).
- Memorial tourism: this is the visitation specifically to memorials or graves of those who have been the victims of tragic events, e.g. the Arnhem Oosterbeek War Cemetery, the Netherlands.
- Thanatourism: this is the visitation of places that denote or have a relationship with death, e.g. the Bodyworlds exhibition created by Gunter von Hagens.

Figure 10.7 demonstrates three dark visitor attractions: (top) the entrance to the former concentration camp known as Auschwitz 2, at Birkenau, Poland; (bottom left) war graves at the Arnhem Oosterbeek War Cemetery in the Netherlands; and (bottom right) Mdina Dungeons, Malta, where visitors may pretend to torture the human exhibits.

The creation of visitor attractions or the preservation of dark sites, such as the Auschwitz-Birkenau concentration camp in Poland, may cause disdain amongst critics who view these as being in bad taste, deviant or immoral (Stone, 2013), and preserving a terrible crime of the past. However, such facilities also serve to educate future generations about such atrocities, in the hope that they will never be repeated.

Dark tourism is not a universally liked or agreeable term, particularly amongst stakeholders of locations that are synonymous with tragic occurrences, who may view the term as being sensationalist or ghoulish. Research by Werdler (2013) noted that some attractions considered the 'dark' label as 'bad for marketing'; however, he also noted that dark tourism was a more accepted term amongst dark visitor attractions that have a 'thrill' element to them, such as the 'Dungeon' attractions operated by Merlin Entertainment. Neering (2013) stated that the Heligoland Tourism board were unhappy with the term dark tourism (Heligoland is a small German island, which during the Second World War was carpet bombed by the British and was the location of the World's largest non-nuclear explosion). It would seem that there is disagreement between academia and industry as to when it is appropriate to use the 'dark' term, but from an academic perspective the 'dark' label works well to identify the association of a leisure form with a historic tragic occurrence.

Fig. 10.7. Dark visitor attractions (see text for attraction details).

Stone (2013) noted that the length of time that has passed between a dark occurrence happening and the perceived connection that an audience has with a dark occurrence impacts upon the motivations of consumers of dark tourism; the same may be said of dark entertainment. This is demonstrated by the matrix in Fig. 10.8, which demonstrates that those who have or perceive that they have a personal connection with a dark occurrence are more likely to be grievers in the time after the occurrence has happened; however, as time passes, they and others may become pilgrims who visit sites or attend events in respect of, and memorial to, those who have been victims of a dark occurrence. Those with less of a personal connection to a dark occurrence may be attracted to dark entertainment through an interest or fascination with what has occurred, and as time passes and a dark occurrence becomes more historic, they and others may wish to learn more about it, why it happened, how it happened, where it happened, whom it happened to and what the longer term impacts of the dark occurrence

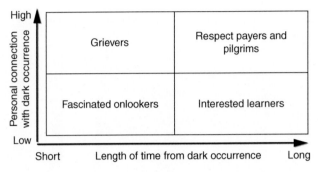

Fig. 10.8. Motivation matrix of consumers of dark entertainment.

have been. In order to help people understand this, over time dark occurrences may be commodified into dark entertainment.

Figure 10.8 can be contextualized using the examples of serial killers 'Jack the Ripper' and Peter Sutcliffe (who became branded through the media as the 'Yorkshire Ripper'). Both were/ are notorious serial killers who operated in the UK and targeted women. Jack the Ripper was active in the late 19th century, and the Yorkshire Ripper was active from 1975 to 1980. Jack the Ripper has become something of a legend and there is a great demand for commodified entertainment products around the crimes he committed, and where there is demand, there is supply of products. These include websites such as the JTR Forums (http://www.jtrforums.com, which has the sensationalist tag line 'THE place to be for all things Ripper'), to 'Ripper Tours' (guided tours around the Whitechapel area of East London), to visit sites that are synonymous with the Jack the Ripper murders.

The crimes of the Yorkshire Ripper are still in many people's minds. Peter Sutcliffe is still alive, and so are many people who are family members or friends of Sutcliffe's victims. As these crimes were committed more recently, and with a greater level of perceived connection with them, perhaps through not wanting to appear ghoulish, there is a lesser demand for entertainment products relating to them. To match this, there has been less inclination to commodify the Yorkshire Ripper crimes into entertainment products such as guided tours of sites relating to murders by the Yorkshire Ripper. Stone (2006, p. 147) states that amongst western society there is an 'apparent contemporary fascination with death, real or fictional, media inspired or otherwise'. It is likely that at some point in the future, possibly after the death of Peter Sutcliffe, something which itself will be well publicized, a renewed interest in his crimes may cause demand to create a supply of new audience attracting Yorkshire Ripper products.

Responsible operation of dark attractions should consider the entire spectrum of visitors to them, and not only ensure that all visitors are catered for but that visitors are educated as to what constitutes appropriate behaviour at such sites. Auschwitz-Birkenau concentration camp attracts visitors from a wide variety of locations and cultures. It has been a personal observation of the author of this section (Moss) on a visit to Auschwitz-Birkenau in 2013, that a group of teenagers were singing and laughing as they walked amongst other visitors – is this appropriate behaviour at a site where an estimated 1.1 million people were killed?

SUSTAINABLE EVENT MANAGEMENT

So far this chapter has approached responsible entertainment management from a societal perspective. This section will add to this, by also exploring issues relating to the physical environment and sustainability, using the context of entertainment events. Since the latter half of the 20th century, various news stories and headlines have helped raise awareness of environmental issues that could impact upon the health of our planet. Issues include (but are not limited to): the burning of the Amazon rainforests, which affects the natural balance of gases in the atmosphere; chlorofluoro-carbonates (CFCs) eroding the ozone layer; the dangers associated with radiation leakage caused by nuclear power; the draining of natural resources including fuels, metals and water; and the burning of fossil fuels, which has been blamed for contributing to acid rain, smog, health problems in people and increased carbon emissions, which in the 2000s have largely been seen as the cause of rising global temperatures, the melting of the polar ice-caps and raised sea levels causing flooding.

Near-apocalyptic news stories, which are designed to capture people's attention, are associated with these issues and have helped to nurture an increasing sense of responsibility towards the health of the natural environment, particularly in 'Western' industrialized nations. Whilst these global issues go way beyond the entertainment industries, a raised environmental awareness means that organizations today in all industries often justify their ways of working from an environmental perspective, particularly where there is a perception (rightly or wrongly) that industry may be harming the environment.

'Green' as both a concept and buzzword for more environmentally friendly ways of working has been used by responsible practitioners, and abused by public relations departments and sales people, since the 1980s. So-called 'green-wash' is often employed as a tactic to mask the true environmental costs of industry. Over the last 50 years, the large-scale entertainment event industry has flourished and changed dramatically. One of the changes is the move by event organizers to incorporate green/sustainable strategies into their event management plans up to the point that some events are labelled as being 'green' or 'sustainable' events.

The Sydney Olympics in 2000 for example were described as the greenest or most sustainable Games ever (Campbell, 2001). For the planning of the London 2012 Olympics, the host city of London embedded sustainability in its planning right from the beginning. Sustainability embedded into event planning is becoming the norm for entertainment events. In the future, it can be expected that events will 'increasingly be evaluated by their reference to the principles of sustainable development' (Getz, 2004, p. 417).

The Convention Industry Council (2004, p. 3) defines a green event as incorporating 'environmental considerations to minimize its negative impact on the environment'. This definition has a clear focus on the natural environment. Definitions of sustainable event management are more inclusive. The definition of sustainable events should incorporate ideas beyond green and environmental objectives alone and include both social and economic sustainability. Sustainable event management (SEM) is the process of designing and organizing an event following sustainable development principles in order to achieve strategic goals that serve the economic, environmental and social interests of organizers, delegates and host communities (Bigwood and Luehrs, 2010).

'Green meetings' are often held as part of the planning process behind organizing events, 'green meetings involve looking at decisions you already make in a green light' (Green Meeting Industry Council, 2010, p. 1). Green meetings are not about additional planning but about different planning, focusing on green solutions – these may sometimes come at additional costs; however, in the long term these should be outweighed by increased environmental and economic efficiency. The UN Climate Conference COP15 in 2009 was the first UN event to achieve CS8901 certification of its management system and made €562,000 (more than US$700,000) savings from sustainability measures (COP15, 2010). The 2010 Business for Sustainability Conference in New York saved US$60,540 by eliminating bottled water and replacing it with water pitchers (Garner, 2011).

Recycling activities in many particularly large-scale entertainment events such as music festivals are today so normal that attendees will often comply without considering it burdensome; additionally the offer of organic local food options can add to the authentic feeling of an event as well as satisfying the increasing demand for healthy dietary options. Overall, it can therefore be argued that green events have a number of economic and environmental advantages. It is therefore worth implementing green and sustainable objectives into event planning.

The Green Meeting Industry Council (2012) outlines a range of tips for making events more sustainable, including:

- developing and writing an environmental statement or policy that can be shared with suppliers and customers;

- using paperless technology, such as websites, electronic registration/ticketing and confirmation, and web-based advertising;

- publishing all printed materials double-sided on recycled paper using vegetable-based inks;

- select host locations that minimize the distance that attendees have to travel;

- using venues that reuse, and provide recycling facilities for, glass, plastic, paper and metal;

- make sure that lights and air conditioning are turned off when rooms are not in use;

- demanding that caterers use bulk dispensers for sugar, salt, pepper, cream and other condiments;

- including 'green' eating options, such as vegetarian meals cooked with local, seasonal produce; and

- making the success of your sustainable efforts public to attendees and the media.

From the above it becomes clear that hosting a green/sustainable event involves all entities along the supply chain of an event, which should comply with international sustainable events standards. These provide a wealth of ideas with regards to sustainable event management systems and indicators of best practice. BS8901 was developed by the United Kingdom National Standards Body (UKNSB) as a voluntary standard for a sustainable management system for events. It is possible to self-certify the standard or to be certified as BS8901 standard compliant, which in an era of environmental concern and awareness can also be advantageous in event promotion. Other sustainable event standards include:

- ISO20121 – this standard was created alongside the 2012 Olympics in London and takes a management systems approach requiring identification of key sustainability issues like venue selection, operating procedures, supply chain management, procurement, communications and transport (ISO, 2010).

• GRI G3 Sustainability Reporting Framework – this reporting framework is intended to be adopted by event organizers for sustainability evaluation and reporting, and includes aspects of environmental social governance reporting, triple bottom-line reporting and corporate social responsibility reporting.

In very general terms, entertainment event planners whose remit is to make their events more sustainable have two broad areas in which to concentrate their efforts. These are: areas under direct management control such as contracts, menus, suppliers, technology and site selection; and those aspects where management can influence and change behaviour such as the education of suppliers and attendees (Henderson, 2008).

This has to be kept in mind when a sustainable or green event strategy is developed. The approach should be based on a vision that is shared by the event team. This needs visionary leaders who understand the process of sustainability with its long-term results and the commitment to invest financial resources and time into training, coaching and research to create a sustainability culture for the event. Overall, there are five key strategic steps to producing and managing sustainable events:

1. Identification of macro-environmental STEEPLE (Social, Technological, Economic, Environmental, Political, Legal, Ethical) factors that may influence the event.
2. Definition of the areas that should be included within the sustainable management system for the event.

3. The creation of measureable, specific, realistic and time-based short-term (less than a year) and long-term (3 to 5 years) objectives and targets as well as key performance indicators (using sustainable event standards) that can be monitored.
4. Determination of priorities upon which resources can be used to achieve the best return on investment.
5. Development and integration of a short policy document (usually no more than two pages), which includes the vision, purpose, principles and objectives of the event. This should be communicated to stakeholders and needs to underline the commitment to constant improvement and learning (Bigwood and Luehrs, 2010).

There are a number of green checklists available that can be used to help shape event sustainability policies, some examples and the areas they are concerned with are contained in Table 10.3.

Whilst carbon emissions and carbon footprints are currently one of the most widely publicized environmental issues, there is an increasing awareness of depleting global freshwater supplies and the 'water footprint' that events may have. The case study overleaf highlights some of The Falls Music & Arts Festival's (TFMAF's) strategies in relation to this, but the responsible event manager of the next decade will need to become more aware of how to reduce their organization's water footprint. According to Hoekstra *et al.* (2011, p. 46) 'The water footprint of a product is defined as the total volume of fresh water that is used directly or indirectly to produce the product. It is estimated by considering water consumption and pollution in all steps of the production chain'.

According to the Water Footprint Network (2008), the production of 1 kg of beef

Table 10.3. Event sustainability checklists.

Source of checklist	Categories
University of Calgary Green Event checklist	Communication and promotion, food and beverage, waste disposal, transportation and energy conservation.
Business Events Australia Key Facts green check-list	Travel selection, venue selection, accommodation, power and water supply, food and beverages, printed material and information, waste reduction and recycling.
DEFRA Sustainable Events Guide	Venue, catering, preparation, social well-being, raising awareness, evaluation, transport.
Musgrave and Raj (2009)	Organization structure, design for duality, avoidance, engagement, legacy, longevity, incentives, strategic management, education and location.
Wall and Behr (2010)	Economic viability/profitability for all stakeholders, guarantee of health and security of all stakeholders, sustainable supply chain management, sustainable resource usage, reduction of emissions, protection of the natural and social environment, satisfaction of stakeholder demands, sustainable development of local communities, distribution and education of stakeholders.

Case Study: The Falls Music & Art Festival

The Falls Music & Art Festival (TFMAF) is a boutique Music and Arts Festival based on European-style events held in environmentally sensitive locations. It is simultaneously held in Lorne, Victoria, Australia and Marion Bay, Tasmania, Australia. Its history goes back to 1993 when then 22-year old Simon Daly developed the music festival in a remote Australian community from a 'campfire idea' (TFMAF, 2012a). The first event was held in Lorne featuring local bands. It exceeded the expected visitor numbers of 5000 when 11,000 turned up. In 2003, demand was outstripping supply and a new venue was added, Marion Bay in Tasmania. In 2012, both events were running at maximum capacity with 16,000 visitors at each (The West Australian, 2012). The organizer stated 'Falls has been recognized internationally as a pioneer in environmental and sustainable initiatives' as 'it makes the world a better place' (TFMAF, 2012b).

In 2010/11 TFMAF undertook a number of responsible management initiatives to enhance its green credentials (TFMAF, 2011). These included:

- undertaking an environmental risk assessment in cooperation with sustainability experts to assess the potential environmental impact of the event;
- appointing a sustainability officer to consider the financial, environmental and social impacts of running the event alongside the site manager;

(Continued)

Case Study. Continued.

- creating a 'Green Team' that was responsible for waste management, e.g. removing general waste bags and recycling bags, and ensuring that there were sufficient waste facilities and regular collections;
- providing written information on environmental strategies to staff;
- measuring the carbon footprint and the management of overall carbon emissions. This incorporated the offsetting of greenhouse gas emission (125.4 tons in 2010) by Climate Friendly, a public transport system connecting the event sites with local townships and campgrounds, and the encouraging of carpooling facilitated by an external online service partner (CoolPoolTas);
- implementing the use of water meters to measure water consumption;
- collecting and storing rainwater all year round to run the patron's showers;
- managing grey water produced on-site, e.g. using environmentally friendly soap dispensers, and water- and chemical-free composting toilets, which produced high grade fertilizer;
- producing an action plan and a litter management policy to make sure that all waste was carefully sorted before it was processed. This was done in a variety of ways such as the distribution of coloured bags to all patrons (general waste and recyclables), appropriate waste stations at various locations, the management of all waste collected in colour-coded bins on-site by the Green Team and the sorting of waste at the so-called skip ramp before being sent off. Other measurements included the treatment of organic waste in worm farms on-site, and the education of staff and patrons by screening green messages on 'Falls TV' to modify their behaviour towards following more environmentally friendly practices with regards to waste;
- maintaining and integrating the events' strict environmental practices into the running of the event management office all year round, e.g. 20% of electricity used is now from renewable resources and paper is sourced from renewable resources;
- creating green policies for on-site traders, which include a list of conditions with strict basic environmental practices that have to be followed;
- implementing the Falls Green Trader award, which goes annually to the most environmentally friendly market stall/caterer and promotes the winning trader during the event;
- producing tree-free tickets using soy inks as well as planting a tree for every ticket sold through Greentix that also includes an option of a carbon offset ticket (+AUS$3.50, calculated by Climate Friendly);
- committing to utilizing local trades and services wherever possible;
- introducing regulations that mean permanent structures on site must have a conditional percentage of recycled materials. Additionally, the damage of on-site temporary

(Continued)

> **Case Study.** Continued.
>
> structures, flooring, general production, local biodiversity and ecology is monitored and restorative measures are taken if damage occurs;
>
> - committing to the community and disadvantaged groups who are seen as an integral part of TFMAF. One Australian dollar of every ticket is donated towards projects in the local communities allocated via an application and community voting process; and
> - providing AUS$54,000 in corporate donations within Tasmania in 2010, which included AUS$31,500 to the Wilderness Society and AUS$6,000 to the Migrant Resource Centre.
>
> The provision of a green responsible management strategy for the Falls Festival has helped it to achieve continued growth and success along with much needed support from stakeholders within the community in which the festival operates.

requires 15,400 l of water, which compared with 1 kg of rice, which requires 2500 l of water, makes the inclusion of beef on the menu of green events of the future a potentially less attractive option. Sustainable event managers will additionally need to consider the water footprint of consumers (attendees), which is defined as 'the total volume of freshwater consumed and polluted for the production of the goods and services used by the consumer' (Hoekstra *et al.*, 2011, p. 52). Water footprints can be expressed in several ways, with the most common being cubic metre per tonne, litres per kilogram and cubic metre per dollar spent. More information on water footprints can be found at http://www.waterfootprint.org.

SUMMARY

Responsible entertainment management relates to the management practices of an organization being beneficial: economically for investors, suppliers and employees; socially for the community in which the organization operates, and its consumers; and environmentally by reducing negative damaging impacts to the environment in which an organization operates. Put simply, responsible entertainment management is designed to protect people and environments from harm by adhering to recognized best practice management principles and is an increasingly integrated component of organizational strategies.

SEMINAR ACTIVITIES

1. Why should organizations care about being responsible?
2. What benefits does integrating CSR into standard management practices bring to an organization?
3. What components might go into the supply chain of a theatre? Using Fig. 10.3 as a template, create your own diagram of a supply chain using the example of a theatre with which you are familiar.
4. What strategies could you suggest to the operators of dark visitor attractions to sensitively educate their customers as to how to behave whilst at the attraction?

5. Consider a music and/or arts festival with which you are familiar. Create a SWOT analysis of the green initiatives that it currently undertakes, highlighting good practice as *strengths*, bad practice as *weaknesses*, things it could do that it currently does not (and things that it could do better) as *opportunities*, and factors that may work against the festival working greener in the future as *threats*.

REFERENCES

Bigwood, G. and Luehrs, M. (2010) The Copenhagen Sustainable Meetings Protocol. Sharing best practice and leadership strategies. Available at: http://www.visitdenmark.com/international/en-gb/menu/mice/news/csmp/csmp.htm (accessed 10 January 2012).

British Broadcasting Corporation (BBC) (2005a) 1997: Diana's funeral watched by millions. Available at: http://news.bbc.co.uk/onthisday/hi/dates/stories/september/6/newsid_2502000/2502307.stm (accessed 1 July 2012).

British Broadcasting Corporation (BBC) (2005b) Indonesia quake toll jumps again. Available at: http://news.bbc.co.uk/1/hi/world/asia-pacific/4204385.stm (accessed 1 June 2013).

British Broadcasting Corporation (BBC) (2006) Castrato superstar disinterred. Available at: http://news.bbc.co.uk/1/hi/world/europe/5171892.stm (accessed 10 December 2011).

British Broadcasting Corporation (BBC) (2011) Frankie Boyle's Katie Price jokes censured. Available at: http://www.bbc.co.uk/news/entertainment-arts-12957309 (accessed 5 June 2012).

Buchholtz, A.K. and Carroll, A.B. (2008) *Business and Society: Ethics and Stakeholder Management*, 7th edn. Southwestern Cengage Learning, Mason, Ohio.

Büchner, L.M. (2012) Corporate social responsibility and sustainability from a global, European and corporate perspective. *Eurolimes* 13, 41–55.

Campbell, N. (2001) *Case Study: Integrating ESD – The Environmental Legacy of Sydney Olympic Park*. The Environmental Symposium, Old Parliament House, Canberra, 14 September 2001.

Carroll, A. (1991) The pyramid of corporate social responsibility. *Business Horizons*, July–August, 39–44.

Centro Studi Farinelli (2012) Centro Studi Farinelli. Available at: http://www.comune.bologna.it/iperbole/farinelli/inglese/index.htm (accessed 10 December 2011).

Convention Industry Council (2004) Green meetings report. Available at: http://www.convention-industry.org/StandardsPractices/GreenMeetingTaskForceReport.aspx (accessed 12 January 2012).

COP15 (2010) COP15: Entry for Imex Green Event Award 2010. Available at: http://www.imex-frankfurt.com/envaward.html (accessed 12 January 2012).

Devine, M. (2005) New Orleans fights on after low blows. Available at: http://www.smh.com.au/news/opinion/new-orleans-fights-on/2005/10/05/1128191784372.html (accessed 1 June 2013).

Font, X. (2013) *Responsible tourism communications for businesses to maximise economic benefits*. Tourism's contribution to communities and their landscapes - the UK experience. Docklands Academy, London, 6 June 2013.

Garner, C. (2011) Event Sustainability Report: 2010 Business for Social Responsibility (BSR) Conference. Available at: http://www.meetgreen.com/resources/casestudies (accessed 12 January 2012).

Getz, D. (2004) Geographic perspectives on event tourism. In: Lew, A.A., Hall, C.M. and Williams, A.M. (2004) *A Companion to Tourism*. Blackwell Publishing, Malden, UK, pp. 410–422.

Green Meeting Industry Council (2010) Myths & reality about green meetings. Available at: http://www.gmicglobal.org/resource/collection/57E31E51-1B17-413D-A3FF-BDC790A6ADD1/Myths.pdf (accessed 12 January 2012).

Green Meeting Industry Council (2012) 10 easy tips for making your event more sustainable. Available at: http://www.gmicglobal.org/?page=BestPractices (accessed 10 January 2012).

Henderson, E. (2008) The basics of green meetings. Available at: http://www.mpiweb.org/Libraries/Research_and_Reports/The_Basics_of_Green_Meetings_April_08.pdf (accessed 12 January 2012).

Hoeffler, S. and Keller, K.L. (2002) Building brand equity through corporate social marketing. *Journal of Public Policy and Marketing* 21(Spring), 78–79.

Hoekstra, A.Y., Chapagain, A.K., Aldaya, M.M. and Mekonnen, M.M. (2011) The water footprint assessment manual. Setting the global standard. Available at: http://www.waterfootprint.org/downloads/TheWaterFootprintAssessmentManual.pdf (accessed 11 June 2013).

International Organization for Standardization (ISO) (2010) ISO to develop sustainable events standard in run-up to 2012 Olympics. Available at: http://www.iso.org/iso/pressrelease?refid=Ref1281 (accessed 11 January 2012).

Kafala, T. (2003) Al-Jazeera: News channel in the news. Available at: http://news.bbc.co.uk/1/hi/world/middle_east/2893689.stm (accessed 1 June 2013).

Lennon, J. and Foley, N. (2000) *Dark tourism*. Cengage Learning EMEA, Andover, UK.

Madden, T.J., Roth, M.S. and Dillon, W.R. (2012) Global product quality and corporate social responsibility perceptions: A cross-national study of halo effects. *Journal of International Marketing* 20(1), 42–57.

Musgrave, J. and Raj, R. (2009) Introduction to a conceptual framework for sustainable events. In: Musgrave, J. and Raj, R. (eds) (2009) *Event Management and Sustainability*. CAB International, Wallingford, UK, pp. 1–12.

Neering, A. (2013) *Current dark tourism research in Germany*. The iDTR International Dark Tourism Symposium 2013. InHolland University of Applied Science, Diemen, Amsterdam, 21 May 2013.

New York Daily News (2013) Apple's Foxconn factory conditions improving but employees still working more hours than China's legal limit: labor group. Available at: http://www.nydailynews.com/news/world/labor-group-apple-foxconn-factory-conditions-improving-article-1.1346431 (accessed 4 June 2013).

Rojek, C. (2000) *Leisure and Culture*. Sage, London.

Ryan, C. (1991) *Recreational Tourism: A Social Science Perspective*. Routledge, London.

Sharpley, R. and Stone, P.R. (2009) *The Darker Side of Travel. The Theory and Practice of Dark Tourism*. Channel View Publications, Bristol, UK.

Spracklen, K. (2013) *Leisure, Sports & Society*. Palgrave-Macmillan, Basingstoke, UK.

Stanford, D. (2013) *Wise Growth communications toolkit for destinations*. Tourism's contribution to communities and their landscapes - the UK experience. Docklands Academy, London, 6 June 2013.

Stone, P.R. (2006) A dark tourism spectrum: Towards a typology of death and macabre related tourist sites, attractions and exhibitions. *Tourism* 54(2), 145–160.

Stone, P.R. (2013) *Deviance, dark tourism & 'dark leisure': (Re)configuring morality in contemporary society*. The iDTR International Dark Tourism Symposium 2013. InHolland University of Applied Science, Diemen, Amsterdam, 21 May 2013.

Tarlow, P.E. (2005) Dark tourism: The appealing 'dark side' of tourism and more. In: Novelli, M. (ed.) *Niche Tourism – Contemporary Issues, Trends and Cases*. Butterworth-Heinemann, Oxford, UK, pp. 45–78.

The Falls Music & Art Festival (TFMAF) (2011) 2010 Falls Festival sustainability report. Available at: http://2011.fallsfestival.com.au/wp-content/uploads/2011/07/Falls_Sustainabilty_web.pdf (accessed 12 December 2011).

The Falls Music & Arts Festival (TFMAF) (2012a) History. Available at: http://2011.fallsfestival.com.au/the-falls-experience/history (accessed 21 December 2011).

The Falls Music & Art Festival (TFMAF) (2012b) Sustainability. Available at: http://2011.fallsfestival.com.au/sustainability (accessed 10 December 2011).

The West Australian (2012) Tasmania could lose Falls festival. Available at: http://au.news.yahoo.com/thewest/entertainment/a/-/entertainment/12483074/tasmania-could-lose-falls-festival (accessed 27 February 2012).

Tierney, J. and Hobbs, D. (2003) Alcohol-related crime and disorder data: Guidance for local partnerships. Available at: http://www.popcenter.org/problems/assaultsinbars/PDFs/Tierney&Hobbs_2003.pdf (accessed 11 June 2013).

Vajda, D. (2012) What's happened to Catalonia's bullrings after the bullfighting ban? Available at: http://www.guardian.co.uk/travel/2012/nov/23/catalonia-barcelona-bullrings-bullfighting-ban (accessed 4 June 2013).

Van Maanen, E. (2013) *What do you do with a World Heritage site that nobody wants?* The iDTR International Dark Tourism Symposium 2013. InHolland University of Applied Science, Diemen, Amsterdam, 21 May 2013.

Wall, A. and Behr, F. (2010) *Ein Ansatz zur Messung der Nachhaltigkeit von Events. Kernziele eines Nachhaltigkeitsmanagement von Events und Indikatoren zur Messung der Nachhaltigkeit.* Centre for Sustainability Management (CSM) e. V., Lüneburg, Germany.

Waller, R.L. and Conaway, R.C. (2011) Framing and counter framing the issue of corporate social responsibility: The communication strategies of nikebiz.com. *Journal of Business Communication* 48(1), 83–106.

Water Footprint Network (2008) Water footprint. Available at: http://www.waterfootprint.org (accessed 11 June 2013).

Werdler, K. (2013) *InHolland dark tourism research.* The iDTR International Dark Tourism Symposium 2013. InHolland University of Applied Science, Diemen, Amsterdam, 21 May 2013.

Williams, D.J. (2009) Deviant leisure: Rethinking 'The Good, the Bad, and the Ugly'. *Leisure Sciences* 31, 207–213.

chapter 11

Enterprise, Creativity and Small Business

Volker Rundshagen, Guido Sommer and Stuart Moss

LEARNING OBJECTIVES

After reading this chapter you should be able to:

- understand the meaning of entrepreneurship from a variety of contexts;
- appreciate the motivations of entrepreneurs;
- know the key components of a business plan;
- know where entrepreneurs seek finance to help carry their plans forward; and
- appreciate how best-practice management techniques have contributed to the success of entrepreneurs at Jever Skihalle Neuss.

Mark Twain once said 'the man with a new idea is a crank until the idea succeeds'. Twain's philosophy fits very well to the development of a business idea, where commonly new ideas are regarded as nonsense. Business is embroiled with risk, there are never guarantees that any

idea will succeed, and indeed the majority of new business ventures do fail. A business idea can be defined as 'an initiating thought, which serves as the starting point for founding an enterprise' (Volkmann *et al.*, 2010, p. 90). Foresight, knowledge and research all play a significant part in entrepreneurial success. The challenge in the entertainment industries is to develop an original idea that will either improve a product or service that already exists, or create a new product or service for which there will be consumer demand.

In the entertainment industries, many products are experiential and therefore intangible, such as club nights, concerts or visitor attraction experiences. Tangible products tend to be ancillary products such as guides, souvenirs, food and clothing. The exception to this is with traditional media-based entertainment such as books, magazines, vinyl records and DVDs. A product idea becomes a viable business idea when a sustainable market can be identified that is willing to pay for the benefits that the product provides. Good product ideas are characterized by their scalability, so that sales revenue outweighs total product costs, which leads to increased profitability. A service is an intangible product, but in terms of scalability this may provide a greater economic challenge to businesses, as service innovations are more likely to come with greater costs in terms of staffing and training.

It is typical in the entertainment industry for new innovative concepts to emerge, where creative thinkers combine their own products with services and thereby generate new experiences for customers. For example, a new theme park product, such as a ride or attraction, combined with an additional queuing experience helps to bundle together a variety of products and services; this could be queue entertainers or themed surroundings. At Disney's Hollywood Studios in Florida, several rides have been bundled with extra added-value services, which increases the overall cost of the ride. The 'Twilight Zone Tower of Terror', which when opened in 1997 was one of the first major and high profile 'vertical drop' rides in the world, uses technology developed specifically for Disney to take riders in a car that could move horizontally as well as vertically. The ride is themed around an old hotel building (see Fig. 11.1) and has been bundled with a pre-ride experience, which includes the playing of 1930s jazz music and a themed snaking queuing area, which takes riders through a mock-up of hotel gardens and a lobby. This helps to build anticipation and extends the experience of the attraction beyond the ride itself.

Fig. 11.1. The exterior of the Twilight Zone Tower of Terror at Disney's Hollywood Studios.

Along the way, costumed cast members interact with the audience to help build anticipation and excitement and to take people's minds away from the boredom of queuing. Riders are taken to the hotel's library, which as well as books includes Twilight Zone memorabilia and a television featuring footage of Twilight Zone creator Rod Serling. In this example, Disney has invested extra resources into extending the attraction beyond the ride itself. There is little doubt that the ride experience is the core product of this attraction, but additionally an enhanced queuing experience beyond this contributes to the success of the ride. The queuing experience comprises a bundled set of products and services that include theming, maintenance, décor, signage and cast member interaction/acting, all of which come at an additional expense but all of which help to generate positive reviews for the ride and the park.

The aforementioned Disney example demonstrates big-business innovation, which comes with the support of significant financial backing; in such a large organization this creative innovation is referred to as intrapreneurship, as the entrepreneurial activity has taken place within a larger organization that has fostered and nurtured the entrepreneurial spirit and ensuing activities.

The majority of entrepreneurial business ideas and activities within the entertainment industries have much smaller and humbler origins, and are predominantly small- to medium-sized enterprises (SMEs) in which individual creativity is the driver of entrepreneurship. It should be noted that the word entrepreneurship means more than business entrepreneurship. An entrepreneur is anybody who is an innovator that uses new ideas to bring a benefit. In business terms the benefit is usually financial, and many business texts are skewed towards this definition. Beyond business, benefits of innovative ideas may be societal, such as a new museum leading to improvements in education, or environmental, such as decreased distribution through printed media formats becoming e-formats leading to a lower carbon footprint. The point to take from this is that entrepreneurs have ideas, and the careful planning and project management of developing these ideas creates benefits. In the entertainment industries and the wider cultural industries, increased levels of competition combined with reductions in public funding often dictate the agenda for entrepreneurial ideas, with the bottom line being financial (Bragg and Bragg, 2005; Hougaard, 2005).

SOCIO-CULTURAL INFLUENCES UPON ENTREPRENEURSHIP

Levels of entrepreneurialism vary greatly in different societies, and there are numerous (particularly macro-environmental) factors that influence this. The so-called American dream is embodied by the success of the late US entertainment entrepreneurs Walt Disney and Steve Jobs, who both began building their now legendary empires from very humble beginnings. An aspirational culture of self-made individualism is reflected in a comparatively high business start-up rate (compared to many other parts of the Western world), and a positive attitude towards entrepreneurs and business characterizes US society (Klandt and Brüning, 2002). In the USA, an encouraging socio-cultural approach towards business start-up has led to an autonomous economic sector, with little reliance on the state for support. This has seemingly facilitated individual entrepreneurialism. The perceived odds of starting a new small business successfully tend to remain comparatively higher in the USA than in other countries. New ventures are considered providers of innovation and employment; in light of the most recent economic downturn, policy makers and business executives are paying greater attention to entrepreneurship and new ventures as job creation catalysts (Kelley *et al.*, 2012).

In Europe, and particularly Germany, there is a mentality rooted more in reliance on the state (Klandt and Brüning, 2002) and there tends to be a more risk-averse behaviour in business or investment contexts, with a real stigma associated with business failure. This is despite Germany's strong economic position as an industrial nation and an exporter of, in particular, engineering products. In a German survey, 50% of respondents indicated that potential failure prevented them from considering starting up a business, which is one of the highest proportions of all industrialized countries (Brixy *et al.*, 2012). This may in part be down to societal 'punishments' such as reduced creditworthiness or a ban from managerial positions in the future. In the UK, the respective percentage of British respondents in a similar survey was 36%, which was the lowest among European nations (Hart and Levie, 2010), indicating potentially higher levels of entrepreneurialism than in other parts of Europe. In the arts and entertainment industries this is self-evident, where innovation by British cultural and creative entrepreneurs has influenced fashionability and trends in particularly music and 'youth' cultures globally since the 1960s.

ENTREPRENEURIAL MOTIVATION

Put simply, motivation is the will to act. It is the force that drives us throughout our lives to achieve goals and accomplishments. Motivation can be intrinsic in that it is something driven by a personal interest or enjoyment, and it can also be extrinsic in that it is driven by something externally such as reward (often but not just financial), praise or promotion. Bridge *et al.* (2003) recognize the need amongst entrepreneurs for achievement, something which is a key driver for entrepreneurial individuals.

Economist and theorist Joseph Schumpeter wrote extensively on the motivational theories of entrepreneurs, coining the term 'Unternehmergeist', which is German for 'entrepreneurial spirit'. Schumpeter (1934) theorized entrepreneurial motivations at various levels, including those that are:

- centred around creating wealth: 'the dream and the will to found a private kingdom, usually, though not necessarily, also a dynasty' (p. 93);
- concerned with social standing and superiority: 'the will to conquer: the impulse to fight, to prove oneself superior to others, to succeed for the sake, not of the fruits of success, but of success itself' (p. 93); and
- engaged in for the pleasure of self-expression: 'the joy of creating, of getting things done, or simply of exercising one's energy and ingenuity' (p. 93).

Schumpeter considered entrepreneurs as carriers and facilitators of innovation and change. He is also responsible for coining the term 'creative destruction': a term used to demonstrate how innovation can lead to new and improved design, rendering older designs obsolete in a continual cycle, something which is easily demonstrated by the rise and fall of numerous audio-visual media formats ultimately to be replaced by media-less digital electronic formats. This clearly demonstrates how creativity, invention and innovation all feed into the entrepreneurial process.

Particularly in the arts there are numerous entrepreneurs who take intrinsic pleasure from self-expression and who are concerned with either not-for-profit endeavours or who gain satisfaction through means that may not necessarily be financial. The appreciation that consumers of their work may demonstrate, or particularly in the case of the arts, discussion and controversy that might arise through audience reaction to their work, can help 'feed' the motivations of creative people. There does seem to be a tipping point between the financial and non-financial motivations of entrepreneurs; it is an old adage that 'everybody has their price', and this notion can also be witnessed throughout the entertainment industries. A specific example of this in practice is with YouTube and Google AdSense, which financially rewards YouTube video uploaders via pay-per-click adverts on YouTube videos. Where once uploading a video may have been for the pleasure of sharing, now it may be for financial reward (Moss, 2011).

TIMMONS THEORY

Timmons theory is based upon a model of entrepreneurship that considers opportunities, teams and resources as the three critical factors available to an entrepreneur and holds that success depends on the ability of the entrepreneur to balance these critical factors (Moises, 2012).

Successful entrepreneurial ventures are shaped by being:

- opportunity-driven;
- creative;
- resource parsimonious;
- lead by an entrepreneur or an entrepreneurial team;
- integrated and holistic with organizational objectives; and
- sustainable for environment, community and society.

The above forces can be assessed, influenced and altered (Timmons and Spinelli, 2007).

At the heart of the process is the opportunity, which can be created by a number of micro- and macro-environmental forces. Examples include: consumers seeking new products and services; technological advancements revolutionizing ways of working; and new legislation that may lead to the opening up of business opportunities to new entrants. Opportunity leads to surges of entrepreneurial activity, particularly from those who are keen to make a competitive foothold. In these early days of entrepreneurial activities, success is by no means a certainty and many lessons will be learned along the way (Fiet *et al.*, 2005).

The entrepreneurial team is crucial in the success of a start-up and needs to be led by a figure who can demonstrate creative brilliance, motivational skills, persistence, risk tolerance, a high level of communication skills and a passion for their goals, particularly through times of adversity. Besides the business plan and any human resources, finance and expertise will additionally often need to be sought in order to carry ideas forward, although this is not always the case. The crucial philosophy in the early stages of creative entrepreneurship is to minimize and control resources rather than own them and become burdened by them. Creativity is often unleashed where finance is minimal and innovative solutions need to be sought; passion and endurance are additionally key personal attributes of successful entrepreneurs.

Timmons (1994) also stated that entrepreneurship involves building something of value from virtually nothing. From a business perspective, entrepreneurship is essential in order for the start-up, survival and growth of companies and organizations. Through a creative process, new products, ways of working and enterprises emerge.

THE BUSINESS PLAN

A business plan is a formalization of a business idea. It should contain specific target goals, which can be expressed in quantifiable ways, e.g. deadline dates, numbers of customers and estimated expenses and revenues. A business plan has several different functions, it:

- serves to convince investors, banks and other external financiers that the project is viable;
- may attract supply-chain associates such as distributors, suppliers and customers by giving them the information to decide whether a partnership will be beneficial;
- allows the entrepreneur to reflect on their skills and any necessary skills that will need to be brought in for the plan to succeed;
- provides a 'road map' of the venture; and
- serves as a performance audit once the plan is underway.

Before beginning, and particularly with creative products, it may be necessary to seek legal protection for intellectual property through copyright, registering patents and trademarking (see Chapter 12). The ever-increasing speed of communication and reproduction in our global economy makes this a real necessity so that an idea can be properly developed before it is copied by imitators. A particular consideration should be non-disclosure agreements with potential partners, service providers and investors.

Figure 11.2 gives an overview of the major elements that should be contained within a business plan. It is essential that a business plan is not ambiguous and is understandable, as it will often be read by potential stakeholders at a distance from the author.

An explanation of each business plan step now follows:

- *Executive Summary* – this is an abbreviated digest of the entire plan. It is usually between one and three pages long

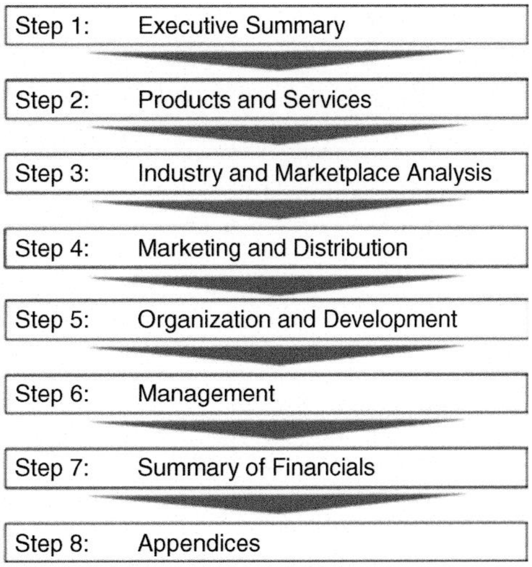

Step 1:	Executive Summary
Step 2:	Products and Services
Step 3:	Industry and Marketplace Analysis
Step 4:	Marketing and Distribution
Step 5:	Organization and Development
Step 6:	Management
Step 7:	Summary of Financials
Step 8:	Appendices

Fig. 11.2. The components of a business plan.

and allows the reader to get a clear idea of what the plan contains. From reading this, they should know whether or not it is something that is of interest to them.

- *Products and Services* – this section gives a detailed presentation of the core and ancillary products and/or services that are at the heart of the business idea. A thorough description of them should include a justification for them, with identified demand and the potential target market. The uniqueness of the product or service should also be identified along with the key features and benefits of using this product instead of other similar products for consumers. This section should also include information about the product costs and what the anticipated pricing strategy will be for the product, as well as the expected lifecycle of the product, considering forecasted demand, and when this is likely to reflect in sales through growth, before maturing and reducing. Strategies for product differentiation and diversification should follow to demonstrate that the business idea is sustainable in the long term and not just through initial demand. Figure 11.3 is a product lifecycle model, which helps to demonstrate the product lifecycle stages. It should be noted that in reality the time periods in the product's lifecycle would vary and not all be alike as in the model itself.

- *Industry and Marketplace Analysis* – this section gives the reader an insight into the industry and its competitive environment. The section shall provide an understanding of the dynamics, challenges and opportunities that characterize the industry and marketplace. Competitors should also be mentioned, and a tool such as a

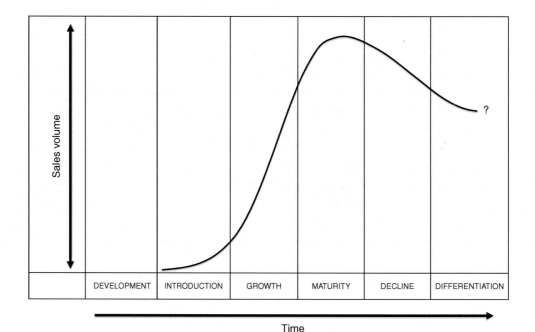

Fig. 11.3. Product lifecycle model.

competitor map (see Chapter 1) should be used to highlight key competitors and demonstrate why your product/idea is unique. For the industry analysis, detailed research is necessary, both academically and/or directly with trade organizations, government statistics, specialized suppliers or others with expert knowledge. When completed, the analysis should give an overview of the size and scope of the industry as well as industry trends. Macro-forces such as STEEPLE factors (see Chapter 14), which have impacted upon and may continue to impact upon the industry and marketplace, should be covered in detail. The marketplace analysis focuses on the specific market, which is likely to be smaller than the whole industry. As an example, for an amusement park the marketplace might be limited to a specific catchment area or maybe to a city. Gaps in the market should be identified so that the proposed product/idea can be seen to exploit these.

- *Marketing and Distribution* – the target market for the product has to be clearly segmented, the size clearly defined and the customers' buying behaviour should be described. This section should include a detailed breakdown of the product's marketing mix (see Chapter 3), particularly details of the price, product, place and promotion (building upon but not repeating what has already been said in previous sections). An effective marketing and distribution strategy, which matches the target market, is critical for the success of the product and this should be clearly stated. The section should also include a product sales forecast, which is based upon short-, medium- and long-term goals, and ideally should be expressed in terms of forecasted numbers of units sold.

- *Organization and Development* – this section provides an overview of how the organization will be structured with specific detail highlighting departments, chains of command and management responsibility. In this section, relationships with suppliers, vendors, partners and associates are defined, as well as what aspects of the business will be done in-house and what will be outsourced. The strategy for development of the business should include time-scales and tools such as Gantt charts (see Chapter 6). Risks should also be identified along with how they can be mitigated. Strategies for dealing with rapid increases in product demand should also be highlighted.

- *Management* – this section needs to clearly identify the managers of the business and highlight their competencies, experience and background knowledge. Ideally it should include similar information that may be found on a curriculum vitae (CV) that backs up these points. This is to persuade potential backers, partners and investors that the people taking this project forward are the right people to do so.

- *Summary of Financials* – this section clearly maps out against a timeline what the forecasted expenditure and generated revenue for the business will be. Commonly this is done using a cash-flow forecast, which is an important tool that demonstrates considerable planning has gone into the financials of the business, so that the business will remain financially healthy and that money that comes into the business overall exceeds money leaving the business. In the early days of a start-up this is unlikely to be the case, but the point when this does happen is called the break-even point. Your plans should identify when this will be and what expected profits will be made from that point onwards. This section of the business plan will also include details of start-up finances and the varying sources of finance that support the business.

- *Appendices* – these should consist of any supporting documentation that helps to back up points made within the business plan. All appendices should be referred to at some point in the text of the business plan. Appendices may include (but are not limited to): research documentation that supports the business idea, such as newspaper/journal articles or original research findings; maps of locations; full and extensive management CVs; website mock-ups; blueprints; and photographs. Additionally, a detailed summarizing SWOT analysis should be included in the appendices that draws together the whole business plan, explaining specific product and organizational characteristics. SWOT stands for strengths, weaknesses, opportunities and threats. Table 11.1 demonstrates how a SWOT analysis may be set out, along with instructions for its content.

It is important when constructing a SWOT analysis to be honest and open, and really demonstrate that thorough research and planning has been undertaken into the product. Any potential investors will certainly have done their own research and be swift to point out flaws in business plans. It is much better for the entrepreneur to demonstrate that they recognize where potential weaknesses and threats may exist than to have it pointed out to them by a potential investor.

FINANCING AND FUNDING A BUSINESS START-UP

Most new ideas will require some kind of financial investment or capital to help them 'off the ground' so that they can develop. There are three predominant sources of financing new ventures:

- banks;
- state subsidy programmes (which may need to be competitively bid for); and
- the 4 Fs – founders, family, friends and foolhardy investors (Bygrave, 2004).

Most ventures will need the services of a banker or lender at some stage. Different institutions have different reputations for how well they work with entrepreneurial start-ups, as do individual bank managers or lenders personally. Therefore, thorough research should influence the selection of which financial institutions to approach and even their individual staff members (Timmons and Spinelli, 2007). European start-ups particularly have to rely more on traditional bank loans, although banks tend to look for assets that can feature as loan securities rather than entrepreneurial opportunities.

Bygrave's above-mentioned foolhardy investors includes professional venture capital (VC) firms and so-called business angels. VC is a major driver of financing entrepreneurial activity in the USA, and increasingly so in Europe and parts of Asia.

Table 11.1. SWOT analysis for a business plan (Osterwalder and Pigneur, 2010; Barrow *et al.*, 2012; Stutely, 2012).

Strengths	Weaknesses
• Identify the unique aspects of the product. • State any successes from product testing or research that has currently been undertaken. • Mention any trademarks, patents and licences already held as a result of developing this product. • Highlight current market demand and predicted market demand for the product. • State why the team behind this idea are the right people to take it forward, including expertise and previous career successes. • Identify any strategic partnerships or networks that may help in the success of the product. • Mention any current sources of capital. • Identify any macro STEEPLE environmental influences, e.g. changes in law that will benefit the future of the product, particularly from a sales and demand perspective.	• Identify where the product could be substituted for other products. • State any continuing negative issues that have arisen as a result of product testing. This may seem like an uncomfortable thing to do, but there is a need for honesty and openness in order to instil faith in potential investors, who may walk away if they sense lies or half-truths. • Mention any trademarks, patents and licences that are not owned, that need to be. • State any gaps in expertise, knowledge or resources that may prevent the team behind the idea taking it forward.
Opportunities	**Threats**
This section should address each weakness and threat individually by identifying as bullet points viable proposed strategies and solutions to counteract these potentially negative influences, so that the product will be successful in future. Opportunities should include details of: • Product development strategies. • Marketing strategies. • Trademark, licensing and patent plans. • Networking strategies. • Recruitment and human resource strategies. • Training and staff development. • Investment strategies. • Supply chain and logistical strategies. • Any other strategies to overcome or work with potentially negative STEEPLE influences.	• Identify key competitors to the product. • Identify any macro STEEPLE environmental influences, e.g. changes in law that may harm the future success of the product, particularly from a sales and demand perspective.

Professional VC firms look for profit maximization options through rigid screening of venture opportunities and risk-diversification. Business angels include wealthy individuals who look for interesting investment opportunities outside financial markets and often want to support business ideas based on their own altruism/idealism or personal background related to specific industries. Professional VC firms usually have a rigorous selection process with only 4% of presented business ideas receiving VC funding (Timmons and Spinelli, 2007).

There are numerous governmental entrepreneurship funding programmes, which may be loan or grant based. In Europe, the High Growth and Innovative SME Facility (abbreviated to the GIF) provides risk capital for innovative SMEs (small- to medium-sized enterprises) through investments of 10–25% of total equity in early business stages and 7.5–15% of total equity in the expansion phase (European Commission, 2012). Such schemes are started with the aim of strengthening the labour market and the long-term competitiveness of the national economy. Research in Germany has indicated that such programmes have increased levels of business start-up (Bergmann and Sternberg, 2007). Other governmental sources of finance that may be encountered are featured in Table 11.2.

Table 11.2. Governmental sources of finance for business start-ups. (From Crimson Publishing, 2013.)

Name of finance	Description
Direct grants	A cash award that is usually given out to develop an idea. These sometimes require a like-for-like investment by the organization applying for the grant.
Repayable grant	This is a loan-based grant, whereby repayment of the grant is only made should the organization succeed and create an operating profit that is enough to pay back the grant – without damaging the business.
Soft loan	This is a loan that comes with 'easier' terms than what may be offered by a high street bank. This may mean leniency in terms of the repayment period, or a reduced amount of interest to pay on the loan.
Equity finance	This type of loan is usually in exchange for a stake in the business. Unlike VC loans, governmental equity finance usually comes with more flexibility for the loanee in terms of repayments.

Case Study: Jever Skihalle Neuss, Germany

Jever Skihalle Neuss (JSN) is a ski-slope visitor attraction located in Neuss, Germany. The core product of the attraction is an indoor 300 m long, 60 m wide and 43.5 m high ski slope, which draws more than 1 million visitors annually. The attraction was founded initially by two entrepreneurs who were both passionate skiers and who spent 5 years planning a vision to bring skiing to the west of Germany, where in winter there is often little snowfall. Together they formed a company called Allrounder Winter World GmbH & Co. KG. The slope was opened in 2001. The indoor ski arena is located in one of the most densely populated areas in Europe, with around 16 million people living within approximately 1 hour of travel, where there are good transport connections and the local population is relatively affluent.

The entrepreneurs behind JSN carried out little in the way of academic research prior to putting their business plan together; they were inspired by the popularity of temporary ski-related events in the region but unsurprisingly were unsuccessful in gaining bank loans. They did find a private investor that was willing to take the risk and provide a major part of the necessary financial resources. The investor was experienced in the business start-up process and gave the entrepreneurs behind the project the necessary advice to help them succeed with their plans. To turn the idea into a reality the entrepreneurial team had to seek a variety of planning permissions and satisfy stringent safety regulations. This was a significant hurdle, and the start-up team demonstrated persistence and resilience in overcoming this.

The entrepreneurs behind JSN wanted to create an alpine-style environment according to how people in the west of Germany may imagine it. Intellectual property rights could not be claimed for the style of the attraction, which has enhanced the pressure to constantly innovate. A successful patent that has been registered at the attraction is a new technology for an indoor snow cannon, which generates more and better quality powder and less icing of the slopes. Twelve such cannons can produce 80 m^3 of snow per day, and the use of these has provided an additional income stream for the attraction, where the cannons have been used to provide snow for temporary ski events in the area including the FIS Cross Country Skiing World Cup.

Through careful cash-flow management and reinvestment into the business, a 32 m high climbing wall was built in 2003 to extend the alpine experience. In 2009, an additional attraction with a climbing park and Germany's biggest free-standing high-wire garden opened, where guests can balance, swing, crawl, jump and climb at a height of up to 9 metres. As well as an active leisure space, the attraction provides visitors with an entertaining spectacle to behold.

An important holistic aspect of the ski resort concept is the gastronomy, and the attraction also includes a themed restaurant and beer garden with costumed cast members helping to create an authentic Alpine feel to the attraction. These additionally attract visitors

(Continued)

Case Study. Continued.

who go to experience the food and drink on offer in a themed environment. In 2011, the product offering of JSN was further differentiated with the addition of 'Fire & Ice', an Alpine-themed four star hotel and 1000 m² of conference area divided between 11 conference rooms. This has encouraged some visitors to stay longer and has opened up the attraction to new potential market segments, including corporate visitors who may be attracted by holding conferences and at the same time engaging in team-building activities by using the facilities. A highlight of the hotel is the foyer that provides a view on to the slopes for visitors to behold. The hotel also offers a wellness area with saunas that allow a view on to the ski slopes. Images of Jever Skihalle Neuss can be seen in Fig. 11.4.

Fig. 11.4. Images of Jever Skihalle Neuss. The ski slope (top left), the themed eating area (top right) and a sauna with a view of the ski slope (below). Images courtesy of Allrounder Winter World GmbH & Co. KG.

(Continued)

Case Study. Continued.

The team behind JSN put their continued success down to the following best-practice management initiatives:

- providing employees with a high quality working environment so that they feel valued, remain in their jobs and take pride in the company;
- maintaining high levels of internal communication, so all employees are continually aware of company developments;
- actively encouraging customer feedback, which is continually solicited and acted upon. Employees are encouraged to regularly seek face to face feedback from customers, including customer opinions of how their visitor experience could be improved. JSN Management believe that this active approach to feedback generates higher quality input from customers than passive feedback methods such as surveys left for visitors to complete;
- regularly running quality product checks, including mystery shopping exercises; and
- cooperating with industry partners, including Austrian skiing destination Salzburger Land and the brewery Jever.

In the future it is likely that the product offer will further diversify and expand to attract new target groups, particularly in relation to travel partnerships and the range of on-site entertainment offerings. JSN management have proven that with an idea, financial backing and persistence, success can follow, which if built upon can lead to expansion and further success in future.

SEMINAR ACTIVITIES

1. How creative are you? In a small group consider and discuss the various creative outputs that you each may routinely generate. This should go beyond written, graphic, and audio/video outputs – think about when you actually make things and what you make. Individually write your own lists and then put these together in a master document, before discussing your collective creativity.

2. Reproduce a copy of your own CV so that it demonstrates your creative side.

3. What motivates you to be creative? In a small group consider this individually and write a list, then discuss within the group common traits and differences.

4. Take one of the following entertainment products: games console; theme park; museum; cinema; live music venue; theatre. Consider an actual real-life example of one of these that you are familiar with and write a detailed SWOT analysis about it.

5. In a small group, come up with a concept for a new entertainment product (media, events or attraction based). Produce a presentation about your concept that follows the business plan steps highlighted in Fig. 11.2.

REFERENCES

Barrow, C., Barrow, P. and Brown, R. (2012) *The Business Plan Workbook*. Kogan Page, London.

Bergmann, H. and Sternberg, R. (2007) The changing face of entrepreneurship in Germany. *Small Business Economics* 28, 205–221.

Bragg, A. and Bragg, M. (2005) *Developing New Business Ideas – A Step-by-Step Guide to Creating New Business Ideas Worth Backing*. Pearson, Harlow, UK.

Bridge, S., O'Neill, K. and Cromie, S. (2003) *Understanding Enterprise, Entrepreneurship and Small Business*. Palgrave MacMillan, Basingstoke, UK.

Brixy, U., Sternberg, R. and Vorderwülbecke, A. (2012) *Global Entrepreneurship Monitor: Länderbericht Deutschland* [country report Germany] 2011.

Bygrave, W.D. (2004) Founders, family, friends and fools. Available at: http://www.businessweek.com/stories/2004-09-02/founders-family-friends-and-fools (accessed 17 August 2013).

Crimson Publishing (2013) Grants for starting a business: what small business grants are available? Available at: http://www.startups.co.uk/grants-for-starting-a-business.html (accessed 15 August 2013).

European Commission (2012) Access to Finance. Available from: http://ec.europa.eu/enterprise/policies/finance/cip-financial-instruments/index_en.htm (accessed 4 July 2012).

Fiet, J.O., Piskounov, A. and Patel, P.C. (2005) Still searching (systematically) for entrepreneurial discoveries. *Small Business Economics* 25, 489–504.

Hart, M. and Levie, J. (2010) *Global Entrepreneurship Monitor United Kingdom 2010 Monitoring Report*. Available at: http://www.gemconsortium.org/docs/download/656 (accessed 10 November 2013).

Hougaard, S. (2005) *The Business Idea: The Early Stages of Entrepreneurship*. Springer, Berlin.

Kelley, D.J., Ali, A., Brush, C., Corbett, A.C., Majbouri, M. and Rogoff, E.G. (2012) 2012 United States report. Global entrepreneurship monitor. National entrepreneurial assessment for the United States of America. Available at: http://www.gemconsortium.org/docs/download/2804 (accessed 10 November 2013).

Klandt, H. and Brüning, E. (2002) *Das Internationale Gründungsklima: Neun Länder im Vergleich Ihrer Rahmenbedingungen für Existenz- und Unternehmensgründungen [The International Founders' Climate: Nine Countries in Comparison in Terms of Their General Conditions for Start-ups]*. Duncker and Humblot, Berlin.

Moises, K. (2012) 'Timmons model of the entrepreneurial process'. Available at: http://kimberlymoises.wordpress.com/2012/08/28/timmons-model-of-the-entrepreneurial-process (accessed 14 August 2013).

Moss, S. (2011) Cultural entrepreneurship. In: Walmsley, B. (ed.) *Key Issues in the Arts and Entertainment Industry*. Goodfellow, Oxford, UK, pp. 161–177.

Osterwalder, A. and Pigneur, Y. (2010) *Business Model Generation*. Wiley, Hoboken, New Jersey.

Schumpeter, J.A. (1934) *Fundamentals of Economic Development*. Harvard University Press, Cambridge, Massachusetts.

Stutely, R. (2012) *The Definitive Business Plan – The Fast Track to Intelligent Planning for Executives and Entrepreneurs*. Pearson, Harlow, UK.

Timmons, J. (1994) *New Venture Creation*. Irwin, Boston, Massachusetts.

Timmons, J.A. and Spinelli, S. (2007) *New Venture Creation: Entrepreneurship for the 21st Century*. McGraw-Hill, New York.

Volkmann, C.K., Tokarski, K.O. and Grünhagen, M. (2010) *Entrepreneurship in a European Perspective – Concepts for the Creation and Growth of New Ventures*. Gabler, Wiesbaden, Germany.

chapter 12

Introduction to Entertainment Law

Dinusha Mendis

LEARNING OBJECTIVES

After reading this chapter you should:

- appreciate the main legal issues affecting the entertainment industries;
- be able to trace the history of copyright law;
- understand the latest rulings on piracy and illegal file-sharing;
- appreciate how and why television formats are protected; and
- gain a detailed insight into defamation and privacy laws and understand how they are applied in practice.

INTRODUCTION

This chapter will deal with selected legal issues that relate to the entertainment industries including parody, television formats, piracy and illegal file-sharing. As these issues all hinge on the laws of copyright, the chapter will begin with a brief introduction to copyright law. The second part of the chapter will consider legal issues arising from the media sector of the entertainment industries, such as the laws of defamation and privacy. The chapter does not intend to provide a detailed insight into all aspects of entertainment law; the aim is to provide an overview of selected legal issues that impinge upon the entertainment industries. Although the focus lies predominantly on UK and English law, the chapter does incorporate international case studies and provide comparative examples from other jurisdictions.

AN INTRODUCTION TO COPYRIGHT LAW

Copyright law comes under the umbrella of Intellectual Property Rights (IPR), which exist to protect the intellectual efforts of human endeavour. Other IPRs include trademarks, patents and design, and the common law rights of passing off and breach of confidence (MacQueen *et al.*, 2010). In the UK, copyright law dates back to 1710 with the introduction of the Statute of Anne. Since then, the advent of technology has meant that copyright law has had to play a 'catch-up' game. The inventions of the gramophone, television, cinema, photocopier, computer and most recently the Internet have led to the introduction of a number of copyright laws including the Copyright Acts 1911, 1956 and 1988. The Copyright Designs and Patents Act 1988 (hereinafter CDPA 1988) was amended most recently by the Copyright and Related Rights Regulations 2003 to take into account issues thrown up by the Internet. The tensions that exist between copyright law and technology have been an ongoing issue, so in the following pages the challenges faced by copyright law in the digital era and within the entertainment industries will be highlighted.

According to sections 1–8 of CDPA 1988, copyright law protects 'original' literary, dramatic, musical and artistic works, together with films, sound recordings, broadcasts and typographical arrangement of published works. Copyright and Related Rights Regulations 2003 provided for the protection of rights in relation to 'wireless broadcasting', which now appears under section 6A(1)(a)–(c) of CDPA 1988.

Furthermore, unlike other IPR, copyright arises automatically subject to the work being 'fixed'. In accordance with CDPA 1988, section 3(2), 'copyright does not subsist in a literary, dramatic or musical work unless and until it is *recorded, in writing or otherwise*'. Whilst the most obvious forms of 'fixation' come in the form of writing and recording,

the section is interpreted to also include fixation in the form of short-hand, electronic mail and content recorded and stored on flash drives for example (MacQueen *et al.*, 2010).

'Originality' in copyright law is determined by the *expression of ideas* not by the ideas themselves. As illustrated in University of London Press v. University Tutorial Press: 'The word "original" does not in this connection mean that the work must be the expression of original or inventive thought. Copyright Acts are not concerned with the originality of ideas but with the expression of thought. The originality which is required relates to the expression of the thought.' But the Act does not require the expression to be in an original or novel form, just that the work not be copied from another work – it should originate from the author.

The case of Designer Guild v. Russell Williams clarified the position further when it established that when deciding whether copyright has been infringed in a work, it is important to consider whether the infringer has incorporated a 'substantial part' of the *independent skill, labour and effort* contributed by the original author in creating that copyright work (Laddie *et al.*, 2011). What exactly constitutes a 'substantial part' is considered on a case-by-case basis, but it is generally accepted to be a test of quality as opposed to quantity (MacQueen *et al.*, 2010).

EXCEPTIONS TO COPYRIGHT, PARODY AND THE HARGREAVES REVIEW

There are certain acts permitted under copyright legislation. These include fair dealing with a literary, dramatic, musical or artistic work for the purposes of research for a non-commercial purpose (CDPA 1988, section 29(1)) and for the purpose of private study. CDPA 1988, section 29(1C) states that fair dealing with a literary, dramatic, musical or artistic work does not infringe any copyright in the work provided that it is accompanied by a sufficient acknowledgement, unless this would be impossible for reasons of practicality or otherwise (CDPA 1988, section 29(1B)). The fair dealing provision also extends to criticism, review and news reporting (CDPA 1988, section 30). The 2003 Regulations (CDPA 1988, section 28A) also recognized that:

> copyright in a literary work, other than a computer programme or a database or in a dramatic, musical or artistic work […] is not infringed by the making of a temporary copy which is transient or incidental which is an integral and essential part of a technological process and the sole purpose of which is to enable (a) a transmission of the work in a network between third parties by an intermediary; or (b) a lawful use of the work; and which has no independent economic significance.

As such, recent changes to copyright law have attempted to keep up with technological developments.

However, the UK's fair dealing exception as outlined above is narrow and does not include exceptions for private copying, format-shifting, time-shifting or parody. This makes the law unclear, as it does not stipulate precisely what an individual can or cannot do. For example, it is unclear whether copying music for private, individual use or format-shifting from a computer to an mp3 player infringes copyright law. Furthermore, the UK does not benefit from a parody exception. According to the Oxford

English Dictionary (Stevenson and Soanes, 2003), parody is the 'imitation of the style of a particular writer, artist, or genre with deliberate exaggeration for comic effect'. The UK's narrow fair dealing exception has meant that such works are not covered by copyright law. Recognizing this gap, the Hargreaves Review recommended some changes to the UK's copyright law, including the introduction of a parody exception and private copying exception (Hargreaves, 2011). In particular, the Review noted that 'video parody is today becoming part and parcel of the interactions of private citizens, often via social networking sites, and encourages literacy in multimedia expression in ways that are increasingly essential to the skills base of the economy'. This view was further compounded by a study carried out by the Centre for Intellectual Property Policy and Management (CIPPM) at Bournemouth University. The study included a detailed analysis of the parody exceptions in Canada, France, the USA, Australia, Germany and the Netherlands and concluded that the UK has much to gain from a parody exception (Mendis and Kretschmer, 2013). Presenting new empirical data drawn from music videos on the YouTube platform, the research further concluded that there is little evidence of economic damage to rights holders through substitution; the presence of parody content is correlated with and predicts larger audiences for original music videos (Erickson *et al.*, 2013).

The existence of such an exception will provide clarity for users and those in the entertainment industries who wish to 'conjure up' the original works for the purpose of creating a work of parody, pastiche or satire. In France, the existence of a parody exception (L 122-5 of the French Intellectual Property Code 1992) led to recognition of the defendant's parody of *Tintin*, whilst in the Netherlands, Nadia Plesner's artistic work was also considered to be a work of parody under Article 18b of the Dutch Copyright Act 1912 (as amended). A parodic version of Roy Orbison's *Oh Pretty Woman* was further held not to infringe copyright under the USA's 'fair use' doctrine (section 107, Copyright Act 1976). During a review of the Intellectual Property Laws in the UK (Gowers, 2006), it was suggested by Arts Council England that an exception along the lines of 'parody, comedy and pastiche' should be introduced on the basis that these were 'particularly strong creative areas in the UK' (Arts Council England, 2006; see also Deazley, 2010).

PIRACY AND ILLEGAL FILE-SHARING

It has been estimated that by 2015, digital piracy will cost the entertainment industries €32 billion and will have caused job losses of 611,300 (International Chamber of Commerce, 2010). Companies such as Napster, Grokster and Pirate Bay, which have offered file-sharing services, brought the issue of piracy to the forefront, highlighting the urgent need for copyright law reform. The advancement of technology has led to widespread piracy, with the web community becoming well-versed in the art of 'uploading and downloading' in the Web 2.0 era – often in breach of copyright (Larusson, 2009).

Whilst rights holders have lamented, and in the cases noted above brought proceedings against both individuals and companies involved in illegal file-sharing activities, this has had very little impact on acts of piracy and illegal file-sharing (James, 2008). Copyright owners and organizations representing them remain unhappy with the current situation, as emphasized in the International Federation

Fig. 12.1. A street vendor sells pirated DVDs in Greece. Image by Stuart Moss.

of the Phonographic Industry (IFPI) Digital Music Reports of 2004–2011. The IFPI Digital Music Report 2010 underlined the fact that despite the wealth of online offerings and the global embrace of digital services, overall music revenues had fallen by around 30% since 2004, with a sales downturn of 12% in the first half of 2009 (IFPI Digital Music Reports, 2010–2011). Since 2004, copyright owners, particularly those in the music industry, have lobbied hard for stricter copyright laws to be implemented in an attempt to curb online piracy (IFPI Digital Music Reports, 2004–2011).

Case Study: The Digital Economy Act 2010

In the UK, the Digital Economy Act 2010 (hereinafter DEA 2010) was introduced to deal with piracy and illegal file-sharing. This controversial Act was rushed through Parliament in early 2010 and is commonly referred to as 'three-strikes-and-you're-out'. It is a controversial piece of legislation, which still requires secondary legislation; and in June 2012, 2 years after the DEA 2010 received Royal Assent, the much-awaited Initial Obligations Code was published. DEA 2010 has also gone through a judicial review hearing (2011) and an appeal hearing (2012), which has delayed its implementation further. DEA 2010 reflects the trend followed in countries such as France, New Zealand, South Korea and more recently Australia and the USA.

Digital Economy Act 2010

Fig. 12.2. Digital Economy Act.

The essence of DEA 2010 (and similar three-strikes laws) is as follows: an alleged infringer, who will be identified by their Internet Protocol (IP) address, will be warned three times before technical obligations (yet to be drawn up as secondary legislation) are imposed. The technical obligations can lead to alleged offenders being disconnected from the Internet altogether; having their Internet speed limited; being prevented from using the service to gain access to particular material or having such use limited; or seeing the services provided to them limited in another way (section 9, DEA 2010). Some of the concerns surrounding this piece of legislation have related to the difficulties in identifying an alleged infringer using their IP address. The issue becomes particularly relevant where the IP address is shared by a number of people in a flat, café, university, library, etc. In such a situation it may be possible to identify the person whose name is on the broadband bill, but it is almost impossible to identify the individual who may have infringed the copyright laws.

(Continued)

The inconsistencies and inaccuracies that arise from identifying alleged infringers through their IP addresses were emphasized by Judge Birss QC in the case of Media C.A.T. v. Adams. In this case ACS:Law representing Media C.A.T. sent hundreds of letters to alleged infringers of copyright by tracking their IP addresses. However, in the court case Judge Birss QC ruled that Media C.A.T.'s monitoring system failed to identify any individual wrongdoing, finding that all an IP address identifies is an Internet connection, which can only identify the person who has the contract with their ISP (paragraph 31).

Section 17 of the DEA 2010, which made it possible for rights holders to gain 'takedown' injunctions against ISPs, forcing them to block access to websites that host a 'substantial proportion' of copyright, was deemed unworkable in May 2011 by the Office of Communications (Ofcom). Ofcom concluded that it is not possible to deliver a framework under the DEA (Ofcom, 2011). In July 2011, the Newzbin II case questioned the validity of Section 17 in view of an existing provision –Section 91A CDPA 1988 – which achieves the same result without the need for 'actual knowledge' of the infringement to be proved. In August 2011, the Government stated that it would not 'bring forward regulations on site blocking under DEA, at this time' (Department for Culture, Media and Sport, 2011).

The heavy-handed approach taken by the DEA 2010 has not gone unnoticed by the United Nations Human Rights Council (UNHRC), which voiced concern about the 'three-strikes' approach in a recent report. The Special Rapporteur Frank La Rue stated in his report that he was 'alarmed by proposals to disconnect users from Internet access if they violate intellectual property rights' and singled out the DEA and the French three-strikes law in particular as pieces of legislation that violate human rights (La Rue, 2011).

As mentioned above, the Act has been plagued by a judicial review hearing and an appeal hearing brought by BT and TalkTalk in March 2011 and January 2012, respectively. Whilst DEA 2010 survived both judicial review and appeal hearings, the challenges for this Act persist and questions remain regarding its future. Producers in the entertainment industries certainly need to be rewarded and incentivized to create original content, and indeed this forms the basis of the cyclical pattern of Intellectual Property Law. However, it remains to be seen whether laws such as the 'three-strikes' law are the answer to the challenges of copyright (Farrand, 2010; Mendis, 2013).

THE PROTECTION OF TV FORMATS

TV formats such as *Who Wants to be a Millionaire*, *X Factor* and *Dragon's Den* have proved to be a lucrative business, and since the 1980s the TV formats industry has boomed. The global expenditure on TV formats has been valued in excess of €9 billion, and in 2007 the TV formats industry was estimated at US$250 billion (Format Recognition and Protection Association, 2011). Therefore, it is not surprising that the creators of successful TV formats wish to protect them from piracy. However, as Coad (2011) points out, nowhere in the world is the existence of a TV format recognized expressly by statute. There is therefore no statutory definition of a TV format, although case law and commentaries in this area have provided for a number of different definitions. Whilst in the American case Murray v. NBC, Circuit Judge Altimari defined a TV format as a 'proposal', Tony Stern of Freemantle Media defined it as 'a recipe of a show that can be remade in various territories' (Stern, 2009). Either way, the collective components of a TV format such as catch-phrases, music, themes, staging, camera angles and lighting arrangements, which are meticulously scripted into a 'format bible', make each TV format unique, thereby requiring some form of protection. This has come about in the form of IPR, in particular copyright law. However, the challenge for creators of TV formats lies in reaching the threshold of originality in copyright law by demonstrating that the TV format is not a 'mere idea' but the *expression* of an idea.

TV formats and copyright law

One of the most significant cases relating to TV formats in the UK dates back to 1982 to the case of Green v. Broadcasting Corporation of New Zealand. The case concerned the well-known show *Opportunity Knocks* created by Hughie Green. In this case, the claimant, Green, brought an action against a TV broadcaster in New Zealand claiming copyright infringement of the *Opportunity Knocks* format, which was also aired under the same name in New Zealand. The court established that the *Opportunity Knocks* script written by Green did 'no more than express a general idea or concept for a talent contest'; and as copyright does not protect ideas, the court

held that the New Zealand TV format did *not* infringe the claimant's copyright.

However, in contrast, the Australian court in Nine Films v. Ninox Television accepted that copyright law can exist in TV formats as did the Dutch court in Castaway v. Endemol. In this latter case, after a long drawn out battle lasting well over 3 years, the Dutch Supreme Court ruled that the format of *Survivor* was a copyright work and therefore protected by copyright law. However, the court held that on the facts of the present case, the TV format of *Big Brother* (produced by Endemol) did not infringe the format of *Survivor*.

Protecting TV formats through unfair competition or passing off

The protection of TV formats through copyright has led to uncertainty, with Logan stating that the 'business is generally run as a series of gentlemen's agreements' (Logan, 2009a, p. 37). It has therefore been suggested that the laws of unfair competition and 'passing off' provide better protection. Unfair competition is 'any act of competition contrary to honest practices in industrial or commercial matters' (Paris Convention 1979, Article 10bis(2)). Whilst countries such as France and the USA provide for a specific unfair competition clause, the UK recognizes it under the common law tort of 'passing off' in order to satisfy the provisions of the Paris Convention.

In 2008, the UK Consumer Protection from Unfair Trading (CPUT) Regulations were brought into force, replacing the Trade Descriptions Act 1968 to give effect to the EU Consumer Commercial Practices Directive.

Section 3(3)(b) of CPUT prohibits commercial practice if it 'materially distorts or is likely to materially distort the economic behaviour of the average consumer with regard to the product'. Whilst the introduction of this provision is encouraging for creators of TV formats, it is important to note that the provision is only applicable between businesses and consumer relationships, and as such does not assist in preventing the copying of TV formats. Therefore, it has fallen upon the law of passing off – a common law tort – to afford protection for TV formats. The law of passing off requires a claimant to satisfy three criteria (known as the 'Classic Trinity') to be successful in a passing off claim. The three ingredients developed by Lord Oliver in the Jif Lemon case require a successful claimant to demonstrate the requirement of goodwill or reputation, misrepresentation and damage.

Establishing the existence of goodwill or reputation where the infringing TV format is broadcast in the same territory as the original is relatively straightforward, as illustrated in the Australian case of Willard and the French case of TFI v. Antenne 2. However, the case of Green (above) declined the existence of goodwill or reputation where two territories were involved and the audiences were unlikely to have seen the UK version of the show. Considering the advancement of technology and the availability of sites such as YouTube, which allows for worldwide viewing of TV formats, it is possible that Green may have been decided differently today.

In establishing misrepresentation, it is necessary to prove that the goods or services in which the defendant trades are those of the claimant, or in some way have a business connection with the claimant, or share particular qualities with the claimant's goods or services (MacQueen *et al.*, 2011). However, it is important to point out that even when the defendant has copied the claimant's badge of identity, passing off will not provide a remedy unless the latter's goodwill has been damaged. When establishing damage, it is necessary to evidence loss of custom (actual and potential); attraction of custom by the defendant using the claimant's goodwill; damage to the claimant's reputation, and hence goodwill, through false association; and damage to the claimant's trading relations.

TV formats can also be protected through the common law right of breach of confidence. However, this claim can only succeed where a confidential concept for a show has been communicated in a confidential situation and subsequently used without permission. Although breach of confidence has its own challenges in attempting to protect TV formats, in the Australian case of Talbot v. General Television Corp Pty Ltd., the Supreme Court of Victoria found that Channel Nine had breached the duty of confidence that it owed to Mr Talbot, who had met with and submitted to Channel Nine a written programme submission and pilot for a show about the development and effect of a millionaire's riches. The court held that the format was to be 'rightly regarded as the property' of Talbot.

It is clearly a challenge to protect TV formats through copyright law, unfair competition/passing off or breach of confidence. The difficulties associated with protecting these formats under the current law are summarized by Lisa Logan (2009b, p. 92) as follows:

> Like the emperor who couldn't see the cloth, TV producers cannot ensure that their TV format rights exist in each jurisdiction but

pretend all the same that the rights exist. For a global format market worth Euro 6.4 billion in 2002/4, the economic justifications for providing greater protection are paramount. However, any change to [...] the Paris Convention [...] will require substantial lobbying from industries likely to benefit from harmonized laws of unfair competition including the TV industry.

THE ENTERTAINMENT INDUSTRIES AND THE MEDIA: DEFAMATION AND PRIVACY LAWS

Defamation and privacy laws exist to protect the reputation and private lives of individuals and corporations. Drawing a line through the case law relating to privacy, and in particular to defamation laws, it becomes clear that almost all claimants are those in the media and are generally affluent. This is unsurprising due to the lack of legal aid in the UK for defamation cases and the high costs associated in bringing these claims (Quinn, 2011). This aspect was well documented following the McLibel case (McDonald's Corp v. Steel and Morris), which concerned two 'ordinary' people of the Greenpeace Group who refused to say 'sorry' to McDonald's for circulating allegedly defamatory statements made against the large corporation (Nash and Crown, 2005; Scolnicov, 2005; Starmer and Hudson, 2005; Stephens, 2005). Lack of legal aid made it very difficult for the two defendants to continue their fight against McDonald's. Having lost their case against McDonald's at the Royal Courts of Justice in London, the 'McLibel Two' took their case against the UK to the European Court of Justice – and won.

However, the lack of legal aid for defamation cases continues, thereby making it a claim available only to the wealthy.

Defamation law

The tort of defamation is regulated by the Defamation Acts 1952 and 1996. On 26 May 2010, the Liberal Democrat peer Lord Lester introduced a Private Members' Bill into the House of Lords, which proposed updating the current defamation laws (Krishnan, 2012). Lord Lester's Defamation Bill was received well, and on 15 March 2011 the Government introduced the Defamation Bill to bring the libel law 'up to date, striking a balance between protecting people's right to free speech [...] while enabling people who have genuinely been defamed to protect their reputations' (Shaw and Chamberlain, 2011, p. 50). The bill was passed by Parliament and received Royal Assent on 25 April 2013, and came into force late in 2013 through secondary legislation. A number of changes in relation to the online environment is reflected in the Act and it swings the balance in favour of freedom of expression. Taking into account these latest changes to the defamation law, the following discussion will make reference to the Defamation Acts 1952, 1996 and 2013 as relevant.

Defamation law exists to protect the reputation of an individual corporation, i.e. companies, schools, universities and associations that are legally incorporated, such as football clubs. It is also worth noting that trade unions, local authorities and central government, and political parties are unable to bring an action in defamation, although the right to bring an action is available for individuals within these groups. As such, where a written or spoken statement, act or gesture injures the *reputation* of an individual, corporation or association by exposing them to 'hatred, contempt or ridicule', a claimant can bring an action under defamation law. The point to note, however, is that defamation law will not permit someone to recover damages in respect of an injury to a character that he *does not or ought not to possess*.

Defamation can be divided into two categories: libel and slander. Libel is defamation in permanent form (e.g. publication in a newspaper, magazine, on the Internet, etc.), whereas slander is defamation in transitory form (such as the spoken word). The following discussion will focus on libel. A further and unusual aspect of defamation or libel law, which comes under the umbrella of civil law, is that until the Defamation Act 2013 was passed these cases were heard by 'libel juries'. Trial by jury has led to unrealistically high awards, far greater than those awarded in cases of personal injury. Recent defamation cases have seen claimants being awarded £500,000 plus £700,000 in damages (e.g. Jeffrey Archer). The Defamation Act 2013 removes the presumption in favour of trial by jury and proposes that libel trials be carried out without a jury unless a court orders otherwise (Section 11, 2013 Act).

Bringing a successful claim

In order for a claimant to bring a successful defamation claim, they must show:

1. That the statement is defamatory.
2. That it referred to the claimant.
3. That it was published to a third party.

The onus then shifts to the defendant to prove one of the defences.

A *defamatory statement*, which can also include innuendos, is one which tends to do any of the following:

- expose an individual or corporation to hatred, ridicule or contempt;
- cause them to be shunned or avoided;
- disparage them in their business, trade, office or profession; and/or
- lower them in the estimation of right-thinking members of society generally.

For example, in the case of Berkoff v. Birchill, Neill LJ stated that calling someone 'hideously ugly' could be defamatory.

Second, the statement must *refer to the claimant*. In other words, the claimant must show that an ordinary, reasonable reader or listener would take the statement as referring to him or her. Whilst it is relatively straightforward for an individual who has been defamed to bring an action, it is less so for a corporation or an association. The requirement is that the claimant(s) must be an identifiable group. In this context, an identifiable group such as a football team can bring an action in defamation, whilst it will not be possible for 'all lawyers in England' to bring an action against an individual who has defamed them. From a practical point of view, it is necessary to consider the amount of damages that will be available for each individual in such circumstances. Where a statement about a claimant's trade defames the claimant, it is 'not sufficient that the statement should simply affect the person adversely in his business; it must point to the discreditable conduct in his business, or else tend to show that he is ill-suited or ill-qualified to carry on' (Hulton v. Jones).

Third, a claimant must show that the *statement has been published* – i.e. communicated to a person other than the claimant or their spouse. The meaning of 'publication' has led to some difficulties in recent times due to the advent of the Internet and due to an archaic rule from 1849, which states that every fresh publication of a defamatory statement gives rise to a new course of action (Duke of Brunswick v. Harmer; see also Jordan, 2010). The 2013 Act proposes a 'single-publication' rule, which suggests a period of 1 year from the date of the original publication for a claimant to bring a claim and which does not restart each time the material is viewed, sold or otherwise republished, provided the publication is 'substantially the same' (Section 8, 2013 Act). The proposed measure strengthens freedom of speech by providing far greater protection to publishers.

Case Study: The Defamation Act 2013: Operators of Websites

Under the Defamation Acts 1952 and 1996, failing to pre-moderate users' comments or failing to take down comments soon after a complaint has been received made the website publisher liable (Godfrey v. Demon Internet; Section 1, 1996 Act). The 2013 Act provides a new provision in this regard, taking into account that comments can arise from individuals who wish to remain anonymous or those who have a pseudonymous identity. Where a complaint arises from a comment made by an identified author, the website should promptly publish a notice of the complaint alongside the comment. The complainant can apply for a 'takedown' order. If this is granted, the comment should be removed to avoid a defamation claim. In the case of comments left by individuals who appear as 'anonymous' or under a pseudonymous identity, websites should immediately remove them on receipt of a complaint (as it is not possible to identify the author), unless the author agrees to identify themselves (Section 5, 2013 Act). This section will primarily apply to operators of forums and blog-sites but will eventually be relevant to all user-generated sites. Ultimately, the effectiveness of this section will depend on the regulations, which are yet to be published and which will set out the procedure to be followed on receipt of notice of defamatory content (Agate, 2013). Under Section 10, the 2013 Act further provides that a court 'does not have jurisdiction to hear and determine an action for defamation brought against a person who was not the author, editor or publisher of the statement complained of'.

With 'publishing' becoming increasingly immediate and convenient in the digital era, and with the increased use of social networking sites such as Twitter, it was important for libel reform to take into account these developments. The complexities that can be thrown up by online services were illustrated in the first ever Twitter libel case in the UK. In March 2012, former New Zealand cricket captain Chris Cairns won his libel case against Lalit Modi, former Chairman of the Indian Premier League (IPL) (Chris Cairns v. Lalit Modi). Modi's tweet of 5 January 2010 alleged that Cairns had been involved in match-fixing. On 26 March 2012, Mr Justice Bean held that Cairns' otherwise clean reputation had been damaged by Modi's tweet and awarded Cairns £90,000 in damages with an order for the defendant to pay the claimant's legal costs of £400,000. The phrase 'be careful what you tweet' is becoming clichéd; however, this case is reflective of the dangers that lurk behind online tools, which allow for the quick-and-easy publishing of potentially defamatory comments.

Bringing a successful defence

In a defamation case, the defendant has the challenging task of proving (on the balance of probabilities) that the published statement was true (Section 5, 1952 Act); that it was a fair comment (Section 6, 1952 Act); or that it was made on a privileged occasion (Section 14, 1952 Act). From a legal point of view, it is therefore relatively easy for a claimant to bring an action in defamation. For defendants, however, it is more challenging, as they must prove:

- the truth or substantial truth of each defamatory statement;
- the truth of any reasonable interpretation which may be understood of the words complained of; and
- the truth of any innuendos lying behind the words.

The main difficulty here is that defendants may be unable to bring enough admissible evidence and prove that the statement is substantially true. Furthermore, pursuing with the justification defence can lead to the award of damages being increased (e.g. Cairns v. Modi).

The Defamation Act 2013 reflects a number of changes to the above position. First, under Section 1 of the Defamation Act 2013, a statement will not be treated as defamatory unless its publication has caused or is likely to cause 'serious harm' to the reputation of the claimant. The existing definition of defamation remains unchanged,

but the bar has been raised to capture the most serious defamatory claims. As Hooper, Murphy and Waite (Hooper *et al.*, 2013, p. 199) state:

> the requirement of serious harm permeates all aspects of the new law of defamation and is likely to lead to an increasing number of claims being struck out or simply not brought. Whenever the court will be exercising its discretion as to whether to allow a case to proceed, it will be asking itself whether the publication has caused or is likely to cause serious harm.

The existing law on justification or truth under Section 5 of the 1952 Act remains largely unchanged although it is codified by Section 2 of the 2013 Act. To prove the substantial truth of part of a statement deemed defamatory, the test will involve establishing whether that part would, or is likely to, cause serious harm (Section 2(3), 2013 Act). The defence of fair comment (Section 6, 1952 Act) has been renamed 'honest opinion' under the new law (Section 3, 2013 Act). Except for the name change, once again the existing law remains largely unchanged, although some of its complexities have been removed (see Hooper *et al.*, 2013).

Other defamation defences include: the defence of privilege (Sections 14, 15 and Schedule 1, 1996 Act); the offer of amends for unintentional defamation (Sections 2–4, 1996 Act); where a claimant has agreed to the publication; where the claimant has died; and if the proceedings were not started within the limitation period of 1 year (Section 5, 1996 Act).

The 2013 Act provides a public interest defence (Section 4), which applies irrespective of whether the statement is a matter of fact or opinion. The Act does not, however, define public interest, leaving it to the courts to decide on a case-by-case basis. Finally, the Act introduces a new area of qualified privilege – peer-reviewed statements in scientific or academic journals. The section is a product of the Simon Singh v. British Chiropractic Association case. Although the section is restricted to peer-reviewed academic or scientific material rather than all scientific debate – which can be defended through honest opinion or lack of serious harm – its inclusion is seen as a welcome addition by the scientific and academic communities.

The journey of the defamation laws in the UK illustrates that there have been attempts made to strike the correct balance between protecting an individual's reputation whilst upholding the defendant's freedom of expression. Section 1 of the new Defamation Act is particularly relevant to this point, requiring serious harm to the reputation of the claimant in bringing a claim. The inclusion of this section in the Defamation Act 2013 is reflective of the law moving in the right direction. Up until now, it has been relatively easy for a claimant to bring an action in defamation, which in turn has encouraged claimants from other jurisdictions to pursue libel cases in England and Wales – known as 'libel tourism' (see Fig. 12.3). Now that the new defamation laws are in place, claimants will have to think twice before pursuing a libel claim in the English courts, thereby providing for a fairer and balanced legislative framework for claimants and defendants.

Fig. 12.3. A protest against libel tourism in London. Image © 2009 ARTICLE 19, made available under the Creative Commons Attribution-Non-Commercial-ShareAlike 2.5 licence.

Privacy and breach of confidentiality

A right to privacy was recognized under the Human Rights Act 1998, which came into force in 2000. Prior to that, an individual wishing to safeguard their privacy relied on the common law right of breach of confidentiality. One of the early cases to have used this right dates back to 1849 and concerned Prince Albert. In Prince Albert v. Strange, the right to breach of confidentiality was upheld in favour of Prince Albert when his private drawings, in the form of etchings between himself and the Queen, were published in a catalogue. However, it was not until 1969, in the case of Coco v. A.N. Clark (Engineers) Ltd, that the court established a three-step test, which provided clear guidance in determining the right. The court held that in order to bring a successful breach of confidence claim, it is necessary to show that the information:

- has the necessary quality of confidence;
- has been imparted in circumstances importing an obligation of confidence; and
- has been used without authorization to the detriment of the party communicating it.

A case in 1991, Kaye v. Robertson, brought the issue of the lack of a privacy right in the UK to the forefront. In this case, the plaintiff, a well-known actor, was recovering in hospital from a serious injury when two journalists gained access to his private room, took photographs and conducted an interview. In this case Glidewell LJ stated:

> In English law there is no right to privacy, and accordingly there is no right of action for breach of a person's privacy. The facts of the present case are a graphic illustration of the desirability of Parliament considering whether [...] statutory provision can be made to protect the privacy of individuals.

Seven years later, transposing Article 8 of the European Convention on Human Rights 1950 (ECHR 1950), the right to privacy was recognized under Section 12 of the Human Rights Act 1998 (HRA 1998), which came into force in 2000. Article 8 states that:

> everyone has the right to respect for his private and family life, his home and his correspondence. There shall be no interference by a public authority with the exercise of the right except such as in accordance with the law and is necessary in a democratic society in the interests of national security, public safety or the economic well-being of the country for the prevention of disorder or crime; for the protection of health or morals; or for the protection of rights and freedom of others.

In addition to the law, the Press Complaints Commission Code of Practice provides further guidance under Clause 3, which states that 'everyone is entitled to respect for his or her private and family life, home, health and correspondence. A publication will be expected to justify intrusion into any individual's private life without consent. The use of long-lens photography to take pictures of people in private places without their consent is unacceptable.'

In Campbell v. MGN Ltd, photographs of the supermodel Naomi Campbell coming out of Narcotics Anonymous (NA) were published by *The Mirror* newspaper. The headline

---

Case Study: Michael Douglas v. *Hello!* magazine

The case of Douglas v. *Hello!* was one of the first cases that attempted to apply the new right of privacy. The case concerned the wedding of Michael Douglas and Catherine Zeta-Jones at the Plaza Hotel in New York. Photography at the wedding was prohibited and the guests were given strict instructions not to use cameras. The couple had an agreement with *OK!* magazine who were given the exclusive rights to publish their wedding photographs. However, a photographer managed to surreptitiously enter the wedding venue and sold six of his unauthorized photographs to *Hello!* magazine within 24 hours of the wedding. The Douglases and *OK!* applied for an injunction to prevent *Hello!* from publishing the pictures, which was rejected by the Court of Appeal. This led to both magazines publishing the photographs the next day. Whilst *OK!* sought compensation for the loss of its exclusive right to publish the wedding photographs, the couple sought damages from *Hello!* for breach of privacy. Interestingly, this long-drawn-out case, which began in 2000 and ended in 2007, was decided in favour of Michael Douglas and Catherine Zeta-Jones based on breach of confidentiality as opposed to relying on the newly established right to privacy (Lavender and Kill, 2007).

---

accompanying the photograph read 'Naomi, I am a drug addict' and the article contained information about the number of NA meetings she had attended. In this case, the court carried out a balancing act of protecting the claimant's privacy against the defendant's right to freedom of expression. Campbell accepted that the public had a 'right to know' that she was a drug addict but argued her case on the premise of breach of confidentiality.

This case also went all the way to the House of Lords and was once again decided on breach of confidentiality. The Law Lords reversed the Court of Appeal decision by a 3–2 majority and held in favour of Campbell, stating that in the present circumstances there had been a breach of confidentiality and the claimant's right to privacy outweighed the defendant's right to freedom of expression (Moreham, 2005).

Case Study: Max Mosley v. News Group Newspapers

A turning point in the law came about with the case of Mosley v. News Group Newspapers. In this case, Max Mosley, the former President of the Fédération Internationale de l'Automobile, the governing body of motor sport worldwide, was filmed engaging in sado-masochistic activities with five prostitutes in a private flat. An edited version of the footage was then made available on News Group Newspapers' (NGN) website in connection with a *News of the World* article. The article that accompanied the footage further alluded to the fact that Mosley had

(Continued)

Case Study. Continued.

been involved in a Nazi re-enactment. Whilst Mosley accepted the events shown, he denied the Nazi element and claimed for invasion of his privacy (as opposed to breach of confidence, which had been used in previous cases). In this instance, the court held that Mosley's privacy had been invaded and awarded him £60,000 in damages. Having won his privacy case in the UK, Mosley took his case to the European Court of Human Rights (ECHR) in Strasbourg, challenging UK laws that allow publication without giving individuals advanced warning. He suggested that reform of privacy law should include a 'prior notification' clause to protect the privacy of individuals. However, in May 2011, Mosley lost his privacy case in Strasbourg.

At the time of writing, privacy law is in a state of flux. The law was brought into question in 2011 following a few individuals who used the social networking site Twitter to publish the names of celebrities alleged to have obtained super-injunctions to protect their privacy. A super-injunction or a legal 'gagging order' is an interim injunction that restrains a person from: (i) publishing information which concerns the applicant and is said to be confidential or private; and (ii) publicizing or informing others of the existence of the order and the proceedings (TSE v. News Group Newspapers Ltd). The significance of super-injunctions is that they not only block the media from reporting the details of a story but also prevent journalists from even mentioning the existence of the injunction (Smartt, 2011). The fact that they were published on Twitter under a pseudonym account revealed the challenges to privacy in the Internet era on the one hand, whilst questioning the restrictions these orders place on freedom of expression on the other. Such challenges have led to the question of whether the law of privacy should be rewritten (Mindell, 2012).

Whilst such questions were being asked, in 2011 Prime Minister David Cameron called for an inquiry investigating the role of the press and police in relation to the 'phone hacking' scandal in the UK. The ensuing Leveson Inquiry aimed to make recommendations for the future regarding press regulation, governance and other areas of oversight. In November 2012, the Leveson Report was published (Leveson, 2012). The report made a number of recommendations, including the setting up of an independent regulatory body backed by legislation. In particular, the report recommended that the independent regulatory body should take an active role in 'promoting high standards' and hold the power to investigate serious breaches and sanction newspapers. Only time will tell whether the recommendations made in the Leveson Report will make a difference to media standards and ethics.

CONCLUSION

The laws considered in this chapter reveal some of the key legal challenges facing the entertainment industries. Whilst each area of the law faces its respective challenges, a common thread that runs through the topics considered in this chapter relates to the tension that exists between law and technology. Whether it is copyright, file-sharing, TV formats, defamation or privacy laws, it is clear that with advancements in technology, in particular the Internet, the law is finding it increasingly difficult to keep up with the challenges technology throws up. In more recent times, social networking tools such as Facebook and Twitter have accounted for a rising number of privacy and defamation cases; illegal file-sharing sites have been the cause of controversy for some time, leading to an equally controversial piece of legislation; and the issue of TV formats has certainly become more complicated with the advent of YouTube and other online tools that provide for dissemination of TV programmes across borders cheaply and swiftly.

Facing up to these challenges in the entertainment industries has led to a call for the reform of certain laws. For example the Digital Economy Act 2010 aims to combat illegal file-sharing and online piracy; the Defamation Act 2013 brings the libel laws 'up to date'; and a consideration of the privacy laws under the Leveson Inquiry has called for regulation to support the integrity and freedom of the press whilst encouraging the highest ethical standards. Whether the suggested recommendations and future reform will be successful is a separate question. For the moment, it is encouraging to see these reforms being proposed in order to bring the law in line with modern developments.

As discussed in this chapter, there are other areas of the entertainment industries, such as TV formats, where the law is riddled with uncertainty. Whilst advancements in technologies also play a role here, the main issue is that the protection of TV formats continues to be unclear. Attempts at protecting TV formats through copyright law, passing off, unfair competition and breach of confidentiality bring their own challenges. Protecting a global format market worth billions can be economically justified. But whether it can also justify the harmonization of European Union laws remains to be seen.

The entertainment industries and the regulations pertaining to them are clearly experiencing a time of major change and uncertainty. But change should not be perceived as being unusual: as technology, society and the entertainment industries develop, reforming the law to reflect these changes will be increasingly important. However, as changes are effected through reform of the law, it is equally important that those changes prove to be effective in serving all stakeholders in the entertainment industries. As we have seen in this chapter, this will ultimately involve a balancing act between these stakeholders. Therefore, in looking to the future, it is hoped that the changes and reforms that are being proposed at present will be translated into a fair and balanced system in order to meet today's challenges in a changing entertainment market.

SEMINAR ACTIVITIES

1. Identify the issues surrounding the protection of copyright content and the problems thrown up by illegal file-sharing.

2. Critically analyse the issues surrounding the protection of parody and TV formats.

3. Identify and explain the grounds for bringing a claim for defamation.

4. Critically discuss the assertion that the Defamation Act 2013 is a step in the right direction.

5. Identify the key developments in the law of privacy and breach of confidence.

6. Discuss the claim that the UK's Digital Economy Act 2010 will be outdated before it can be implemented.

7. With reference to relevant case law, discuss the development of the common law right of breach of confidentiality and a right to privacy as recognized in the Human Rights Act 1998.

8. Discuss the future of the press and privacy laws with reference to the recommendations made in the Leveson Report.

REFERENCES

Agate, J. (2013) The Defamation Act 2013: Key changes for online. *Computer and Telecommunications Law Review* 19(6), 170–171.

Arts Council England (2006) Submission to Gowers Review of Intellectual Property (24 August). Available at: http://www.hm-treasury.gov.uk/d/arts_council_england_476_37kb.pdf (accessed 15 May 2012).

Coad, J. (2011) How do you stop your TV formats idea being stolen? Available at: http://www.ifla.tv/howdoyoustoptvformatideabeingstolen.htm (accessed 20 May 2012).

Deazley, R. (2010) Copyright and parody: Taking backwards the Gowers Review? *Modern Law Review* 73(5), 785–823.

Department for Culture, Media and Sport (2011) *Next Steps for the Implementation of the Digital Economy Act.* Department for Culture, Media and Sport, London.

Erickson, K., Kretschmer, M. and Mendis, D. (2013) Copyright and the economic effects of parody: An empirical study of music videos on the YouTube platform and an assessment of the regulatory options. Intellectual Property Office, London. Available at: http://www.ipo.gov.uk/ipresearch-parody-report3-150313.pdf (accessed 15 July 2013).

Farrand, B. (2010) The Digital Economy Act 2010: A cause for celebration, or a cause for concern? *European Intellectual Property Review* 32(10), 536–541.

Format Recognition and Protection Association (2011) FRAPA Report 2011. Available at: http://www.frapa.org/services/frapa-report-2011 (accessed 13 December 2012).

Gowers, A. (2006) *Gowers Review of Intellectual Property.* HMSO, Norwich, UK.

Hargreaves, I. (2011) *Digital Opportunity: A Review of Intellectual Property and Growth.* Intellectual Property Office, London.

Hooper, D., Waite, K. and Murphy, O. (2013) Defamation Act 2013: What difference will it really make? *Entertainment Law Review* 24(6), 199–206.

IFPI Digital Music Reports (2004–2011) Available at: http://www.ifpi.org/content/section_statistics/index.html (accessed 8 January 2013).

International Chamber of Commerce (2010) Building a Digital Economy: The Importance of Saving Jobs in the EU's Creative Industries. Available at: http://www.iccwbo.org/uploadedFiles/BASCAP/Pages/Building%20a%20Digital%20Economy%20-%20TERA%281%29.pdf (accessed 15 April 2013).

James, S. (2008) The times they are a-changin': Copyright theft, music distribution and keeping the pirates at bay. *Entertainment Law Review* 19(5), 106–108.

Jordan, B. (2010) Existing defamation law needs to be updated so that it is fit for the modern age - the Government's consultation on the multiple publication rule. *Entertainment Law Review* 21(2), 41–47.

Krishnan, S. (2012) Lord Lester's Defamation Bill: Striking a balance? *Entertainment Law Review* 23(2), 5–31.

Laddie, H., Prescott, P. and Vitoria, M. (eds) (2011) *The Modern Law of Copyright and Designs*, 4th edn. Lexis-Nexis Butterworth, London.

La Rue, F. (2011) Report of the Special Rapporteur on the promotion and protection of the right to freedom of opinion and expression. Available at: http://www2.ohchr.org/english/bodies/hrcouncil/docs/17session/A.HRC.17.27_en.pdf (accessed 14 April 2013).

Larusson, H.K. (2009) Uncertainty in the scope of copyright: The case of illegal file-sharing in the UK. *European Intellectual Property Review* 31(3), 124–134.

Lavender, D. and Kill, L. (2007) When breach of contract might be OK! *European Lawyer* 69, 18–19.

Leveson, B.H. (2012) Leveson Inquiry: An Inquiry into the Culture, Practices and Ethics of the Press. Available at: http://www.levesoninquiry.org.uk/about/the-report (accessed 20 June 2013).

Logan, L. (2009a) The emperor's new clothes? The way forward TV format protection under unfair competition law in the United States, United Kingdom and France: Part 1. *Entertainment Law Review* 20(2), 37–43.

Logan, L. (2009b) The emperor's new clothes? The way forward TV format protection under unfair competition law in the United States, United Kingdom and France: Part 2. *Entertainment Law Review* 20(3), 87–92.

MacQueen, H., Waelde, C., Laurie, G. and Brown, A. (2011) *Contemporary Intellectual Property: Law and Policy*. Oxford University Press, Oxford, UK.

Mendis, D. (2013) Digital Economy Act 2010: Fighting a losing battle? Why the three-strikes law is not the answer to copyright law's latest technological challenge. *International Review of Law, Computers* and *Technology* 27(1–2), 60–84.

Mendis, D. and Kretschmer, M. (2013) The treatment of parodies under Copyright Law in seven jurisdictions: A comparative review of the underlying principles. Intellectual Property Office, London. Available at: http://www.ipo.gov.uk/ipresearch-parody-report2-150313.pdf (accessed 15 July 2013).

Mindell, R. (2012) Rewriting privacy: The impact of social online networks. *Entertainment Law Review* 23(3), 52–58.

Moreham, N.A. (2005) Privacy in the common law: A doctrinal and theoretical analysis. *Law Quarterly Review* 121, 628–656.

Nash, A. and Crown, G. (2005) McLibel: The Last Supper for denying legal aid? *New Law Journal* 155(7166), 316–317.

OFCOM (2011) 'Site Blocking' to reduce online copyright infringement: A Review of sections 17 and 18 of the Digital Economy Act. Available at: http://stakeholders.ofcom.org.uk/binaries/Internet/site-blocking.pdf at Section 6 (accessed 14 July 2013).

Quinn, F. (2011) *Law for Journalists*. Pearson, Harlow, UK.

Scolnicov, A. (2005) Supersized speech: McLibel comes to Strasbourg. *Cambridge Law Journal* 64(2), 311–314.

Shaw, R. and Chamberlain, P. (2011) Libel reform: draft Defamation Bill seeks a legal balance but ignores the costs issue. *Communications Law* 16(2), 49–51.

Smartt, U. (2011) Twitter undermines super-injunctions. *Communications Law* 16(4), 135–139.

Starmer, K. and Hudson, A. (2005) McLibel Two win in Europe. *Legal Action*, 9–10.

Stephens, M. (2005) McLibel decision could even odds in David and Goliath disputes. *European Lawyer* 49, 15–16.

Stern, T. (2009) Freemantle Media Bournemouth University international trade of formats and the relevance of format rights/CEMPVIDEOS. Available at: http://tvformats.bournemouth.ac.uk/overview (accessed 15 June 2013).

Stevenson, A. and Soanes, C. (eds) (2003) *Oxford English Dictionary*. Oxford University Press, Oxford, UK.

Case Law

Berkoff v. Birchill [1996] 4 ALL ER 1008

Campbell v. MGN Ltd [2004] UKHL 22

Castaway v. Endemol 16 April 2004, no Co2/284HR

Chris Cairns v. Lalit Modi [2012] EWHC 756 (QB)

Coco v. A.N. Clark (Engineers) Ltd (1969) RPC 41

Designer Guild v. Russell Williams [2001] 1 ALL ER 700

Douglas and another and others v. Hello! Limited and others [2007] UKHL 21

Duke of Brunswick v. Harmer [1849] 14 QB 185

Godfrey v. Demon Internet [2001] QB 201
Green v. Broadcasting Corporation of New Zealand [1989] RPC 700
Hulton (E) and Co v. Jones [1910] AC 20 (HL)
Kaye v. Robertson [1991] FSR 62
McDonald's Corp v. Steel and Morris [1997] EWHC (QB) 366
Media C.A.T. v. Adams [2011] EWPCC, 6
Mosley v. News Group Newspapers Ltd [2008] EWHC 1777 (QB)
Murray v. NBC 844 F.2d 988 (2d Cir. 1988)
Nine Films and Television Pty Ltd v. Ninox Television (2005) FCA 1404
Prince Albert v. Strange [1849] EWHC Ch J20 (8 February 1849)
Simon Singh v. British Chiropractic Association [2011] 1 WLR 133
Talbot v. General Television Corp Pty Ltd [1980] VR 224 (Vic SC), RR 489
TFI v. Antenne 2 (1993) ELR E-63 Cour d'appel de Versailles
TSE v. News Group Newspapers Ltd [2011] EWHC 1308 (QB) 23 May 2011
University of London Press v. University Tutorial Press [1916] 2 Ch 601

Legislation

Article 8 European Convention of Human Rights 1950
Commission's proposed directive amending the term of protection of copyright and certain related
    rights (COM (2008) 464/3)
Consumer Protection from Unfair Trading (CPUT) Regulations 2008
Copyright Act 1976 (USA)
Copyright, Designs and Patents Act 1988
Defamation Act 1952
Defamation Act 1996
Defamation Act 2013
Digital Economy Act 2010
Human Rights Act 1998, Section 12
Paris Convention for the Protection of Industrial Property 1979, Article 10*bis*(2)
Press Complaints Commission Code of Practice clause 3
Term extension (COM (2008) 464/3)

chapter 13

Managing Strategic and Financial Performance

Martin Piber and Ben Walmsley

LEARNING OBJECTIVES

After reading this chapter you should be able to:

- discuss the relationship between an organization's mission and management cycle and the way it evaluates its strategic performance;
- analyse the role of stakeholders in informing organizational objectives and performance;
- define and discuss the key principles behind financial accounting in arts and entertainment organizations;
- understand how production and exhibition budgets are drafted and managed; and
- apply and critique different tools and frameworks designed to manage and evaluate organizational performance.

INTRODUCTION

The key question explored in this chapter is how arts and entertainment organizations ensure the sustainable survival of their organizations by managing the quality of their performance effectively. However, defining quality is not an easy endeavour because quality is invariably a subjective and shifting phenomenon which depends on each organization's particular mission, environment and perspective. Arts and entertainment organizations are usually entangled with audiences, artists and funders, either on a public or private basis, so they almost always appeal and answer to a diverse range of stakeholders. This is relevant for both subsidized arts organizations and for commercial entertainment companies.

This chapter is organized as follows: first, we will outline our understanding of the management cycle and discuss its relationship with performance management. Second, we will address the key issues and challenges of financial accounting in arts and entertainment organizations. We will then study the role of financial planning and budgeting, focusing briefly on the acquired art of managing production and exhibition budgets. Finally, we will move on to critically explore more holistic ways of managing and measuring organizational performance and consider a range of tools and frameworks that are particularly useful for evaluating the strategic performance of arts and entertainment organizations.

THE MANAGEMENT CYCLE

In general, performance measurement is built upon the vision and the mission statement as well as upon a set of strategic organizational objectives. The vision outlines the projected long-term development of an organization and forms a basis for its organizational objectives and targets. The mission frames the purpose and tasks of the organization. Both are seminal for the development of targets. But given that they set out the long-term strategic direction of an organization, it is advisable to allow for flexibility in the vision and mission statements in order not to be bound to the environmental conditions prevailing at the time of generating the vision.

On the basis of organizational targets, management teams can establish both an annual planning cycle and an appropriate performance measurement system, which should comprise both financial and non-financial data. On a strategic level, issues relating to organizational change, corporate culture and the development of vision and mission are all on the agenda here. On the operational level, the basic planning dimensions are based on revenues and costs.

A budget represents the translation of an organization's targets into clear-cut figures. After the planning period, the management team will consider their latest financial figures and compare them with their planned set of figures in order to identify any problem areas or deficiencies. The result of this deviation-analysis will be integrated into the planning process for the following financial periods. Considering the particular output and outcomes of cultural and entertainment organizations, other performance measures such as customer and employee satisfaction, the share of self-generated income and sponsorship revenue are also useful in this context. We will address these issues later in the chapter.

So an organization's budget enables it to learn and improve over time. If the targets of the budget are not met, the people and the departments involved should reflect on the relevant issues in order to improve the situation for the next financial period. It is also important to adjust financial targets according to the current situation. This is known as 'strategic feed-forward control' and it enables an organization to establish a learning process in the second dimension, which is referred to as 'double-loop learning' (Argyris and Schön, 1978). This essentially means that an organization adjusts not only its past practices (which Argyris and Schön call 'single-loop learning') but also its future-oriented targets.

The management control process draws on methods that enable an organization and its employees to act in the interest of the mission and fulfil its strategic goals. By reviewing both operational and strategic data, the organization will be able to take more informed decisions. However, many entertainment organizations, especially arts and cultural organizations, face major challenges in setting their target systems because of the diverse stakeholder interests to which they must respond. Key stakeholders generally include funders (national, regional and local), audiences/consumers, artists/producers and the general public. In some cases these groups might even have conflicting interests. For example, museums or art galleries might exhibit famous artists like French impressionists in order to maximize their visitor figures. On the other hand, curators might prefer to exhibit unknown artists to maximize the gallery's artistic reputation. This strategy would automatically attract fewer visitors. These conflicting interests make it more difficult to align the targets of an organization, as profit is not always the only clear and commonly accepted denominator for success.

On a strategic level, many arts and cultural organizations are increasingly having to cope with shrinking public subsidies, especially in Europe. This can cause severe planning problems, as these organizations might face a cut in the short term without any clear warning in advance. This means that cultural organizations have to maintain a certain flexibility to be able to adjust their operations according to the available funding. As for profit-based organizations, with increasing demands on people's leisure time, it is crucial

for entertainment organizations to keep their costs under control. This requires sound and detailed financial information. So at the heart of any cost accounting strategy lies a robust and fit-for-purpose financial accounting system.

FINANCIAL ACCOUNTING

Most entertainment organizations now rely on professional financial software and accounting tools and systems to support their operational and strategic planning. In certain sectors of the entertainment industries, for example in arts and cultural organizations, which often receive some form of public subsidy, the most important line in the profit and loss account is public funding, which is generally distributed via a public or arm's length body such as an arts or regional council. When we consider the expenses of cultural organizations we will see that the biggest expenses are usually related to staff. This is typical of the wider service industry where personnel costs comprise on average two-thirds of an organization's overall costs.

Case Study: Income and expenditure in an art gallery

Table 13.1 displays the profit and loss account of an art gallery in Austria. It indicates the percentage of each income and expenditure item in relation to the overall budget.

This example shows that the gallery has a high self-financing ratio. The self-financing ratio represents the extent to which the gallery is able to bear its own costs. In the current era of reduced public funding, this is becoming an increasingly significant ratio. However, we can see in the table that almost two-thirds of the gallery's income still comes from government funding. This means that one-third of its budget is self-earned, which is a relatively high level for a subsidized museum or gallery in Europe, where the average self-financing ratio is around 20%.

(Continued)

Case Study. Continued.

Table 13.1. Profit and loss statement for an art gallery.

Item	% of total budget
Income	
Governmental funding	63
Entrance fees	21
Gallery shop sales	7
Fees for lending of artwork	2
Exhibition sales to partners	1
Income from rent of event spaces	2
Sponsorship and donations	1
Grants for research projects	2
Other income	1
	100
Expenses/Expenditure	
Cost of goods sold (in the gallery shop)	3
Staff expenses	60
Rent of building and maintenance	13
Purchase of artwork	1
Collections and restoration	2
Exhibition expenses	8
Publications and catalogues	2
Marketing costs	3
Events and exhibitions	1
Travel expenses	1
Consultancy	1
Other expenses	2
EBITDA	
Depreciation	3
EBIT	
Financial income	0
	100

The income side of this account statement reflects the different sources of income such as entrance fees, shop sales and the renting out of event and hospitality spaces. This highlights the fact that in order to gain additional revenue, arts and cultural organizations

(Continued)

Case Study. Continued.

are increasingly concerned with generating new and diverse sources of income. In this example, the gallery sells exhibitions to major sponsors and rents out its rooms for private hire or business meetings, conventions or other events in order to generate additional income. Likewise, shops, cafés, restaurants and bars are becoming more and more important in raising additional income for entertainment organizations.

We can see here that the most significant cost for the gallery is its expenditure on staff. However, in some cases, the supporting functions of an entertainment organization might be outsourced. Therefore, a comparison or financial benchmarking exercise of different organizations only works where organizations share a similar level of activity. For example, the figures provided here include the cost of security staff, but many entertainment venues will have lower levels of staff expenditure due to the outsourcing of specialist services such as security (Fig. 13.1) – especially bars and nightclubs, where security staff are often regulated by local or national government or industry bodies. To further complicate the financial issues, many not-for-profit entertainment organizations have cafés, bars and restaurants inside their venues, which are often run by a trading company that gifts its profits back to the host organization via a rental or lease agreement, thereby providing a further source of much needed extra income for arts and entertainment organizations.

After the staff costs, we can see that the second biggest draw on the gallery's financial resources is the cost of renting its space. In this case, the organization does not own its building but rents it on a lease. However, many buildings owned by entertainment organizations, especially established arts and cultural institutions, form part of a nation's cultural heritage. This can lead to significant extra costs for conservation and restoration, as well as placing heavy restrictions on what the organization can do with its building.

Fig. 13.1. Security officer at Nelson Atkins Museum of Art. Image by David Reber's Hammer Photography.

The previous case study illustrated an arts organization that generates a high proportion of its own income. But just as business models vary widely in the entertainment industries, so do ratios of earned income to overall income. With the restriction of public funding for the arts, many European countries have witnessed a drive towards a greater diversification of income. But this is easier for some organizations to achieve than it is for others. As we saw in Chapter 9, corporate sponsorship and personal giving is often concentrated in a tiny minority of flagship organizations, which are often based in a capital city. This tends to leave smaller, less well resourced regional and local organizations fighting over the scraps left over. Figures 13.2 and 13.3 illustrate the discrepancy in income distribution between England's London-based National Theatre (NT) and one of its largest regional theatres, West Yorkshire Playhouse in Leeds.

A quick comparison of these pie charts highlights the significant discrepancies in the breakdown of income for these two organizations. While the NT generates a huge 77% of its own income and receives only 23% in public funding, West Yorkshire Playhouse receives 35% of its income from public funding bodies and generates only 65%. It also raises significantly less through fundraising and sponsorship. This comparison reveals the practical challenges of fundraising in the regions and illustrates how regional organizations are therefore often much more vulnerable if their public funding is cut.

Now that we have explored the key issues pertaining to income and expenditure, we will move on to explore the role of the balance sheet. A balance sheet records an organization's assets, liabilities and equity and therefore provides a financial snapshot of a company's cash value or financial condition (Williams *et al.*, 2012). Balance sheets in the entertainment industries, even in the arts and cultural sector, do not differ very much from those in other industries, at least in terms of

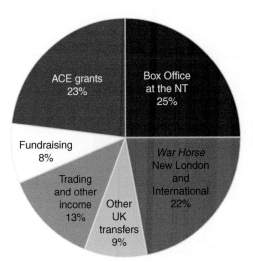

Fig. 13.2. National Theatre's Income Breakdown 2011–2012. (From National Theatre, 2012, p. 43.)

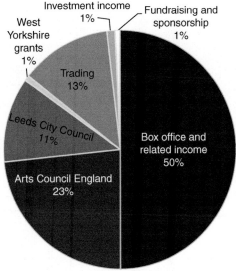

Fig. 13.3. West Yorkshire Playhouse's income breakdown 2011–2012. (From West Yorkshire Playhouse, 2012.)

liabilities and equity. But how artistic and cultural assets are recorded on the balance sheet differs from country to country and even from one organization to another. As most entertainment organizations are not listed on the stock exchange, their financial affairs are governed by national regulations and are not subject to the new International Financial Reporting Standards (IFRS), which are designed to promote global financial accounting standards and produce comparative data. To refer back to our case study of the art gallery, it does not make much sense to activate the value of art, even on its purchasing price, because galleries do not usually sell their art collections. Some galleries list their artworks with a nominal valuation in their accounts (e.g. one cent or one pence per piece), whereas others are not allowed to list them at all because they do not actually own them. This is especially the case for many national galleries and museums, whose collections are often owned by the state or by the general public.

On the passive side of a balance sheet there are two specific entities that we need to consider here. As a significant number of entertainment organizations are not-for-profit organizations and therefore balance their budgets to zero, they have very limited reserves for investment. Normally, large investments are provided by their owners (ultimately the general public) or through national lottery schemes. Some cultural institutions therefore have an item called an *investment grant* on the passive side of their balance sheets. On the active side of the balance sheet, this grant refers to expenditure against this investment (e.g. the refurbishment of a theatre). This grant is reduced annually according to the depreciation of the invested asset, to account for wear and tear, etc. Another special feature of many entertainment organizations is *philanthropy*, which can take the form of donations for future investments – for example, if a fundraising campaign is instigated for a capital investment that will be carried out in 2 years' time. This income is listed as a passive accrual until the investment is actually spent.

ACCOUNTING SYSTEMS

There are two basic accounting systems: *cash accounting* and *accrual-based accounting*. Cash accounting is just a simple calculation of all cash inflows minus all cash outflows so that at the end of the month or quarter (or whatever the organization's reporting period) the total balance becomes visible. The main drawback of cash accounting is that it fails to show debtors and creditors (or in other words how much an organization owes to others and how much others owe to the organization). In order to be informed about an organization's true and longer-term financial status, it is therefore necessary to use an accrual-based accounting system, because this includes information about future commitments and receivables. For example, if an organization buys five computers by credit card, this expenditure will not show in the cash accounting system until the credit card company collects the money (which may be almost 2 months after the money was actually spent). In an accrual-based accounting system, however, the accounts will immediately indicate that the debt of the organization has increased with the purchase.

Usually profit-based organizations generate a *profit and loss statement* (P&L) or an *income statement*, which compares the revenue and expenditure of an organization. If there is a net income at the end of the year the organization has been profitable. Not-for-profit organizations usually generate a *statement of financial activities* (SOFA), which also comprises revenue and expenditure. If the total amount of revenue is greater than total expenditure then the organization will increase its net assets or reserves. Unlike profit-based companies which can spend their net profits as they choose, not-for-profit organizations are obliged to reinvest any surplus into their charitable activities, which in the entertainment industries generally translates to artistic or educational activities. Both profit and loss statements and statements of financial activities are carried out over a specified financial period – typically a financial year, which varies from organization to organization.

PLANNING AND BUDGETING

Krug and Weinberg (2004) developed a performance measurement system for cultural organizations which refers to three dimensions: mission, money and merit. The first dimension measures the strategic contribution to the mission of the organization. The second dimension covers the financial performance of an organization and the third dimension (merit) addresses the *quality* of an organization's performance by using both qualitative and quantitative measures. The strategic contribution to the mission needs to be evaluated by experts, whereas the money and merit dimensions can be evaluated via a set of specially designed performance measures. Krug and Weinberg propose that organizations present their results in a three-dimensional cube.

The comparison of an organization's mission with its achieved performance is particularly useful for planning purposes. The mission is the most future-oriented element of the corporate planning process. On a short-term basis, organizations generate both strategic and operational plans, and the extent to which an organization is fulfilling its mission needs to be evaluated through a process of strategic control. On an operational basis, this strategic control works via the process of budget management.

A budget can be understood as the financial translation of all the elements related to an organization's operational planning, to its planned activities. In the budgeting process, a forecast for all the significant expenses of the organization is established, which provides the basis for the corporate budget. A short-term budgeting period would usually cover 1 year of operational activity, although of course many entertainment organizations operate also via production or exhibition budgets, which are usually operational for a period of weeks or months. However, on the corporate level, the typical short-term plan is covered by the annual budget, which is an organization's most important financial planning tool. Strategic budgeting includes larger investments, especially in buildings or IT facilities, which have to be planned in the long term and budgeted over a period between 3 and 5 years.

For larger organizations, the process of generating the annual budget should begin a couple of months before each new budgeting period (see Fig. 13.4).

We can distinguish three methods of budgeting in this simple Gantt chart (Fig. 13.4): the top-down approach, the bottom-up approach and the mixed approach.

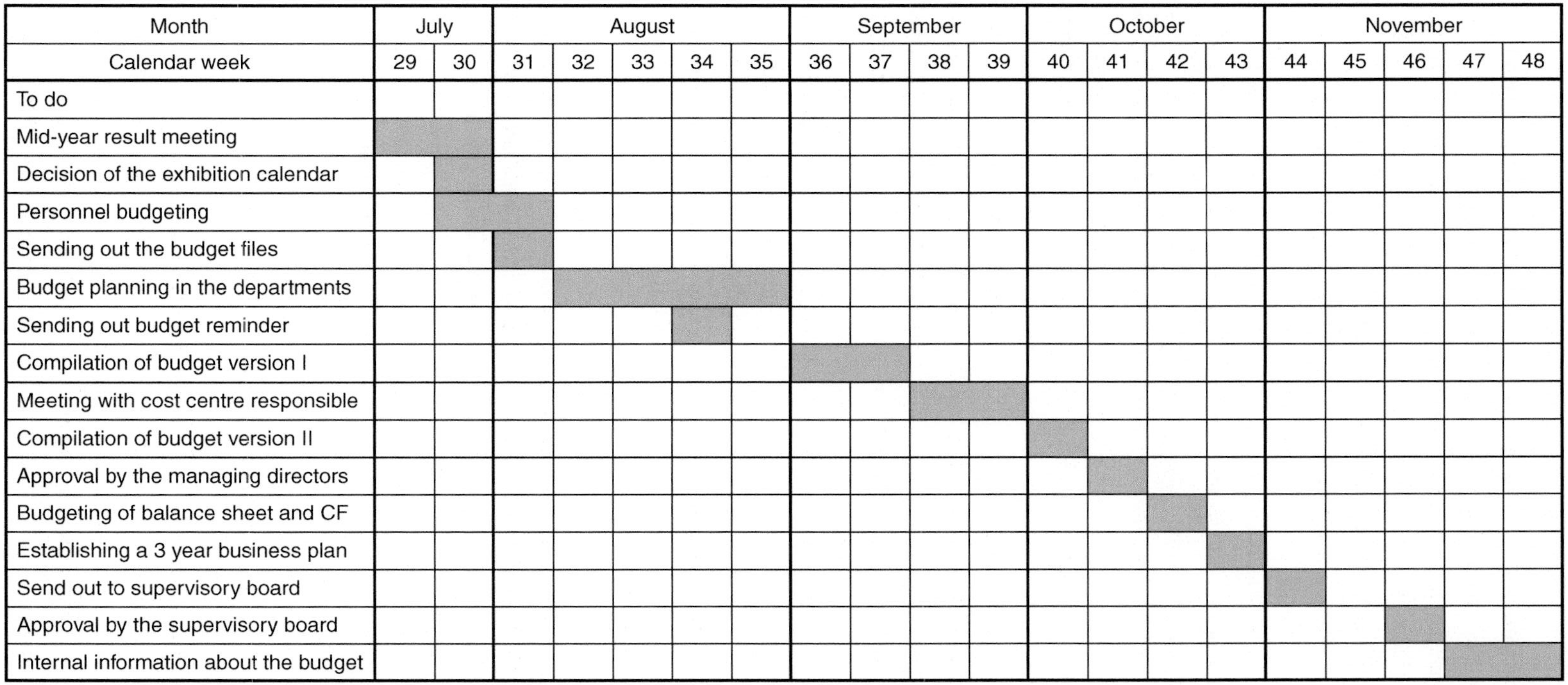

To do	July			August				September				October					November			
Calendar week	29	30	31	32	33	34	35	36	37	38	39	40	41	42	43	44	45	46	47	48
Mid-year result meeting	■																			
Decision of the exhibition calendar		■																		
Personnel budgeting			■																	
Sending out the budget files			■																	
Budget planning in the departments					■	■	■													
Sending out budget reminder						■														
Compilation of budget version I									■											
Meeting with cost centre responsible											■									
Compilation of budget version II												■								
Approval by the managing directors													■	■						
Budgeting of balance sheet and CF															■					
Establishing a 3 year business plan																■				
Send out to supervisory board																■				
Approval by the supervisory board																		■		
Internal information about the budget																				■

Fig. 13.4. The planning process of an art gallery.

A top-down budget is generated by the senior management, whereas a bottom-up budget represents the total of the collated departmental budgets. The mixed approach starts with a proposal from one side and is finally developed through a communicative process between the senior management and each department in the organization.

At the end of the budgeting period, the management compares the budget with the performance achieved in order to learn how to improve (single-loop learning). In a double-loop learning process, the accuracy of the budget targets will also be reflected and translated into corrective action to guide future planning, with targets adapted to current or future requirements.

Budgets are established for different units or cost-centres of the organization such as the marketing or production department. As discussed above, budgets can also be implemented for one-off projects or events. These are activities with a clear starting point and a clear terminal point. Production and exhibition budgets comprise all the expenses for a specified activity. They are flexible financial plans, which need to include a contingency to allow for any inaccurate budgeting or unanticipated costs. Like departmental budgets, production and exhibition budgets need to be monitored and reconciled both during and after the event.

Budgeting is a key process in the achievement of financial success and stability. But accurate budgeting and financial forecasting are acquired skills, which take years of industry experience. Organizations therefore need to designate budget holders clearly and carefully, because these key individuals will be tasked with balancing an organization's financial situation according to its available means.

They will ultimately determine the organization's financial success.

PERFORMANCE MEASUREMENT

The financial data provided by the statement of financial activities and the balance sheet provide sound information about the financial status of an organization. However, it is also necessary to consider other key data such as individual production or exhibition costs and the related marketing spend. In addition to this, the comparison with past or historical data can quickly alert an organization to any potential dangers facing the organization and highlight any seasonal or longer-term trends. But even then, financial data do not provide enough information to fully understand an organization's long-term development, and they certainly fail to provide sufficient insight to enable a management team to take informed and rounded strategic decisions. This is especially the case for many entertainment organizations, whose concerns are often far wider than just the bottom line. An arts organization, for example, may often place its artistic achievements and reputation above its financial performance. For this reason, financial accounting data should always be complemented by other key performance indicators (KPIs), which should cover the main areas of an organization's activity and reflect its vision, its core purpose and its mission. An example of broader, strategically focused targets and KPIs is provided in Table 13.2.

The development of KPIs is a vital part of the strategic and financial management process as it works alongside financial data to inform an organization's decision-making.

Table 13.2. Example of key performance indicators.

Strategic focus	Target	Key performance indicator (KPI)
Artistic quality	Improve the quality of exhibitions	Positive media coverage in quality media Number of awards and distinctions
Commercial development	Generate more external revenue	Shop sales per visitor
Marketing	Raise interest for exhibitions amongst new audiences	Increase in visitor figures from first-time visitors
Exhibitions	Increase the satisfaction of visitors	Improvement in visitor satisfaction surveys
Finance	Decrease dependence on public funding	Raise self-generated revenue ratio

This holistic approach to organizational analysis is called *multi-dimensional performance measurement*.

Although organizations can learn a lot by benchmarking themselves against similar organizations, every organization should also develop its own specific KPIs, which should reflect its strategic goals. Performance measures are generally used to evaluate the following organizational achievements:

- inputs (e.g. the budget for a restoration project);
- processes (e.g. the number of innovative projects or collaborations);
- outputs (e.g. the number of films, shows or exhibitions produced); and
- outcomes (e.g. developing a new audience base).

The advantage of using performance measures in the entertainment industries is that they can also address the artistic and educational targets, outputs and outcomes of cultural and creative organizations, which financial data alone cannot capture.

THE BALANCED SCORECARD

One of the most popular multidimensional performance measurement systems in use is the *balanced scorecard*. The balanced scorecard was developed by Kaplan and Norton (1992) as a strategic management tool to evaluate performance based on an organization's mission and strategic objectives. It combines financial data and other KPIs with softer, less tangible assets such as organizational culture, processes and innovation. Arts and entertainment organizations have been encouraged to adopt it by many commentators, including Boorsma and Chiaravalloti (2010), who argue that it places the mission (rather than profit) at the heart of performance management and explicitly addresses the different types of value demanded by the diverse range of stakeholders often involved in the funding and operations of arts and entertainment organizations.

The use of performance measurement systems such as the balanced scorecard in many arts and entertainment organizations reflects the fact that they do not have one single bottom line (profit). Different target systems require multiple bottom lines, which should reflect and represent an organization's core areas of activity. For example, it might be strategic for a museum to lend out more of its permanent collection, both to increase its earned income and to enhance its artistic reputation. Likewise, a local performing arts venue might decide to measure its success by how well it engages with its local community, which could not only increase its ticket sales income but also improve its local

visibility and diversify its audience base. The following case study illustrates how an art gallery might use a balanced scorecard approach to evaluate its strategic performance.

However, even when a sophisticated multi-dimensional performance measurement tool such as the balanced scorecard is employed, management systems are only ever as robust as the people and data that populate them and they are always open to interpretation. Artistic quality and reputation and other issues relating to brand equity will always remain very difficult to measure. Indeed some people would argue that they are so subjective that they cannot and should not be measured at all. When exploring the value and impact of cultural activities, for example, we might argue that any attempts to measure them are doomed to be reductive and incomplete. In order to fully understand

---

Case Study: A balanced scorecard approach to evaluating an art gallery

A scorecard-based performance measurement system analyses an organization by evaluating its most important strategic dimensions. Table 13.3 presents the balanced scorecard for an Austrian art gallery. The key dimensions in this particular example are the contribution to the mission, the stakeholder orientation, the employee perspective and the financial perspective. For each dimension you can see the most important strategic targets identified by the gallery and the performance indicators selected to assess the organization's state of development and measure its success in achieving its organizational goals.

This example illustrates how the balanced scorecard can be utilized by arts and entertainment organizations to provide a holistic analysis of their strategic performance, which goes far beyond their financial performance to address issues of culture, quality and service. In this example, the scorecard is mainly based on hard data that can be measured in an objective way, but it is worth noting that one of the advantages of the balanced scorecard is that it can incorporate softer data and more subjective performance indicators such as the intrinsic impact of art on audiences or an organization's propensity for change or risk.

(Continued)

Case Study. Continued.

Table 13.3. Balanced scorecard for an art gallery.

Strategic dimension	Strategic targets	Performance indicators
Contribution to mission	Improve the quality of exhibitions Develop the art collection	Excellent coverage in quality press Enhance curators' expertise
Stakeholder orientation	Increase visitor satisfaction Improve the gallery's reputation	High visitor satisfaction index Positive comments on visitor feedback forms Invitations by well-respected institutions to (co-)curate exhibitions
Employee perspective	Knowledgeable gallery staff Motivated employees Adequate professional development	Number of complaints by visitors High employee satisfaction index High employee satisfaction index Improvement in employees' qualifications
Financial perspective	Reduce dependence on public funding Increase sales per visitor Increase efficiency in security	Increase in self-generated income Increase in shop sales per visitor Fewer false alarms

such important spheres of organizational performance and integrate them into the corporate decision-making process, it is necessary to rely on the experience, skills and intuition of well-trained and highly experienced arts and entertainment managers.

CONCLUSION

This chapter has explored how arts and entertainment organizations evaluate their strategic performance. It has also analysed some of the challenges involved in measuring subjective notions such as organizational culture and artistic quality. In the course of the chapter we have seen how management cycles and financial accounting processes help managers to assess the financial health of their organizations. We have also discussed the importance of adopting an accrual-based accounting approach to generate a long-term picture of an organization: cash accounting and even balance sheets only provide a simple snapshot of financial performance, so they are of limited use for long-term strategic planning.

We have highlighted the importance of accurate budgeting to operational aspects of entertainment management. Given the entertainment industries' dependence on live events such as shows, exhibitions and performances, many organizations need to budget on both a short- and long-term basis. Budgets and budget holders play a vital role in entertainment management because budgets act as financial translations of an organization's planned activities. Budget management can be improved by adopting a 'double-loop learning' approach, which can improve the accuracy of budgeting and guide future financial planning.

However, financial data do not provide enough information to fully understand an organization's long-term development nor to enable a management team to make balanced strategic decisions. This is especially the case for arts and entertainment organizations, which, as we have seen, are founded on missions, business models and income streams that do not always prioritize profit. Financial data should therefore always be complemented by other key performance indicators, which should reflect an organization's core purpose, activity and mission. Entertainment organizations now have a range of tools and frameworks at their disposal to measure and evaluate their strategic performance in a multidimensional way. Krug and Weinberg (2004) developed a three-dimensional performance measurement system for cultural organizations, which takes into account the importance of mission, money and merit. But the most popular multidimensional performance measurement system remains the balanced scorecard, which places mission rather than profit at the heart of performance management. This is of particular importance in the entertainment industries because it reflects the different types of value demanded by the diverse range of stakeholders often involved in the strategic success and sustainability of arts and entertainment organizations. However, even the most sophisticated management system cannot fully capture the soul and essence of an organization, and aspects such as value and impact will always need to be assessed and articulated in human terms by experienced entertainment managers.

SEMINAR ACTIVITIES

1. Why does an entertainment organization's vision need to be flexible?

2. How would you define deviation analysis?

3. What is the main drawback of the cash accounting system?

4. What is the alternative system called and what are its key benefits?

5. What is the difference between strategic and operational budgeting and how might this differ in the entertainment industries?

6. What are the key advantages of the multidimensional performance measurement system?

7. Think of an entertainment organization you know well and make a list of what you think its key performance indicators should be.

8. What do you think are the main advantages of the balanced scorecard for entertainment organizations? Prepare a balanced scorecard analysis for an entertainment organization of your choice.

REFERENCES

Argyris, C. and Schön, D. (1978) *Organizational Learning: A Theory of Action Perspective*. Addison-Wesley, Reading, Massachusetts.

Boorsma, M. and Chiaravalloti, F. (2010) Arts marketing performance: An artistic-mission-led approach to evaluation. *Journal of Arts Management, Law and Society* 40(4), 297–317.

Kaplan, R.S. and Norton, D.P. (1992) The Balanced Scorecard – measures that drive performance. *Harvard Business Review* 70(1), 71–79.

Krug, K. and Weinberg, C.B. (2004) Mission, money, and merit: Strategic decision making by nonprofit managers. *Nonprofit Management & Leadership* 14(3), 325–342.

National Theatre (2012) National Theatre Annual Report 2011-2012. Available at: http://www.nationaltheatre. org.uk/sites/all/libraries/files/documents/National-Theatre-Annual-Report-2011-2012.pdf (accessed 12 April 2013).

West Yorkshire Playhouse (2012) *Financial Statements for the year ended 31 July 2012*. Leeds Theatre Trust Limited, Leeds, UK.

Williams, J.R., Haka, S.F., Bettner, M.S. and Carcello, J.V. (2012) *Financial & Managerial Accounting*, 15th edn. McGraw-Hill Irwin, New York.

chapter 14

Consultancy

Simon Woodward, Amanda Peacock and Peter McQuitty

LEARNING OBJECTIVES

After reading this chapter you should be able to:

- appreciate why organizations within the entertainment industries use consultants;
- learn the information gathering process undertaken by consultants for projects along with research methodologies and key analytical tools used to better understand collected data;
- know how to write a consultancy report and present findings to clients; and
- understand the importance of monitoring the impacts of interventions proposed by clients.

In a highly dynamic entertainment and leisure sector, which is sensitive to a range of economic, political and social factors, organizations sometimes need to call upon consultants to provide additional expertise and knowledge that will help them respond to changes in the external operating environment. This chapter explains the role of the management consultant and explores the practical steps they take as they provide well-informed, expert recommendations to industry. A case study from leading UK heritage consultancy PLB Ltd describes what happened when they were commissioned by Oxford City Council to identify a way forward for the struggling Museum of Oxford.

DEFINITIONS

The term 'consultant' is generally used to describe any person or organization that provides technical support or advice to decision-makers in private, public or third-sector organizations. Inserting the word 'management' in front refines the area of interest and indicates that the advice and intervention provided by the consultant is more closely focused on issues surrounding the efficient management of a business, organization or operation (Kubr, 1993).

Within the entertainment sector of the economy, there are many different types of consultant who can provide support. There are generic consultancies working in areas like general business strategy, market research, marketing and PR, whose experience covers many sectors of the economy. There are also more specialist consultants whose business model is based around the specific needs of the entertainment, leisure and tourism sectors.

The consultant will be commissioned to carry out work by a 'client', who may be a single individual or it can refer to a whole organization. The client will set the terms of reference for the consultancy assignment, establishing the scope of the work to be carried out on their behalf. All types of client organizations (public, private and third sector) in almost every part of the entertainment, leisure and tourism industry can benefit from the use of management consultants.

WHY USE CONSULTANTS?

The UK's Management Consultancy Association (MCA) (2012) defines the process of management consulting as 'the creation of value for organizations, through improved performance, achieved by providing objective advice and implementing business solutions'. So the emphasis is very much on finding solutions to improve the performance of an organization. This might be through ways to generate more revenue from existing products and services, opportunities to save money or identifying new products and services.

Whilst the MCA definition might imply that the consultant helps implement the appropriate changes, in reality this is not always the case, particularly in the entertainment industries. The main point to remember

is that the purpose of the consultant is to help whoever they are working with to do a better job than they were doing before the consultant was engaged.

So why do people hire consultants? There are generally three reasons, which reflect Rassam's (2001) categorization of consultant roles:

- 'Expert' – the client *does not have the skills* to undertake the work and believes that an external consultant will be able to do it better.
- 'Pair of hands' – the client *does not have the time or resources* to devote to a particular task and thinks that external support will get it done more quickly.
- 'Collaborator' – the client *wants an independent perspective* on the issue (and in some cases may even want to be disassociated from the findings if they are likely to be sensitive). For instance, if an organization thinks it needs to make redundancies or budget cuts, it may get an external consultant to identify where these should be so that the risks of conflict with colleagues in the workplace is lessened.

To learn more about the history of management consultancy and its role in today's society, two good introductions to the subject can be found in Sadler (2001) and Whickham and Wilcock (2012).

CHOOSING A CONSULTANT

Once a client organization has decided that it needs external help, selecting a consultant will normally be done through a tendering process whereby the client issues a brief that specifies the support they are seeking. The brief may be advertised widely through procurement websites or may just be sent to a few consultants already known to the client or recommended to them by other people working in the same area.

How a client approaches this initial stage depends partly on whether they are bound by certain procurement rules and regulations (for instance, public sector organizations are generally obliged to broadcast calls for tender widely) and also on their past experience of commissioning consultants. Consultants will then respond to the brief with a proposal that sets out: their credentials (skills, previous relevant experience, awards or certification, testimonials from past clients); their proposed approach to carrying out the assignment (including an initial assessment of issues and possible solutions); and a financial proposal (costs and time commitment by the team). They will also provide evidence of their financial standing and commitment to good practice.

The client may select the successful consultant on the basis of the proposal alone or may invite a selection of consultants along to make a presentation so that they can examine the expertise and team dynamics in a little more detail. This latter point is particularly important since consultancy is a 'people' business and one of the keys to a successful assignment is a good working relationship between client and consultant.

Once a preferred consultant has been identified a contract will be drawn up and agreed before both parties get together to start working on the project. Next we explore the main stages in a consultancy assignment,

before looking in more detail at some of the main skills required to carry out this work.

THE CONSULTING PROCESS

One of the leading writers on management consultancy, Cope (2010), has identified a seven-phase cycle that can be used as a framework for structuring almost any consultancy assignment (Table 14.1). This 'Seven Cs' framework illustrates the consultancy lifecycle and demonstrates the general sequence of events in any project.

In reality, not every contract will involve all of these stages and in many cases the contract will end at Stage 3 'Create'. This is because resources may not be available within the lifetime of a contract to implement the changes identified by the consultant and to monitor the impacts. In such cases, a consultant may help the client develop monitoring tools to help them assess on their own the impact of the interventions made. And in cases where the consultancy is about helping to deliver a capital project, such as the installation of new management or accounting software, or the installation of a new exhibition gallery in a museum, then the assignment may well jump from Stage 4 'Change' to Stage 7 'Close'.

Cope's contention is that within each of these seven stages the consultant will use various tools and diagnostic models to address the problem or challenge facing the client and their business, and that only once all possible solutions have been identified and addressed should the client and consultant 'close' the assignment. Whether this happens in reality again depends on the level of resources available to both parties. Some of the main tools

Table 14.1. The 'Seven Cs Framework', based upon the work of Cope (2010).

Client	Define the client's mission, values and objectives for the assignment. Identify internal champions and those who have the power to influence the outcome, i.e. understand the person and the problem.
Clarify	Determine the nature and detail of the problem to be addressed. Agree what is to be included and excluded from examination, and identify any areas of risk, i.e. understand what is going on.
Create	Use creative techniques to develop a sustainable solution to the problem, that can be measured against clear success criteria. This requires the collation of relevant data, the implementation of some form of diagnostic process and the identification of appropriate solutions.
Change	Understand the factors that drive and underpin the change process within that organization, in particular the human factors that need to be managed. Commence the appropriate intervention(s).
Confirm	Ensure that the change has taken place, using quantitative and qualitative measures.
Continue	Ensure that the change is being sustained, using learning that emerges from the early implementation phase.
Close	End the engagement process with the client, reviewing and recording the final outcomes, the added value, new learning (for both parties) and what further action might be undertaken in the future.

used by consultants to gather and analyse data in a little more detail will be discussed later in this chapter, but first the key to every successful assignment – good quality information – should be considered.

INFORMATION – THE KEY TO A SUCCESSFUL CONSULTANCY ASSIGNMENT

As indicated above, every assignment should begin with the consultant gaining a good understanding of the client, their problem and the parameters within which the solutions will be delivered. Key to the success of this stage will be an in-depth review of all relevant management information. This can take many forms and will relate both to the organization for which the work is being carried out and also the wider context.

Table 14.2 summarizes the key areas of understanding needed for some of the main types of consultancy study that might be commissioned in the entertainment industries and indicates, where appropriate, relevant sources of information.

Table 14.2. Data requirements for different types of assignment.

Type of assignment	Key area of understanding needed	Possible information sources
Strategic business review	Current business performance The wider operating environment – current status and likely changes Organization's capacity and willingness to change	Organizational records Employees Trade associations Industry experts External stakeholders including customers, suppliers, government
HR or organizational review	Company/organizational performance Organization's capacity, ability and willingness to change Employment legislation Current paradigms on management theory and practice	Organizational records Employees Trades Unions Government
Product or service development study	Current demand (satisfied and unsatisfied) Technological and other developments in the sector Projected changes in the relevant marketplace Profile of users/non-users Organizational capacity to develop/change/implement new products or services	Organizational records Employees Suppliers Trades associations Industry experts Customers Competitors

ETHICS, INFORMATION GATHERING AND THE CONSULTANCY PROCESS

A key requirement for management consultants is that they behave ethically at all times. Most consultants will already be bound by a code of ethics prepared by a relevant professional body such as the MCA, the Market Research Society (MRS) or a more sectoral-specific organization such as the Tourism Society Consultant's Network. Even when consultants are not signed up to a formal protocol, there is an expectation that they will behave ethically at all times. A good review of ethical considerations in consultancy is provided by Lynch (2001), whilst Gill and Johnson (2010) present an overview of ethics from an academic research perspective.

There are three fundamental points to remember when considering the ethics of any particular piece of consultancy or research.

- *Informed consent of participants*, meaning that all participants should be given full and accurate information in order for them to decide whether to take part in the research or not. Whilst in consultancy there is normally an assumption that the person providing information, for instance during a stakeholder interview or as part of a round-table discussion, will have given their consent for their views to be recorded by the very fact that they turned up and participated, in academic research this usually requires a properly developed 'participant information and consent' form.
- *Confidentiality and anonymity*, meaning that explicit consent must be gained from participants in order to publish any information that may enable them to be identified. This is the case whether their views are recorded and disseminated in a consultancy report that is prepared for the client's eyes only or whether the information may be used later on within a formal publication (e.g. a monograph, journal article or book chapter). Consultants should also consider data protection law in terms of how confidential data are stored or disposed of at the end of the contract.
- *Beneficence* – 'do positive good', and non-malfeasance – i.e. 'do no harm'. This means that all research should be assessed for potential risks concerning participants. The interests of subjects and participants should always come before those of the investigation itself.

Assuming that a consultant has addressed all of these points in an appropriate fashion then there should be no cause for concern.

RESEARCH METHODS

Consultants use the same basic research skills as do academic researchers. Indeed, many of the larger consultancies have their own 'research observatories' that gather information and publish on topics that they regularly consult on. Such groups include the US-based McKinsey Institute and the Global Thought Leadership team based in PriceWaterhouseCoopers' London offices.

In addition to their in-house teams, consultancies may work closely with accredited market research companies on specific projects. There is also a growing body of specialist professionals working in the emerging field of Strategic and Competitive Intelligence (SCI), which is basically an applied form of market research. Perhaps one of the most well-known organizations in this field is Mintel, who regularly publish reports on topics relevant to our discipline. Themes explored in recent Mintel reports include UK Nightclubs (January 2012), US Entertainment Venues (May 2011) and International Cultural & Heritage Tourism (May 2010).

The types of research methods used in any consultancy assignment, and the balance between them, will depend partly on the budget available (is there funding to commission original market research, for instance) but mainly on the data requirements, which themselves are determined by the problem being addressed in the study. So returning to the 'Seven Cs' model (Cope, 2010), it is essential to understand the client's aspirations and to clarify the scope of the project early on. Much time can be lost collecting the wrong data and delays will occur if you do not gather the right information.

The following are the main research methodologies used by consultants:

- desk research;
- primary research:
  - quantitative;
  - qualitative;
- site audits, including mystery shoppers.

A key feature of good consultancy, as with good academic research, is the importance of triangulating findings. In other words, consultants will use different sources or methods to check the validity of their findings before they present them to the client. This is to ensure that they are not distracted or misled by incomplete or even erroneous information. So in preparing a research plan, the consultant may identify a number of parallel or sequential data-gathering exercises to make sure that sufficient data are collected to allow for this triangulation.

Two good introductions to research techniques for our industry are the recent book by Veal (2011) and the slightly older book by Ritchie *et al.* (2005). Each of these broad methodologies will be briefly explored below.

Desk research, including reviews of secondary data

The starting point for almost every consultancy study will be a period of desk research as the consultant gains deep knowledge of the client organization, the broader operational context and the particular challenges being faced at the time. Sources of information can include the following:

- The records and archives of the organization in question.
- Academic journal articles. There is likely to be a journal – or several – relevant to almost every subject area; many have a practical focus and are important for influencing policy and practice. In the entertainment sectors, journals such as *Managing Leisure*, *The International Journal of Hospitality Management* and the *International Journal of Arts Management* all contain relevant articles on a regular basis.
- Trade journals that contain a mixture of news, opinion, case studies and longer reviews of policy and practice. Examples in the entertainment sector include *The Stage*, *Leisure Management*, *Caterer & Hotelkeeper* and *Museums Journal*.
- The 'grey' literature (i.e. material that has not been formerly published such as consultancy reports, government documents – sometimes available on the Internet, sometimes from NGO or government offices in the field).
- Websites, including competitor organizations (to seek out benchmarking data or ideas on good and bad practice), trade bodies and government agencies (for contextual information, guidance on relevant legislation etc.).

Reviewing this secondary data must be done in a structured fashion, so the consultant will identify key themes within the research and make sure that all appropriate areas have been covered. Again, this means that the consultant must have a very clear understanding of the scope of the study from the outset. Prior to commencing the desk research, it is helpful to draw up a set of key words that will guide the data-gathering exercise, particularly when it is web-based.

Primary research

Primary research is the collection of original new data that does not already exist. Data are raw, unprocessed facts, figures and opinions, which when analysed provide information that consultants can use to underpin theories and support proposed actions. Consultants gather two different types of data, these are quantitative and qualitative.

Quantitative

Quantitative techniques used by consultants are numeric in nature; this does not necessarily mean that all data consist of numbers, but it does mean that gathered data can be portrayed using statistical and graphical analysis. Common quantitative techniques include questionnaires, consumer surveys and gathering financial data from the client organization and competitors (it should be noted that questionnaires commonly also gather qualitative data). As indicated earlier, the scope of the data-collection exercise will be determined by the nature of the issues under investigation and also by the resources available. Often there are not the resources to commission large, tailor-made market studies, so the consultant may try to get around this by implementing a small-scale piece of research and comparing the findings with larger, industry generic studies.

Qualitative

Whilst quantitative sources and techniques may yield much useful management data, it is almost always necessary to support this with additional data that allows respondents to express their opinions and feelings beyond figures or tick-boxes. Most organizations have an 'institutional memory' that is rarely written down anywhere but that exists in the minds of the workforce; it is also important to understand the perspectives of other stakeholders outside the client organization. Getting at this information requires a good deal of skill in qualitative research techniques including structured, semi-structured and unstructured interviewing, focus groups or from longer written answers to questionnaire questions. Jennings (2005) provides a useful introduction to the different types of qualitative research techniques available.

It is rare for a consultancy study not to include a programme of interviews with key informants. The key to success is being well-prepared, recording accurately the discussion and also agreeing with each interviewee which points are 'on-' and which are 'off-the-record'.

The Delphi Technique is helpful when trying to establish the overall situation in a discipline or subject area and is both a data collection method and a diagnostic tool. It is particularly useful for forecasting studies. The researcher or consultant will ask a panel of experts inside or outside the client organization, or both, a series of fundamental questions about how they see the topic under consideration. The responses to this initial series of open-ended questions are reviewed and a relative score or weighting accorded to each response that indicates the overall level of importance given to it by the panel. Panel members are then contacted again and asked to review their initial responses in the light of the combined replies of other panel members. It is proposed that through a process of iteration, the researcher will be able to eventually arrive at the 'true' answer. A key point to note is that participants in the process are (or should be) granted anonymity at all stages, even when the report is published. This is to ensure that panel members can speak freely without compromising their own professional relationships with the client.

Focus groups are slightly different as panel members are brought together into a room and, with the aid of a facilitator, explore together the topic under examination. The composition of the focus group will be determined by the client and/or consultant beforehand to represent particular stakeholder interests or market segments. Thus an entertainment company wishing to invest in a new family attraction in a seaside destination could commission a research company to run focus groups with parents of young children living within the catchment area, parents already on holiday locally and representatives of the destination's tourism and hospitality sector. The discussions in focus groups tend to be recorded and transcribed, to provide quotes that support a broader narrative in the resulting report. It is possible to perform a content analysis on the text of the focus group discussion using software such as Nvivo, although care must be taken when interpreting the findings as the direction of the conversation is normally led by the facilitator and not the participants.

Observation/site audits

In the entertainment, leisure and tourism sectors much time is spent on developing new site-based products. The list of such products is almost inexhaustive and will include visitor attractions, nightclubs, arts venues, museums, visitor centres, pubs, clubs, restaurants, hotels, theme parks, wildlife parks and zoos. It may be necessary to carry out a site audit

of the client's own premises or facilities, or those of competitors. These audits might be achieved in the form of 'mystery-shopper' visits (where the auditor is not known to the staff running the facility) or may be more formal and even escorted by site management. Procedures for carrying out such site audits are straightforward, though there is always the ethical issue of whether or not the visit is overt or covert. Again, this relates back to the issues of professional ethics and the extent to which the consultant or researcher is seeking to uncover hidden secrets about the site rather than merely assess its quality and positioning.

There are already many evaluation forms for the industry associated with quality assurance schemes such as VisitEngland's Visitor Attraction Quality Assurance Scheme (VAQAS) and more specialist initiatives such as the National Accessible Scheme (NAS) or the Green Tourist Business Scheme (GTBS) for tourist accommodation. Most consultants will be familiar with these schemes and will usually adapt one or more of the evaluation frameworks to their own purposes, to make sure that when carrying out a site audit they cover all of the relevant points.

TRANSFORMING DATA INTO MANAGEMENT INFORMATION

It is important to reflect for a moment on the difference between data and management information. Data are the raw material produced by research and can stand alone, but without any analysis it is of limited use. Information is data that has been analysed using some form of diagnostic tool (which may be very basic or an incredibly sophisticated computer program) and that can then inform decision making.

In order to transform data into management information, consultants will tend to use diagnostic or analytical tools. Some of these have been developed by particular consultancy companies and adopted more generally across the sector, whilst others have emerged from academic work on organizational management and some have been developed to suit the needs of a particular sector.

A review carried out by Fehringer *et al.* (2006) revealed that many consultants rely on a small number of basic analytical techniques to make sense of their data so that it becomes useable management information. What tools consultants use depends largely on the field of management consultancy they are operating in. For example, in the UK heritage sector consultants tend to use tools recommended by client organizations such as the Heritage Lottery Fund, which favours the Ansoff Matrix.

STEEPLE

A STEEPLE (Social, Technological, Economic, Environmental, Political, Legal, Ethical) analysis enables a consultant to explore the external macro-environment, and how this can influence the way a client operates. To make use of a STEEPLE analysis, a consultant needs to consider the main factors under each heading that is influencing the client's business or organization. STEEPLE is typically used for structuring reviews of how an organization operates and what constraints have been placed upon it, as well as what has facilitated

the organization, and how these are likely to influence the organization's operations in future.

Tools for diagnosing the current situation in an organization

- Benchmarking – the consultant identifies key performance indicators (e.g. sales revenue per guest, staff members against venue capacity, energy costs per 100 m^2 floorspace) and will compare the data for the client organization against competitors.
- Forcefield Analysis – a tool borrowed from the social sciences in which the consultant considers the various forces for and against a proposed change. Particularly useful for organizational reviews.
- Johari Window – a tool from cognitive psychology, sometimes adapted to establish how organizations see themselves in relation to the broader marketplace or operating environment.
- Product Lifecycle or Tourism Area Lifecycle (TALC) – TALC was developed by Butler (1980) and allows the consultant to consider whether the destination, business or organization is in a growth phase, whether it has reached its full potential and is stagnating, or whether it is in decline.
- SWOT (Strengths, Weaknesses, Opportunities, Threats) Matrix – a simple way of summarizing the key factors facing an organization or operation at a particular point in time.
- Value Chain Analysis – looks at the key stages of any business operation (including manufacturing, storage, sourcing and procurement, transport, sales, marketing, servicing, HR) to identify which offer

competitive advantage and which do not. This then allows the consultant to identify where the client should focus its own activities and where it can outsource work so that competitive advantage is sustained.

Tools for structuring development proposals

- Ansoff's Matrix – helps businesses decide their product and market growth strategy by identifying opportunities for increasing market penetration, developing new markets or products, or diversifying the business operations. Requires an understanding of the performance of existing markets and products and of the size of potential new markets.
- Boston Matrix or Boston Box – developed by the Boston Consulting Group and evaluates the products of an organization according to their market share and growth prospects.

Tools for reviewing the likely impacts of, or prospects for, interventions

- Green Book (Her Majesty's Treasury, 2013) – provides a framework for the technical appraisal and evaluation of programmes, policies and projects. Required reading for any consultant working for Central Government.
- VICE (Visitor, Industry, Community, Environment) Model – originally developed to plan sustainable tourism in the New Forest in England, this framework is designed to help organizations frame any interventions or actions in terms of

the impacts that they might have on the four pillars of sustainability (cultural, economic, environmental and social).

WRITING A CONSULTANCY REPORT

Once the data have been analysed, a diagnosis of the issues prepared and appropriate solutions or strategies identified, the consultant will need to present the information to the client. There are four types of report that may be produced during a consultancy assignment.

- An *inception report* confirms terms of reference, organizational arrangements, timeframe, deliverables and will also detail any variations that might have arisen after the original brief and proposal were prepared. By its very nature it will be prepared before the main stage of information gathering and analysis has been completed.
- An *interim* or *progress report* that details work done, findings to date and issues arising. It might mark a particular milestone in the assignment against which partial payment is made.
- A *discussion paper* that sets out key issues for consideration by the client team, possibly also relevant stakeholders and also by the consultants themselves.
- The *end of assignment report*.

Whichever type of report is being produced, there is great virtue in communicating complex issues in a straightforward manner. Consultancy reports should be clearly written, not least because they need to avoid any ambiguity in meaning. The client is looking for clear recommendations not obfuscation. It is important that the writing is simple but not simplistic.

Hints for producing a well-written consultancy report include:

- avoid over-long sentences;
- avoid passive constructions where possible (for instance, do not say 'agreement with the community must be reached');
- avoid meaningless or redundant phrases;
- avoid going off at a tangent;
- include 'signposts' within the text that guide the reader; and
- consider how different presentation techniques such as imagery, charts or plans may assist in conveying the key messages, e.g. using graphs to present key data.

Where professional jargon is used it should be explained clearly and concisely. Where text is peppered with technical terms, acronyms and abbreviations, a consultant should include a glossary at the beginning of the report. In order to ascertain whether or not a consultancy report is complete and ready for submission to the client, the author(s) should ask the following questions:

1. Does the report address all the objectives of the consultancy assignment?
2. Is the structure of the report clear?
3. Is there a clear line of argument or 'golden thread' throughout the narrative?
4. Is the conceptual framework appropriate? Has the consultant used the most relevant concepts and theories and have these been explained properly?
5. Is the evidence presented in the report relevant and does the interpretation of the data support the recommendations?
6. Is everything in the report factually accurate? Are data sources and references clearly

stated so that the client can also review the information for themselves if necessary?
7. Are any graphics contained within the report accurate and are they sufficiently distinctive and imaginative to get the point across that the author wants to make?
8. Are the recommendations clearly stated, and does the report indicate the resource implications for implementing them, likely outcomes and appropriate monitoring procedures?

Only once all of these questions can be answered in the affirmative should a consultant submit the report to the client. This may initially be a draft report that may be further amended after the client has had time to consider the contents and discuss them with the consultant, but the same questions also will be asked when submitting the final document.

PRESENTING FINDINGS TO CLIENTS

Why present findings?

At some point the consultant will be expected to deliver their findings to the client team. There may in fact be several such events throughout the assignment, as the consultant needs to secure the client's 'buy-in' to the work done to date and perhaps to confirm the details of the next stage of the project. Certainly, a client will want to hear the consultant present key findings from any research stages and they will also want to hear first-hand the main recommendations being put forward. It is at this stage that the collaborative aspects of consultancy are particularly important, as the client is able to share any concerns about the recommendations and implications for their business. From the consultant's perspective, this type of presentation provides the best opportunity to demonstrate the progress that has been made and the value that has been (or will be) added to the organization as a result of their work, as well as providing an opportunity to 'sell-on' additional services that might not have been thought about or included in the original brief.

Presentations

Typically these presentations will be done via face-to-face meetings, but alternatives include teleconferencing or Skype calls. Generally, the larger the audience, the more structured the presentation will need to be.

Something that will guide the content and focus of the presentation will be whether or not the client has already had sight of an interim or final report. Thus the findings may come as a surprise or the client may already have had time to consider them and their implications. But in any case, it is normally good practice to focus on recommendations rather than on analysis and findings. Another point to consider is the composition of the audience in terms of their position within the client organization and the impact that the issues raised in the presentation may have on their own professional (and possibly personal) interests.

It is crucial that the consultant is well prepared before any feedback session with the client and that the presentation is appropriate to the audience in terms of both content and format (e.g. PowerPoint display, talk with supporting hand-outs or notes, or even a more interactive 'workshop'-style event).

In particular, it is important for the consultant to consider very carefully how the various options or recommendations will be received by the client, as there may be some resistance to certain proposals. It is also vital to present the case for any interventions with clarity and sensitivity, particularly when the client has not already had sight of a written report detailing the findings. Finally, the consultant must make sure when presenting the final recommendations that any changes in the internal or external operating environments that may have occurred during the course of the assignment are taken on board in the final presentation so that the client is getting the most up-to-date advice possible.

The recent emergence in the creative industries of the PechaKucha style of presentation, which time limits the presenter to a maximum of 6 minutes 20 seconds, is encouraging more and more people to focus on the efficient delivery of a lot of information without going into great detail.

There are several useful reference books on preparing persuasive presentations using standard computer-generated visual displays such as Microsoft PowerPoint, Apple Keynote or Prezi. Key points to remember include keeping the display simple, focusing on implications and anticipated outcomes of benefits rather than detailing the supporting data, and, most of all, tailoring the content and focus of the presentation to the needs of the audience rather than to the interests of the presenter.

Whether or not visual aids are used, the individual or team presenting the findings will need to be extremely accomplished public speakers, able to deliver short, pithy presentations that convey the overall sense of the meaning of an often complex scenario or large amount of data. For inspiration, prospective presenters should look at the selection of talks available on http://www.ted.com, where internationally renowned experts present their ideas clearly and concisely. Above all the key to a successful presentation is planning, preparation and practice, which contribute to perfectly prepared and performed presentations (Hind and Moss, 2013).

MONITORING IMPACTS OF CONSULTANCY INTERVENTIONS

Public organizations in particular are increasingly being required to demonstrate the value that they have received from any expenditure, including funds spent on hiring consultants. But it is important for all types of client to evaluate the impacts of the interventions identified and perhaps implemented by consultants. This not only helps the client understand the benefits associated with the contract but also provides the consultant with evidence of their skills and contributions that they can use when tendering for future work.

As indicated earlier, one of the key tools used by consultants is benchmarking, a technique that requires the identification of appropriate performance indicators and the collection of baseline data to compare the client organization with competitors. It is good practice, therefore, for the client organization to continue collecting this information on a regular basis, to track changes in these indicators. In our sector, typical indicators include numbers of guests or users, levels of customer satisfaction, turnover, profitability and revenue expenditure. It is sometimes difficult to be able to ascribe these changes directly to the interventions identified by the consultant and implemented by the client organization, so a strategy for data collection should be developed that allows such links to be made, wherever possible.

Case Study: Future strategies for the Museum of Oxford

In 2010, heritage consultancy and design firm PLB Ltd was commissioned by Oxford City Council to help find a viable way forward for the Museum of Oxford.

The Museum of Oxford is a community museum and tourist attraction owned and managed by the Council and is the only museum in Oxford to tell the story of the city, as opposed to the story of the university. It is situated within Oxford Town Hall, a Victorian Grade II* listed building in the centre of the city.

The Museum of Oxford had been under severe financial constraints for several years. While the museum continued to mount high quality and popular temporary exhibitions, the permanent exhibitions suffered from a lack of investment. Financial pressures on the City Council were such that serious consideration was being given to closing the museum.

The City Council was keen to secure an external perspective on the future direction of the museum, including guidance on whether it could and should remain in its current location within the Town Hall given the broader context of ongoing cuts to local government spending and major organizational changes linked to the use of office and income-generating space within the Town Hall.

(Continued)

Case Study. Continued.

Methodology and research

The consultancy team assembled brought expertise in organization development planning and business planning together with interpretive planning and exhibition design, and structured their approach to the exercise as follows.

- A start-up meeting and site visit, to help define and clarify the client's mission, values and objectives, and to understand the scenario the Council faced in relation to the existing museum.
- A desk-based review of the context for the study, including review of previous studies undertaken and data on the current audiences/markets for the museum; and a review of the current performance/management of the museum.
- A review of the museum collections and spaces within the Town Hall.
- Identification of additional qualitative and quantitative research needed to inform the team's understanding of the project, and appropriate routes for undertaking tasks.
- Stakeholder consultations and comparator research.
- Undertaking an options appraisal as a diagnostic technique for identifying a potential solution to the problem.
- Business forecasting against the different options, including exploration of the possible benefits of different governance models for the museum.
- Developing an outline interpretive framework and concept designs for the preferred option and design cost planning.
- Action planning for both the preferred design development scheme and for organizational development, including producing a 3-year business plan.
- Assisting with the preparation of a funding application to enable the development.

From the outset, it was important for the consultancy team to understand the following:

- current demand for the museum (satisfied and unsatisfied);
- the profile of users/non-users (or audiences) for the museum;
- projected changes in the relevant marketplace;
- the museum's current business performance;
- the wider operating environment – current status and likely changes; and
- the organization's capacity and willingness to develop/change/implement new products or services.

Information sources used included:

- existing/previous studies and management plans (e.g. the Conservation Management Plan and Access Plan for the Town Hall);
- existing performance/budget and organizational management information, supported by consultations;

(Continued)

Case Study. Continued.

- organizational information derived from web research and consultations;
- qualitative and quantitative research, including online questionnaires, on-site ques- tionnaires, a Citizens Panel survey, consultation at local events, focus groups with representatives of different audiences and a review of demographic and tourism statistics; and
- comparator and competitor research derived from site visits to other attractions in Oxford, consultations and online research.

The scope and scale of information used to inform the research was influenced by the resources available within the project team, in particular time and expertise, and also by the direction of the client team. A great deal of information was available from previous research carried out into the museum's future, including qualitative and quantitative data. To support the research process, museum staff ran focus groups aligned to the brief and fed this information back to the consultants. The Council was also able to facilitate access to their community consultation tools including Citizens' Panels. Finally, the PLB team gathered established industry data such as museum audience studies and tourism market information.

Analysis, reporting and completion

The main analysis tool used to bring the disparate areas of the study together (organiza- tional options, business performance, spatial and interpretation concepts) was an options appraisal, which enabled specific options to be tested against key criteria defined in col- laboration with the client team, such as an option's income-generating potential or ability to support community engagement with the museum.

Having identified a preferred option for the museum, the consultants then developed a vision for the future museum, supported by concept design and phased development recommendations.

Reporting was undertaken in stages, with an interim report detailing the results of all research undertaken and the outcomes of the options appraisal, including early design development. This was followed by a workshop with members of the client team to develop the vision for the museum and agree a way forward for its implementation, which allowed the consultants to undertake a final research phase and develop the action plan plus more detailed costs and the 3-year business plan within the programme dictated by the client's brief, budget and timescale.

The results of the study were presented to Officers and Councillors from Oxford City Council, as well as representatives from other partners in the city including other museum attractions. A round-table meeting was held with this group, allowing the team to formally present the findings of the study and then discuss and clarify any implications for this broader group of stakeholders.

(Continued)

Case Study. Continued.

Since the study findings focused on the need for the Council to make a decision on capital and revenue funding resources it could commit to the museum in the future, including the enabling of physical and capital works within the Town Hall, the actual interventions made as a result of PLB's work were left unconfirmed with the report's completion.

This scenario is entirely typical for this type of consultancy assignment in the heritage sector, where there are sufficient resources for the consultant to recommend a preferred way forward, which the client team can then, as far as possible, take the decision to implement themselves.

What happened next? The client's perspective

PLB's recommendations were exciting and ambitious, though in the context of increasingly constrained local government finance it was felt by Oxford City Council that they would struggle to attract the necessary level of financial support. Whilst the political leaders of the Council sincerely wished to keep the museum open, their final decision had to be made in light of budget realities.

In order to provide a solution that would win the Council's support and be consistent with the need to make better use of Town Hall office and income-generating space, the client prepared a modified strategy that retained some of the key principles underpinning the recommendations but which significantly simplified their implementation. For example, a key recommendation had been to move the museum into the main body of the Town Hall, with access through the main Town Hall entry. This recommendation was implemented although with a reduced museum footprint. A supporting recommendation was to move the existing café into two rooms at the front of the Town Hall and to theme this accordingly. This was ultimately considered too expensive at the time. Instead, the Council is upgrading the existing café and converting it into a licensed venue, a move that requires minimal capital investment but which will still deliver increased revenue for the organization. The two rooms that PLB envisaged as the themed café have become two new permanent galleries, loosely based on interpretive concepts put forward by the consultants.

This modified approach won political and budget support within the Council and also attracted around £90,000 of external investment. The original aim has been secured, in the sense that the museum operation has been retained, although with a smaller footprint.

The two new galleries were officially opened on 21 June 2012 with over 70 key stakeholders attending the opening celebration. The public opening on Saturday 23 June 2012 attracted over 600 people, with overwhelmingly positive responses. On the basis of what has been achieved with this renovation, the client feels that it is in a strong position to begin fundraising for the next stage of development. The aim of this phase is to bring the rest of the original museum footprint back into use. Planning for this will involve the client looking again at the original PLB proposals in the light of the developing needs of the museum.

Images of the Museum of Oxford can be seen in Figs 14.1 and 14.2.

(Continued)

Case Study. Continued.

Fig. 14.1. The Museum of Oxford entrance in Oxford Town Hall.

Fig. 14.2. Visitors to the Museum of Oxford experience traditional and technological interactive exhibits.

This chapter has introduced the role of the management consultant and explored the main stages of consultancy assignments, illustrating it with a number of examples from real-world situations. Some of the main analytical tools used by consultants to structure their work have been introduced and a wealth of practical guidance given to help entrants into the profession understand what makes a good consultant.

SEMINAR ACTIVITIES

1. Review a recent copy of a professional journal such as *The Stage*, *Leisure Management*, *Museums Journal* and see how many references there are to the work of consultants in sectors of the entertainment industries. Make a note of who the clients are, what the consultants have or will be advising and what type of research work the consultants are doing.

2. Write a list of the information you would need to collect, and the sources you would consult, to advise a theme park operator on whether or not it is financially viable for them to open a new attraction on a site in central Scotland.

3. Read more about how Forcefield Analysis and the Johari Window are used by consultants. Then prepare a briefing note for a nightclub owner detailing how you could use those two tools to help them understand whether or not they should open a second club in the same town in which they are already operating.

4. You are a local authority wanting to increase public interest in your local history museum. Prepare a draft brief for consultants stating what you would like them to investigate, how they should carry out the work and how you would like the findings presented.

REFERENCES

Butler, R.W. (1980) The concept of a tourism area cycle of evolution: Implications for management resources. *The Canadian Geographer* 24(1), 5–16.

Cope, M. (2010) *The Seven Cs of Consulting*, 3rd edn. Pearson Education Ltd, Harlow, UK.

Fehringer, D., Hohhof, B. and Johnson, T. (2006) *State of the Art: Competitive Intelligence*. Competitive Intelligence Foundation, Alexandria, Virginia.

Gill, J. and Johnson, P. (2010) *Research Methods for Managers*, 4th edn. Sage Publications Ltd, London.

Her Majesty's Treasury (2013) The Green Book: appraisal and evaluation in central government. Available at: https://www.gov.uk/government/publications/the-green-book-appraisal-and-evaluation-in-central-governent (accessed 11 August 2013).

Hind, D. and Moss, S. (2013) *Employability Skills*, 2nd edn. Business Education Publishers, Sunderland, Massachusetts.

Jennings, G.R. (2005) Interviewing: A focus on qualitative techniques. In: Ritchie, B.W., Burns, P. and Palmer, C. (eds) *Tourism Research Methods. Integrating Theory with Practice*. CAB International, Wallingford, UK, pp. 99–118.

Kubr, M. (1993) *How to Select and Use Consultants: A Client's Guide*. International Labour Office, Geneva.

Lynch, P. (2001) Professionalism and ethics. In: Sadler, P. (ed.) *Management Consultancy. A Handbook for Best Practice*, 2nd edn. Kogan Page, London, pp. 60–79.

Management Consultancy Association (2012) The consulting industry. Available at: http://www.mca.org.uk/about-us/the-consulting-industry#def (accessed 10 December 2012).

Rassam, C. (2001) Presenting advice and solutions. In: Sadler, P. (ed.) *Management Consultancy: A Handbook for Best Practice*, 2nd edn. Kogan Page, London, pp. 143–154.

Ritchie, B.W., Burns, P. and Palmer, C. (2005) *Tourism Research Methods. Integrating Theory with Practice*. CAB International, Wallingford, UK.

Sadler, P. (ed.) (2001) *Management Consultancy. A Handbook for Best Practice*, 2nd edn. Kogan Page, London.

Veal, A.J. (2011) *Research Methods for Leisure and Tourism: A Practical Guide*. Pearson Educational Ltd, Harlow, UK.

Whickham, L. and Wilcock, J. (2012) *Management Consulting: Delivering an Effective Project*, 4th edn. Financial Times/ Prentice Hall, London.

chapter 15

Visitor Attraction Management

Peter D. Dewhurst and Edwin Thwaites

LEARNING OBJECTIVES

After reading this chapter you should be able to:

- identify a range of visitor attractions;
- appreciate the levels of product for a visitor attraction;
- realize the impacts that a wide array of STEEPLE factors are having upon visitor attractions; and
- identify best practice management solutions to these impacts.

Visitor attractions are a vital component of any country's entertainment and tourism industries. They can function as a stimulus encouraging people to travel to destinations (Cooper *et al.*, 2005). Indeed, they have been cited as providing 'the *raison d'être* for tourism' itself (Boniface and Cooper, 2001, p. 30) as 'for many tourists, the attractions on offer at a destination form the major reason for visiting' (Page *et al.*, 2009, p. 197). In other

words, they have been recognized as the primary component or 'first power' (Gunn, 1988) in what is termed the 'tourism system' (see Chapter 2). Attractions bring in visitors, who once at the attraction may become enthralled and captivated audience members, either passively or through interaction with the attraction. Attractions can offer visitors an experience that is either unique to that particular attraction or something which is engaging that can have an emotional impact upon the visitor, and often both. Figure 15.1 illustrates visitors who have been captivated by the architecture, décor and size of Cologne Cathedral.

In spite of the widespread acceptance of the economic significance of attractions, it is noteworthy that this sector remains under-researched and is relatively poorly understood (Leask *et al.*, 2002; Swarbrooke, 2002; Benckendorff and Pearce, 2003; Prideaux, 2003). Changing patterns of tourism and

Fig. 15.1. Captivated visitors in Cologne Cathedral.

shifting patterns of visitor demand continue to place pressures on the management of visitor attractions, and survival in the future will depend on effective management responses to current and future challenges.

DEFINITION OF VISITOR ATTRACTIONS

There remains a lack of consensus as to the definition of visitor attractions and this creates problems in understanding their structure and role in both the entertainment and tourism industries. If we give the name 'destinations' to the places we visit – Paris, Egypt, Sydney, Rome – then the major visitor attractions may well be the Eiffel Tower, the Pyramids, the Opera House, the Coliseum. However,

many destinations consist of a wide variety of different visitor attractions, with some being so important they become destinations in their own right. We can therefore see at one end of the spectrum the giant corporate Walt Disney World, Florida, as both a destination and a visitor attraction, whilst at the other extreme are the very small and often family-run visitor attractions such as tea rooms and petting zoos. In the broadest sense we could argue that visitor attractions may be defined as anything that serves to attract visitors to a location. This could include a locality's climate and scenic beauty, distinctive cultural patterns, the friendliness of local residents, special events and even retail outlets (Inskeep, 1991). However, such a broad definition inhibits the detailed comparative analysis preferred by academics (Middleton, 1988) and industry bodies (Scottish Tourist Board, 1991) who have sought more precise definitions. This quest for a shared understanding led the UK's national tourist boards to agree a definition, which states (ETC, 2001, p. 8) that a visitor attraction is:

> A permanently established excursion destination, a primary purpose of which is to allow public access for entertainment, interest or education; rather than being primarily a retail outlet or a venue for sporting, theatrical or film performances. It must be open to the public without prior booking, for published periods each year, and should be capable of attracting day visitors or tourists as well as local residents. In addition, the attraction must be a single business, under a single management...and must be receiving revenue directly from the visitors.

This definition reflects terminology used by the World Tourism Organization (WTO) and the World Travel and Tourism Council (WTTC) and has been cited by many commentators who value its capacity to narrow the focus of attention to managed sites, whilst simultaneously accommodating a wide range of attraction products.

CATEGORIZATION OF VISITOR ATTRACTIONS

Attempts to categorize visitor attractions has led to a similar level of debate with commentators proffering varied listings of attraction types. One of the most broadly cited categorizations, as presented in Table 15.1, was used by the English National Tourist Board over a

Table 15.1. Categories of visitor attractions (ETC, 2001).

Cathedrals and churches	Other historic properties	Wildlife attractions and zoos
Country parks	Leisure and theme parks	Workplace attractions
Farms	Museums and art galleries	Other attractions
Gardens	Steam railways	
Historic houses and castles	Visitor centres	

number of years in an annual survey of visitor attractions.

This listing has been criticized for being restrictive and outdated and of limited use for any purpose other than counting and segregation. A more comprehensive categorization emerged from an investigation into England's most-visited attractions (Dewhurst, 1996). Visitor attractions are identified as belonging to distinct groupings each of which contains a number of sub-groupings, as shown in Table 15.2.

The over-simplification in such a categorization can also present problems in so far as many attractions have for a number of years been engaged in a process of 'product diversification and the consequent blurring of attraction distinctions' (Dewhurst, 1996). An example of this phenomenon is provided by Beaulieu, which is 'one of the South of England's top visitor attractions' (http://www.beaulieu.co.uk/). Beaulieu comprises two historic properties, gardens, museum and also rides

Table 15.2. Categories and types of visitor attractions (adapted from Dewhurst, 1996).

Attraction category	Attraction types	Constituent attractions
Historico-cultural	Religious sites	Abbeys, cathedrals, chapels, priories
	Museums and galleries	Art galleries, open air museums, traditional museums, science centres
	Historic sites	Castles, landmarks, monuments, palaces
	Interpretative heritage sites	Interpretative centres, heritage sites
	Multi-faceted historic sites	Castles, docklands, historic houses, palaces
Environmental	Animal attractions	Safari parks, wildlife parks, zoos, rare breed farms, nature centres, aquaria
	Parks and gardens	Botanic gardens, outdoor activity parks, public parks
	Country parks	Country parks, reservoirs
Entertainment[a]	Leisure and recreation complexes	Leisure centres, leisure pools, recreation centres, water parks
	Amusement parks	Pleasure beaches, pleasure parks
	Theme parks	Indoor parks, outdoor parks, beach resorts
	Themed retail outlets	Antique centres, garden centres, retail and leisure parks
	Workplace industrial visit centres	Craft workshops, factory shops
Miscellaneous other		Arboretums, piers, themed transport

[a]It should be noted that whilst the word entertainment has been used as a category of visitor attractions, that all attractions by their very nature can captivate audiences through sensory stimulation and emotional engagement and are therefore by default entertaining.

that would be more typically found in theme parks. At the same time many theme parks also have extensive 'other' facilities for those who may not wish to go on rides (including those too young, parents and grandparents). Alton Towers in Staffordshire, England, has extensive gardens, and Flamingo Land in North Yorkshire, England, is also a zoo and has gardens.

Whilst debates over classification can become protracted and unhelpful, they do demonstrate the scale and variety of visitor attractions available.

THE VISITOR ATTRACTION OFFERING

Each visitor attraction, however it is categorized, is required to provide more than the base attraction if customers are to be satisfied, as the experience of visiting other attractions acts as a benchmark for expectations that each visitor will bring with them. If visitors arrive by car they will need a car park; if no other facilities are nearby, a toilet and a place to eat and drink will also be essential. These constituent parts of visitor attractions have been discussed by Swarbrooke (2002), who adapted Kotler's (1994) three-category classification of marketing components. The first comprises the *core* element of a visitor attraction, which can be regarded as providing the central appeal for customers. This category includes such intangible features as the excitement and/or atmosphere of an attraction. The *tangible* component is the marketed product – the features of the attraction; the reason the attraction is there. This is what most people associate with the attraction and the way it is presented. The third component is that extra element that ensures customer satisfaction. This *augmented* aspect includes those tangible and intangible features that seem peripheral to the attraction but are essential to the whole experience. Included in this category are car parking facilities, toilets, catering and retail outlets that are all under the influence of management, but also include the weather and traffic problems outside their control but which

still impact on enjoyment. These three components together form the visitor attraction offering. Figure 15.2 demonstrates this using the example of a museum; the core elements are highlighted in the centre circle, some or all of which motivate the museum visit; the middle circle contains the tangible elements that museum visitors will come into contact with and are what have been marketed to visitors. The outer ring contains the augmented elements that are not intrinsic in bringing in visitors but can have a significant impact upon the visitor experience.

What is clear from this discussion is that attractions are complex and amorphous businesses that act as drivers for the local, regional and international movement of people. As such they operate within the wider socioeconomic context and it is this that gives rise to a series of significant strategic and operational challenges presently confronted by attraction operators.

PRESSURES FACING VISITOR ATTRACTIONS

The first decade of the 21st century started with the 'war on terror' following the terrorist attacks on the World Trade Center in New York and a war in Iraq and Afghanistan. The decade ended with banking collapses and the realization of heavy debt burdens both for a wide range of countries and also large sections of many Western countries' populations who had borrowed too much in the economic good times. At the same time, new hope is emerging for the citizens of a wide range of countries that have managed to lift themselves out of dictatorship, whilst in contrast others are struggling to free themselves from

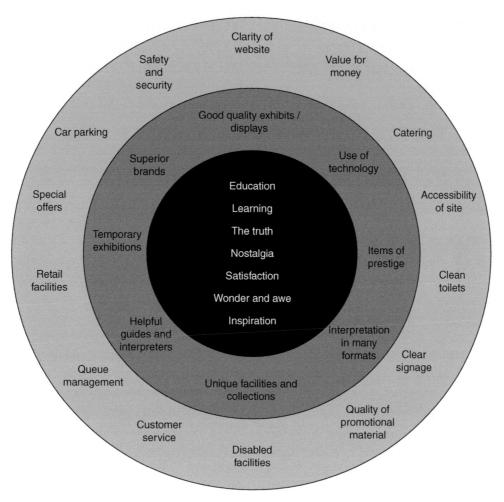

Fig. 15.2. The levels of product for a museum (adapted from Swarbrooke, 2002).

despotic regimes. With the as yet unappreciated consequences of climate change and steady year-on-year increases in fuel costs, it is hardly surprising that visitor attractions face an uneasy future. Increased technological integration into our everyday lives means that potential customers are now more aware and also able to share their experiences with global audiences. Structural changes to the population at a time of changing leisure patterns, where rising customer expectations sit uneasily with increasing competition for leisure spend, add to the pressures on attraction managers, many of whom must also contend with increasing legislative burdens.

Many of the challenges confronting the world's visitor attractions vary both in scale and nature according to their location and the sub-sector to which the individual attractions belong. However, there is evidence to show that maturing markets and shifting patterns of demand bring with them a series of pressures that are common to many visitor attractions and these can be considered in more detail.

STRUCTURAL CHANGES IN THE POPULATION AND CHANGING LEISURE PATTERNS

Changes in population demographics can impact on visitor attractions in a number of ways. Many developed and industrialized countries have ageing populations, an increasingly diverse ethnic mix and a growing number of single parent households and both pre-family and no family adults, factors which together serve to both diversify and magnify the demand for novel and appropriate visitor attractions. This changing pattern of demand can prove problematic to the operators of visitor attractions, especially established small family attractions that have limited resources with which to update the product content, the style of product presentation and the tools used to promote the product offer.

The emergence of leisure time as a precious commodity has occurred at the same time as increasing work-related pressures are being experienced in most developed and developing countries. These pressures, seen in the increasing prevalence of weekend and evening working, have ensured an increase in the home-based leisure and 'bite-sized' leisure activities that are consumed before and after work. The recent advances in the variety and quality of in-home leisure products support this trend. Unfortunately, these trends increase the pressure on visitor attractions, many of which are located some distance from their intended markets, with most typically requiring their customers to commit to an out-of-home leisure experience of between a couple of hours' and a full day's duration. In some cases the visit requires a much longer time commitment.

RISING CONSUMER EXPECTATIONS AND INCREASING COMPETITION FOR REDUCING LEISURE SPEND

Time available for leisure activities is a precious commodity to those in employment and the pressure this places on attractions to deliver a high quality experience is compounded as large sections of the population of many developed countries have begun to experience shrinking levels of personal disposable income (PDI). The result is more discerning consumers who are less tolerant of poor products and services and increasingly prepared to vote with their feet. Of course the problems arising from dissatisfied customers are compounded by the increasing use of social media, as not only will disgruntled visitors inform their friends, relatives, co-workers and neighbours, they are also now likely to notify their Facebook friends and post comments on Trip Advisor and Twitter about their poor experiences. Unfortunately, many attraction operators have failed to recognize the requirement to manage the quality of the service encounter with their customers, in spite of the fact that research has shown the quality of the product, ease of access and value for money to be of key importance to the leisure consumer (Morgan, 1998). This represents a major challenge to attraction operators competing for often shrinking levels of PDI, many of whom are faced with falling demand and declining sales.

In contrast with the present time, the late 20th century and up to 2005 was a time of increasing PDI in most Western countries, and this together with the increasing emphasis on leisure activities helped to persuade many individuals and organizations to move into the attractions sector especially in the period up to the millennium celebrations of 2000. Within the UK, the Government had a direct impact on the 'explosion in the number of visitor attractions' (Mintel, 2002) by directing some of the income secured from the National Lottery into a variety of new attraction development schemes. This growth in attractions took place at a time of growth in competition for leisure spend and so led to stagnating or falling demand. In such circumstances it was inevitable that there would be clear winners and losers. In 2002, Mintel noted that within the UK around 60% of all attractions received less than 6% of all visitors at a time when the top 7% of attractions received around 60% of total visits (Mintel, 2002). A more detailed analysis of the data from this period reveals that the larger more flexible attractions were better equipped to respond to the changing market conditions. More recently, the same larger operators, such as the Merlin Entertainments Group, have been better placed to benefit from shifts in the focus of economic development away from the Western countries and towards the BRIC nations of Brazil, Russia, India and China, by choosing to invest in these new and potentially lucrative markets.

MULTIPLE EXPECTATIONS OF DIFFERENT STAKEHOLDER GROUPINGS

In addition to the obvious need to satisfy the expectations of an increasingly diverse range of customers, there is a need to address the needs of employees, as it is increasingly being recognized that effective customer management is predicated on good staff relations (Williams and Thwaites, 2007a). Other key stakeholder groups include the investors in the attraction together with a wider constituency of local residents and special interest groups such as wildlife conservation bodies in the case of zoos and safari parks and heritage conservation bodies in the case of castles and stately homes. This disparate range of potential stakeholders and the fact that they can hold conflicting views makes the visitor attraction managers' task of securing support or at least consent for activities and developments an extremely challenging one. Failure to achieve this consent has the potential of bringing bad publicity, conflict and possibly the business failure of the attraction.

Perhaps the most extreme stakeholder-related pressures arise from investment programmes that form part of broader strategies to encourage the economic development or regeneration of regions. Within the UK, the Millennium Commission contributed £15.65 million to The Lowry Art Gallery at Salford Quays as part of a plan to regenerate an area to the west of Manchester that had suffered from a lengthy period of industrial decline. In this and other instances (including the development of the Guggenheim Museum in Bilbao, Spain; the National Museum in Wellington, New Zealand; and the Royal Armouries Museum in Leeds and the Millennium Dome in Greenwich, UK) the developments have brought with them an expectation of a growth in visitor numbers both to the attraction and the host environment, leading to an increase in spending, economic activity and further private-sector investment. With such politically oriented pressures there is a danger that those externally imposed strategic priorities that serve as the initial rationale for the development of an attraction can take precedence over sound business planning. This can in turn serve as a contributory factor in the ultimate failure of the attraction as indicated in the case studies of Crinkley Bottom and the Millennium Dome.

Case Study: Crinkley Bottom's failed strategic alliance

In 1994, Lancaster City Council in partnership with The Unique Group Ltd decided to develop a visitor attraction based upon the television show *Noel's House Party* that featured a UK TV celebrity Noel Edmonds and a fun character called Mr Blobby. The attraction was to be built in Happy Mount Park in the UK seaside resort of Morecambe at a planned cost of £100,000 and with an assumed 150,000 admissions in the first year giving rise to an expected profit of £85,000. Initially the profit was to be shared between the partners on a 50:50 basis but this changed during negotiations until a profit share of 60:40 in the favour of the council was agreed, with the Unique Group Ltd receiving £40,000 for design ideas; a further £300,000 was to be paid to the Unique Group Ltd over 3 years with a 50:50 share of the profits if the admissions figures exceeded 350,000. Admission numbers were much lower than expected and capital and revenue costs were allowed to rise with limited opportunities for secondary spend once the entry price was paid. The lack of things to do, items to buy and the extended waiting times between the appearances of the star attraction – Mr Blobby – left customers with time on their hands, in direct contrast to expectations. The site of the temporary café was an aesthetic disaster and the choice of food and beverages was well below the standards normally experienced by theme park customers. The theme park closed within 13 weeks with an estimated loss to the local council of £2 million, of which £90,000 was an out-of-court settlement to The Unique Group Ltd. The failure of the attraction and the loss of public money resulted in a campaign by the local press and subsequent investigations by the District Auditor. The investigation concluded that whilst the construction of the theme park in a public park was lawful, the subsequent decisions as to the financial agreements were 'irrational and unlawful' (Williams and Thwaites, 2007b).

Case Study: The Millennium Dome – a case of false expectation

The London Millennium Dome was developed as the centrepiece of the UK's millennium celebrations and was intended to serve as a vehicle for the economic regeneration of the eastern side of London. During its 1 year of operation the Dome succeeded in attracting 6.5 million visitors, making it the most visited admission-charging attraction in the country. Yet this was 50% short of its visitor target of 12 million customers. A subsequent Parliamentary review concluded that meddling politicians were involved in the decision-making processes with a loss of business-planning focus and a lack of attraction-related management experience. Not surprisingly it was claimed that the attraction offered a mundane and generally uninspiring product that lacked cohesion and which had set unrealistic visitor admission targets (Select Committee on Culture, Media and Sport, 2000; Wickens *et al.*, 2000).[1]

(Continued)

Case Study. Continued.

Fig. 15.3. The London O2 Arena, formerly the Millennium Dome.

MANAGEMENT RESPONSES

Any visitor attraction manager aiming to respond to the shifting patterns of demand and the variety of competition in the sector needs to focus attention on four key areas of integrated management responsibility to maintain and enhance future success. The first of these areas is the product being offered to the attraction visitor and its contemporary presentation. The second area is the market in its widest sense, in particular the way promotion can be significantly improved with appropriate strategic partnerships. The third and often neglected area of responsibility is revenue management; that is, the ability to optimize the earnings potential of attractions so as to facilitate the generation of profits or surpluses that can in part be used to re-invest in site improvements and developments. The fourth priority concerns the management of the visitors on site, including everything from service quality to hiring and training of staff. Underpinning all of these priorities is a need to recruit and develop high calibre and motivated staff capable of driving the attractions from both a strategic and operational perspective.

PRODUCT DEVELOPMENT, DIVERSIFICATION AND DIFFERENTIATION

Product developments and diversification are recognized as key means of boosting market demand with many attraction operators continually engaged in the development of programmes to improve and enhance the visitor experience. Theme parks, such as Blackpool Pleasure Beach in the UK, provide an example of this kind of continual development with new white-knuckle rides, stage shows and food courts with 'brand' franchise outlets forming part of the ongoing and regular improvements. Technological innovations are also used to improve the core product offering, with an increasing emphasis being placed on providing visitors with a high quality interactive experience. A notable example is provided by Seaworld Orlando, set to launch Turtle Trek, which will provide visitors with a state of the art 3D animated film to be shown in a 360-degree dome theatre. Similarly, the Särkänniemi theme park in Tampere, Finland, is to develop the world's first Angry Birds themed attraction, which is to include what the developers term a 'Magic Place' where physical and virtual worlds are set to combine to provide an interactive entertainment experience (Attractions Management, 2012).

Indeed, as attraction-going consumers become increasingly familiar with the latest digital and online technologies, there is a need for attraction operators to invest in high quality design solutions that make effective use of technological innovations to attract customers and maximize the likelihood of repeat visitation. The Odysseum Science Adventure in Cologne is a 7000 square metre facility developed at a cost of £9.4m, which includes seven themed areas with a total of 200 interactive exhibits embedded in the scenery rather than displayed in traditional gallery settings. The building has an annual upgrade schedule intended to refresh the product offer, whilst the design specification has helped to reduce operating overheads by minimizing energy consumption.

Many attraction developments serve to diversify the product offer thereby helping to attract repeat visitors whilst simultaneously opening up new markets. Such an approach contributes to a blurring of the boundaries between previously distinct categories of attractions. For example, theme park-style rides at zoos and educational resource centres at theme parks can be used to deliver both an educational and entertainment-based product (van Aalst and Boogarts, 2002). In addition, a number of operators have sought to diversify

by introducing new customer services such as the themed hotel at Alton Towers, which mirrors similar developments at attractions in the Netherlands and Germany (Mintel, 2002).

In 2004, the Tussauds Group chose to embark on a strategy of product differentiation rather than diversification to reposition their Chessington World of Adventures and Thorpe Park theme parks to target two separate and more narrowly defined markets. The operators of the sites, which had both formerly catered for a family market, reviewed the product components of the attractions with a view to developing the Chessington site specifically for young families and the Thorpe Park site for a young adult market (Attractions Management, 2004a). This strategy reflects the difficulty of providing an excellent visitor attraction to a diverse public on the same site.

STRATEGIC PARTNERSHIPS, MARKETING AND PROMOTION

Many attraction operators choose to develop strategic partnerships with other businesses to expand their activities. Whilst many alliances are centred on marketing and promotional activities, some also share resources and provide and share sector-specific expertise. Madame Tussauds provides a valuable example of promotional alliances with its operators having developed strategic brand partnerships with Coca Cola, Fuji, Disney, Universal, Columbia (Attractions Management, 2004b) and United Biscuits (Attractions Management, 2004c).

In some instances, strategic marketing alliances have been established between attraction operators that in the past were viewed as competitors. Research conducted in Scotland has revealed a willingness for attraction managers to work together, as well as with transport and accommodation providers, in order to develop joint brands, themes and packages (Fyall *et al.*, 2001). Indeed, the managers of many rural attractions regard such approaches, which can include the development of shared advertising, printed promotional material and websites, as being essential for their very survival.

Another manifestation of collaborative working is provided within urban centres where cultural quarters have been established, which have at their core clusters of historico-cultural attractions. This approach has emerged as a popular vehicle for raising the profile of districts and thereby increasing the numbers of visitors accessing the attractions and adjacent shops, bars and restaurants (van Aalst and Boogarts, 2002). An additional benefit of such a collaborative approach can be the emergence of a deeper working relationship, which can be manifested in the shared use of resources and even shared management practices.

Many attractions have utilized the Internet to develop sophisticated websites that are used to attract visitors. A notable example is provided by New York's Museum of Modern Art, which offers a virtual tour of the museum as well as online booking and retailing services. Ullswater Steamers in the English Lake District have a dedicated website in Japanese to attract the significant numbers of Japanese visitors who visit the Lake District each year. Computerized booking systems are now very common and the promotion of attractions via tour operators increases market penetration (Market Assessment International, 2000). Attractions are now developing integrated promotional strategies that embrace the new forms of social media with attractions appearing on Facebook and Twitter, providing potential and regular visitors with frequent updates about events and new product offerings. The introduction of a wide variety of customer loyalty schemes across the sector is also utilized for the maintenance of marketing databases to help target mailings and special offers as the electronic manipulation of customers and potential customers has been fully integrated into the sophisticated marketing of attractions.

Case Study: Technology use at the Cathedral of St John The Baptist, Warsaw

The Cathedral of St John The Baptist in Warsaw's 'old town' is an exemplar of best practice in how its management have embraced and utilized technology in order to enhance the visitor experience. In recognition of the rapid proliferation of portable Internet-ready devices such as smartphones and tablet computers that many visitors carry, the Cathedral's management have provided a free Wi-Fi network which visitors may use to connect to the Internet. Many visitors to the cathedral are from foreign destinations, so using devices with SIM cards such as smartphones to access the Internet may be expensive and dissuade visitors from doing so. By providing free Wi-Fi the cathedral's management are not only providing an additional service to visitors, they are also using it to promote information about

(Continued)

Case Study. Continued.

the cathedral via 'Quick Recognition' (QR) codes that are displayed about the cathedral. Visitors with smartphones or tablets can use their device's camera to scan the QR codes for information about the cathedral to be displayed directly on to their device, and if using the cathedral's Wi-Fi network this is at no cost. This also reduces the need for staffed information points and interpreters. Information is also offered via Bluetooth, which again can be transmitted to mobile devices and displayed on the device's screen.

Fig. 15.4. QR codes, Wi-Fi and Bluetooth in use at the Cathedral of St John the Baptist in Warsaw.

REVENUE MANAGEMENT

An increasing level of competition for what in many countries is a plateauing or even a shrinking market, combined with a growing emphasis on commercial priorities even amongst long-established historico-cultural attractions (van Aalst and Boogaarts, 2002), has meant that there is increasing pressure on attraction operators to ensure that they optimize the earnings potential of their sites. This can be achieved through the introduction of revenue management techniques that provide 'a systematic approach to maximizing revenue from the sale of intangible tourist services and

facilities through pricing, market segmentation and service enhancement' (Leask et al., 2002). A wide range of options is available to managers to aid the financial management of attractions. These need, however, to be closely related to an understanding of demand in relation to time and price and also the marketing concept of the attraction. The varying of admission prices according to (i) the time and duration of the visit; (ii) the category of visitor; (iii) the volume of visitors; and (iv) the number of resources being accessed by the visitors, is a well-practised approach (Leask et al., 2002) that is not always fully understood by visitors. The development of additional income streams, frequently through the introduction of a conference and events programme, has been an approach adopted by many attractions, as has the maximization of a return from secondary spend activities such as the delivery of a food and retail offer and enhanced customer services (Leask *et al.*, 2000). Indeed, visitors to a range of attractions including castles, historic houses and gardens often undertake repeat visits on account of the *augmented* product offering, as they see little value in seeing, or paying to see, the main attraction. The presence of these often local, repeat visitors represents a contribution to the overall profitability of the attraction. Yet, as Harris (2011, p. 11) has indicated, it is not sufficient just to know about these methods to improve profitability – the information needs to be used by managers in the 'routine day-to-day profit planning decisions'.

Increasing numbers of visitor attractions are confronting a growing variety of pressures, many operating as small businesses at the margins of viability and always with the fear of business failure. However, whilst such failures are considered by many to be inevitable, especially where attraction operators either will not or cannot make the necessary changes to maintain some degree of viability, the application of good management practices should make it possible for many to continue in operation. A shrinking attractions sector is not in anyone's interests as it may well contribute to the overall decline of the tourism/leisure economy. This would in turn undermine one of the key vehicles for economic development and regeneration that is increasingly being deployed by governments around the world. Every effort must therefore be taken to create a stable environment in which it is possible for the attractions' sector of the visitor economy to

prosper. A key measure for delivering effective support to attraction operators is to focus on what has been termed the 'management deficit'. To this end the onus should be on academics to engage more fully in attractions-oriented research that can be of direct benefit to attraction operators. There is also a need to further develop benchmarking schemes and training support packages that provide attraction operators with enhanced and applied insights into best business and financial practices.

MANAGING THE VISITOR EXPERIENCE AND IMPROVING SERVICE QUALITY

Visitor attraction operators are faced with the conflicting demands of having to safeguard and protect their sites and exhibits whilst at the same time encouraging as many visitors as possible to access their sites. The tension created by these two demands inevitably places a requirement on the operators effectively to manage their customers at the same time as ensuring that they enjoy a satisfying visit experience. Effective visitor management techniques are needed to avoid congestion outside, and overcrowding inside, the attraction. The former can result in the alienation of local residents and the latter in increased wear and tear of the product components within the attraction. Effective visitor management also enhances the visit experience for all and contributes to a sense of customer satisfaction amongst visitors who will be more inclined to make a repeat visit and less inclined to make negative comments about the attraction to their friends, neighbours and relatives.

Effective visitor management techniques, which are essential if customers are to enjoy their visit experience, address issues of demand and supply. Demand-related management techniques include differentiated pricing to encourage visits at some times and provide a disincentive at other times and even using de-marketing to control and manipulate the peaks and troughs in demand. Supply-oriented visitor management techniques are used to manipulate capacity levels in such a way as to avoid the physical degradation of the site whilst ensuring customer satisfaction. These techniques include queue management, site hardening initiatives and capacity-raising schemes that may involve new product developments that extend the existing site (Garrod, 2003). The FastPass at Disneyland Paris (Market Assessment International, 2000) is an example of a queue management technique that has grown in popularity in recent years. This involves visitors reserving a time when they can access a particular attraction component, thereby enabling the visitors to enjoy other facets of the attraction at the same time as they are 'virtually queuing' for their booked activity.

As visitors continue to benchmark against previous outstanding experiences, the range and quality of the *augmented* offerings need to be of a high standard. The excellent attractions can therefore seek to differentiate themselves from their competitors by ensuring the highest standards of customer support features; in other words they may choose to introduce facilities for the disabled that go way beyond legal requirements. Similarly, as both access to mobile telephones and mobile telephone technology itself has improved, so the leading attractions are producing apps that deliver useful pre-visit information, whilst the same technology can then serve to enhance the visit experience by making available downloadable audio guides.

Case Study: Downloadable Audio Guides for Fountains Abbey and Studley Royal, North Yorkshire, England

The management of Fountains Abbey and Studley Royal, which is a World Heritage Site in North Yorkshire, England, have created a very comprehensive website, which also hosts a range of mp3 audio files that can be downloaded to mobile phones/tablet computers and played by visitors to make an audio tour as they wander around the attraction, thus enhancing their visitor experience. These are available in several languages. The English language guides can be found at: http://www.fountainsabbey.org.uk/html/visiting/audio-guide-download/english/.

This initiative is also a cost-saver for the attraction, which now has less of an onus to provide their own equipment for customers to use to play audio guides. With the increasing proliferation of smartphones and tablet computers that have an mp3 playing capability, this need will continually reduce in future as more visitors will arrive already 'equipped'.

In an increasingly competitive mature market, attraction operators are required to deliver an efficient and effective operating performance at the same time as ensuring effective customer satisfaction. Front-line staff are essential here in the management of the customer experience. The demands of the modern consumer can only be met through the professional management of customer contact staff, which is best achieved through the development and implementation of effective human resource strategies (Graham and Lennon, 2002; Nickson, 2007) that comprise human resource planning, recruitment and selection, induction orientation, training and development, as well as performance monitoring (Taylor, 2004).

Unfortunately, the current human resource environment, especially in the European visitor attraction industry, is one of low pay, long unsociable hours and staff often on casual or part-time contracts with a high turnover rate. Yet an increasingly discerning customer base is demanding a higher quality and professional service that is not always delivered by an untrained casual workforce. Using the idea of the 'service-profit chain' (Heskett *et al.*, 1997), the relationship between good human resource strategies and effective customer satisfaction can easily be developed in a way that will ensure that newly recruited front-line staff working in visitor attractions can develop those decision-making skills essential for customer satisfaction (Williams and Thwaites, 2007a). Good customer relations do not occur by accident. Staff need training to respond to a wide range of potential problems and they need to be empowered to act, if and when the need arises, for service recovery (Thwaites and Williams, 2006).

Furthermore, as many attraction operators look to exploit the shifting focus for economic development by extending their product portfolios into new operating regions, they will need to take into account local climatic conditions and cultural values. As an example of the former, attractions that are being developed in Asia and the Middle East must minimize outdoor queuing, whilst cultural traditions in some Muslim countries mean that waterparks are required to provide separate male and female bathing areas as well as making provision for fully clothed bathing (Galbraith, 2012).

The variety of challenges faced by attraction operators and the complexity of the responses needed to address them inevitably means that success is often dependent upon the quality of workforce. Yet the workforce at many attractions is largely comprised of part-time, seasonal and/or voluntary staff managed by a team which is frequently under-resourced and potentially lacking in key management skills. It is this human resource challenge that is perhaps the single biggest threat to effective visitor attraction management. This latter point is emphasized in a research investigation into managerial competency requirements, which revealed that the managers of Scottish visitor attractions attached relatively little significance to either strategic or people management skills (Watson *et al.*, 2004). Yet it is just such skills that need to be demonstrated by the managers of attractions who are increasingly required to take a lead in innovative developments as a response to the rapidly evolving and increasingly competitive marketplace.

CONCLUSION

Visitor attractions are a major part of the entertainment industry. The whole rationale behind their existence is the tourist or day visitor who spends part of a vacation or a day free from work visiting somewhere for a high quality and engaging experience. Attractions, therefore, are in competition for consumers' leisure spending with other providers of entertainment-related experiences. Money spent at the cinema and concerts, at sporting events or even on the latest computer downloads and games cannot be spent a second time at a visitor attraction.

It is not appropriate, therefore, for visitor attractions to just benchmark themselves against other attractions or regard other attractions as their only competition. The modern visitor arrives at a destination with a wide range of experiences and expectations derived in part from a lifetime of experience of entertainment. Quality of food and drink, quality of the augmented products, quality of customer/staff interaction – these are all considered by customers, and compared to other entertainment experiences and not simply other visitor attractions.

The modern visitor attraction manager must embrace the whole concept of entertainment and manage the experiences of customers who will always have other opportunities for being entertained.

SEMINAR ACTIVITIES

Create a proposal for a new visitor attraction in your town or city. Thoroughly explain what your attraction is and how it might work. Justify your choice of attraction by answering the following questions:

1. What type of attractions are not currently in your locality that there could be demand for?
2. Who would be your target market?
3. What would be your attraction's main draw in terms of product offering?
4. What would be your attraction's unique selling point?
5. Using Fig. 15.2 for guidance, what would the levels of product be for your attraction?
6. Where could your attraction be physically built?
7. What objections might you come across to your attraction being built and how might you overcome these?
8. What STEEPLE factors might impact upon your attraction and what strategies would you put in place to overcome these?
9. What would be the short-, medium- and long-term goals for your attraction?

NOTE

[1] It should be noted that since the closure of the Millennium Dome, and its subsequent re-branding to the O2 Arena, that this venue has become extremely successful as both an entertainment venue and visitor attraction, particularly for hosting live events and temporary exhibitions, as well as being the permanent home of a multiplex cinema. It was used as a venue in the Summer 2012 Olympics and Paralympics when it was referred to as the North Greenwich Arena.

REFERENCES

Attractions Management (2004a) Tussauds repositions Chessington and Thorpe Park. Available at: http://www.attractions.co.uk (accessed 7 April 2004).

Attractions Management (2004b) Tussauds looks to strategic partners. Available at: http://www. attractions.co.uk (accessed 5 August 2004).

Attractions Management (2004c) Hula Hoops team up with theme parks. Available at: http://www. attractions.co.uk (accessed 13 April 2004).

Attractions Management (2012) Attractions Management. Available at: http://www.attractionsman- agement.com (accessed 25 March 2012).

Benckendorff, P.J. and Pearce, P.L. (2003) Australian tourist attractions: The links between organiza- tional characteristics and planning. *Journal of Travel Research* 42, 24–35.

Boniface, P. and Cooper, C. (2001) *Worldwide Destinations: The Geography of Travel and Tourism*, 3rd edn. Butterworth-Heinemann, Oxford, UK.

Cooper, C., Fletcher, J., Fyall, A., Gilbert, D. and Wanhill, S. (2005) *Tourism: Principles and Practice*, 3rd edn. Pearson Education Limited, Harlow, UK.

Dewhurst, P. (1996) England's most visited tourist attractions: An evaluation of success and taxonomic review. Unpublished PhD thesis, Manchester Metropolitan University, Manchester, UK.

ETC (2001) *Sightseeing in the UK 2000*. English Tourism Council, London.

Fyall, A., Leask, A. and Garrod, B. (2001) Scottish visitor attractions: a collaborative future? *International Journal of Tourism Research* 3, 211–228.

Fyall, A., Garrod, B. and Leask, A. (eds) (2003) *Managing Visitor Attractions*. Butterworth-Heinemann, Oxford, UK.

Galbraith, S. (2012) Culture Club. *Attractions Management* 1, 63–64.

Garrod, B. (2003) Managing visitor impacts. In: Fyall, A., Garrod, B. and Leask, A. (eds) *Managing Visitor Attractions*. Butterworth-Heinemann, Oxford, UK, pp. 124–139.

Graham, M. and Lennon, J.J. (2002) The dilemma of operating a strategic approach to human resource management in the Scottish visitor attraction sector. *International Journal of Contemporary Hospitality Management* 14(5), 213–220.

Gunn, C. (1988) *Vacationscape: Designing Tourist Regions*, 2nd edn. Van Nostrand Reinhold, New York.

Harris, P. (2011) *Profit Planning for Hospitality and Tourism*, 3rd edn. Goodfellow Publishing, Oxford, UK.

Heskett, J.L., Sasser, E.W. and Schesinger, L.A. (1997) *The Service Profit Chain: How Leading Companies Link Profit and Growth to Loyalty, Satisfaction and Value*. Free Press, New York.

Inskeep, E. (1991) *Tourism Planning*. Van Nostrand Reinhold, New York.

Kotler, P. (1994) *Principles of Marketing*, 6th edn. Prentice Hall, Englewood Cliffs, California.

Leask, A., Fyall, A. and Goulding, P. (2000) Revenue management in Scottish visitor attractions. In: Ingold, A., McMahon-Beattie, U. and Yeoman, I. (eds) *Yield Management*, 2nd edn. Continuum, London, pp. 211–232.

Leask, A., Fyall, A. and Garrod, B. (2002) Heritage visitor attractions: Managing revenue in the new mil- lennium. *International Journal of Heritage Studies* 8(3), 247–265.

Market Assessment International (2000) European Tourist Attractions 2000. *Market Assessment International*, July.

Middleton, V.T.C. (1988) *Marketing in Travel and Tourism*. Heinemann, Oxford, UK.

Mintel (2002) *Visitor Attractions – UK*. Mintel International Group, London.

Morgan, M. (1998) Market trends in leisure. In: Buswell, J. (ed.) *ILAM Guide to Good Practice in Leisure Management*. ILAM/Pitman, London.

Nickson, D. (2007) *Human Resource Management for the Hospitality and Tourism Industries*. Butterworth- Heinemann, Oxford, UK.

Page, S.J. and Connell, J. (2009) *Tourism: A Modern Synthesis*, 3rd edn. Cengage Learning, Andover, UK.

Prideaux, B. (2003) Creating visitor attractions in peripheral areas. In: Fyall, A., Garrod, B. and Leask, A. (eds) *Managing Visitor Attraction*. Butterworth-Heinemann, Oxford, UK, pp. 58–72.

Scottish Tourist Board (1991) *Visitor Attractions: A Development Guide*. Scottish Tourist Board, Edinburgh.

Select Committee on Culture, Media and Sport (2000) Marking the Millennium in the United Kingdom. Eighth Report. Available at: http://www.publications.parliament.uk/pa/cm199900/cmselect/ cmcumeds/578/57802.htm (accessed 1 August 2000).

Swarbrooke, J. (2002) *The Development and Management of Visitor Attractions*, 2nd edn. Butterworth-Heinemann, Oxford, UK.

Taylor, T. (2004) Managing human resources in sport and leisure. In: McMahon-Beattie, U. and Yeoman, I. (eds) *Sport and Leisure Operations Management*. Thomson Learning, London, pp. 58–74.

van Aalst, I. and Boogaarts, I. (2002) From museum to mass entertainment. *European Urban and Regional Studies* 9(3), 195–209.

Thwaites, E. and Williams, C. (2006) Service recovery: A naturalistic decision-making approach. *Managing Service Quality* 16(6), 641–653.

Watson, S., McCracken, M. and Hughes, M. (2004) Scottish visitor attractions: managerial competence requirements. *Journal of European Industrial Training* 28(1), 39–66.

Wickens, E., Paraskevas, A., Hemmington, N. and Bowen, D. (2000) The Dome – The perception and the reality. English Tourism Council, London. ETC Insights A137–A142.

Williams, C. and Thwaites, E. (2007a) Adding value to tourism and leisure organisations through front-line staff. *Tourism Recreation Research* 32(1), 95–105.

Williams, C. and Thwaites, E. (2007b) Public parks: A service perspective from the northwest of England. *Managing Leisure* 12, 61–76.

Afterword:
The Future

James Roberts

A wide range of factors have the potential to influence the future growth and evolution of the entertainment market including technological, economic and social issues (Fig. A.1). Many of the trends already evident in the industry are likely to continue and intensify, with significant implications for consumers and companies alike.

Technology has already transformed the way in which we interact with entertainment. Developments in devices and networks have created new opportunities to access and consume content in ways that could not have been imagined in the 1980s. Whilst this *proliferation* can only continue, with the delivery of ever more complex forms of entertainment on different platforms and devices, many of the changes in the industries in the near future will be driven by the issue of *interoperability*, that is the consumer's ability to acquire, consume and move content on to different platforms and devices. The immediate challenge for firms is to make this interoperability seamless.

But there are challenges. Electronic networks have traditionally grown up quite separately, designed to have different characteristics including specific content and associated devices, different business models and different dominant companies, e.g. the television network, data networks like the Internet and communication networks like the telephony system. However, over the last 10 years we have seen the emergence and widespread dissemination of what might be called converged networks, e.g. broadband networks, used for the delivery of a wide variety of different content and services to a vast array of common devices (e.g. the telephone, computer and mobile phone) from providers who have traditionally kept to their own networks but who are all having to learn to survive in a converged environment.

Companies have different reasons for moving into this new space, but for many the main motivation is to secure as much of

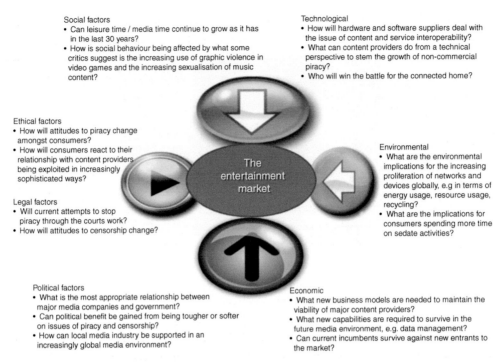

Social factors
- Can leisure time / media time continue to grow as it has in the last 30 years?
- How is social behaviour being affected by what some critics suggest is the increasing use of graphic violence in video games and the increasing sexualisation of music content?

Technological
- How will hardware and software suppliers deal with the issue of content and service interoperability?
- What can content providers do from a technical perspective to stem the growth of non-commercial piracy?
- Who will win the battle for the connected home?

Ethical factors
- How will attitudes to piracy change amongst consumers?
- How will consumers react to their relationship with content providers being exploited in increasingly sophisticated ways?

Legal factors
- Will current attempts to stop piracy through the courts work?
- How will attitudes to censorship change?

The entertainment market

Environmental
- What are the environmental implications for the increasing proliferation of networks and devices globally, e.g in terms of energy usage, resource usage, recycling?
- What are the implications for consumers spending more time on sedate activities?

Political factors
- What is the most appropriate relationship between major media companies and government?
- Can political benefit be gained from being tougher or softer on issues of piracy and censorship?
- How can local media industry be supported in an increasingly global media environment?

Economic
- What new business models are needed to maintain the viability of major content providers?
- What new capabilities are required to survive in the future media environment, e.g. data management?
- Can current incumbents survive against new entrants to the market?

Fig. A.1. STEEPLE analysis of key factors affecting the development of the entertainment market.

the consumer's attention and leisure spend as possible. Broadcasters are concerned about losing their valuable television audiences to other advertising mediums (e.g. online) and that younger audiences are becoming less interested in television programming, generally preferring to engage in social network activities and console gaming. Most broadcasters have moved online to augment their core broadcasting service with new programme-related content, social network-based applications and advertising initiatives. Whilst for some companies this move is a tactical approach to defending their current operations, for others the move is part of a bigger strategy to transform their business. Channel 4, a major UK commercial channel without its own production arm, has argued at various times that it cannot maintain its current business model

(and the complete reliance on external ideas and independent producers that is part of its public service remit) without further financial support from the Government or the opportunity to form commercial agreements with suitable partners (e.g. BBC Worldwide or Channel 5). Its latest strategy, according to its new Chief Executive, is to focus on the generation and exploitation of consumer data to fill potential funding gaps (Abraham, 2011), a radical extension of the core advertising model on which most commercial broadcasters have built their businesses.

Network infrastructure providers like the cable and telephony companies have increasingly augmented their core services with the 'triple play' of access to telephony (land-line and mobile), television and broadband. The constant challenge for such companies is how far and how fast to upgrade their existing networks and how the cost of such investments is met by launching new services and increasing the average revenue per user (ARPU). In many cases they have been forced to become media as well as infrastructure companies, owning channels and branded TV services, and in some cases the tensions of running both distribution and content businesses under one roof have been difficult to overcome. But perhaps their biggest challenge in the future is how they manage and address their customer base across multiple platforms; customer service management has always been a challenge to such companies, but its importance can only increase in a multi-platform environment.

Companies in broadcasting, publishing and music are all finding themselves compelled to move to new platforms to defend and enhance their prospects. In some cases there is evidence of the synergy of such moves (e.g. broadcasters enhancing the relationship of audiences with key brands through the provision of social network applications), in others questions remain about if moving on to these platforms is cannibalizing their existing 'real-world' businesses (e.g. film studios and record companies offering their films and music via new streaming services and publishers offering online versions of their newspapers) and what the overall effects are on revenue and profit levels.

In terms of *interoperability*, in the recent past, the ability of such firms to develop cross-platform applications was hindered to a degree by the sheer number of new platforms and platform variants emerging. It was expensive to launch new products on new platforms and to develop the in-house expertise to do so, and their relative lack of interoperability,

for example: music bought on iTunes service that could only be played on Apple devices; games that had to be re-versioned for three or four different console systems; applications that might only work on a single mobile-phone operating system. Hence content and services often had to be re-versioned multiple times to work on all available platforms and devices. In some ways, hardware manufacturers supported these barriers. Keen to be at the centre of the networked home, they launched equipment that would only work seamlessly with other equipment supplied by the same manufacturer or a very limited number of partner companies. This locked consumers into hardware silos and ensured that such suites of hardware had to be accommodated in the list of required platforms for which content had to be re-versioned.

Increasingly, however, consumers are expecting a higher level of interoperability. Not content to only move their content between a limited set of hardware or applications, they increasingly expect all of their content to be playable on all of their hardware wherever they are in the world. Efforts by some service providers to move to cloud-based media storage solutions are encouraging these expectations, though in many cases the services still limit the range of applications and hardware on which content can be consumed. Still there is early evidence of some hardware providers opening up previously proprietary applications for use on a greater range of hardware (e.g. Apple's Air-Play, Samsung's Allshare), though we are still very far from the vision of seamless interoperability of all content, on all platforms, all the time and anywhere.

As content becomes more available on a variety of platforms, new forms of consumer behaviour are also emerging. Whilst simultaneous multiple media usage is not a new thing (consumers have long read the newspaper whilst listening to the radio), technological developments offer new ways for consumers to *actively* engage with multiple media simultaneously, switching rapidly between applications such as gaming, watching TV, listening to music and communicating with friends on converged devices such as tablets, laptops and increasingly televisions. Whilst this offers consumers the potential ability more actively to avoid the intrusion of commercial interests into their media experience (e.g. through skipping advertising by temporarily moving to a different activity) it also creates an incredibly rich potential dataset of consumer media behaviour for those organizations in a position to capture it, and perhaps more significantly to turn raw data into usable and saleable information. Whilst the development of social media applications was initially seen as a potential threat to more traditional media activities like watching TV or listening to music, their development and integration into other media may actually secure the existence of these more traditional forms well into the future by producing useful new revenue streams for providers.

In other areas of traditional media behaviour, consumers appear to have been slower to change their activities. The early emergence of services like pay-per-view films on television promised an environment where consumers would entirely give up conventional television channels in favour of 'do-it-yourself' scheduling. Early forecasters felt that their predications were vindicated with the subsequent launch of online-based catch-up TV services like the BBC's iplayer and online streaming services such as Netflix. Similarly,

early predications of music consumption in the online environment portrayed consumers as constantly searching the Internet for up and coming bands and user-generated content, ignoring the efforts and protestations of the major record companies. The reality of the situation, however, is that consumers have been relatively slow to move to these more active models of consumer consumption. Pay-TV, catch-up TV and streaming services have displayed relatively slow growth rates. The majority of consumers still spend most of their time watching programmed channels. In a similar way, record companies are still in a position to dominate how most consumers spend their music dollars, pounds and euros, despite the availability of a hugely increased pool of artists online. This points to a number of key issues that are relevant for the evolution of entertainment at home in the near term.

Not all consumers necessarily want to spend time and attention on programming their own media experience. Many appear happy to rely on existing providers to do this for them. Broadcasters and music companies have over the years become very proficient at selecting appropriate material and packaging it into an appealing form (e.g. the TV channel, the magazine, the album). This content is typically designed to appeal to a wide variety of consumers and to offer them the convenience of consuming it rather than spending time on an extended search for content, the technical challenge of accessing multiple content on multiple platforms and the risk of accessing very poor quality content. At least at the moment, this guarantee of convenience and quality appears to outweigh the attractions of 'going it alone' for the mass market.

For some early adopters of new technologies, there are other appeals for going it alone however. One of the major ones is that, having invested the time in becoming sufficiently technical to access these legal and commercial services, it is only a small step to a level of technical expertise that will allow them to access a huge amount of free content through applications like Bittorrent. The rise of non-commercial piracy in the latter part of the 20th century is seen by many as a sign of the growing technical capabilities of media consumers, as well as a sign of their willingness to ignore traditional rules of commercial exchange and to threaten the traditional business models of media suppliers. The response of content suppliers to date has been an appeal to consumers' reason and sense of fair play through advertising campaigns, and an appeal to the courts, most recently with the various European initiatives against Swedish file-sharing service 'The Pirate Bay' in 2012. But even as some services are shut down and others re-brand as legal commercial services (e.g. Napster), more illegal file-sharing services emerge.

The longer term effect of this may be a more fundamental re-balancing of the value of media content in the minds of consumers and companies alike, leading to a range of new business models for firms. In the future some entertainment content may be given away free in return for a 'relationship' between consumer and supplier that generates data that is monetized through the sale of information on that relationship. Consumers may be getting services and content for free but in doing so they become the product, to be sliced, diced and sold according to the whim of the supplier. How consumers will respond to this, and hence their view of what relationships they are willing to form with content suppliers in the future, is the subject of much current debate and speculation.

The speed of change and its degree in the entertainment market is partly a function of major companies' willingness to be innovative in their practices and content. When a small number of companies dominate a market (e.g. the early history of broadcasting, the music market for much of its history) they have no real incentive to be innovative. But this can often lead to unmet demand in the marketplace and as new firms enter the industry to meet this unmet demand, levels of concentration drop and a new cycle of more innovative activity and content is instigated. If we look at the entertainment market today, different sectors appear to be at very different stages in these cycles.

For much of the history of the popular music industry it has been dominated by a very limited number of major record companies. Over the last 10 years, however, we have witnessed a period of rapid and radical change as major record companies, once completely dominant in the distribution and marketing of popular music, have found it harder to maintain their position in an increasingly dynamic and fragmented music market. As a result we have seen rapid and ongoing innovation in how music is sourced, marketed and distributed. Major record companies have finally come to the realization that they have to change. Whilst the music sector remains in a state of flux, with many new entrants, new technologies and rapidly evolving consumer usage of music, this innovation is likely to continue.

In the broadcasting sector, a long period of market concentration up to the early 1990s led to a relative lack of innovation in how content was sourced and distributed. Dramatic change with the growth of digital platforms led to more open forms of innovation as major networks and channels sought new content from independent companies and had to adapt content to new distribution opportunities. Now, however, broadcasters are increasingly seeking to originate and build major programme brands themselves (rather than relying on independents to supply them) to ensure they capture all of the value of the brands they are building with their airtime. As a result, conglomeration has led to the alignment of broadcasters and content companies in the USA (e.g. 20th Century Fox, Fox Studios and Searchlight aligned to the Fox Network as part of News International; Paramount aligned to CBS and UPN within Viacom; Universal and NBC Studio aligned to NBC), and in Europe commercial broadcasters are looking to acquire independent companies to boost their in-house production capabilities. Here we are at the beginning of what may be a new cycle of concentration in media ownership and potentially a decline in the innovativeness and diversity of content available to consumers.

In the newspaper publishing market, circulation of hardcopies appears to be on a slope of inevitable decline and publishers are struggling to maintain advertising revenues. But here providers are faced with a dilemma. Should they go all out to re-launch their services online? What will be the implications for their 'real world' businesses? Will it disappear? And if so, how quickly? And if they are successful in moving their businesses to new platforms, what new competitors will they face? As major publishers struggle with these questions but remain relatively dominant, innovation remains at a relatively low level (experimenting with pay walls and launching digital versions of their newspapers on various platforms) as they try to work out what the implications of their actions are. Innovation is appearing amongst new entrants in the market, however, such as relatively new online firms who do not fear the implications of their online activities for real-world brands.

So what can we be certain about in the future entertainment market? If the last 30 years are anything to go by, it is probably going to keep on growing in terms of the sheer range of opportunities to consume entertainment content. It is more questionable if the industries can expand much further in terms of how much of consumers' disposable time entertainment activities can occupy. The story of the latter half of the 20th century was the growth of disposable time allocated to entertainment activities, with a significant expansion occurring after the launch of TV. But subsequently we may have reached a ceiling in terms of the sheer amount of time consumers have every day to consume entertainment content. If so, the next decades may be much more about the substitution of one form of entertainment for another (with significant implications for the growth in the overall value of the entertainment sector and the prospects for companies focused on single platforms, devices or forms of content). Recent years have witnessed an explosion in the growth of 'lean forward' forms of entertainment, that is entertainment in which the consumer plays an active role in creating it (e.g. console games, music and film creation software). To date, there are still debates about the degree to which 'lean forward' forms are substituting for, rather than adding to, 'lean backwards' forms (e.g. passive watching of linear TV or visits to the cinema); it is certainly a subject for debate in the boardrooms of major media companies like Warner Bros and the BBC. In the next 10 years, we will get a sense of this if the days of generally passive media are over and if the new entertainment market will be dominated by forms that are more actively chosen and engaged in by consumers. But this is unlikely to play out in a predictable and linear fashion over all entertainment sectors. The one thing we have learned about the sector over the last 30 years is that what constitutes entertainment and how it is created, distributed and consumed is constantly changing and evolving, creating a complex and shifting environment to be navigated by companies and consumers alike.

REFERENCE

Abraham, D. (2011) What we're 4. Available at: http://www.rts.org.uk/sites/default/files/David-Abraham-2011.pdf (accessed 2 February 2013).

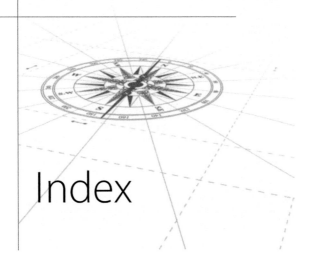

Index

Page numbers in **bold** refer to illustrations, tables and boxes.